The ancient ruins of Rhodesia : Monomotapae imperium

Richard Nicklin Hall, W G Neal

JAMES MILL.

A. KING AND COMPANY,
PRINTERS TO THE UNIVERSITY
OF ABERDEEN.

JAMES MILL.

A

BIOGRAPHY.

BY

ALEXANDER BAIN, LL.D.,

EMERITUS PROFESSOR OF LOGIC IN THE UNIVERSITY OF ABERDEEN.

———————

LONDON:
LONGMANS, GREEN, AND CO.
1882.

PREFACE.

AN account of the circumstances that led me to undertake the present biography will be the best apology for its defects.

It occurred to Professor Masson, after he went to Edinburgh to occupy the chair of English Literature in the University, to make a search in the registers for facts bearing on James Mill's career during the seven years that he was a student there. The results were more interesting than either of us expected, and I preserved them on the chance of their one day being available.

About the same time, I happened to meet the Rev. John Bain, Free Church minister of Mill's native parish, Logie Pert, in Forfarshire. In the course of conversation, he imparted to me a number of traditions that he had gathered up in the parish respecting Mill's family and connexions. He farther volunteered to make still more particular enquiries, in order to gratify my curiosity; and the information that he thereby procured, I treasured up along with the college facts.

In 1867, John Stuart Mill was engaged in editing his father's *Analysis of the Mind*. Thinking that he might make this an opportunity of saying something as to his father's general character and history, I mentioned to him that I had become possessed of those biographical particulars. His answer was, that he was almost entirely unacquainted with his father's early career in Scotland, which he himself hardly ever alluded to, and could not undertake the trouble of getting it up. He added—"Most of what I could tell about my father from my own knowledge is already committed to writing, in an autobiographical paper, which I shall leave behind me for publication if I do not publish it sooner ; and will be better reserved for that purpose."

This was of course decisive. I thought no more about collecting facts until the *Autobiography* should appear. That was a great disappointment, so far as the father was concerned. Admirable and authoritative as an *éloge*, it was nothing as a biography. There were many interesting statements that would have taken their place in a biography, but such an account of James Mill's career as the public expect in any work that is called a Life, was certainly not forthcoming.

In order that a complete Life might some day be possible, I thought it right to push a little farther the enquiries that had been already begun, and to fix the traditions that were in danger of perishing. I visited the parish of Logie Pert, under the guidance of my namesake, the Free Church minister, and saw the site of Mill's father's cottage, and the places identified with his early years. I interrogated all the persons that could give me information, and pushed my enquiries by correspondence, and by a search in public registers.

From the facts thus obtained, I compiled an article for MIND No. I., comprehending Mill's early Life in Scotland. Some of the materials already gained bore upon the commencement of his career in London ; and, having received all the assistance that the surviving members of his family could give, I prepared two more articles, extending over the remainder of his life; the aim being to fix and preserve all the information, as well as to obtain corrections and additions from whoever might be able to furnish such.

The consideration was naturally forced upon me, that I had become possessed of advantages for a complete biography such as hardly anybody after me could attain to. This, however, necessarily involved a new class of labours. I had to face the circumstance that the materials are unusually scanty. Time had already been lost; those that, from personal knowledge, could have given information as to Mill's early history, were nearly all dead. Several invaluable collections of letters have been destroyed. Instead of making a selection from a copious mass of documents, I have been obliged to use almost everything that came into my hands.

Inasmuch as those writings of Mill that made great part of his influence on his time are not accessible, except in a small number of Libraries, I thought it right to make a full abstract of the more important of them; including the contributions to the *Encyclopædia Britannica*, and the chief articles in the periodicals. It was only in this way that the general reader could be made to taste of his characteristic vigour and originality.

Another requisite was to supply the needful elucidations of Mill's exertions from the history of the time, and from the biographies of persons whose career was mixed up with his. I have done this part to the best of my ability; but, not being specially versed beforehand in the matters needful, I may have made mistakes as well as omissions.

The help that has been rendered by various persons will be seen as the occasions arise. I have, however, some debts of general acknowledgment, to be paid in advance. From one of the very few surviving friends of James Mill, Mr. Andrew Bisset, who wrote his biography in the *Encyclopædia Britannica*, and in the *Penny Cyclopædia*, I have received a large amount of valuable assistance.

The published correspondence of the late Macvey Napier contains a number of important letters from Mill. The editor of the correspondence, the present Mr Macvey Napier, has allowed me to peruse a number of other letters not included in the published volume. He has also been helpful in other ways, from having been an official in the Examiner's Office, in the India House, while Mill was yet alive.

I am indebted to the courtesy of Lord Brougham in permitting me to copy the letters in his possession from Mill to his late brother, the renowned Henry Brougham. The value of these letters will be appreciated in their place.

The portrait is from a drawing that belonged to Mrs. Grote. I am informed that a still better likeness was at one time in her possession ; but I cannot learn what became of it.

ABERDEEN, *January, 1882.*

CONTENTS.

CHAPTER I.

EARLY LIFE IN SCOTLAND.

1773-1802.

CHAPTER II.

START IN LONDON.

1802—1808.

CHAPTER III.

HISTORY OF INDIA ; EDINBURGH REVIEW ; PHILANTHROPIST ; EDUCATION MOVEMENT.

1808-1818

Preparatory Surveys.

CHAPTER IV.

APPOINTMENT TO THE INDIA HOUSE.

1819-1823.

1823.

CHAPTER V.

ARTICLES IN THE SUPPLEMENT TO THE ENCYCLOPÆDIA BRITANNICA.

1816-1823.

Government.

Colony.

Law of Nations.

Education.

Beggar.

CHAPTER VI.

WESTMINSTER REVIEW: ANALYSIS OF THE MIND.

1824-1829.

1824.

1825.

CHAPTER VII.

CLOSING YEARS :—INDIA CHARTER ; LONDON REVIEW : · FRAGMENT ON MACKINTOSH.

1830-1836.

India Charter Renewal.

1830-1833.

Chapter VIII.

REVIEW OF LATEST WRITINGS · POLITICAL ECONOMY: ANALYSIS OF THE HUMAN MIND: FRAGMENT ON MACKINTOSH.

Chapter IX.

CHARACTER AND INFLUENCE.

REFORM MOVEMENT.

APPENDIX.

CHAPTER I.

EARLY LIFE IN SCOTLAND:

1773-1802.

JAMES MILL was born on the 6th of April, 1773, at Northwater Bridge, parish of Logie Pert, county of Forfar or Angus.

The spot of his birth is not far from being a central point in that part of Strathmore, extending into the two counties Forfar or Angus and Kincardine or the Mearns, called " Howe of Angus," and " Howe of the Mearns". The strath or plain is four to six miles wide, and lies between the Grampians (here rising to an average of nearly two thousand feet) and a line of coast hills of much lower elevation.

Northwater Bridge is a bridge on the Northwater or North Esk, a river inferior to the Tay and the Dee, but still a considerable stream, rising not far off in Glenesk in the Grampians, flowing across the country from west to east, and entering the sea three miles north of Montrose. Of its various bridges, the oldest and most important is the one that gives the name to Mill's birth-place; a three-arch stone bridge built about two centuries before his time, on the great central line of communication from the north of Scotland to the south; the bridge near the sea for the coast road being built only in the end of last century. The river is for a great part of its course the boundary of the two counties of Forfar and Kincardine.

1

The parish of Logie Pert, a union of two older parishes, Logie and Pert, lies along the right bank of the North Esk, and is the last of the Forfar parishes northward. Across the river is Marykirk, lower down St. Cyrus—the coast hills and coast parish.

The account of Logie Pert Parish, in the old Statistical Account of Scotland, was drawn up by the parish minister, Mr. Peters, in the year 1791. It is most careful and minute, and will enable any one to form a very accurate picture of James Mill's life and surroundings, both physical and social. The parish is about four miles long by three miles broad; it contained in that year a population of 999 persons. It was mainly an agricultural parish; but had also two bleachfields—Craigo and Logie, a small flax mill, and even a snuff mill, besides meal mills. There were also limestone quarries then largely worked. The river yielded a good supply of salmon. The land for agriculture was distributed among thirty-six farmers; five or six paying from £100 to £200 yearly rent.

Northwater Bridge became the name of one of the leading farms, of which the farm-house was contiguous to the bridge on the south side; an unusually large and good farm-house, of four rooms in length and two storeys in height. This was also in Mill's time an inn and posting-house, kept by the tenant of the farm. Right and left of the high road south of the bridge, there were other houses, perhaps fourteen or fifteen, making up a hamlet, the largest in the parish, with a population of seventy persons. Blacksmith, wright, mason, carrier, small grocer or merchant—were all found here; in addition to which were cottages attached to the farm, and let by the farm-tenant—Barclay, by name, whom we shall hear more about. One of these was a clay-built thatched cottage, a hundred yards south of the farm-house of the bridge, and on the same side of the road (right hand going south). It stood some twenty yards off the road, and at right angles, the gable towards the road. It had two doors and three windows; the door farthest from the road was the entry to the usual two rooms of a cottage—" but an' ben " ; the other door entered a single room, the room next the road. This was the cottage where James Mill was brought up.* In front was the kail yard or garden : behind, running at right angles, was a similar cottage inhabited by the head labourer or manager of the farm ; at the south end of that cottage was the byre belonging to Mill's cottage.† The elder Mill's family rented also a cow's grass ; and continued to have a cow to the last.

The father of James Mill (also called James) was a shoe-maker, and had a good country business, employing usually two or three men. Of his own previous history we know only that he worked at his trade some time in Edinburgh, before settling at Northwater Bridge. There are plenty of his name all over that part of Scotland, but the spelling varies, " Milne" being perhaps more common : his own name in the register of his son's birth is spelt so. In general character, all we can say is, that he was industrious and steady in his calling, good-natured in disposition, pious and devout, but with no special claim to intelligence or any high mental quality. In the prime of his age he seems to have been in good circumstances, and to have saved money.

Mill's mother was Isabel Fenton, the daughter of a farmer in the Kirriemuir district of the county. She was born in 1755, at Kirriemuir, and must have been married at 17. A correspondent supplies me with the following facts as to the family.

---

* According to the best information, Mill was not actually born in that house, which was the abode of his family for more than sixty years. His birth took place, before the house was built, in a cottage at the river side, near the lower end of Barclay's garden ; it was thus more in the centre of the little hamlet made up of the tradespeople's houses. The tradition is that his father obtained a site on lease from Barclay and built himself the cottage so long identified with his family. This, however, could not be ; for he paid rent regularly to the tenant of the farm. The other children were born in the new house, which must therefore have been occupied in 1775.

† Before the cottage was pulled down, some twenty years ago, a photograph was taken, which preserves its appearance.

The father was born and resided in Kirriemuir.   Two children
of his, Alexander Fenton and Margaret Fenton, owned two
thatched houses where the Airlie Arms Hotel is now situated,
and lived in one of them.   Alexander was a handloom weaver,
Margaret a dressmaker, and both were unmarried and in good
circumstances.   Alexander died in 1826, and Margaret, far
advanced in years, about 1839.* They had a sister, who went
to Edinburgh as a servant, and did not return to Kirriemuir.
This was Mill's mother.

There have long been a number of substantial farmers of the
same name on the Airlie and other estates in that neighbourhood.†   In the thirteenth and fourteenth centuries the Fentons
had landed property in the district, and were called the Fentons
of Baikie.   It is said that Isabel Fenton's father had fallen
from much better circumstances, in consequence of joining in
the Stuart rising of 1745.   Forfarshire was the chief part of the
Lowlands that was so infatuated as to take the field for the
Pretender.   The then heir of Airlie, Lord Ogilvie, led out a
large band of tenants and residents, including, it is said, Isabel
Fenton's father, who, with the rest, suffered severely by the
ravages of Cumberland's troops, and was thenceforth a much
poorer man.   It is even said that he was himself a proprietor
before 1745, but the circumstance is not verified.   Isabel, at all
events, looked upon herself as one that had fallen from a better

---

* In 1840, Mr Barclay wrote to John Mill, intimating that a property in
Kirriemuir seemed to fall to him as his grandmother's heir, the occasion must
have been the death of Margaret Fenton. Mill's reception of the news was
characteristic   He would not take advantage of any mere informality in a will ;
but if there were a case, he would do whatever might be necessary to secure
the property for his paternal aunt's family, the Greigs. They, it seems, were
met by a remote male heir turning up.

† By desire of Lady Airlie, the minister of Lintrathen, Mr. Chree, furnished me
with an account of the best known families of the name of Fenton in the Airlie
district.   One family possessed formerly a considerable property in Forfarshire.
An anecdote, illustrative of Scottish life and character in the last century, is
given by Mr. Chree, relating to a Fenton, tenant of Balintore, in Lintrathen :
he was ejected by his landlord, at the instigation of the Earl of Airlie, for
violently opposing the settlement of a former minister of Lintrathen.

estate. It was in Edinburgh that she became acquainted with James Mill. Her character is difficult to rescue from various conflicting traditions. All admit that she was a proud woman; her pride taking the form of haughty superiority to the other cottagers' wives, and also entering into her determination to rear her eldest son to some higher destiny. She could do fine work, but was not so much in her element in the common drudgery of her lot; neither could she accommodate herself to the coarse food of the cottage, but relied mainly on her tea. A saying of hers to her husband is still remembered :—" If you give me porridge I'll die, but give me tea and I'll live". Of course the tea had to be accompanied with butter, and that was among the luxuries of those times. All this led to her being accused of luxurious habits; but was more probably a proof of delicacy of constitution. She was the object of no small spite among the villagers from her presumption in bringing up her eldest son to be a gentleman ;* but the Barclays always treated her with marked distinction. When she came to tea with them they always took out their best set of china. In any family distress, they sent for her.

It was the fancy of those that knew her, that she was the source of her son's intellectual energy; but the only proof now attainable is the apparent absence of any unusual force of character in her husband.

The biography of James Mill requires a special notice of the tenants of the farm where his father's cottage lay. This farm, consisting of about two hundred Scotch acres, is on the Earl of Kintore's estate of Inglismaldie, and was commonly called " the bridge," or " the brig". The tenant was a member of the family of the Barclays of Montrose; long known as tenant farmers also in Kincardineshire, in the proximity of the more

* The common saying was " What right has she to suppose that her son will be called *Mr.* Mill, and his wife *Mrs.* Mill". It was usual among the lower ranks in Scotland to go on giving married women their maiden name. Mill's own married sister, Mrs. Greig, was designated " May Mill". She was so named to myself in her native locality.

renowned family of the Barclays of Ury; although not known to be related to these, except by a certain personal resemblance to that Quaker and athletic race. The one that occupied the farm, when Mill was born, died in 1794, leaving a widow and large family, with whom James was very intimate. The eldest son, who succeeded to the farm, Mr. David Barclay, was four years younger than Mill, and is the medium of much of our authentic information respecting him. One of the sisters, the youngest of the family, still lives (1881), and is able to testify to some important events in Mill's early history.

The children of James Mill and Isabel Fenton were—James Mill (1773), William Mill, two years younger, and a daughter, May Mill, two years younger than William. There are no family events to record for the early years of James Mill. He went, of course, to the parish school (in the centre of the parish) as soon as he was able to walk two miles and back. Of his schoolmaster I have heard no special accounts. It is a matter of fair inference that his superior talent was unmistakably shown in very early years. In fact, James Mill could not have reached his seventh year without disclosing his superiority over the other children of his years. His talent was of a kind that the common school elements would soon make manifest. He must have been distinguished in all the three R's. He had voice and elocution for a reader, he was a neat writer, had abundant arithmetical faculty and an admirable turn for languages. His parents at home could not be ignorant of his powers. As a matter of course, the parish minister would soon learn that an extraordinary boy was growing up at Northwater Bridge. His mother's ambition resolved that he should be a scholar; by her he was nurtured and petted, and exempted from all distracting occupation. It is a very rare thing, indeed, for a boy to live in a humble rural family, be he ever so scholarly, without having to take some share in manual occupations, either field labour or artisan employment within doors. I have received the most emphatic assurances, from good authority, that James Mill neither assisted in his father's trade, nor took any part in the labour of the field, whereby he might have been less dependent on his parents. He saw what was going on, contracted an interest in farming, but his own sole occupation was study. His brother William was put to work in his father's shop, and so continued during his short life.

After mastering the R's with a little English Grammar, Mill would enter the Latin class of the parish school; the fee at this stage being *2s 6d* a quarter. What with the little attendance he got at school, and with his studious habits at home, he must have got on very rapidly: and, in fact, at ten or eleven years, he would be at the end of the schoolmaster's curriculum.

It is much to be regretted that we have nothing but a few plausible conjectures to make up the history of his studies to his eighteenth year. It is certain that he was sent to Montrose Academy. This led to his being boarded in Montrose, where he had to pay for his board half-a-crown a week. He walked home every Saturday and returned on Monday morning. He had for a class-fellow Joseph Hume, who was four years younger than himself, but left the school at thirteen, to study medicine with an apothecary. As Mill apparently did not leave till nearly eighteen, they must have been together for several years; but at very unequal stages of advancement. There are traditions of walking excursions undertaken by the two, one said to be as far as Aberdeen. Both were highly muscular youths; but the broad, short figure of Hume had the superiority. It is said that on the Aberdeen excursion, they climbed the famous castle rock of Dunnottar, by Stonehaven, and that Mill had to hold Hume by the collar while he was venturing down the precipices of the rock.

The Montrose Academy was one of the most renowned burgh schools of Scotland. After the Reformation, Erskine of Dun is stated to have established a Greek School at Montrose. The famous scholar and reformer, Andrew Melville, was born at Baldovy on South Esk, a mile from Montrose, and educated at the Grammar School of the town. The head master, called "Rector," in Mill's time was presumably a good classical scholar. The following is the title of a school book preserved in Mill's Library :—" Grammar of the Latin Tongue, by Hugh Christie, M.A., Rector of the Grammar School of Montrose. Printed by D. Buchanan, 1789."

Mill boarded in the house of a shop-keeper, named Christie, who often had the teachers of the Academy at his house; and these were always overflowing with the praises of Mill's cleverness and perseverance, which was a little galling to poor Christie, from his having a son of the same age at the Academy, who never got a word of commendation.

We can but guess the time when he went to the Academy; it would depend upon how long the parish schoolmaster was able to carry him forward. He would certainly be ripe for being transferred any time after nine or ten, but may have delayed as long as possible to save the expense. If he remained at Montrose till he went to college in his eighteenth year, he could not have been there less than five or six years; during which time he must have become a very accomplished scholar in every branch of learning included in the school course. Indeed, it was a very rare thing for ordinary boys to remain at any Grammar School to that age; and I do not quite understand how Mill was kept occupied, as he could have had no class-fellows at his stage of advancement. An alternative supposition will be offered as we proceed.

We should not omit at this stage the assistance he received from the excellent and able minister of the parish, Mr. Peters, his friend all through. It is within allowable conjecture that if the schoolmaster ever staggered under the pressure of Mill's rapid advances, Mr. Peters would come to the rescue; would help the boy over difficulties, lend him books both for scholastic purposes and for general study, and guide and encourage him in his aspirations. Mr. Peters would also advise his parents, and confirm them in their determination to set him apart for a student's career.

A passage in a letter written long after, in an interesting moment of his life, may be quoted here as the only existing testimony borne by himself to his early feelings : " My plea- sure shall consist . . . . . in establishing to myself that name in the world for wisdom and knowledge which was the darling object even of my infant years to think I should one day attain ; and which I know I do not deceive myself when I think that few men, at my years (31), have laid so good a foundation for attaining " The circumstances probably gave an undue warmth to his language on this occasion.

I now approach what appears to have been the most im- portant event of his early career, his connexion with the Fetter- cairn family.* The beginnings of this connexion are hopelessly

---

* It is necessary to know a small portion of the family history of Sir John Stuart. The following particulars will suffice. He was a descendant of the great Stuart family. His mother Emilia Stuart, in 1752, married her cousin William Belsches, the heir of Belsches, of Tofts, in Perthshire. Her husband died the year after, leaving an infant son John Belsches. This son she educated for the Edinburgh Bar. In 1775, when he was 22, he married Lady Jane Leslie, eldest daughter of the Earl of Leven and Melville. Two years after happened the event that lifted him to fortune. His mother, on the death of her uncle Sir William Stuart, in 1777, became heir to her grandfather Daniel Stuart, who was a man of wealth, but not seemingly in land. No estate is mentioned as transmitted ; but in the same year was purchased by her the estate of Fettercairn, which had descended for generations in the family of the Earl of Middleton An ancestor of Emilia Stuart Belsches had served in the army under William III., and in 1706 received a baronetcy, this title was inherited by John Belsches. He was now Sir John Belsches, of Fettercairn, and his wife, Lady Jane Belsches. They had an only child, a daughter Wilhelmina, born in October, 1776. In 1797, Mrs Belsches, the mother of Sir John, executed a settlement enforcing upon her son the name of his great-grand father Daniel Stuart, and he was henceforth Sir John Stuart, of Fettercairn whence we have the name John Stuart Mill.

Sir John was elected member for Kincardineshire, in the Union Parliament 1801 ; an occurrence that had an important bearing on James Mill's fortunes. He continued to serve in Parliament till 1807, when he was made a Baron of Exchequer, a promotion conferred for being a good adherent to his party. It was an honourable appointment (with a salary of £2000 a year), but the duties

obscure; but, before stating the traditions bearing upon the event, I will make a few preliminary remarks.

A young man born on the banks of the North Esk, in humble circumstances, and possessing superior abilities, would, as a matter of course, turn his thoughts to the colleges at Aberdeen. The distance from Northwater Bridge is thirty-eight miles, an easy student's journey. The distance to St. Andrews is much greater, to Edinburgh more than double. The Aberdeen colleges possessed numerous bursaries open to competition, the exercise being a "version," or translation from English into Latin. A £10 bursary would pay all the fees and in those days cover half the maintenance of a student for the college session. Moreover, there were in the patronage of the family of Ramsay, of Balmain (in Mill's neighbourhood), four bursaries of £24 a year, tenable for four years: so that one was vacant every year. Such a bursary would pay the fees and give a sumptuous maintenance to the student. A boy so distinguished as James Mill could have been put forward to the patron as a candidate for one of these bursaries, and notwithstanding the claims of factor's sons, clergymen's sons, &c., would eventually have succeeded. Add to all this, that the parish

---

were light in comparison to those of a Lord of Session; and although Sir John studied for the bar, he could scarcely have ever practised. He held the office till his death in 1821.

It is not easy to find out what sort of man Sir John Stuart was. Few people can give any account of him. He was not even honoured with a newspaper paragraph on his death. The popular tradition makes him out haughty and ill-tempered; but, after hearing all that could be said in his own locality, I was led to the conclusion, that he was a just-minded and really generous man, though somewhat imperious, he could not bear to be thwarted. Lady Jane was revered for every virtue. Sir John's steady attachment to James Mill entitles him to honourable remembrance.

It was surmised by Dr. Thomas Thomson, and, on his authority, believed by various friends of Mill in London, that he was related to Sir John Stuart by blood. The insinuation admits of positive disproof. Sir John did not acquire the property of Fettercairn, so as to be resident in the neighbourhood, till 1777, when Mill was four years old. I could mention other decisive circumstances, but refrain from giving more importance to what was a mere creation of Thomas Thomson's cynical fancy.

minister, Mr. Peters, was brother-in-law to Professor Stuar
of Marischal College, in Aberdeen, and in frequent communica
tion with the professor, who was a man of some property ir
Kincardineshire, and came every year to visit his brother-in
law; while it is known that he became well acquainted witl
Mill, and was useful to him at a later stage. The ministe
and the professor would certainly have discovered a way o
sending him to Marischal College. The sons of the clergy anc
of the farmers in that district, we know, went to Aberdeen; ?
younger brother of Mr. David Barclay studied there. Hac
it been proposed to send Mill to Aberdeen, he was quite
ready to go in his thirteenth, or at latest, his fourteenth year
Starting at that age he would have kept abreast of every brancl
in the curriculum, and probably have been the first man of hi·
year. That he was detained at home till his eighteenth year
to be then sent to the University of Edinburgh, shows tha
some powerful hand had interposed at an early stage to diver
him from what I must deem his obvious and natural career.

The account given by John Stuart Mill (*Autobiography*) o
his father's introduction to the Fettercairn family is a some
what loose version of the statement made to him by Mr. Davi?
Barclay in a letter written after his father's death in 1836.
We do not possess that letter, but we know the substance
and we have Mr. Barclay's own words in another communi
cation, which he made to the *Montrose Review* in the sam
year. It was to furnish a biography of his father, for the *Enc?*

---

* The following extract from John Mill's letter to Mr. David Barclay show
the ignorance of the family as to their father's early history.—

"The chief points are the time and place of his birth; who and what h
parents were, and anything interesting that there may be to state about them
what places of education he went to : for what professions he was educate?
I believe he went through a medical course, and also that for the Church, an
I have heard that he was actually licensed as a preacher, but I never heard hi?
say so himself, and never heard of it till after his death. I do not kno
whether it is true or not; perhaps you do. How long did he remain at tl
University, or prosecute his studies for the Church? The history of his co?
nection with the late Sir John Stuart."

clopædia Britannica, that John Mill applied to Mr. Barclay for information. He placed the letter that he received in the hands of Mr. Andrew Bisset, who with some assistance from Mill himself, composed the article. Mr. Bisset had the advantage of being locally connected with James Mill's birth-place, and of having independent information respecting his early days. I therefore accept his rendering of the circumstances of the introduction to the Stuart family as the best now attainable; although it is not so satisfactory as we should wish. "Some pious ladies," he says, "amongst whom was Lady Jane Stuart (she was then 'Belsches'), having established a fund for educating one or two young men for the Church, Lady Jane applied to the Rev. Mr. Foote, minister of Fettercairn, to recommend some one. Mr. Foote applied to Mr. Peters, of Logie Pert, who recommended James Mill, both on account of his own abilities, and the known good character of the parents." Mr. Barclay's published statement is to the same effect. He was himself rather too young to have remembered from personal knowledge what happened somewhere between 1783 and 1790; his account is a tradition from the elder members of his own family. Mill might naturally enough be brought to the notice of Sir John and Lady Jane Stuart, either by their own parish minister, or by Mr. Peters of Logie Pert. (The house of Fettercairn is only five miles from Northwater Bridge.) How far Lady Jane was associated with other ladies, and whether Mill was but one of several young men that received the same assistance, tradition leaves entirely in the dark. We know that Lady Jane was reputed in her neighbourhood as foremost in every good work; and, if the educating of a promising youth to the ministry had come before her as a proposal, she would have readily taken a part in carrying it out; and we are safe in giving her the chief credit of obtaining for Mill the higher start that he gained, in being taken at a mature age to the University of Edinburgh, instead of going to Aberdeen as a mere boy.

Whatever may have been Lady Jane's intentions as to bringing Mill forward for the ministry, this much is clear that for many years the principal bond of connexion between him and the Stuart family was the education of their only daughter. We do not know when Mil entered on this task, nor how it was reconciled with hi private studies and his attendance at the University. The family resided in Edinburgh in winter, and at Fettercairr House in summer. In Edinburgh, Mill had his own lodging and probably went to Miss Stuart during certain hours eacl day. In summer he lived much at Fettercairn. It is possible that he may have been Miss Stuart's tutor before he went to Edinburgh, and may have ceased attending the Montrose Academy for some time before entering the University; ir which case, he would be resident the whole year at Fettercairn excepting the portion of time that the family may have beer in Edinburgh. All this is completely in the vague. The one thing certain is that the Stuarts took him to Edinburgh insteac of allowing him to proceed to Aberdeen, like the other young men of the neighbourhood, and that their only motive was the education of their child. It is true also that both Sir Johr and Lady Jane contracted a liking for himself that lasted with their lives; they were never tired of his company. If thei patronage had been a mere matter of charitable help to a promising young man, the sending him to Aberdeen woulc have cost them less than any other mode of effecting the object; but I repeat that this could have been perfectly accomplished without their assistance.

We now pass to his career at Edinburgh University. He first appears in the records in 1790: so that he enterec college at the unusually advanced age of $17\frac{1}{2}$ years. For thi session he is entered in the Senior Latin Class (Prof. Hill), anc the Senior Greek Class (Dalziel). That is to say, he skippec the junior classes in both Latin and Greek, and entered at

once into the senior, which gave him the rank of a second
year's student. I reserve comments till I give his whole Arts
attendance. Next year, 1791-92, he is entered again for
Senior Greek, Logic (Finlayson), Natural Philosophy (Robison). Third year, 1792-93, Senior Greek.*

This is all that we obtain from the College books, and it
lands us in uncertainty. Besides the omission of the junior

* Lord Cockburn's impressions of the professors of the time may be here
referred to. Of the Latin teaching (Hill) he speaks very unfavourably. "Little
Latin was acquired. The class was a constant scene of unchecked idleness,
and disrespectful mirth. Our time was worse than lost."

Of Dalziel, the professor of Greek, he speaks at least some differently. To
those that had the elements of the language to learn he imparted very little : but
as an enthusiast about learning, he excited the minds of the students, as well as
secured their affection. From his text-books, which were long used in the
Scottish Universities, we know that he was an accomplished Greek scholar.

The professor of Logic, Finlayson, "was a grim, firm-set, dark, clerical man ;
stiff and precise in his movements ; and with a distressing pair of black,
piercing, Jesuitical eyes, which moved slowly, and rested long on any one they
were turned to, as if he intended to look him down, and knew that he could do
so ; a severe and formidable person. Though no speaker, and a cold, exact,
hard reader, he surprised and delighted us with the good sense of his matter.
Until we heard him, few of us knew that we had minds ; and still fewer were
aware that our intellectual operations had been analyzed, and formed the
subject of a science, the facts of which our own consciousness delighted to
verify. Neither he nor his class were logical, in any proper sense of the word.
But no exposition of the mere rules of reasoning could have been half so useful
as the course which he adopted ; which was first to classify, and explain the
nature of, the different faculties, and then to point out the proper modes of
using and improving them. This, though not logic, was the first thing that
wakened our dormant powers. He did not work us half enough at composition "

Cockburn next eulogizes Stewart at some length. His "voice was singu-
larly pleasing ; and, as he managed it, a slight burr only made its tones softer.
His ear, both for music and for speech, was exquisite, and he was the finest
reader I have ever heard. His gesture was simple and elegant, though not
free from a tinge of professional formality ; and his whole manner that of an
academical gentleman.

"To me his lectures were like the opening of the heavens. I felt that I had
a soul. His noble views, unfolded in glorious sentences, elevated me into a
higher world. I was as much excited and charmed as any man of cultivated
taste would be, who, after being ignorant of their existence, was admitted to all
the glories of Milton, and Cicero, and Shakespeare. They changed my whole
nature."

classes in the Classics there is no Mathematics (Playfair), and, more still, no Moral Philosophy (Dugald Stewart). As we know that he was destined for the Church, the first thing to ask is, what attendances did this necessitate? It is curious that such a matter should be doubtful, yet so it is. The Act of Assembly in operation at the time merely specifies a course of Philosophy corresponding to the course for the M.A. degree at each university; but, in Edinburgh, the M.A. degree was rarely taken, and the regulations for it at that time are unknown to me. The subjects of the usual curriculum for a degree in Arts are understood to be Latin, Greek, Mathematics, Natural Philosophy, Logic, and Moral Philosophy. In Classics there were in all the universities junior and senior classes, but it may have been allowable to pass over the junior class if the student were sufficiently advanced to enter the senior, which Mill certainly was. Then as to Mathematics. I have heard, on good authority, that the subject was not, at that time, obligatory on students for the Church.* But that James Mill should fail to attend Playfair's classes seems to me very strange. If Playfair's oral teaching could be judged from his printed writings, Mill lost a great deal by not attending him. With all his ability and devotion to study, and with the very best help that the Montrose Academy could give him, he could not have been so accomplished a mathematician as he was a classic. Moreover, for him to enter the Natural Philosophy class in his second year, without a previous mathematical course, would be anomalous. He might have had enough of geometry to enter the school of Plato, but certainly he had not enough to enter the school of Robison

---

* The late Professor Cruickshank, of Marischal College, had heard his colleague, Dr. Glennie, state that he remembered a discussion taking place in the General Assembly on the question whether students going into the ministry should be required to attend Mathematics. The smallness in the attendance in the Edinburgh Mathematical classes clearly shows that students for the Church could dispense with the subject, the numbers being less than half of those attending Latin and Greek.

—the last of the adherents to the tough geometry of the *Principia*.

But it is when looking to the entry of his third year that we must express doubts as to the accuracy of the Register, in this instance; the more so that it has been occasionally found to be defective. It may be quite true that Mill gave a second unnecessary attendance on Dalziel's class, for Greek was his delight, and Dalziel was an admirable teacher, and seemed to notice Mill's aptitude; but that he should have attended no other class is very unlikely. He must have attended Dugald Stewart this year: the Church never dispensed with Moral Philosophy; and, if it had, Mill would not have neglected Stewart. The following passage occurs in a letter addressed, in 1821, to Macvey Napier:—"All the years I remained about Edinburgh, I used, as often as I possibly could, to steal into Mr. Stewart's class to hear a lecture, which was always a high treat. I have heard Pitt and Fox deliver some of their most admired speeches; but I never heard anything nearly so eloquent as some of the lectures of Professor Stewart. The taste for the studies which have formed my favourite pursuits, and which will be so till the end of my life, I owe to him."

The biography of John Leyden, Mill's contemporary and class-fellow, is of some use here. Leyden entered, in 1790, the Senior Latin and Greek classes, and, although his biographer does not say so, the college records show that he attended Senior Greek with Mill, and Junior Greek also. In 1791, he took Logic (with Mill, of course), Mathematics, and Classics again. His third Session he devoted to Moral Philosophy, Rhetoric, Natural Philosophy, and Natural History*; thus, like Mill, finishing the Arts course in three years. With this information we may fairly say that Divinity students found three years enough.

---

* A mistake on the part of Leyden's biographer: Natural History was then, as now, a summer class.

As to the Logic class, Leyden's biographer seems to believe that Professor Finlayson must have been an able teacher, from the number of able thinkers that passed through his hands. More particularly he remarks that Finlayson "recognised the native energy of thought and the assiduity of Leyden, and not only bestowed on him particular notice, but found employment for him in the preparing of other students, and acting as his own amanuensis". I take this to mean that Leyden assisted him in reading class exercises; a proof that Finlayson did not prelect merely (like Stewart and Robison), but gave the students at least some work to do. That Leyden should have risen to the leading position in the Logic class of that year shows that James Mill, in those days, was disposed to hide his light under a bushel: an explanation is obviously wanted. The Logic class of the year following contained Thomas Brown, thus treading on the heels of Mill, and we are quite prepared for the statement (given in Brown's *Life*) that "Finlayson's approbation was decidedly expressed".

Mill might have followed Leyden's example, and taken Rhetoric in his third year. I cannot account for John Mill's supposition that he may have studied in the Medical classes. Perhaps, in conjunction with Thomas Thomson, he may have attended the lectures of Black, which drew students from all parts.

Excepting this strong testimony to Dugald Stewart's fascination, which, no doubt, was the stirring of his own philosophical aptitudes—" I, too, am a metaphysician "—we have not a shred of information as to his doings or feelings those three Edinburgh winters. From extraneous sources we know what Edinburgh was in those years; the local colouring—political, literary, and social—has been given in connexion with many memoirs, as well as in the general history of the time. We can tell who were his distinguished contemporaries and class-fellows; but let us first pass on to complete his college career.

His Divinity studies commence in 1794, and occupy four

winters. The Theological professors were—Divinity, Andrew Hunter; Church History, Thomas Hardie; Hebrew, William Moodie. Of Dr. Hunter I know only that he was a man of weight in the General Assembly of the Church, and, in the famous Leslie debate, took the liberal side. The professor of Church History, Hardie, is cited by Mill himself, in his translation of ' Villers,' in terms of high praise. The passage there quoted does credit to Hardie's vigour as a reasoner. It is directed against ritualism and superstition. Hardie must have been of the stamp of Principal George Campbell, of Aberdeen, and his lecturing would probably be in keeping with Mill's intellectual phase at the time.

But what interests us most is the Librarian's Register of the Theological Library, which contains the titles of the works taken out by the students, with their names appended chiefly in their own hand. Here we have a clue to Mill's reading during those four winters. Of course he had other sources : he might have access at the same time to the General Library; and, besides his own private collection of favourite authors, he could borrow from friends. Making allowance for all these, we can discern a marked character in his studies. The list of books taken out by him has been extracted by Professor Masson; and I here give it entire.

The first entry is for January 2, 1794; the book is not very legibly given. Jan. 20; Ferguson's History of Civil Society. Feb. 6; Alison on Taste. Feb. 13; Rousseau's Emile, vol. 1. Feb. 20; Emile, vol. 2. March 3; Cudworth's Morality. March 6; Gregory's Essays. March 13; Smith's Theory (of Moral Sentiments), vol. 1. April 3; Smith's Theory, vol. 2. April 10; Massillon's Sermons. April 30; Reid's Intellectual Powers. This last was probably returned in a week, and he would then leave town. No books are borrowed in the recess.

The second Divinity session (1794-95), shows the first entry in November 20; Ferguson's Philosophy, vol. 2. Without giving dates, I will quote the rest: Discours par Rousseau;

Mélanges de Litterature; Hume's Essays, vol. 1; Jortin's Dissertations ; Bolingbroke's Dissertations ; Hume's Essays, vol. 2 (four weeks after vol. 1) ; Sermons par Massillon ; Alison on Taste ; Smith's Theory, vol. 2 ; Kames's Sketches ; Theological Repository, vol. 1 ; Gregory's Sermons ; Necker's Religious Opinions ; Platonis Opera, folio ; Hakewell's Apology (a very peculiar book) ; Campbell on Rhetoric ; Platonis Opera ; Campbell on Rhetoric (permission to have Plato and Campbell together) ; Ferguson's Essay ; Oeuvres de Maupertuis ; Hume's Essays. This brings us down to August 12, showing that Mill resided in Edinburgh this summer, and was absent only in September and October, being then probably either at Fettercairn House, or, for a holiday, at Northwater Bridge.

The third session opens with the entry, November 26, Oeuvres de Fénélon ; Plato's Works ; Ferguson's Philosophy ; Plato's Works ; Ferguson's Philosophy ; Plato's Works ; (for six weeks an alternation of the two) ; Massillon's Sermons ; Oeuvres de Fénélon ; Massillon ; Plato's Works ; History of Man ; Plato's Works—April 27, 1796, last entry of the session.

He has now made three full sessions in Divinity. His fourth and last might be what is called a partial session—two or three weeks, during which his principal duty is the delivering of the last of his prescribed discourses in the Hall. Only three entries occur :—December 26 ; Locke's Works, vol. 2. December 29 ; Whitby on the Five Points. January 2 ; Abernethie's Sermons. The two last may have had some bearing on his discourses.

The foregoing list speaks for itself. Mr. Masson remarks that it is very unlike the lists of the other Divinity students. Mental Philosophy is the foremost subject of his choice ; but it surprises us that he had not yet become privately possessed of such leading authors as Locke and Reid. There is also a beginning of his studies in Historical and Social Philosophy ; a dead set at Plato ; and an attempt upon the flowery vein of Massillon. He is already a fair French scholar.

A word or two now on his college companions.   I doubt if
there were ever at one time gathered together in one spot
such a host of young men of ability as were at Edinburgh College in the last ten years of the last century.   Thomas M'Crie
as well as John Leyden sat with Mill in the Senior Greek Class
in 1790-1.   Brougham was at college at the same time,
although young, and must have then commenced his intimacy
with Mill.*   Jeffrey should have gone to Edinburgh College
for his whole education, but seems to have attended only the
class of Law.   Whether Mill knew him here I cannot say.
Thomas Thomson, the chemist, was a class-fellow both in Arts
and Divinity, and was all through life an intimate friend.   Sir
D. Brewster knew Mill, but their college careers only touched :
Mill ended in the Divinity Hall in the year that Brewster
began.   Another of Mill's life-long friendships may have
commenced here : Professor Wallace began to study in Edinburgh at that time, although mainly in the scientific classes.
In the *Life of Constable* is given an interesting sketch of his
first start.†   Among many other names of after-repute may be
mentioned also Mountstuart Elphinstone.   We may readily
imagine Mill's conversational encounters with such men, but
we have nothing to record as to facts.   An Aberdeen life in
the same years, would, I must admit, have been a dull affair.
These were the closing years of Beattie and Campbell in
Marischal College ; and the young men of the period were
undistinguished.   In the previous decade (1781-5) James

---

* Brougham's biography shows that he attended Playfair in 1792-3, Mill's
third year.

† Constable's description of Hill's book shop, in Parliament Close, where he
and Wallace were fellow-shopmen, and which was frequented by the professors
and clergy (Burns came there when in Edinburgh), can be used as a help in
our imagination of James Mill's Edinburgh life.   Most probably he here
became acquainted with Wallace , and, at all events, their intimacy would
bring him here.   Wallace was an admirable mathematician, but was neither a
metaphysician nor a sceptic.   James Mill's sociability was much wider than his
tastes and opinions.

Mackintosh and Robert Hall were fellow-students at King's College.

Having thus presented his college life in unbroken narrative, because of the continuity of the known facts, I may as well go on to the date of his being licensed as a preacher, making use of the records of the Presbytery of Brechin, to which I have been allowed to refer. He finished the Divinity Course in January, 1797, and had now to present himself to be taken on trial for license. The first entry in the Presbytery records is on the 19th of October, 1796, at which date he was allowed to make an appearance in anticipation ; being introduced by his friend, Mr. Peters. At the subsequent meeting in December, notice is given by Mr. Peters, that at the next ordinary meeting, Mr. James Mill, student in Divinity, upon producing proper certificates, be admitted to his questionary trials. On the 1st of February, 1797, he accordingly appears ; produces his certificate from the Professor of Divinity that he had regularly attended the Divinity Hall and had delivered the usual exercises with approbation, and that his conduct had been suitable to his views. He was then subjected to questionary trials, or, as we call it, a *vivâ voce* examination, and gave satisfactory answers. Whereupon he was reported to the ensuing Synod, which had to authorise the Presbytery to proceed with the rest of his probationary trials. He is not mentioned again in the Presbytery books till the 28th of June, although in the meantime the subjects of some of his discourses must have been prescribed to him. He delivered his "Homily" on Matthew v. 8 ("Blessed are the pure in heart, for they shall see God"), and, more interesting still, his "Exegesis" (Latin) on the foundations of Natural Religion, "Num sit Dei cognitio naturalis?" The Presbytery is satisfied, and farther prescribes, as a "Lecture," the 14th chapter of John's Gospel. On the 30th August, he delivers the Lecture, together with his "Exercise in addition" on Galatians ii.

20 ("I am crucified with Christ," &c.).   Both are approved of,
and there are prescribed farther, Revelation xxii. 14, for a popular sermon, the fifth century for a discourse on Church History, and the 23rd Psalm in Hebrew to be explained.   On the
11th of October, he gives the popular sermon.   An unexplained blank of a year occurs between this appearance and
his next, which was the last.   On the 4th of October, 1798, he
is examined at large upon his knowledge of Chronology and
Church History, and of the Hebrew and Greek languages, and
is approved.   "And the Presbytery having taken the whole
of his trials under their consideration, Did and hereby Do
unanimously approve and sustain them, and therefore after he
had given satisfying answers to the usual Questions, and subscribed the Confession of Faith and Formula, *coram*, and after
Act Eight of the Assembly, 1759 [directed against obtaining a
church by Simony] was read to him, the Presbytery Did and
hereby Do Licence him, the said Mr. James Mill, to Preach
the Gospel of Jesus Christ.   The Moderator [his friend, Mr.
Peters] having given him suitable Directions, the above was
intimated to him."

Being now qualified to preach, he would display his powers,
in the first instance, in the churches of his own neighbourhood.   Very few records of his preaching exist; but there is
good evidence of his officiating in the church of Logie Pert.
My informant, the last survivor of the Barclay family, distinctly
remembers hearing him on one occasion; and knows of his
preaching twice.   She remembers his loud clear voice, which
filled the church; that his text was from Peter; and that the
generality of the hearers complained of not being able to understand him.   Sir David Brewster said to myself, "I've heard
him preach; and no great han' he made o't".   This would be
at the Divinity Hall, not the best place for a young preacher
to show all that was in him.   His discourses would no doubt
be severely reasoned, but wanting in the unction of the popular evangelical preacher.

It was known in Mill's own family that in a saddle bag in
the attic at his house in Queen's Square, there was a parcel o
his sermons. At the time of the family's removal to Kensing
ton these had disappeared; the belief was that he had destroye(
them. The "saddle bag" suggests a curious coincidence witl
the traditional equipment of the "probationer" or license(
preacher of former days, who rode on horseback from parish t(
parish to supply pulpits in the temporary absence of the minis
ters. The ordinary probationer spent his time in going abou
in this fashion: as is the case still; but Mill having othe
engagements could hardly have been for any length of time s(
occupied. It is curious, however, that John Mill should pr(
fess uncertainty as to whether his father had been licensed t(
preach.

It is no easy matter to trace Mill's movements and occupa
tions from 1790 to 1802, in that part of his time not spent a
college. That he acted as private tutor in various familie
must be received as a fact, but the particulars handed dow
are very confusing. The best attested of these engagements i
that connected with the Fettercairn family. We know that h
acted as tutor to Miss Stuart. She was three years younge
than himself; being fourteen at the time he went to college
In the year 1797 she was married, being then twenty-one
and we may reasonably suppose that her connexion wit
Mill as a tutor may have ceased some time before that even
If she was done with him at eighteen, in 1794, he must hav
taught her from the beginning of his college life, if not als
before; either at Fettercairn House, in his vacations, or partl
there, and partly in Edinburgh while attending classes.* A
any rate it must have been at an early period of his studie

* I gather from Lockhart's *Life of Scott*, that Sir John and Lady Ja
Stuart lived for a long time secluded (that is, in their country house), but th
several years before 1797 they resided in Edinburgh part of the year; no dou
to educate and bring out their daughter. Mill would thus be very much wi
them both in summer and winter during his first college years.

She had reached an interesting age, and made a lasting impression on his mind. He spoke of her in later years with some warmth; putting it in the form of her great kindness to him; although, if we believe the traditions, the first source of all the friendship displayed towards him by the family was her mother.

The romance that surrounds this lady is now well known. Lockhart gives the incidents of Scott's passion for her. In marrying the son of the banker, Sir William Forbes, she became the mother of James David Forbes, the distinguished Natural Philosophy Professor of Edinburgh. In the *Life of Forbes* is given her portrait along with her husband's; and one could easily fall into the opinion that her cast of expression and mind is what was reproduced in the professor, as he unfortunately participated in her constitutional delicacy. Beloved of so many gods, she died young.

It is thus certain that Mill resided for a length of time in the family as Miss Stuart's tutor: it is equally certain that the house was always open to him as a guest. He might walk across any day from Northwater Bridge to Fettercairn House, a distance of four miles, and he was counted upon when company were in the house.

The House of Fettercairn, being the only extant domicile that we are able to associate with Mill in Scotland, deserves a brief notice. The village of Fettercairn, containing 400 inhabitants, is considerably off the line of rail between Forfar and Aberdeen, being five miles north-west from Laurencekirk. It is a mile and a-half from the Grampians, and between it and them, is Fettercairn House and the more stately House of Fasque, belonging to the Gladstone family: the grounds of the two being about contiguous. Fettercairn House is half a mile from the village. Modern additions have been made to the original building, which, however, is still distinctly apparent. It is upwards of two centuries old, and as regards extent, convenience, and comfort, would be midway between the cramped old castle and the spacious modern country house; its external decoration in the way of turrets and ornamental projections is very limited. Stripped, by the new additions, of all smaller adjuncts of former days, the main block is a plain three-storey building, a hundred feet in length. The lower floor was the kitchen and offices : the first floor a range of fair-sized public rooms, the house being only room thick. The upper floor contained a range of good bed-rooms large and small; imagination readily fixes on one of them as Mill's room. In this house, with its pleasant grounds, surroundings, and walks to the mountains, Mill spent many happy and studious days. The portraits, still preserved in the house, enable us to conceive the figures of his host and hostess. Sir John is seen to be a man of very fine features, as well as of stately height. Of his daughter in girlhood, there is no portrait; the existing picture must have been taken after her marriage; it is, however specially venerated by being kept in a shut-up frame.

The Fettercairn estate is now the property of Lord Clinton's eldest son, a minor (Hon. Chas. H. R. Trefusis), whose mother was the great-grand daughter of Sir John Stuart.

Passengers in the railway between Dubton and Laurencekirk can see, right and left of them, the scenery where Mill's boyhood rambled; on the left is the Grampian chain, with the intervening strath of four or five miles in width. The Craigo station is the nearest to the Northwater Bridge.

It is curious to think of the close geographical proximity of Scotch metaphysical talent in that neighbourhood. Beattie was born at Laurencekirk. In a long forenoon walk, through the Grampian pass, by Fettercairn and Fasque, Mill could reach the birth-place of Reid (manse of the parish of Strahan) and four miles farther, the manse of Banchory-Ternan, on the Dee, where Campbell wrote the *Philosophy of Rhetoric.*

But now as to his other tutorships, say from 1795 to 1802. One engagement, not mentioned in any tradition, I have been able to trace out by the assistance of a daughter of Professor

Stuart of Marischal College (born in 1792), who distinctly
remembers having seen James Mill in Aberdeen.   This was to
me an entirely novel circumstance.   No one had ever heard
him say that he had been in Aberdeen, or mention any fact
that implied it.   As the lady in question was the niece of Mr.
Peters, and often visited his manse as a child, she probably
saw Mill there; but she farther states that she knew him as a
tutor in Aberdeen, in the family of Mr. Burnet of Elrick, one
of the branches of the family that gave birth to Bishop Burnet.
At the time when I first received this information, one of the
sons that would have been his pupils was still alive.   From him
I received this statement: "It is quite true that *a* Mr. Mill was
private tutor in my father's family, whom I am aware my father
held in high estimation, and kept up an intimate correspondence with for years afterwards, but I am sorry to say that my
memory does not serve me sufficiently to give any reliable
information, and I was not even aware of the Mr. Mill in
question being the father of John Stuart Mill".   That an intimate or extensive correspondence was kept up I should very
much doubt; but if the letters are ever forthcoming, they will
be a valuable contribution to the biography, assuming that
there is no mistake.   A farther confirmation, however, occurs
in Mill's own letters to Mr. Barclay, who had a brother that
studied in Marischal College.   Mill promises to introduce this
brother to "his friends in Aberdeen".   Now he might have
had one or two friends in Aberdeen, without ever being there;
but the unqualified plural seems to imply that he had made
friends there by residence.

This engagement must have been subsequent to his leaving
the Divinity Hall in the beginning of 1797; for although he
might have been tutor to families in the south while attending
college, seeing that the high families often wintered in Edinburgh, he could hardly have been a tutor in Aberdeen so long
as he was a student.   His introduction to Mr. Burnet was,
without doubt, through Professor Stuart.   The professor's

daughter related a tradition to the effect that Mill threw up his appointment suddenly, owing to an affront given him at a dinner party; but this cannot be received if we are to trust Mr Burnet's own statement. The story will re-appear presently in an altered form.

On the above supposition as to the time of this engagement Mill would have been in Aberdeen after being a licentiate o the Church; and I therefore thought it worth while to search the records of the Kirk Session of Aberdeen, in which a regula insertion is made of the preachers and texts every Sunday in the three parish churches. I found his friend, Mr. Peters twice mentioned, but Mill's name does not occur. There were other churches, called chapels of ease, but their records I have not seen.

Some illumination of these dark years is supplied by a series of letters addressed by Mill to Dr. Thomas Thomson the celebrated chemist. They were written from London, and therefore, relate to a subsequent stage, and will be made use o when we come to that stage. They indirectly, however, assis us in reference to the Edinburgh period. The intimacy sub sisting between Mill and Dr. Thomson makes a large part o his early biography. A nearly equal intimacy obtained between him and the brother of the chemist, James Thomson, after wards Dr. James Thomson, minister of Eccles, in Berwickshire Short biographies of the brothers Thomson were drawn up and printed by the late Dr. Robert Dundas Thomson, Lecturer a St. Thomas's Hospital, son of Dr. James Thomson, and son-in-law of Dr. Thomas Thomson, as well as his assistant in Glasgow, during his last years. These biographies impar some valuable information respecting Mill.

The brothers Thomson were successively engaged as as sistant editors to the *Encyclopædia Britannica*, from 1796 til 1800, the period of publication of the Supplement to the Third Edition: the chief editor being George Gleig, after

wards Bishop of Brechin and Primus of Scotland.   Both
brothers contributed largely to the work—James, theological
and miscellaneous articles, Thomas, his first scientific compositions, the foundation of his subsequent works.   The contributions of the brothers seem to have extended into the Fourth
Edition, which began to be published in 1805.   The allowance
for the editorial part of the work was £50 a-year, with house,
coal and candle, in the office.   The pay to contributors was
three guineas a sheet.

    Mention is made, in both Memoirs, of the fact that, besides
the standing Theological (debating) Society, there was in
Edinburgh, a Select Literary Society for general subjects, composed of six persons—James and Thomas Thomson, James
Mill, John Barclay, the anatomist; James Carter, afterwards of
Liverpool, a medical writer; and Dr. Miller, who, I suppose,
was James Miller the editor of the Fourth Edition of the
Encyclopædia (the two memoirs differ somewhat in the enumeration).   These represent Mill's most intimate friends in Edinburgh, as regarded study and discussion.   At least four out of
the six ultimately embarked in lay occupations.

    It was in 1800 that Dr. Thomas Thomson, having finished
editing the Supplement to the *Encyclopædia*, found a more
commanding and lucrative sphere as a lecturer on chemistry.
He associated himself with Barclay, who had been giving lectures in anatomy in a hired house since 1797.   One of the
memoirs states, as if a coincident fact, that "James Mill obtained a tutorship in the family of a Scottish nobleman in East
Lothian"; the other memoir adds—on the recommendation of
Finlayson, professor of Logic.   The inference would be that
before that time Mill was resident in Edinburgh; his occupation is not stated.   He was certainly as well qualified for
writing articles in the *Encyclopædia* as either of the Thomsons,
and seeing that they were editors in succession, he must have
had it in his power to contribute, but we have no information
as to the fact.   One of the traditions floating in his father's

family, and given me by an old man, his relative, whom I had been able to interrogate, was that he had been a corrector for the press in Edinburgh.

The name of the nobleman is not given; but the narrative, repeated in the same words in both memoirs, goes on to say that "he gave offence to the heads of the family by drinking the health at table of one of the junior female members of the house," and in consequence "gave up his situation, and determined to trust to his pen and his own exertions". This is a curious echo of the story told me by the daughter of Professor Stuart, of Aberdeen, who laid the scene in the family of Burnet of Elrick, but stated that the precise offence to Mill's pride consisted in his being, on one occasion, motioned to leave the dinner table with the ladies. It must be the same story, and the version coming to us from the Thomsons is the most to be relied on. If connected with his resolution to go to London, the fact must have been well remembered by both brothers, and we have it from their nearest relative.

Supposing, as appears to be implied, that Mill entered upon this tutorship when Dr. Thomson began lecturing, and gave it up previously to going to London, he would probably have been a little more than a year in the family. Now one of the particulars stated by Mr. David Barclay, and confirmed by at least one other testimony (an insertion by Lord Brougham, in the biography in the *Penny Cyclopædia*), is that Mill was for some time tutor in the family of the Marquis of Tweeddale. The other noble houses of East Lothian are those of Wemyss and Haddington; in neither of which was there a young family under tuition in 1800. In the house of Tweeddale, a large family was just growing up; the eldest son was thirteen, and a daughter next to him was twelve. This eldest son was the venerable Marquis, not long since deceased; and to him, before his death, I applied for information on the point. He responded to my enquiries with great courtesy, and took pains to recall the particulars of his early education, from which it would appear that he could not have had Mill as a tutor. I regard his statements as decisive up to the year 1800, when he went to a succession of schools in or about London, to finish his education, before entering the army. Excepting that the Marquis should not have entirely forgotten what was going on at home during the years 1800 and 1801, there is nothing to preclude Mill's being tutor in the family to the next children, from some time in 1800 to the end of 1801. Unfortunately, at the time the Marquis wrote, his sister, who was next him, was too ill to be interrogated, and soon after died. She would be the beauty that Mill had rashly toasted. The next eldest brother, after the Marquis, Lord James Hay, married a lady of property near Aberdeen, and lived there the greater part of his life, but has been dead for several years. If the point had been raised in time, Lord James could no doubt have set it to rest. We must be content with supposing that within the limits mentioned the connexion actually took place, but terminated in a way to make both parties willing to forget all about it. There seems no alternative mode of accounting for the origin of a tradition authenticated both by David Barclay and by the brothers Thomson, as well as by Lord Brougham.

I will now present in one connected view the notices of Mill " at home," or in his family at Northwater Bridge. He would not reside there continuously any year after first going to college, but he was known to be there occasionally in vacations, and on longer or shorter visits.

Taking our stand about 1795, we discern that his parents without being gone in years, were yet not " what they had been "; indeed the mother was only forty, but was prematurely feeble. Perhaps as yet there was no failure in their circumstances, but the decline was not far off. William was twenty, and had for years been in his father's shop; another of the workmen is identified at that date, a married man, who lived apart from the Mills. These would probably be

Mill's usual complement of workmen; although it is admitted that he might have three men at work. The household would thus be made up of father and mother, James (when at home), William, and May (eighteen), on whom would fall a chief part of the housework, as well as the shoe-binding for the shop.

The west room of the house contained two beds along the right hand wall; in that room the mother hung up a canvas curtain ("cannass" it was called, being what is laid on the threshing-floor to keep the corn together); thus cutting off from the draught and from the gaze, the farther end of the room, including James's bed, the fire, and the gable window. This was his study; and the whole arrangement was vividly retained in the memory of contemporaries. Here he had his book shelves, his little round table and chair, and the gable window sill for a temporary shelf. He spent great part of his day in study. He had his regular pedestrian stretches; one secluded narrow glen is called "James Mill's walk". He avoided people on the road; and was called haughty, shy, or reserved, according to the point of view of the critic. He went often in the evening to tea with the Barclays, being thoroughly at home there. Their little library would be an extension of his compass of reading. One of the sons of the house, Robert, studied for the church, and was assisted in his studies by Mill. Writing to David Barclay from London, many years after, he reverts with much warmth to his early friendship with the family. Referring to a letter from another correspondent, his words are, "He stated that your mother whose age must now be very great, is in a melancholy state of health. I beg you will present to her my most affectionate remembrance, and tell her that few things on earth would give me greater pleasure than to see her again. The tears come in my eyes when I think of her and the excellent man your father; whom I always loved next to my own, and in whose house I was for so many years as much at home as in that of my own. Tell me of your brothers William and Robert, and of all your sisters; I know but little of your movements, since I saw your brother Robert in London."

Besides the minister, he had as friends the most important people in the parish, among whom special mention is made of Lord Kintore's factor, or steward.

His meals he took alone in his screened study; they were provided by his mother expressly for his supposed needs. Among the other members of the family who would take their meals in the kitchen, there is said to have been a line of demarcation on the score of rank, but authorities are not agreed as to how it was drawn. Some accounts represent the mother as having, in her dignified and luxurious fashion, a table apart; others say that she and her husband were at one table, and the workmen with the two younger children at the other.*

The latest recorded incident of his career in Scotland is his being defeated in the attempt to become minister of the pleasant village of Craig, a long narrow strip of uplands lying on the coast between Montrose and the Bay of Lunan. Mill could have taken care of such a parish, and yet have found time for his favourite studies, working his way to authorship, and almost certainly to a chair in a university. The patronage was in the hands of the Divinity professors of St. Andrews, who might be expected to favour one of their own pupils; but

---

* James Mill, the father, regularly fasted on Sunday till he returned from church, and it is not likely that the less strict members of the household would breakfast very sumptuously on Sunday mornings. He had an inconvenient habit of whistling in a low "sough" while at his work; and the neighbours remarked that he was never known to give way to it on the Sabbath day. He was very strict in all observances of a religious nature: but as regards the discipline of the children, he and his wife were (in their eldest son's judgment) blameably lax

In the dearth of characteristic illustrations of Mill in his home relations, the following anecdote may be excused. One day his sister coming to serve his dinner, found him inclining his little table to his lap. She exclaims, " Hoo can the things *sit* there?" He replies, "If they wunna *sit*, try if they'll *stan*'". It may be going too far to interpret this as showing his early resolution to conquer Scotticisms, which he carried out in after-life with admitted success.

in this case the contest turned upon other considerations. Mill was said to rely on Lady Jane Stuart, whose family, all-powerful in Fifeshire, would have influence with the St. Andrews professors. On the other hand the Rossie family (chief in the parish itself) preferred James Brewster, the brother of Sir David.

As the vacancy did not occur till the resignation of the minister in June, 1803 (more than a year after Mill left Scotland), the contest must have taken place in anticipation, and must have been virtually decided against him. Brewster was a man far more acceptable to an ordinary congregation than ever Mill could have been. It is said that the disappointment was the immediate cause of his going to London—a mere guess.

I cannot conclude this first chapter, embracing Mill's twenty-nine years' life in Scotland, without another remark or two that I could not conveniently incorporate in the narrative.

Reverting to his Edinburgh contemporaries (afterwards men of more or less distinction), and to the various societies where they began to exercise and display their talents, I am struck with the absence of Mill's name from the Speculative Society, the oldest and greatest of all the Edinburgh Debating Societies, and adorned by nearly all the highest names of the time. In fact, to have been a member of this society, between 1790 and 1800, was of itself a distinction; to have been in Edinburgh and not to belong to it, seemed to argue a man unknown.* It

* Take Lord Cockburn's enumeration of the contemporaries of Jeffrey, who became a member in 1792 "In the course of those nine or ten years, he had a succession, and sometimes a cluster, of powerful competitors. It is sufficient to mention Sir Walter Scott, with whom he first became acquainted here ; Dr. John Thomson, John Allen ; David Boyle, now Lord President of the Court of Session, the Rev. Dr. Brunton, the Marquis of Lansdowne, the late Charles, Lord Kinnaird, Dr. Headlam ; Francis Horner ; the late William Adam, Accountant General in the Court of Chancery ; John A. Murray, and James Moncrieff, both afterwards Judges, Henry Brougham, Lord Glenelg, and his late brother Robert Grant ; James Loch, the Honourable Charles Stuart, and William Scarlett. The political sensitiveness of the day at one

is vain to ask why he did not enter the Speculative Society.
We can see, however, that the absence of his name from the
brilliant company that composed it in those years, has led to
his being usually passed over when the roll of his Edinburgh
contemporaries is mustered in history.

As in so many other things, we are entirely in the dark as to
the first impulses of his mind towards liberal politics and political philosophy.   He went to Edinburgh the year following
the outbreak of the French Revolution.   There was a very
good twice-a-week paper in Edinburgh, the *Courant*, which
regularly reported the proceedings in France; and these,
together with the home politics, must have been closely
followed by every earnest and enquiring mind.

The home excitement in the beginning of 1793, was at fever
heat.   Every number of the *Courant* was crowded with reports
of meetings in the counties (chiefly the gentry) at which were
passed votes of confidence in the British Constitution, supposed to be in danger from French infection.   How Mill, at
the age of 20, took all this, we have no indication.*   There
can be little doubt that the merits and demerits of the Revolution would be a subject of stirring debate among all those that
he came in contact with.   He was now reading the best acces-

time obtruded itself rather violently into this hall of philosophical orators; but
it soon passed away, and while it lasted, it only animated their debates, and,
by connecting them with public principles and parties, gave a practical interest
to their proceedings.   The brightest period in the progress of the society was
during the political storm that crossed it in 1799."

The energy of Brougham started another smaller society in 1792, which included Francis Horner, and Andrew Thomson, the great Scotch preacher of
after years, and a few lawyers, but not Mill.   Andrew Thomson would be with
Mill in the Theological Society.

* On the 30th August this year, occurred the memorable trial of Thomas
Muir, who was sentenced to 14 years' transportation for sedition, as the mildest
form of political agitation was then called.   Cockburn tells us that Jeffrey and
Sir Samuel Romilly were present.   "Neither of them ever forgot it.   Jeffrey
never mentioned it without horror."   Next January, 1794, occurred the trial
and banishment of the other Edinburgh political martyrs.   These atrocities
would affect Mill no less than they did Jeffrey and Romilly.

sible books on the theory of Government, as Millar, Ferguso[n] and Hume. He must also have read a good deal of History ancient and modern. Probably his Greek studies imbued hin with the democratic ideal of Government: but this suppose an independent bias on his part; for very few have ever bee[n] made liberal politicians by classical authors alone.

The extent of his acquired knowledge and original thinking when he left Scotland at the age of twenty-nine, will be judge[d] by what he was able to do in the next few years. He kep[t] back from the aspiring Scotchman's venture upon London until he had attained an unusual maturity of intellectua[l] power; while possessed of good ballast in the moral part Moreover, we are to conceive of him as a youth of great bodil[y] charms. One of my lady informants spoke of him with [a] quite rapturous admiration of his beauty. His figure an[d] proportions were fine; the short breeches of the time showe[d] a leg of perfect form. His features beamed with expression Nothing was wanting that could prepossess people's favourabl[e] regards.

CHAPTER II.

START IN LONDON:

1802-1808.

MILL went to London in the beginning of 1802. It may be held as certain, that he made the journey in the company of Sir John Stuart, whose movements may be judged from the date of the opening of the Parliamentary session. In point of fact that session had been opened the previous winter, and had been kept adjourned for short periods till February; but the business of the year may be said to have commenced about the 9th of February.

If Mill had journeyed on his own resources, he would have followed the plan that he afterwards recommended to his correspondent in Logie Pert, to "go on board a Montrose smack". His friend Thomas Thomson, whose pecuniary circumstances were then much better than Mill's, went to London a few months later in a smack from Leith; the fare was £4 4s., and the entire cost of the journey (lasting a week) was £5 7s. 8d. By coach the expense must have been twice or three times as much. Perhaps Sir John posted, and gave Mill the spare seat.

The first account of him in London is a letter that he addressed, on the 13th March, to Thomas Thomson, which, it appears, had been preceded at a very short interval by another not found in the collection. The one half of the letter recounts his operations with a view to literary employment, the other half is on politics.

His first introduction, how obtained he does not say, was to Dr. Bisset,* who promised to recommend him. But the great object he had in view was to be introduced to Dr. Gifford,† and for this he had already applied to Thomson in the previous letter, and now iterates the request; Bisset also having promised to mention him. It appears that Thomson was not personally known to Gifford, but undertook, solely on the strength of his scientific reputation, to write a testimonial in Mill's behalf. The letter goes on :—" I am extremely ambitious to remain here, which I feel to be so much the best scene for a man of letters, that you can have no notion of it till you be upon the spot. You get an ardour and a spirit of adventurousness, which you never can get an idea of among our over-cautious countrymen at home. Here everybody applauds the most romantic scheme you can form. In Scotland everybody represses you, if you but propose to step out of the beaten track. On the idea of remaining here, I have even formed schemes for you and me already. You must of necessity come here, where you may do anything you like. You may make £500 a year by your pen, and as much by a class. I have mentioned to several people my idea of a class of Juris-

* Dr. Robert Bisset, a Scotchman, born in 1760, author of a *Life of Burke*, *History of the Reign of George III.*, and some novels. He also published an edition of the *Spectator* with notes. He died in 1806. Mill says of him, in the letter, that he has not a single pretension to genius, nor " half the knowledge that you or even I have," and yet makes six or seven hundred a year by his pen solely. He does not appear to have been an editor, so that he could not himself provide employment for Mill.

† This was John Gifford (born 1758), whose real name was John Richards Green. He had squandered a fortune, and took to writing. Besides his voluminous authorship he edited the *Anti-Jacobin Review*, a monthly periodical of good standing From a double coincidence of name, he is apt to be confounded with William Gifford, editor of Canning's *Anti-Jacobin*, and subsequently editor of the *Quarterly Review*. Among other things John Gifford wrote the *Political Life of Pitt*. For his adherence to the government, he was made a police magistrate, and died in 1818. It was as editor of the *Anti-Jacobin Review* that he was so important in Mill's eyes. Possibly also he could be the means of opening a newspaper connection to a qualified aspirant.

prudence, who have assured me that it could not fail to succeed, and have advised me for that purpose to enter myself in
one of the Inns of Court the first term ; by which means too
I may become a lawyer, if I shall ever think proper to make
that attempt.* If you were here, and we had made to ourselves something of a name, which I think we surely might do,
what would hinder us to produce a periodical work of our own,
of any description that we might approve ? I am sure we
might make it more interesting than anything which is published at present. And the profits of these things, when they
have a good sale, are immense. And our classes might go on
at the same time, as well as larger undertakings which we
might carry on. The great difficulty here is a beginning—
when you have got that, you can make your own terms."

The second half of this interesting letter is on politics. Mill
entered with the utmost zest into the political situation, notwithstanding a disclaimer to the effect that the newspapers
tell all the news except what was kept secret from everybody.
He had not been idle the few weeks of his stay. He had seen
almost everything worth seeing in London. He had been at
every tolerable debate, and had heard all the ministers speak,
but had not yet heard Pitt, Fox, or Sheridan. The eloquence

---

* The proposal to set up a class of Jurisprudence is very suggestive. It
would seem to show that, while yet in Edinburgh, he had pushed his study of
the Moral Sciences not merely into Politics and Political Economy, but also
into Law and Jurisprudence. The moment chosen for the proposal would be
a trying one. Bentham had published enough to upset the credit of previous
jurisprudence, but his more important constructive treatises were still unpublished The *Fragment on Government*, the *Principles of Morals and Legislation*, the *Defence of Usury*, the *Panopticon or Prison Discipline* were published,
and these I can infer from an expression of Mill's he had studied early.
Dumont's Treatise was published in Paris this very year, and may have caught
Mill's wakeful eye I observe in a note to his translation of Villers's work on
The Reformation (1805) that he professes acquaintance with the Prussian and
the Danish Codes. His article on Jurisprudence written long afterwards is
dependent on the later works of Bentham. Of course, in thinking of a subject
for lectures, he had in view the demand, and found that there was a sphere
among the law students.

of the House of Commons, he says, is nothing to the Genera Assembly, no speaker that he had yet heard was equal t twenty in the Assembly. "They speak such silly stuff, an are so much at a loss to get it out, that they are more like boy in an evening society at college, than senators carrying on th business of a great nation. The old political stagers of bot sides are standing completely aloof at present." *

The particular moment of public affairs was the discussio of the pending treaty of peace, called the peace of Amien: The preliminary articles had not yet been signed, but suc points as the giving up of Malta to the Knights of St. Joh were freely canvassed, and much objected to. Mill had mad up his mind in favour of peace at the cost of the various cor cessions, and not only so, but had written a short paper on tha side, and had sent it to Dr. Bisset to show what he could do a an occasional writer on politics. His activity did not sto there. "I inserted a squib in the *True Briton* (newspaper) c 12th March (yesterday) against the Pic-nic Theatre."† I d not know whether Bisset had anything to do with this pape or whether Mill obtained, or tried to obtain, admission to it a a writer.

* The only debates of interest that had yet occurred were Feb. 17—o the Civil List, chiefly with reference to the affairs of the Prince of Wales, i which Pitt and Fox both spoke; March 3—on the Army Estimates—a grea War debate; March 5—on the American Treaty Bill, also of considerabl length. Mill probably heard the two last.

He afterwards returns to his comparisons between the House of Commor orators and the orators of the General Assembly, at whose debates he had ofte been present. In those years among the men that wielded the Scotch eccles astical democracy were Principal Hill (who succeeded Robertson, the historiar as leader), Sir H. Moncrieff, Dr. Bryce Johnstone, Dr. Grieve, Dr. Alexande Carlyle, and the theological professors Hunter and Hardie. Distinguishe judges and non-theological professors, as well as the pick of the nobility an gentry, sat as lay representatives, and often took part in the debates

† The squib is a very small affair, consisting in all of a few lines. I reflects somewhat broadly upon the dissipated morals of the " Pic-nic Pro prietors," as they are called by their young satirist. No clue worth followin out is afforded either as to their actual proceedings or as to the new comer interest in them.

We have not another letter to Thomson for eight weeks; in the middle of the interval occurs his first communication to his friend David Barclay (17th April). This last is our evidence that he went to London by road. He gives his impressions of English farming, as seen on his way. The first thing that struck him was the absence of waste land. The next was the inferiority of English farming, of which he gave two illustrations. One was that their ridges were more crooked than the worst even of the old ridges at home. The second was their ploughing with three, four, and even five strong horses all in a line; the plough itself being "a great ill-contrived, abominable instrument". On the other hand, "they excel us in the rearing and fattening of cattle".

Then for London itself. He works up a considerably exaggerated picture for Barclay's astonishment. On all sides streets filled, almost choking, with people, horses, waggons, carts, carriages, and every sort of bustle. Another very fine sight, Hyde Park, especially on a Sunday, where all the nobility and gentry go to air themselves. You see thousands of carriages and horsemen; and the walks, for miles, filled with the finest-dressed people walking almost as thick as the passages of your church when the people are coming out. Another sight was sailing down the river through thousands and tens of thousands of ships, of all sizes and all nations, with myriads of small craft plying around. He repeats to Barclay his having been often in the House of Commons. In the interval since he wrote to Thomson, he has heard Fox make one of the greatest speeches he was ever heard to deliver; it lasted two hours and a half.*

---

* In the interval, March 13 to April 17, Fox made three great speeches. First on March 16, in moving for a new writ for Tavistock, occasioned by the death of the Duke of Bedford, he indulged in a lengthened panegyric on the deceased Duke. On March 29, with reference to the everlasting worry of the Civil List, he delivered an animated speech occupying more than six of Hansard's dense pages, Pitt replying. On March 31, the same subject came up with more special reference to the Prince of Wales, on a motion by Manners Sutton relative to the Duchy of Cornwall. Fox supported the motion. The second of the three speeches must be what Mill alluded to.

He has another incident to relate. Walking yesterday in a solitary part of Hyde Park (he does not say where that was) up came two gentlemen riding behind, and talking togethe most earnestly. He looks once round; they are Pitt and Ad dington. He stared at them, Pitt stared back at him two o three times. To complete his chain of adventures, he nex overtakes the Prince of Wales on horseback, and finally meet the Princess of Wales in an open chaise.

More to business is his second letter to Thomson on th 10th of May. He is now at work for Gifford in the *Anti Jacobin Review*. He has written an article on Belsham' *Elements of Logic and Mental Philosophy*,* it is printed and i to appear on the 1st of June (out in May). He now wishe to review Thomson's own book (first edition of his *System o Chemistry*, 4 vols.); he has half read it, and but for Belsham stopping the way, would like it to be the leading article of th next number of the *Review*. (It appeared in the June number.

He gives a full picture of his situation and prospects. A yet his chief stay seems to be Gifford, who is full of friendly demonstrations, advises original composition, promises him books for review, but does not give him much encouragement In fact, the return from the *Anti-Jacobin Review* would be but a small part of his maintenance. He doubts whether it would be prudent to stop in London on this precarious footing. " I may

---

* This is Mill's first article on Mental Philosophy known to us. It i sufficiently mature and decided in its views; and his stern logic is already in the ascendant. His mode of stating his positions is not exactly what he fol lowed afterwards. He attacks Belsham's definitions, his logic, his order o putting logic before metaphysics, his theory of memory. He attacks the vib rations of Hartley, and praises Reid's arguments against them. He quarrel with Belsham as to the purpose of Locke's *Essay*, which he calls—"an achievement of thought, the greatest perhaps on record in the treating of the human mind" Attacks his selfish theory of morals "it imposes an obligation to be vicious, removes the moral character of the Deity, and renders it impos sible to prove a future state". "Till you have first proved the moral attributes of God, it is absurd to offer a proof of Revelation. For, however certainly you prove revelation to be the word of God, unless I know that God is true, how do I know that his word is true?"

tell you, however, that I am a good deal more than half
inclined to do so, and risk everything rather than abandon the
hopes I have allowed myself to indulge. I can support myself
for a year, as you propose, by the *Encyclopædia* [*Britannica*,
the fourth edition now getting forward under the editorship
of Miller], and during the time bring forward too, perhaps,
some little thing to make myself known : I am willing to
labour hard and live penuriously, and it will be devilish hard,
if a man, good for anything, cannot keep himself alive here on
these terms."

He recites a long conversation he had with Gifford (at a
Sunday dinner) upon public affairs ; but not interesting to us.
It reveals the type of partisan that could criticise his party
very freely (of Pitt he even says, " when a man deserts his
principles I give him up "), but took care never to vote on the
other side.   I cannot tell whether any value now attaches to
the fact (given by Gifford) that Sir Sidney Smith never heard
Napoleon called a great man without getting into a rage, &c.

He has another House of Commons debate to describe :
one of the great debates of the session, on a motion by Nicholls
for censuring the late Administration, and Pitt more especially
(May 7). It was a fine opportunity for hearing all the good
speakers of the Opposition. Nicholls, who opened, showed a
good deal of knowledge ; but very inelegant both as to language
and delivery. Lord Belgrave, on the other side, had small
merit. A number of silly fellows followed, and iterated Pitt's
praises—saviour of the country—financial abilities—eloquence
—firmness, manliness, integrity—sedition—danger of the constitution—morality, religion, social order, &c. The first speech
worth mentioning was by T. Erskine, *apropos* of whom Mill
denounces the speaking generally for diffuseness, want of
arrangement, disproportion, &c. Wilberforce spoke tolerably
well in favour of ministers—a flowing, wordy style, a clear
though effeminate voice—says common things in a pleasing
manner—only an ugly little wretch to look upon. Grey—a

tallish, rather young, genteel man. His eloquence, ver
powerful, is described with great minuteness and in a strain o
high compliment. Lord Hawkesbury—able in Pitt's defence
his speaking very much resembling Pitt's peculiar style o
vehemence. But now Fox rose—the foremost man in th
House of Commons by many degrees ; the most profound an
philosophical as well as the most generous and liberal ; sucl
an appearance of good humour ; does every thing with so mucl
nature and ease.

In three weeks (31st May) another letter to Thomson, com
municating an improvement in his prospects. The good fortun
consists in a proposition made to him to co-operate in a grea
literary work with Dr. Hunter.* It was to re-write a popula
book called *Nature Delineated*, keeping the plan, but freshenin
the material. Hunter had been entrusted by two booksellei
with the work, and, at his request, Mill drew the scheme
after Bacon's famous classification of knowledge. He goe
into some detail, asks Thomson's advice upon the physica
topics, and does not shrink from undertaking to write th
greater part himself. He expects liberal terms, and also t
become known to the booksellers. Hunter's name, he say;
is pretty high.

He had already delivered an introduction from Thomson t
"Spankie," who promised to procure newspaper work for hir
next season. This was Robert Spankie, afterwards Serjean
Spankie, who was the editor of the *Morning Chronicle*, whil
Perry was occupied in a manufacturing speculation. We d
not hear that the promise was fulfilled : Mill's sway in th
Chronicle was reserved for another day.

The letter then intimates that his review of Thomson's boo

* This was evidently Dr. Henry Hunter, a native of Perthshire, and livin
in London as minister of the Scotch Church, London Wall He was a volu
minous writer—as compiler, editor, and translator—now completely neglectec
Three of his translations were of well-known works—Euler's *Letters*, St. Pierre'
Studies of Nature, and Lavater's *Physiognomy*. He was a very good man fc
Mill to get hold of, and Mill would be the square peg in his square hole.

is to appear as leader in the next number of the *Anti-Jacobin Review*. He never so much regretted his imperfect knowledge of the subject; wished to compare the book with some other elementary treatises, but was afraid.* His friendly interest in the success of the book is warmly expressed.

In the same letter we have the two days' debate on the Peace (May 13, 14) which may be considered *the* debate of the session. For this he had to be in the gallery from eleven forenoon to four next morning, and again from eleven till five in the morning. Very little good speaking. Windham—a disagreeable, squeaking voice, little animation, and all the obscurity of dulness. Lord Hawkesbury—able, but unmercifully long; the fault of them all, for want of method. The rest of the first day, clumsy panegyrics upon Pitt. Next day, somebody whose name he forgot (Sir W. Young) made a tolerable speech on Windham's side. Lord Castlereagh replied: fire and fluency, but not much in what he says—second rate. Dr. Laurence—a great coarse man, but has more knowledge than most of them. The Master of the Rolls (Sir William Grant) made one of the best speeches in the debate; calm, and thinks and argues more closely than most in the House. Near three in the morning, Sheridan rose and delivered " a piece of the most exquisite wit and raillery that I fancy ever came unpremeditatedly from the mouth of man. It was not a number of fine sparks here and there—it was one blaze from beginning to end: he wrote down every part of the antagonists' speeches that struck him, and these he ridiculed with inimitable success. The discussion has hurt the popularity of the ministry, and Pitt will be in as soon as he can gracefully."†

---

* The article is of course intelligent. It summarises the work, and praises the method and the style, but is not critical. I cannot explain how it was that Mill's intimacy with Thomson in Edinburgh should not have given him a better hold of the doctrines of chemistry. Perhaps, the circumstances of his Edinburgh life did not permit him to work at the subject.

† See Wilberforce's Diary, 14th May:—"House till near four again—Sheridan infinitely witty, having been drinking." The greatest witticism

The letter farther intimates that Mill is now sufficiently settled to take rooms by the year, in 33 Surrey Street. He is joined by an old pupil of Thomson's, Macdiarmid, also devoted to literary work, who did not long survive. They have a sitting room, "about as good as yours" (in Bristow Street) and two bed-rooms for 50 guineas: they have to dine at the coffee-house, and get their boots cleaned by the shoe-black. There is still an important postscript :—"I had almost forgot to thank you for your care in providing me work from the *Encyclopædia*. You will see that now I shall have enough to do without it. I intend still to review for Gifford, because I wish to cultivate his acquaintance, and because I think I can review a few books without hindering my other work. You will hear from me again very soon: but now we shall be obliged to pay one another's letters (elevenpence, no franking by Sir John at present)."

Two days afterwards, he writes to Barclay in connexion with his own family, being then in the hurry of moving. Another letter to Barclay of 9th Sept., is little to our purpose, unimportant political comments, and a discussing of harvest prospects; with family matters to be referred to afterwards. There is no letter to Thomson till the 20th Nov. The reason of the blank is that Thomson was in London for ten days in August, but although he has a diary of the humours of his fellow-passengers on board the smack, he gives no record of his dealings with Mill.

Meanwhile the scene of his activity has changed. We left him, in the end of May, planning with Hunter the new edition of *Nature Delineated;* we find him in November, in the advanced stage of a project for a new literary periodical. The

of the speech is the comparison of Pitt to Theseus, who sat so long in one posture that he adhered to the seat; so that when Hercules came to snatch him away, in the sudden jerk a portion of his sitting-part was left behind. Leigh Hunt quotes an anecdote to the effect that Sheridan got this simile from some one as he walked down to the House.

only assignable link in the transition is the fact that Hunter
was seized with inflammation of the lungs and died at Bristol
Wells on the 27th October.   In the new enterprise Mill is
in connexion with the publisher Baldwin, a connexion that
became still closer and lasted his life.* We cannot tell whether
Baldwin was one of the two booksellers that Hunter was employed by for *Nature Delineated ,* nor how the scheme came
to be exchanged for a periodical.   That Mill had considerable
faith in the success of a well-conducted useful-knowledge
periodical we saw before.

The work now planned, in which Mill was to be occupied as
editor and contributor for the next four years, was *The Literary
Journal.* In the prospectus drawn up by him, the key-note
is this:—the projectors "have long been of opinion, that a
publication devoted to the dissemination of liberal and useful
knowledge, on a more comprehensive plan than any which has
yet appeared in this country, would, if rightly executed, be a
work of great utility". A sentence relative to the more rapid
communication of discoveries, hitherto overlooked by our
periodicals, is very likely the insertion of Thomson.   The work
was to be arranged in four divisions—Physics (or Physical
Science), Literature, Manners, Politics.   "Literature" was pretty
wide, including Theology, Mental Philosophy, History, Biography, Geography, Chronology, Travels, Criticism, Poetry, &c.
An unoccupied department of literary criticism is pointed out,
namely, to select and analyse such works as exhibit the literary
spirit of the times.   "Manners" was to cover all the refined
amusements of the country, with dissertations on the usages
of other nations.   "Politics" kept out daily politics, and took
in general views of Politics, Political Economy, Jurisprudence,
and Police.   The work, it is said, has received promises of
support from eminent literary characters.   It was to be issued
weekly, in shilling numbers, commencing in January (1803).

* The biographer of Dr. Thomas Thomson says that Thomson, on the
faith of his reputation solely, gave Mill a letter to Baldwin, as he had done
to Gifford.

The letter of 20th Nov. is occupied with the preparation then far advanced. The prospectus is in course of circulatio Thomson is asked to see to the copies being distributed Edinburgh and Glasgow; Mill himself is to attend to Abe deen. The fear is expressed that it will be too expensive f Scotland: the Scotch, however, are familiar with the devi of half a dozen persons clubbing for a periodical.

The arrangements for supplying the matter are still incomplet Thomson, it is understood, has the whole scientific departme on his shoulders; he was quite equal to it. All the scientif periodicals were ordered for his use. Some one that Mill do not yet know is engaged by Baldwin for the important branc of Manners. For Literature, David Macpherson, a Scotchma is engaged; he is at present occupied with a work on the Hi tory of Commerce (published in four vols., quarto, in 1805 There remain History, Biography, Travels, Theology, Phil sophy, and original essays. Mill had advised Baldwin, apply through Thomson, to Gleig (the former editor of tl *Britannica*). There was another Edinburgh friend, M Christison, to be thought of. (There is an Alexander Chris son, an Edinburgh author of this time). More help is to l found in Edinburgh than in London.

The letter alludes to the labour that had been gone throug in correcting the prospectus. Thomson of course sent sugge tions. Mill is pleased that so few things had been found t correct. Thomson's corrections all adopted, except where h wanted to erase the word "pleasure," as coupled with "advan tage". Mill stands out upon this; people may be found to tak a paper that promises *pleasure*, who are not much allured b mere advantage.

Our remaining letter of the year, 16th December, alludes t a previous one not preserved, which obviously treated of hitch. "Matters will all be right." Thomson had evidentl been busy in looking out contributors to fill the blanks. H own brother James is to do Literature and the Philosophy c

Mind, to Mill's great satisfaction.   Increasing distrust is shown of the London literary labourers; a great many proffered articles already rejected.   Thomson is to use his judgment in employing "Darwinian Brown," or any other, for a purpose not stated. (This is Thomas Brown, the metaphysician; "Darwinian" would be his Edinburgh nickname, from his juvenile work on Darwin's *Zoonomia*).

The prospectus is now afloat.   The publisher has communicated with Ross and with Blackwood in Edinburgh: Mill has written to Aberdeen.   Thomson is to despatch the copies thither, and to leave some with Mr. Forbes, Sir John Stuart's son-in-law, at the Bank.

The letter goes on to express satisfaction at the success of Thomson's own book (*System of Chemistry*); the first edition nearly sold out.   Advice to drive a good bargain over the second; to make the publishers pay sweetly for emendations. Buchan gets £20 for every amended sheet of his *Family Physician*.   Had done something to get a publisher for a work of his brother James's (theological, no doubt); but too much of the kind in the warerooms already.   He lately met James's old pupil (Stirling of Kippendavie) at a ball.

He has now thoughts of taking chambers in one of the Inns of Court, and means to enter as a student of law next term (did neither).

Such is our record of this eventful year.   Probably Mill wrote many things besides those that we have been able to trace; partly for newspapers and partly for reviews.   He plainly intimates that he would go on with the *Anti-Jacobin Review*. But his energies and his hopes are concentrated in the success of his bold design.   It was no small achievement for a young man to have induced a publisher to make the venture.   But he had the power of getting people to believe in him.   He was also cut out for a man of business, and shows it now as an editor; in which vocation, first and last, he must have been occupied for a good many years.

Accordingly, the year 1803 is marked by the publication of the *Literary Journal*, whose pages are our only biographical materials for that year. The letters to Thomson have unfortunately ceased. There are four letters to Barclay, but almost exclusively on family affairs, with occasional political allusions to the breaking out of the war. One dated 3rd January, 1804, informs us that he has been enjoying himself this Christmas season, as well as the hurry of business would permit. It gives farther an account of his part in the general volunteering. "I have been a volunteer these six months, and I am now a very complete soldier. It has cost me a shocking sum of money however, not less I am sure than one-and-twenty or two-and-twenty guineas; and I have been one of the least expensive in the corps. We are still talking about the coming of Bonaparte. Whether he will come or not, God knows; but we are well disposed to receive him. We are 30,000 volunteers in London, and made a very fine figure when we were reviewed by the King in Hyde Park. Our regiment is altogether formed of Scotsmen, and was taken particular notice of by the King. When riding along the lines, he stopt opposite to us and spoke several minutes to our colonel. I was very near, and heard him say: 'A very pretty corps, a very pretty corps indeed—all Scotsmen, my Lord, all Scotsmen?'"

A cursory glance at the *Journal*, enables us with great probability to identify his contributions; and from these we may gather the course of his studies, and the character of his views at this period.

Each number is methodically laid out, beginning with an article on Physical Science, by Thomas Thomson; the succession of articles being a regular course of the natural sciences.

The other subjects in like manner have their appropriate places. In two successive numbers in January appears a complete view of the Human Mind, which I at first supposed, as a matter of course, was Mill's own, but found to be James Thomson's. There is a survey of the political situation of the

chief modern nations, with a very detailed theory of the
French Revolution; whether by Mill, I cannot say. The influence of his opinions must have told upon his contributors.
His own hand appears most clearly in certain Historical and
Biographical Reviews, which, however, make a small proportion
of the Journal; so that his labour must have been mainly
editorial. If we consider that it was a shilling number issued
weekly, that labour could not be small.

I give a few illustrative jottings. In a review of Tytler's
Roman History, there is a strong protest against accepting the
truth of the records of the Kings, and of the transactions generally, prior to the destruction of Carthage—almost exactly the
position of Sir G. C. Lewis. A correspondent's attack on this
article is vigorously met. Stewart's *Life of Reid* is reviewed;
and some pertinent remarks introduced as to the necessity of
a biographer's tracing the early influences operating on the mind
of his subject. The same strain recurs in other articles. An
essay on the structure of the Platonic Dialogue may not be
Mill's, but it must have been prompted by him. A paper occurs
to prove that Utility is not the foundation of virtue; this might
be editorial licence, and not necessarily his own opinions.

The opening number for 1804 is a survey of the literature of
the previous year. The review of the political works and of the
biographies is clearly Mill's. In reference to an affected life of
Chaucer, which he condemns, there is this remark—" Religion
without reason may be feeling, it may be the tremors of the
religious nerve, but it cannot be piety towards God, or love
towards man." A long review of Degerando may be his, but
it is not specially remarkable. His hand is pretty evident in
Theology, especially the apologetic treatises. He views all
such treatises with constant misgivings; remarks how seldom
defences of Christianity answer their purpose, and advises
writers to adhere more to one another.

In connexion with the long-standing discussion on the Corn
Trade, he published a pamphlet in 1804, entitled, *An Essay on*

*the Impolicy of a Bounty on the Exportation of Grain, and o
the Principles which ought to regulate the Commerce of Grai*
This pamphlet I have not seen; it is given by Macculloc
in his *Literature of Political Economy*.   It is the earliest know
publication bearing his name.*

He continues at the *Journal* through 1805.   This year h
published his translation of Villers's work on *The Reformation*
a task that must have occupied a good deal of his time; it is
volume of 490 pages.   The original work was written for
prize proposed in 1802, by the Institute of France: the subjec
was—"What has been the influence of the Reformation c
Luther on the Political situations of the different States c
Europe, and on the Progress of Knowledge."   In the prefac
to the Translation, Mill states that the subject attracted hi
interest at the time it was propounded, as a proof of liberality c
view on the part of an assembly belonging to a Roman Catholi
country (surely this could not be wonderful after the Frenc
Revolution).   His surprise was increased by the work itsel
which was an unsparing display of the vices of the papal system
and an impartial view of the blessings of the Reformatior
Accordingly he undertakes the translation, and adds copiou
notes, embracing quotations from English authors as well a
observations of his own.   He looks upon the publication c
the work as important in its bearing upon the much agitate
Catholic question in Ireland; and thinks that if Catholics wer
once put in a position whence they would no longer regar
Protestants as their enemies, they might be reasoned out c
their Catholic predilections by such a work.

The notes give a very good idea of Mill's reading an
favourite authors at the time.   Long quotations occur fror
Dugald Stewart, George Campbell, Millar, Robertson, Hardi

---

* In Alibone's enumeration of Mill's publications is placed first—"*A
Examination of E. F. Jones's System of Book-keeping, 1796.*"   This is an errc
copied from the *Bibliotheca Britannica*.   The real author was a Londo
accountant of the same name.

(his Professor of Church History). He reinforces all the author's expressions as to the value of free inquiry. He has a very indignant and disparaging note on Voltaire :—" His authority is of very little value "; "he used not only lawful but poisoned arms against religion and liberty": "anything that would abate the admiration so long attached to his works, would be a public benefit". (Notwithstanding all this, Mill was an assiduous reader of Voltaire.) Another curious note, (p. 304) takes Villers to task for speaking of the books of the Bible as mere scraps of the literature of distant ages. "These books comprise the extraordinary code of laws communicated by a benevolent divinity to man." "I am unwilling to ascribe infidelity to any man who does not give certain indications of his being an unbeliever. But I could not allow expressions concerning the Bible, which appear to be not sufficiently respectful, to pass without notice." Villers is also reproved for being a Kantist.*

Villers's book must have been part of his occupation in 1804. The solitary letter preserved for this year gives his mode of spending his day: "Breakfast, and to his office as usual about 8 (office of the *Journal*, presumably at Baldwin's, Southampton Buildings), dined on the way home (by the Strand); read or wrote with great diligence till towards seven; had tea with his fellow-lodger; walked two hours; studied till between eleven and twelve." On the evening of writing the letter, his reading was Xenophon, περὶ οἰκονομίας. This was in the midsummer heat (6th July). Holidays were unknown things to Mill.

To the year 1805, and two, if not three, subsequent years attaches another of Mill's engagements, the editorship of the *St. James's Chronicle* newspaper; on which there hangs nearly

---

* He was the author of a book on the Philosophy of Kant, (Paris, 1801), on which Thomas Brown wrote a long condemnatory criticism of Kant, in the first number of the *Edinburgh Review*.

as great darkness as on the Scotch tutorships. It was know
in his family that he had edited this paper, but the fact wa
never mentioned by himself, and rarely alluded to by any on
The paper was started in 1761, and continued till a few yea
ago, as a clerical and conservative journal. On this footin
Mill's editorship seemed a discord. As Baldwin was the pr
prietor of the paper (it was in the Baldwin family long before
the connexion is explicable enough. The only trustwortl
tradition in the matter makes him editor at the time of h
marriage, which took place this year; so that he carried on th
Journal and the *Chronicle* together. Proceeding upon th
fact, I turned over the file of the *Chronicle* of 1805-6, if po
sible to track his presence. The paper was published evei
second day. The only part that could support an inferenc
was the leading articles. To newspapers readers of our tim
it needs to be explained that the leading article of those day
(at any rate in the *Chronicle*) was but a puny affair; vei
like the introductory Notes now given in the *Spectator*, bi
fewer of them. Generally speaking there was one such artici
or note; very rarely did it amount to a discussion or an argi
ment; most usually a brief recital and slight comment on th
chief topic of the day's news. Now and then, once in two (
three weeks, there was an article of half a column or thre
quarters; when the editor rose to his legs, and descanted i
earnest on what was doing. Of course, this at least would k
Mill's part as editor; how much else he did, we cannot knov
Taking then the file for 1805, the first thing I noticed wa
(January 8) a pretty severe handling of Pitt in connexion wit
Taxes on Knowledge. On February 9, the suspension (
Habeas Corpus in Ireland is styled a melancholy transactioi
On February 19, Pitt's war-tax on farm-horses is condemnec
Generally speaking, the criticism of the Government is fair an
candid. On March 23, the comments made on the recentl
granted Dutch constitution accord with what we should hav
expected. In April occurred one of the greatest episodes (

the Liberty of the Press, second only to the trial of Peltier two
years before. A Tory journal (*The Oracle*) had used very disrespectful language towards the House of Commons with
regard to the proceedings against Lord Melville. On the 25th
of April, Mr. Grey brought the article under the notice of the
House, and moved that the proprietor of the paper be called to
the bar. Long debates followed. The proprietor was called
to the bar, reprimanded, committed, and afterwards set free.
The proceeding was supported by the Whig party. In the
Chronicle's article on this affair (April 27), I think James Mill's
hand is apparent; the defence of liberty against all the plausible
pretexts of Grey and Fox is to my mind conclusive. In some
other articles, I fancied I could discern his hand, but the conduct of the paper is marked by the absence of pronounced
opinions. There is no truckling to the ministry: neither is
there any violent condemnation. Mill certainly did not discredit himself by the connexion. Possibly, as an ardent
liberal politician, there were many occasions when he would
have wished to speak out, but was not free to do so.
Certainly, the worst that could be said of the paper in those
years was that it was milk-and-water. To obtain some clue to
the beginning and end of Mill's connexion, I examined, along
with a sagacious friend, the file for a number of years. The
date of his commencing cannot be shown by any transition in
the style of the editorial remarks; but it could not well be
before 1805. In 1807 there are traces of his hand;* he con-

---

* This passage is very like him (July 7, 1807), on Whitebread's motion
for an inquiry into the state of Public Affairs :—"In regard to the debate of
last night, it is a matter of trivial consequence. It is easy to see that it would
contain merely an attempt on one side to prove that the nation was very safe
in the hands of the late ministry, and in great danger in the hands of the
present ministry. The people, on the contrary, seem to be of opinion that it is
not in very good hands between them both. We may rest assured that that
great circumstance by which the happiness of the nation is chiefly affected, the
grievances and unparalleled taxation under which we groan, was not placed
foremost in the rank of national dangers, and pointed out as the first and most
indispensable work of reform. Till this become earnestly and effectually the
subject of deliberation, the affairs of the nation will continue to move in the
direction which they had lately and for some considerable time pursued."

tinued in all probability till towards the close of 1808. He
conspicuous by his absence in the notice taken by the pape
of the celebrated proceedings in Parliament (1809) against th
Duke of York for the delinquencies of Mrs. Clark.

I shall now dispose of the last year of the *Literary Journa*
1806, which contains a good many interesting matters. Afte
going on three years as a weekly, it now starts as a monthl
and is designated "Second Series": the general plan bein
varied. It is said in the memoirs of Dr. Thomas and D
James Thomson, that they both ceased to contribute in th
end of 1805; I should think it more probable that they wer
on to the last. The editor would have had great difficulty i
replacing Thomas Thomson as his chief scientific contributor.

An article on Tooke's *Diversions of Purley* is obviousl
Mill's own; while approving of much, it contains his characte
istic handling of abstract ideas. Dugald Stewart's pamphlet o
the renowned Leslie case comes up for notice; and strangel
the reviewer takes the side of the clergy against Stewart an
Leslie. This must have been from an Edinburgh contributo
whom Mill accepted *simpliciter*. In a review of Good's *Lucretu*
the attempt to show that Epicurus was not an atheist is refute
with scorn. In the February number, as the leading articl
Payne Knight's *Principles of Taste* is handled at length an
with great severity. There is a somewhat elaborate review
Sir James Stewart's writings on Political Economy; the co
duct of the French Monarchy towards Sir James himself
freely commented on. A volume of sermons by Sir Hen
Moncrieff Wellwood is praised; said to contain fewer absurd
ties than usual, but yet a sufficient number to make the auth
inconsistent. In the review of an anonymous pamphlet on th
state of Britain at the close of Pitt's administration in 180
the writer is very pungent and severe on the East Ind
Company. A notice on Professor Playfair's pamphlet on th
Leslie controversy declares both sides in the wrong (might
Thomas Thomson). The writer objects to the use that ha

been made of Principal Robertson's name by the combatants; and affirms that the Principal, in exerting his influence in the appointment to chairs, put great stress on the religious views of the candidates (if he knew them). A work on Intellectual Philosophy, by Robert E. Scott, Professor in Old Aberdeen, is praised as of no ordinary class. The arrangement of the intellectual powers differ from Reid and from Stewart and is superior to both, but still wants a combining principle. The work is calculated to be extremely useful. There is no mistaking the review of Millar *On Ranks*. Judging from the two works—*On Ranks*, and *On the English Government*, we shall be disposed to reckon the lectures of Millar "as among the most instructive things that were ever offered to the minds of youth". Much dissatisfaction, as usual, is expressed with the biography. I cannot help making room for a passage on the duties of a biographer in reference to the early history of men of eminence; the readers of the present sketch will then justify me in protesting that, if a biographer has his duties, he has also his rights. Almost every one of the requisites here put down, Mill has in his own case (and he quite looked upon himself as a man of eminence), by studious concealment, rendered it all but impossible to supply.

"We shall not attempt an abridgement of it (the Life), because, in fact, a naked enumeration of dates would be as dry in our Review as in the pages of the author. With regard to the early part of Mr. Millar's life, the materials must either be very scanty, or his biographer has been very negligent in collecting them.

"It appears to us that few biographers have the same opinions which we have formed respecting the importance of the early part of life. When a man has risen to great intellectual or moral eminence; the process by which his mind was formed is one of the most instructive circumstances which can be unveiled to mankind.

"It displays to their view the means of acquiring excellence,

and suggests the most persuasive motive to employ the
When, however, we are merely told that a man went to such
school on such a day, and such a college on another, our cu
osity may be somewhat gratified, but we have received
lesson. We know not the discipline to which his own w
and the recommendation of his teachers subjected him. V
may conclude that young Millar studied hard, from the effec
which afterwards appeared. But we are not introduced to t
particulars of his studies. We have no hint with regard to t
circumstances which kindled his ardour, or those by which t
flame was fed. This is the matter of primary importance
the life of any man. To this is owing whatever excellence
may discover in the labours of Science, or the active busine
of mankind. With regard to this important particular mu
more we think might be discovered by those who write t
lives of eminent men, near the time when they flourished, th
we generally find. At any rate, in whatever obscurity t
causes of their ardour might remain, the degree of it whi
they exhibited in early life might in most cases be pretty accu
ately described, as well as the direction in which it impell
them. We might learn the studies in which they delighte
the books which they chiefly perused, the hours which th
were accustomed to give to labour, and those which th
resigned to relaxation; even the nature of the sports in whi
they indulged, might be a circumstance frequently not unwortl
of regard.

"The people among whom an eminent man spent the days
childhood and youth; the character of his parents and teacher
and the style of behaviour which they manifested towards hi
ought always to be an object of peculiar attention. Our bi
graphers, like our historians, aiming only at the magnificer
seem to think that the occupations and character of the scho
boy are altogether below their notice. But if the business
education be of that importance which we suppose, their m
take is egregious. If too our knowledge with regard to educ

tion, our knowledge of the means by which intellectual and moral excellence may be communicated, is so imperfect, of what consequence should it not be deemed, to obtain the most minute information with regard to the means actually employed in producing those instances of great talents and virtues which have really appeared?"

The next article that I account his with certainty, is on Sir William Forbes's *Life of Beattie* (Sir William was the father-in-law of his favourite pupil and friend); and he again goes into the scope and sources of biography, and complains of the hurrying over of Beattie's life previous to his becoming professor in Marischal College, when it becomes profuse enough. He notices at some length the reception of the *Essay on Truth* in England. The article is another of the many indirect indications that Mill must have resided at one time in Aberdeen; the writer is thoroughly at home in local gossip about Beattie. He talks of an impression very general among the people about Aberdeen, that Beattie dangled too much after the Duchess of Gordon; and remarks, as if from personal knowledge, that Sir William has not shown great exactness in giving the style and manner of Beattie's conversation. In an article on Milton's prose writings, there is a defence of his public character and also of his conduct to his wife and daughters. In reviewing Woodhouse *On the Apocalypse*, the critic gives an unceremonious go-by to all the author's orthodox conclusions. *Apropos* of Filangieri's *Science of Legislation*, there is a long review of the provinces of Politics and Political Economy. In Van Mildert's *On Infidelity*, the reviewer praises the author's intention and the execution of the work, but throws cold water on every one of the arguments against infidels. We unexpectedly find an article on Malthus, full of sentimental horror of his opinions. Brackenbury's *Discourses on Christianity* receives the usual carping at all the arguments on the Christian side. On Colquhoun's *System of Education for the Labouring Poor*, there is

a pretty full article arguing the whole question of Educati
in Mill's usual style.

If we allow for the double editorship of the *Journal* and t
Chronicle, the contributions that we have pronounced to
Mill's own represent a pretty hard year's work. This was t
year after his marriage, and the birth-year of his first chil
We can see further how thoroughly he impregnated the *Journ*
with his own views on the greater questions. The attack
Malthus was an exception, if he was then a Malthusian; bu
whether he was or not, the rousing of sentiment against reas
was repugnant to his whole being, so far as we know anythi
about him.

At this stage we are called upon to give some account of 1
marriage and domestic relations. Soon after coming
London he became acquainted with a family named Burro
who kept an establishment for lunatics in Acton Place, Kin
land Road, Hoxton.

The head of the family was dead, but the establishment w
conducted by his widow, whose ability was equal to t
occasion, and under her management the institution w
prosperous. She had two sons and three daughters. S
came originally from Yorkshire, and was a woman of gre
beauty, a circumstance which re-appeared among her childre
In 1804, Mill was engaged to be married to Harriet, her elde
daughter, then in her twenty-second year (he thirty-one). S
was an exceedingly pretty woman; had a small fine figure, a
aquiline type of face (seen in her eldest son), and a pink ai
dun complexion. One letter of Mill's to her she preserved,
perhaps the fullest and strongest of all his affectionate outpoi
ings. The depth and tenderness of the feeling could not w
be exceeded; but, in the light of after years, we can see that .
too readily took for granted that she would be an intellectu
companion to himself. Without anticipating the view of Mil
domestic interior, as it appeared when he was surrounded by

numerous family, I may say at once that Mrs. Mill was not wanting in any of the domestic virtues of an English mother. She toiled hard for her house and her children, and became thoroughly obedient to her lord.   As an admired beauty, she seems to have been chagrined at the discovery of her position after marriage.   There was disappointment on both sides : the union was never happy.

They were married on the 5th June, 1805, and took up their abode in a small house, 12 Rodney Terrace, Pentonville (an interpolated house makes the number now 13).   As his wife's marriage portion, under her father's will, Mill received £400.   The house was bought for him by Mrs. Burrow, to whom he paid a rent of £50 a year.

Coming from a well-to-do family, Mrs. Mill would bring with her a good outfit.   There was thus ample means of beginning housekeeping, without the drag of being in debt ; and Mrs. Burrow was always ready to assist her daughter in her struggling years.

A younger sister of Mrs. Mill, who was never married and died a short time ago at an advanced age, retained a distinct recollection of the marriage and the early circumstances of Mill in connexion with it.   We know independently that he was editing the *Literary Journal* ; we have the highest circumstantial evidence of his being also editor of the *Chronicle* ; and the traditions all agree that he was then obtaining £200 a year for *an* editorship, though the double editorship was not clearly conceived, and the salary was spoken of sometimes as attached to the *Journal* and sometimes to the *Chronicle*.   By Miss Burrow's account, Mill stated to her mother that he was capable of earning £500 to £800 a year.   If he held both editorships in 1805 and 1806, his income in those years ought certainly to have exceeded £500 a year.   If he continued the *Chronicle* two years longer, he would still without difficulty earn £300 or £400.   Mrs. Mill, according to her sister, was very sorry when he gave up the *Chronicle* ; it made of course a great

difference in their means, as it left him, for the time, nothir
that we know of but Review-writing, from which the incor
stated by him was simply impossible.*

The giving up of the *Journal* at the end of 1806 beir
unexplained, we may assume that it was not a success. It b
came in the second form so like the other magazines, of whic
there were plenty, that, however well it might have been got u
it could not command a very large public. Moreover it had
large tincture of Mill's own severe views both in politics ar
religion. In the biography of Thomas Thomson it is said, tl
Journal "ultimately ceased in consequence of the conducto
being engrossed by more profitable employment". This did n
to all appearance apply to Mill.

The commencement of the *History of India* dates from tl
end of 1806. We can see distinctly from his first letters th
writing some permanent works was a part of his plan of livir
by literature ; and it was by the help of paying books th
Bisset and others made their seven or eight hundred a yea
But then a man must find the means of support in the interva
Mill's calculation was that in three or four years he cou
finish such a history as he projected. He probably saw h
way well enough to maintaining his (as yet) small househo
by his savings and by the work that he proposed to do alor
with the History. The utter failure of his calculations—tl
demand of twelve years' labour instead of three—may be take
as the sole and sufficient explanation of what he had to endu
in regard to his means of support. Writing in October, 181

* Mill came to have nine children :—1. John Stuart, born 1806 (20th Ma·
2. Wilhelmina Forbes (named from Sir John Stuart's daughter) ; died 186
3 Clara. 4. Harriet. 5 James Bentham ; in Civil Service of India, died 186
6. Jane (named from Lady Jane Stuart). 7. Henry ; died 1840. 8. Mai
9. George Grote ; entered India Office ; died 1853.

At their father's death, all the nine were alive , and except James, who h
gone to India the year before, they were all at home, and had been so almo
throughout. None of the sons left children to continue the name. Four of t
daughters were married, and three had children.

he says of the History :—"Thank God, after nearly ten years since its commencement, I am now revising it for the press. Had I foreseen that the labour would have been one half, or one third, of what it has been, never should I have been the author of a History of India."

In 1807, a pamphlet appeared by William Spence, entitled *Britain, Independent of Commerce.* It was immediately met by a rejoinder from Mill, in a pamphlet of 154 pages, in fact, a book. The title is *Commerce Defended: An Answer to the Arguments by which Mr. Spence, Mr. Cobbett, and others, have attempted to prove that Commerce is not a Source of National Wealth* (first edition, 1807; second edition, 1808). The Introduction states the motives of the writers attacked. "People are always gratified by paradoxes, and this paradox coming at a time when the commerce of Great Britain was in extreme difficulty and peril, it was consolatory to be enabled to believe that we shall not suffer by its loss." Mill was followed in the same strain by Colonel Torrens, then commencing his career as a political economist.

Of his contributions to the periodicals in these years, we know almost nothing. There is no indication of his continuing to write for the *Anti-Jacobin Review.* It is said on good authority that he contributed at various times to the *British Review,* the *Monthly Review,* and the great organ of the Evangelical Dissenters—the *Eclectic Review.* I have heard John Mill speak of the *Eclectic* as one of his father's chief connexions when writing for Reviews. I could not undertake to trace his hand in any of the periodicals named, without at least some special guidance as to the dates of his articles. In the *Eclectic,* he would have to restrain some of his more marked peculiarities. On referring to the volumes of these various Reviews about the years when Mill may have been a contributor, I was deterred by the multitude of short articles that would need to have been studied.

Most important for us are his articles in the *Edinburgh Review,* the greater part of which are traceable. They range from 1808 to 1813. They embrace the leading subjects of his writings in those times—Political Economy, Politics, Jurisprudence, Toleration, Education. The only subject notably absent is Mental Philosophy, which, however, would appear to be in abeyance with him during all those laborious years of the *History*.

I now go back to gather the little additional information that we possess down to the end of 1808.

Only two letters exist for the two years, 1806, 1807; they are to Barclay. The second, 7th Feb., 1807, is suggestive:—

" I would have written to you long ago, had I not been unwilling to put you to the heavy expense of postage (over a shilling to Forfarshire). I have been in good health, and going on in my usual way ever since you heard from me (4th April, 1806). I had a letter about the beginning of the winter from Mr. Peters (parish minister), which informed me that you were all well, and managing your affairs with your usual prosperity, which, you may believe, gave me no little pleasure to hear. I should be happy to see it too. Have you no good kirk yet in your neighbourhood, which you could give me, and free me from this life of toil and anxiety which I lead here? This London is a place in which it is far easier to spend a fortune than to make one. I know not how it is: but I toil hard, spend little, and yet am never the more forward."

The remainder refers to his father's affairs which brought upon him a demand for £50: " If I am obliged to find the sum it will not a little distress me ". As he could have only very lately begun to divert his strength to the unproductive labour of the *History*, we cannot suppose him in want of means, but to any man in his circumstances a sudden demand for such a sum might be unhinging. His only family burden yet was a healthy, fair-complexioned, bright-eyed, sweetly-smiling babe of nine months.

This year, Sir John Stuart was withdrawn from Parliament, by being appointed a Baron of Exchequer. The circumstance made a considerable blank to Mill. Sir John brought him every year the local doings, in which he never lost interest; and all through the session they were constantly coming together. Mill's radicalism was no stumbling-block in the way of their attachment. Subsequent to 1807, Sir John's visits to London were only occasional, but they invariably took him to Mill's house. The surviving children can remember his latest visit in company with Lady Jane. It was his own special wish that the eldest child should bear his name.

Of his friends and associates up to this time, we have only incidental mention; but he had a very extensive acquaintance among London literary people. A man could not be an editor for four or five years without knowing nearly everybody that drove the literary pen.

I have purposely kept back the references in the letters, from 1802 to 1808, to what was going on in the father's cottage at Northwater Bridge, in order to present the whole in one unbroken narrative.

The numerous local traditions respecting the members of Mill's family are tinged with dissatisfaction, not to say censure, of his conduct towards them. Many years ago I heard from a native of Montrose that he had allowed his only sister to become a pauper without rendering her any assistance. My recent inquiries have revealed a similar strain of disapproval. He is commonly styled "a hard unfeeling man". There is a confidently received tradition, that he was in vain applied to for a contribution to purchase a cow for his father in place of one that had died; another version putting his sister in place of his father. Fortunately, the letters to Mr. Barclay make us aware of the true state of his relations with his family, and are calculated to produce an impression considerably at variance with the popular view.

At the time of Mill's going to London (Feb., 1802) his family may be said to have been a wreck. His mother was dead. The precise date is unknown; but she listened to her son's sermon, formerly described, sitting not in a pew of her own but out of sight behind the stair. She had then a consumptive cough, and was in a state of great debility. The father had become paralysed, and was unfit for work. As if this was not enough, the only brother, William, who worked with his father, and should have been the stay of the house, was also disabled (said to be from some accident), and soon after died. The one active person was the sister, May, and she was not equal to the burdens thrown upon her. A journeyman, named William Greig, had worked with the father for some time, and on him devolved the carrying on of the business. Soon after James Mill went to London, Greig married May, and so became the head of the house, with its invalid charge.

The picture is not yet at its darkest. The old man was bankrupt. The explanation is casually furnished by his son, in a letter written long after. He had been asked on one occasion to give his name as a security, and in answer wrote as follows :— "You will not wonder that the risks of being security for others should appear to me terrible, when I tell you, as I think you must know already, that my own father ruined himself by that means and, instead of being (for his station) a man of opulence, lived and died a poor one; and that the horror of being liable to risks in this way was therefore one of the earliest and deepest of my impressions." No farther light is gained as to the circumstances referred to; and the fact was entirely unknown to all my informants in the locality. Indeed, the surviving relations are not disposed to credit the circumstance.

This complicated situation of distress was what Mill had to deal with while he was commencing his career in London. Every one of his letters to Barclay contains some reference to the subject; and, indeed, most of them are written expressly on that account, although other matters are thrown in by the way.

In the first communication, April 17 (the letter where he
describes his journey and first impressions in London), there is
a thankful acknowledgment of a letter from Barclay respecting
the family, but no particulars stated, except in a postscript
anxiously desiring another letter of information, in case his
brother William should not be well enough to write. The next
letter, June 2, implies that Barclay has written very fully about
the family, and taken much pains with their affairs, and it is
emphatic in thanks, while disclosing the depths of their misery :
" By long distress they are less able to manage their affairs than
I could wish, and their affairs are more difficult than they have
been " ; " I shall never forget the friendship of you and of a very
few more" ; "you understand their circumstances better than
any other body" ; " I shall look upon it as a very particular act
of friendship, if you will pay them some attentions, and not let
them be in want of anything, and whatever assistance they
receive from you, I shall be most happy to repay ". The third
letter, three months later, states that he has not heard from
the family in the interval, which he attributes to William's inability to write, and desires to hear again from Barclay soon,
not, however, exclusively with regard to his own relations. The
next letter is at an interval of five months, Feb. 11, 1803, and
makes the first reference to his father's bankruptcy ; Barclay
being still his indefatigable deputy. The creditors are soon to
be called together. Mill is impatient to hear that they have met,
and announces his own intentions. " I want them to get fairly
divided among them all that is to divide. Peter Laing, of
course too, must get his share, for that for which I became
security to him. And as to that particular at which you hinted
in your last letter, I cannot but be obliged to you, for you
desire to ease me of my burden, which I am not obliged
to bear—but I am resolved to pay every farthing of debt
which my father owes to every creature, with all the haste
that I possibly can ; and he and I both must try to live as
moderately as possible, till that be accomplished. I wish

you to let his creditors know that this is my intention." He then adverts to the arrangements of the household, and gives us the truth of the story of the cow. Approving of Barclay's advice that his father and May should have the 'ben' house, and W. Greig and his sister the other (the marriage had not yet taken place), he thinks they will do better to part with the cow, which had hitherto been a part of the family *ménage;* milk, &c., they could get from Barclay's farm, and May would be able to turn her time to profitable work, probably in shoe-binding. The next allusion is to William's death; and the letter expresses pleasure at Barclay's information that he was "perfectly happy till his death, his spirits not sunk, nor had he lost hopes of recovery"; circumstances strongly suggestive of consumption. At an interval of three months, we have another letter charged with troubles. William Greig, who has just become May's husband, has written to his brother-in-law complaining that he is not communicated with respecting the state of the family; he has further detailed some very unpleasant interference with him and his wife on the part of the neighbours, who are indignant at their neglect of the old man. Mill is very much distressed at all this. He exculpates his sister from any cruelty to her father, but dilates upon her youth, her inexperience, and her being a *spoiled child;* on this last head, he had often remonstrated with her father, with the usual amount of thanks for his pains. He laments that he is thwarted in his attempts to make his father happy in his last years. At the same time, he strongly censures the neighbours for their interference, and trusting to Barclay to give him "a true and sensible account," he reiterates his thanks for the management of his father's affairs. In less than a month he writes again. He has received a satisfactory explanation of the disagreeable incident, and is well pleased with the advice given to his sister by Barclay and Barclay's mother. "She (May) has now, poor creature, but few friends about her, to whom she can look either for advice or for protection; and though her conduct has often vexed me, and still more the conduct of both her parents with regard to her, I cannot forget that now she is not in a very happy situation." He ends by desiring Barclay to ask his mother to give "some idea of what will be necessary in the year to maintain my father". Six weeks afterwards, we have a letter chiefly occupied with the settlement of his father's affairs. One of the creditors had been raising an action on his own account before the business could be wound up. He reiterates his "sincere and unalterable resolution" to pay off the whole of the debts, as he is able ; but refuses to be pressed by any individual creditor, or to give a pledge as to time. He is at this date (Aug. 15, 1803), "oppressed with business". No further communication till the new year. In the intervening months, his father's affairs had been advanced towards a settlement through Barclay and Mr. Peters, who had both written to him. He is full of gratitude for their friendship. He returns to the point of his father's maintenance. William Greig declined to mention a sum, although putting in strong terms the trouble of keeping him. Mill wished to give as much as any other creditable family would think reasonable. We are left to infer that an arrangement speedily followed this letter. There is no other till August, when he writes to clear up some misapprehensions about the payment of the money to Greig. He apologises for writing few letters, "from the necessity of writing so much every day, that I am glad to take a little rest when my necessary task is done". There is now a gap in the correspondence of nearly two years. On April 4, 1806, he writes from Rodney Street, seemingly with no other object than to get some personal news of his old friends. He had had, as usual, from Sir John Stuart, a pretty full history of the recent doings in the neighbourhood, but he wants other particulars still. The same flank enclosed a letter to Mr. Peters about his father. On the 7th Feb. following, there is a letter on another unpleasant incident in the bankruptcy. One creditor, Laing, a tanner in Brechin, had been harrassing his father, before he left Scotland, and he had stopped his mouth by a written promise to pay the debt as soon as he was able. Laing is now bankrupt, and has given up Mill's letter to a London creditor, who bases on it a sudden demand for £50. Mill writes for information, as the immediate payment of this sum will not a little distress him. The interval separating this from the only other letter that has been preserved, is thirteen years. Before mentioning its purport, I may state what is known of the circumstances of his family in the meantime. His father appears to have died in 1808. His sister has given birth to three children, a daughter and two sons. All accounts represent her as extremely poor in the early years of her wedded life. Very strong expressions on this head were used in my hearing, by those that remembered her well. There was no good reason for such a state of things; and it is attributed to the want of business steadiness of her husband, who carried on the father's occupation. When her two sons were old enough to enter the shop, they, by their industry, redeemed the fortunes of the family, and strove, with ultimate success, to better their position. In October, 1820, when the eldest son was fifteen, and the second about nine, Mill writes once more to Barclay. A friend named M'Conachie had said that it was both his and Barclay's opinion, that "it would be a good thing for my sister and her family if they were enabled to open a little shop". He now asks what is the sum that would be necessary for him to advance; " much cannot be expected, both because my income is small, and because my own family is large "; " however, I am anxious to be of use to them according to my means ". What was the result of this application, I cannot tell; but probably nothing came of it. Mill had now been a year in the India House, but his salary was as yet only £800, and we do not know what liabilities may have survived from previous years; he certainly would have been as good as his word. May's family remained in the cottage long after this date; she herself died in 1837, in the bed where she was born. Some time later, her sons went to Montrose, and set up business as drapers, which the elder (James) still carries on. Their father died in Montrose, at an advanced age.

These are the facts as given in Mill's own letters. I have now to add that there is in the minds of his sister's family a strong conviction that their mother was unjustly treated in consequence of the large sums spent by the father in the education of his eldest son; they hold that there was even some express stipulation whereby May was to be repaid her share of this money, which she never was. There is no collateral testimony bearing upon this point : and the statement being *ex parte*, I cannot give an opinion upon it. If the claim rests solely on the fact that Mill's parents expended a good deal more upon him than upon the other children, I suspect that neither in the higher nor in the lower ranks would usage support it. Moreover, as Mill cleared off his father's debts, he must have made up in that way for what his education had cost. He also took upon himself the exclusive burden of his father's declining years; and we see that he was ready to listen to any proposal for helping his sister. It is evident, too, that, from the moment of May's marriage, her husband took up a hostile position towards himself, such as to repel whatever good offices he might be disposed to render to her family.

The only other matter that I will notice in this painful part of the biography is that, among some members of the Barclay family, there still lingers a complaint of the want of gratitude on Mill's part for all the kindness he had received from them. The feeling has not been expressed to me by those that I have conversed with. I cannot learn that it is borne out by any facts; and it is belied by the existing correspondence. Two members of the family, who especially exerted themselves to procure information for me, were greatly moved in Mill's favour by perusing the letters, after these had been put into my hands by their cousin, the daughter of Mill's correspondent.

CHAPTER III.

HISTORY OF INDIA: EDINBURGH REVIEW: PHILANTHROPIST: EDUCATION MOVEMENT.

1808-1818.

THE present chapter will cover eleven years of intense activity. The *History of India* is the main occupation throughout; concurrent with which is a large mass of miscellaneous writing, and a considerable amount of occupation with public schemes.

The narrative can be greatly simplified, by preliminary sketches of some leading topics that are best given in unbroken connexion.

We may first review the more important personal connexions that start with this period; the most important of all being the connexion with BENTHAM.

In the *Fragment on Mackintosh* occurs the following remark, in reply to a saying of Mackintosh, that the disciples of Bentham derived their opinions from familiar converse with himself:—"It is also a matter of fact, that till within a very few years of the death of Mr. Bentham, the men, of any pretension to letters, who shared his intimacy, and saw enough of him to have the opportunity of learning much from his lips, were, in number, two. These men were familiar with the writings of Mr. Bentham; one of them, at least, before he was acquainted with his person. And they were neither of them men, who took anybody for a master, though they were drawn to Mr.

Bentham by the sympathy of common opinions, and by the respect due to a man who had done more than any body else to illustrate and recommend doctrines which they deemed of first-rate importance to the happiness of mankind."

Of these two persons one was Mill; the other, I presume, was Dumont, Bentham's first and fullest interpreter to the world at large.

There is no record of how or when the intimacy began, but it was not later than 1808. The wonder is that Mill was six years in London before obtaining the introduction, having already been familiar with Bentham's writings. We are to bear in mind that Bentham was now sixty years of age, although scarcely at the beginning of his fame. Many of the incidents of the connexion with Mill are given in Bowring's *Life of Bentham*, and some very important letters are printed there. Unfortunately, the narrative of facts is not always correct, as we shall see. The form of intercourse at first consisted in Mill's walking down at short intervals from Pentonville to Queen Square to dine with Bentham. This went on for two years. In 1810, Bentham gave Mill for a residence Milton's house, which adjoined his own and was also his property. The family lived there a few months, but it was found to be unhealthy, especially for Mrs. Mill, and had to be given up. To make matters worse, Mill seemed unable to find a house to his liking nearer than Newington Green, a mile and a half farther off than Rodney Street. It was the house No. 45; and next to it is one much larger, No. 43, where lived the grandfather of Mr. Taylor, the first husband of Mrs. J. S. Mill. Mill, nevertheless, trudged down as often as before to see Bentham. There is a tradition in the family that during the panic of the Williams murders (Dec. 1811), Mrs. Mill used to sit trembling for his return from Bentham late in the evening. At last in 1814, Bentham succeeded in obtaining Mill as a neighbour. The intercourse of the previous six years, however, was agreeably varied. In 1809, Bentham hired as a summer residence, a fine country

house, Barrow Green House, Oxted, in the Surrey hills. Here
Mill and Mrs. Mill and John spent two or three months of the
summer of 1809; and for several successive summers the visit
of the family was renewed. This house, in 1859, became the
residence of Mr. and Mrs. Grote; and I remember meeting
John Mill there, and hearing his early recollections of the place
and neighbourhood, and of Bentham's walks and habits.

In 1814, Bentham leased the house, No. 1 Queen Square,
now 40 Queen Anne's Gate, and let it to Mill at the rent he
had been paying for his previous houses, £50 a year; ultimately,
however, Mill paid the full rent, which was about a hundred a
year. It is a large house, and gave good accommodation to the
growing family for sixteen years; being, in fact the residence
principally identified with Mill's London career. At the very
same time, Bentham entered upon a still grander summer
residence, Ford Abbey, near Chard, in Devonshire. Here too,
he insisted on having the society of Mill; and the whole family
went there every year, for four years, and spent, not the summer
merely, but nine or ten months at a stretch. We shall have to
make numerous references to this domicile, and shall have
to recount an incident at the very outset, which seemed likely
to bring the connexion to a premature end. The last year of
the residence was 1818; Mill had then finished his *History of
India*, and was very soon afterwards appointed to the India
House. Bentham gave up Ford Abbey, although greatly
attached to it, on the ground of suffering money losses; but even
apart from this, however, he would not have gone back in 1819,
all alone, in his 71st year. He henceforth lived in his Queen
Square house, close to Mill, so that the intercourse was as easy
as need be. Mill, when in the India House, used to keep
certain evenings for dropping in upon him. There was, however, a growing coolness latterly, of which I cannot describe
the steps for want of exact information. Some time before Mill
left Queen Square, but I do not know the exact date, a painful
transaction occurred that was either the proof or the cause of

the estrangement of the two. Mill had always had the range of Bentham's library, and made free use of the privilege. One morning, he being absent at his official work in the India House, Bentham, without warning, sent and removed all his own books from Mill's shelves, including, by mistake no doubt, some of Mill's own.

Bowring has given some notes of Bentham's conversations regarding Mill, which contain an exceedingly harsh opinion of his motives as a politician, ascribing his sympathy for the oppressed many to his hatred for the oppressing few. The notes also give a number of anecdotes relating to Mill's career, which we can now value at their proper worth. When Bowring's Edition of Bentham came out, an article appeared on it by Empson, in the *Edinburgh Review*, which quoted the saying above mentioned. This drew out from John Mill a strong letter of remonstrance; it was printed in the *Review* (vol. 79, p. 267). He controverted the obnoxious sentiment with becoming warmth, and also replied to many of the other statements as to his father's personal history. Bentham was blameably inaccurate and disparaging throughout, and we have ample means of correcting his mistakes.

Mill's acquaintance with RICARDO began in 1811, probably through Bentham; and John Mill celebrates their intimacy and mutual attachment. Ricardo, himself shy and timid, greatly relied for counsel and encouragement on Mill; at whose instigation, he published his book on Rent, and entered Parliament. Among Bentham's sayings we read this:—"I was the spiritual father of Mill, and Mill the spiritual father of Ricardo"; the degrees of the relationship were, however, very unequal in the two cases. Ricardo amassed an enormous fortune on the Stock Exchange, but, if we may trust Bentham, he was stingy on small matters. "Considering our intercourse, it was natural he should give me a copy of his book (on Rent)—the devil a bit." I quote a sentence or two from John Mill's *Autobiography* :—" During this first period of my life, the habitual frequenters of my father's house were limited to a very few persons, most of them little known to the world, but whose personal worth, and more or less of congeniality with at least his political opinions (not so frequently to be met with then as since) inclined him to cultivate; and his conversations with them I listened to with interest and instruction. My being an habitual inmate of my father's study made me acquainted with the dearest of his friends, David Ricardo, who by his benevolent countenance, and kindliness of manner, was very attractive to young persons, and who, after I became a student of political economy, invited me to his house and to walk with him in order to converse on the subject."

Mill's only outing during his first years in the India House, was an annual visit of two or three weeks to Ricardo's house in the country.

There is another intimacy deserving a preparatory mention, namely, with HENRY BROUGHAM. That the two met in Edinburgh, may be regarded as highly probable; and they came to London nearly at the same time, Brougham arriving in 1803. I have heard Mrs. Grote say that they met in London, at the house of Whishaw, a well-known barrister, a friend of Bentham.* At all events their intimacy was close and uninterrupted to the last. It is just shown in Brougham's inducing Jeffrey to accept Mill as a contributor to the *Edinburgh Review*.† In the stirring public questions, Brougham was always eager to

---

* John Whishaw of Lincoln's Inn, is apt to be confounded with a cousin of his, James Whishaw, of Gray's Inn, the author of various Law books. John was well acquainted with all the politicians and men of society of the time. He was Bentham's arbiter in his Panopticon dispute with the Government; and was executor to Sir Samuel Romilly, and guardian of his children.

† "When we got beyond the 20th number (July, 1807) we had other contributors, such as John Leslie, Malthus, *Mill*, Bloomfield and Mackintosh." Brougham, *Autobiography*, Vol. I., 256. Again, in a letter to Jeffrey, 19th March, 1810, Brougham writes—"Can't you suggest some theme for Playfair, or a job for Mill?"

have a talk with Mill, who while admiring his extraordinary energy, endeavoured to give it a good direction. John Mill, who early conceived a repugnance to Brougham, states that his father's attachment to him was for the sake of his public usefulness; but he acknowledged in private to myself, that Brougham's fascination was very great when he set himself to gain any one, and that his father always succumbed under the influence. Not that he overlooked Brougham's faults. On one occasion, when Brougham in his Chancellor days, gave public utterance to a panegyric upon the Christian religion, declaring that he had examined its evidences, and found them satisfactory, Mill vented his astonishment and indignation in two pages of foolscap. He says nothing of his private means of judging of Brougham's opinions, or want of opinions, but places him in a series of alternative positions:—either he had examined the evidences, or he had not; if he had, and was satisfied, his judgment in regard to evidences was so worthless, that no weight could be given to any opinion he might hold upon any subject, &c., &c.*

I shall have to quote letters to Brougham for much personal information during Mill's last years (1831-6); and, in the midst of much obloquy cast upon Brougham's conduct during those years, the favourable estimation of Mill can always be adduced as a counter-testimony in his behalf.

It was some time before Brougham came into direct personal contact with Bentham, and the communications between them were made through Mill.

The friendship with JOSEPH HUME, begun at Montrose

---

* In private conversation, Mill remarked of Brougham's habits of reasoning, that he did not know when his premises and conclusion were converted. Francis Horner, while admiring Brougham's oratorical powers, thought him weak as a reasoner. "Precision and clearness in the details, symmetry in the putting of them together, an air of finish and unity in the whole, are the merits of the best style of legal reasoning; and there is not one of those qualities in which he is not very defective."

Academy, was resumed and continued for public objects, on Hume's settling in London after his returning from India. Hume had not much independent resources in the way of political knowledge; but his dispositions and tendencies in public matters led him to Mill, who could provide him with ideas to work upon. His indomitable perseverance is inscribed in our history; his judgment when he relied upon himself, was by no means unerring. The absence of high intellectual faculty could be discerned in his speeches which were often confused, and full of tedious repetitions. His wonderful *physique* cast for endurance, was instrumental to his success in the House of Commons; his short, broad figure, being probably the perfection of human strength. I remember, in company with Grote, passing him in the Regent's Park, and Grote turned round, and said, "Do you see what a depth of chest Hume has got?" He attained considerable opulence, and kept a hospitable house, where Mill was often entertained; the families also being very intimate.

We should not omit from the list of Mill's friends, the radical tailor of Charing Cross, FRANCIS PLACE, who played a conspicuous part in politics, both local and general for nearly half a century. As he did not often appear in the front ranks of public movements, his name is but little known hitherto; probably not one in a hundred of Sydney Smith's readers have caught the humour of the allusion to him in the posthumous pamphlet of Sydney, in the Irish Church.* Reared as an apprentice tailor in the end of last century, he had not much education, and to the last was deficient in culture. He took a

---

* Sydney is illustrating the way that the Irish priests are paid, and supposes his friend Dr. Hodgson of St. George's, Hanover Square, in the same position. "Soon after this he receives a message from Place the tailor, to come and anoint him with extreme unction. He repairs to the bed-side, and tells Mr. Place that he will not touch him under a suit of clothes, equal to £10; the family resist, the altercation goes on before the perishing artisan, the price is reduced to £8, and Mr. Place is oiled."

part in advanced liberal politics from his earliest years, and
bore the stamp of the men that have achieved for us our
liberties. His house and shop in Charing Cross became the
resort of all liberal politicians. He collected a considerable
library which he made available to his friends. Although not
either profound in thought, or in any way accomplished or
refined, he was an admirable man of business, precise and
methodical in all his transactions. He was also very generous
both to the public and to individuals. He kept a full diary of
what he saw and did, and preserved the interesting pamphlets,
squibs, and newspaper cuttings, connected with all the exciting
events. Fifty volumes of MSS., now in the British Museum,
are the result; and are essential to the historian of the first
third of the present century. He prepared also an Autobiography, but that unfortunately is not found in the collection,
neither is there a letter book, often referred to by him, containing many letters from men of importance, including Mill.
A few of Mill's letters occur in the volumes in the Museum.
The topics that bring Mill under our notice are (1) the History
of the Lancasterian Schools, wherein Place is very exhaustive,
mixed up with which was a long-continued but abortive attempt
to erect a High Class School, after the model of the great
Scotch Grammar Schools; (2) the Westminster Elections, and
chiefly those of 1818; and (3) the founding of the University
of London.*

Place's introduction to Mill is recorded by himself, in his

* Romilly met Place when on a visit to Bentham at Ford Abbey, in 1817,
and, in a letter to Dumont, writes thus, " Place is a very extraordinary person;
by trade he is a master tailor, and keeps a shop at Charing Cross This situation—a humble one enough—has, however, been to him a great rise in life,
for he began his career in the lowest condition. He is self-educated, has
learned a great deal, has a very strong natural understanding and possesses
great influence in Westminster—such influence as almost to determine the
elections for members of Parliament. I need hardly say that he is a great
admirer and disciple of Bentham " The history of his influence in the Westminster elections, has been well traced in a paper in the *Statesman* for August
1881, by Mr. A. F. Munson.

documents connected with the Lancasterian Association. " My acquaintance with Mr. Wakefield* must have commenced towards the close of 1811, or in the beginning of 1812. . . . Mr. W. was at the time remarkably desirous to promote education amongst the poor, and I found in him an excellent co-operator for many useful purposes. . . . Soon after we became acquainted, Mr. Wakefield introduced Mr. James Mill to me. Mr. Mill at this time resided in Stoke Newington, whence he came occasionally, generally once a week, I believe, to dine with Mr. Bentham, who lived in Queen Square Place, Westminster. Our acquaintance speedily ripened into friendship, and he usually called on me on his way to Mr. Bentham, when we spent an hour together."

Place managed Mill's money affairs, during his long absences from London, from 1814 to 1818, and possibly at other times.

One more friendship must be mentioned. Probably it was through Bentham that Mill became acquainted with General MIRANDA, a native of Venezuela, who spent his life in endeavouring to emancipate his native province from Spanish rule. He had an eventful and chequered career ; and at various times resided in England, being well received by the highest political personages. He was an admirer of Bentham, and was to have introduced into his own country a Benthamic code. His last residence in England seems to have included the years 1808, 1809, and 1810; he left for good on his final revolutionary attempt, in October, 1810. By an act of basest treachery, he was delivered, in 1812, into the hands of the Spanish Government, conveyed in chains to Madrid, and there immured under the Inquisition, till his death in 1816. In the last years of his stay in London, he was one of Mill's frequent

---

* Mr. Edward Wakefield, a well-known man of those days, was the author of a good book on Ireland, published in 1812. His son, Edward Gibbon Wakefield, came forward about 1831 as a political writer. He was well-known as the promoter of a great scheme of Colonisation.

visitors. There has been preserved a record of one of his visits
to Mill's house at Pentonville, on the 16th May, 1810. On
that occasion, he told an anecdote of Pitt so curious that Mill
jotted it down at the time, and it remains among his papers.*

The commencement and progress of the friendship between
Mill and Sir Samuel Romilly will appear in the narrative.

The name of Joseph Lowe will turn up presently, and will
re-appear on various occasions. Lowe too was of Scotch origin,
but not a successful man. He wrote on Statistical Subjects,
and was always on the look-out for some profitable vocation.
He attached himself to Mill, and often received assistance
from him. When, at last, he got an official appointment, he
had not sufficient conduct to retain it.

The much lamented Francis Horner, Mill's contemporary in
Edinburgh, was, in London, thrown among Mill's friends, and
was on familiar terms with Brougham, Romilly, Dumont, Sharp,
Whishaw; but does not seem to have contracted an intimacy
with Mill himself. He mentions Mill casually, in connexion
with a visit to Ford Abbey, in 1814, as "a gentleman who writes
a good deal in the *Edinburgh Review*".

Considering the great repute of William Godwin, as a writer
of advanced views in Politics and Ethics, we may wonder that
Mill and he did not fraternize. They never did come together,
so far as I know; and Godwin's looseness in money matters
inspired Mill with dislike, whatever he may have thought of
the *Political Justice*. It is quite certain, that Godwin would,
with all his liberality of views, be reckoned by Mill as too
much of a sentimentalist.†

---

* Count Woronzow, the Russian Ambassador in England, frequently complained to General Miranda of the vagueness and uncertainty of Mr. Pitt's
communications. He said that, after a three hours' conversation, expressly
carried on for the purpose of ascertaining the most important points, he had
found himself totally at a loss to write to his Court to say what had been the
result of the conversation

† In the *Life of Godwin* (II. 183), we find him running a bill on Place for

I am a little surprised at Mill's never becoming acquainted with Thomas Campbell, the poet; who settled in London, only a year after him, and took up the literary profession. Their lives were doubtless different, but both were miscellaneous contributors to magazines; and there was no reason apparent why they should not be in mutual sympathy. Campbell was anything but a bigot; indeed, it is doubtful whether he clung to Theology any farther than was essential to his poetical and literary vocation. The Grotes knew him at a later period, and were wont to visit him; Mrs. Grote wrote an article for his Magazine. The first recorded occasion of Mill's meeting him was at the founding of the University of London.

I must now advert to another connexion that Mill kept up during the years that follow 1808. In the *Life of Macaulay*, Mr. Trevelyan adverts to the great services rendered to this country and to mankind by the Clapham brotherhood, which comprised Wilberforce, Zachary Macaulay, Babington, Thornton, and others. He remarks, that, in their mode of carrying out their anti-slavery and other philanthropic enterprises, "they can be regarded as nothing short of the pioneers and fuglemen of that system of popular agitation which forms a leading feature in our internal history during the past half-century". The services of these men are, indeed, great and undeniable; although, in politics, they were mostly Tories. But justice demands an equal reference to another sect, and another set of names, who were in active co-operation with the Claphamites, and not inferior to them in self-sacrificing zeal—I mean the Society of Friends, whose foremost representative for a long time was William Allen, the chemist of Plough Court. Rivalling Wilberforce in the intensity of his subjective piety, he was inferior to none in energy and devotion to every good

£140. In connexion with Godwin's laboured reply to Malthus, a friend, H. B. Rosser, is to talk with both Place and Mill, and get a distinct statement of their objections, if Place has any, to the book (II. p. 273, 4).

work ; and, besides being devoted to philanthropy, he was very considerable as a man of science. Allen became acquainted with Mill, not later than 1810, and secured his active co-operation in a literary enterprise—a quarterly journal, called the *Philanthropist*, published for seven years at Allen's own risk. He also obtained the advice and support of Mill in public gatherings for agitating his various schemes ; and, in fact, Mill was one of the philanthropic band of the time, and knew many of them intimately, and, among others, Zachary Macaulay. Allen was worthy of a biography; but the three volumes devoted to him, although bodying forth his piety, his energy, and his science, by the help of diaries and letters, are exceedingly out of proportion to the facts of his life. Thus, the *Philanthropist* was projected in the summer of 1810, and only one page and a quarter are devoted to it. Again, in 1812, while it was going on, it receives mention in less than three lines ; and in all the three volumes, I have not discovered another reference. Mill is mentioned only twice : once he and Ricardo accompany Allen (May, 1811) to a great meeting at the Freemasons' Tavern, for a subscription to Lancaster ; and, again (November, 1813), he and Fox are taken to a Finance Committee on the Lancasterian School business. Now, although the *Philanthropist* was only an instrument of propagandism for the numerous schemes that Allen worked at, it occupied a very large share of his attention for seven years ; and, while he had many contributors, Mill and himself were the mainstay of the work : they were in constant communication, and many of his letters to Mill are preserved. The deep-seated divergence of their opinions on religion nowise interfered with their mutual esteem. Robert Owen's infidelity was a grief to Allen, and he made some vain attempts to combat it ; but Mill's views were never obtruded in an unsuitable place. Different was the impression he made on Wilberforce, who, according to Sir James Stephen, was the most charitable of judges.

One more preparatory survey is requisite to the explanation of the course of the narrative from 1810 to 1818; namely, a sketch of the Lancasterian School controversy. A good deal has been published concerning the Bell and Lancaster schemes of education, and the tremendous controversy they gave birth to between the liberals and the church party in England; but the consecutive history has not yet, so far as I know, been written, as it might be, by the help of the existing documents; Place's MSS. being an essential contribution to the record of the proceedings of the Lancasterian Committee.

Dr. Bell published the account of his Madras System in 1797, and it was first adopted in the parochial charity school of St. Botolph's, Aldgate. In the following year, Lancaster opened a school, well known as the Borough Road School, which he conducted on the monitorial plan, and from him, it became known as the Lancasterian system. Bell identified himself with the Church of England, and his religious teaching was strictly on church principles; Lancaster, a Quaker by persuasion, would have nothing but the Bible. The liberal and philanthrophic men among the Dissenters, who had long sought some means of promoting Education among the Poor, conceived they saw in the new system a machinery both effective and cheap; and they attached themselves to Lancaster, and formed a Society, in 1809, for multiplying schools on his plan —the Royal Lancasterian Institution, afterwards called the British and Foreign School Society.

The rival institution of the church, which linked itself with Bell, was founded the year after, and became the National Society. In 1810, the controversy was alive, as may be seen in the *Edinburgh Review* of that year (November), which took the Lancastrian side, while the *Quarterly* embraced the other.

The first start of the Society was formidable indeed. Its title is the "Royal British System of Education," patronized by their Majesties, the Prince Regent, and the Royal Family. Presidents—the Duke of Bedford and Lord Somerville. The

finance committee contained a number of the best names in
London: Lord Lansdowne, Lord Moira, Lord Carysfort, Henry
Brougham, T. F. Buxton, Thomas Clarkson, Joseph Fry, Samuel
Gurney, Francis and Leonard Horner, Luke Howard, John
Merivale, James Mill, Basil Montagu, Samuel Rogers, Sir S.
Romilly, &c., &c. William Allen was one of the Trustees.
Secretary—Joseph Fox.

The first volume of the *Philanthropist* (1811) and the article
in the *Edinburgh Review* of November the same year, describe
the early operations of the Society. On the 11th of May, there
was held at the Freemasons' Tavern, a great "General Meeting
of the Friends of the Poor". The Duke of Bedford was in
the chair, and was supported by the Dukes of Kent and Sussex.
There is an Address (*Philanthropist*, No. III.) which may not
be wholly Mill's work, but which bears unmistakable traces of
his hand. The resolutions may be seen at length in the
Edinburgh Review, vol. XIX., p. 14. Mill, we know, was
present.' In those *Edinburgh Review* articles will be found
a very complete history of the Bell and Lancaster dispute.
It will be seen that Bell, although the founder of the Madras
system—which, in essential features, agreed with Lancaster's
method, remained inactive after his return to England, and
certainly never thought of commencing an agitation for the
general education of the poor. He lived in retirement in an
obscure living at Swanage, where he remained eight years
(1798-1806) doing nothing for education beyond keeping up
a Sunday school in his parish.* It was the alarming progress
of Lancaster's operations that made the church dignitaries turn
to Bell as the convenient instrument of their rival organization.

The most curious part of the affair was the management
necessary to get out of the fix of the Royal Patronage of

* This was said at the time; but, according to Professor Meiklejohn, in his
recent Memoir of Bell, is not correct. "Education, under the enthusiastic
fostering of Bell, spread in the parish, until there were no fewer than thirteen
day-schools in it, and three Sunday schools." p. 35.

Lancaster. The King and the Prince of Wales, as well as the two royal dukes, were sincere and zealous in their support of the Lancasterian schools; and various were the devices tried by the church party to overcome this obstacle. The "No Popery" cry was raised, but did not answer. Then a daring falsehood was hit upon. The king having at this time had an attack of his malady, the rumour was industriously circulated, that he had withdrawn his countenance and sub-scription from Lancaster; but this too was, in a great measure, although not entirely, foiled, by the increased zeal of the Prince Regent. At last, however, the church mustered resolution, under the auspices of Professor (afterwards Bishop) Marsh, to proceed with their own organization, and to denounce the Lancasterians, regardless of Royalty. A sermon of Marsh's delivered at St. Paul's, gave the cue, and, in consequence, was marked out for the criticism of the *Edinburgh*, the *Philanthropist*, and the other Lancasterian organs.

Lancaster's personal character was opposed in nearly every point to the true Quaker type; he was hot, reckless, and ex-travagant. He appears to great disadvantage in the records of the Committee, and was a perpetual source of embarrassment. As Place puts it, he became a sad nuisance.*

The following extract from Place introduces Mill's part at the stage best known to us:—"Mr Wakefield, Mr. Mill, and I were all well acquainted with the controversy which would be going on between the partisans of Bell and Lancaster; we had read most of the publications not only relating to the con-troversy, but those which related to the modes of teaching and discipline of schools; all three were very desirous to extend

* Bentham calls him "this self-styled Quaker," and speaks of the movement thus —"*Lancaster*—the first adopter, and, in some particulars, the improver of the intellectual mechanism—saw in it an instrument of that reputation, that opulence, and that power, which he actually attained, and so notoriously and scandalously abused. *His supporters*—his generous and public-spirited sup-porters—saw in it those admirable capacities which it possesses, and pushed on the application to the utmost of their power."

Lancaster's system, and to teach the children of parents of every denomination of religion. We were not religious ourselves, and had therefore no sectarian notions to teach; we wished the improvement of the people, knew that reading and writing and arithmetic were important steps in the process," &c. . . . . . "As our desire was to teach all, we saw very clearly that the way to teach all was to teach no religious doctrines." . . . . So out of those opinions grew the project of the "West London Lancasterian Institution,"—to establish schools for the whole of the poorer children west of Temple Bar. "Mr. Fox was known to Mr. Mill and Mr. Wakefield personally." . . .; and they thought Fox would be a great acquisition to help them. The movement went on, and by-and-bye we come to the drawing up of an address to the public, by a sub-committee (Wakefield, Place, and Fox). "The matter of the address had been previously settled between Mr. Mill, Mr. Wakefield, and me."

A public meeting was held on 2nd August, 1813 : Sir James Mackintosh in the chair. The Address seems to be Mill's work. The first resolution was moved by Joseph Hume. In " a short speech, replete with feelings of true philanthropy," William Allen proposed the fifth resolution. Joseph Fox was secretary.

Fox presently became " refractory ". Troubles arose, of the most singular description. Sir Francis Burdett had taken up the odd notion that Place was a Government spy. Place consults Mill as to withdrawing from the Committee; Mill advises him not to withdraw; but he did withdraw nevertheless. This was only one of many hitches; and, while it is apparent that Mill kept in the background and put other people forward, it was always to him that recourse was had, when difficulties came.

The scheme of a Superior, or *Chrestomathic* School, was launched in 1813. Mill was an active promoter, and Bentham went heartily into the project; turning aside for a time from his juridical work, to compose his book on Education. The details of the plan were worked out by Place and Wakefield. Fox visits the High School of Edinburgh and the Perth Academy ; Gray of the High School (Edinburgh) writes a long letter to Wakefield ; Mill is to assist in procuring money. The Association is formed in February, 1814 : £3000 to be raised in 300 shares of £10 each. The Trustees to be—Mackintosh, Brougham, Mill, Allen, Fox, and Wakefield. Place wrote an interesting exposition of the project, in the form of a letter to William Allen. Plans and sections are sent to Ford Abbey to Mill, who writes, " I am anxious to show them to Mr. Bentham, and he is anxious to see them. His views on the plan of instruction are now on paper and are all with me. The treatise only wants revising to be ready for publication ; but his eyes are too bad for revising, and it must wait till they are better." This was the *Chrestomathia.* Bentham offers "part of his garden at the back of the Recruit House in the Bird-cage walk, St. James's Park, as a site for the school". This was considered very eligible; and further, plans are sent to Mill for Bentham, at Ford Abbey. Mill writes, 14th October, expressing much interest in the school, but warns Place " that Bentham's mind may, and will probably, work round to finding it a nuisance in his garden," and bids him keep his eye open for any other suitable spot. He is hopeful, nevertheless : " we shall build, I hope, early in spring ". In point of fact, Bentham imposed so many restrictions, and made so many difficulties, that his garden was presently abandoned. On the 31st December, Mill writes again, " Bentham is hard at work upon his treatise, and is infinitely hot upon the subject ; and wishes to complete it before coming to London". In March, 1815, the return took place ; Bentham bringing with him his *Chrestomathia.* This being a considerable book, Mill and Place prepare for circulation a short paper of " Proposals," &c. Mill at this time had one of his attacks of gout, and "was intensely occupied on his *History,* and on other literary matters which his family made perpetually necessary". So, the chief stress of the business fell on Place. Sir S. Romilly is induced to join by pressure from Brougham, Mackintosh, and Bentham. Things, however, move slowly, and for a year no great advance is traceable. In the intervals of the Ford Abbey residence, Mill is at meetings about it, time after time. In 1818, he had induced Sir Francis Burdett, to offer to transfer the interest of £1000, which he had given to the West London Lancasterian School; but legal difficulties stopped the way. Finally, in 1820, several meetings took place, Mill being present : the site has never been settled, and the scheme is abandoned. Thus ends a well-meant and laborious attempt at Higher Education. It produced Bentham's treatise ; but nothing more. The next move towards the object in view was the founding of the London University.

There is reason for supposing that Mill's views on Religion took their final shape between 1808 and 1810. What little I am able to add to John Mill's explanations on this point (*Autobiography*, p. 38) I will state here. When he left Scotland, he was undoubtedly a believer in Christianity, although attached more to the 'moderate' than to the 'evangelical' school. His attitude towards religion during the years of the *Literary Journal*, we have already seen ; he might then be on the way to scepticism, but he had not reached the goal. His mental history from 1806 to 1808 can only be conjectured. That his acquaintance with Bentham would have hastened his course towards infidelity, it is impossible to doubt. Bentham never in so many words publicly avowed himself an atheist, but he was so in substance. His destructive criticisms of religious doctrine, in *Church-of-Englandism and its Catechism examined*, and still more his anonymous book on Natural Religion, left no residue that could be of any value. As a legislator, he had to allow a place for Religion ; but he made use of the Deity, as Napoleon wished to make use of the Pope, for sanctioning whatever he

himself chose, in the name of Utility, to prescribe.* John
Austin followed on the same tack; but the course was too dis-
ingenuous to suit either of the Mills. It is quite certain, however, that the whole tone of conversation in Bentham's more
select circle, was atheistic. In Mill's own family, there is a
vague tradition that his breaking with the church and religion
followed his introduction to Bentham. Strange to say, the
most authentic fact that I have been able to procure is, that
the instrument of his final transformation was General Miranda.
Unfortunately, we have nothing but the bare fact; it was stated
by Mill himself to Walter Coulson, one of his intimate friends
of later years, but the circumstances have been withheld.
Neither Bentham nor Miranda, nor any one else, would have
made him a sceptic, except by the force of reason; but they
may have set his mind to work to sift the question more
completely than he had ever done before. Miranda's biography gives us no assistance on this point; his patriotic
struggles are described, but his phases of faith are not touched
upon, except in the incident of his ignominious burial by the
Spanish priests. We can fall back upon the observation,
often made, and repeated by Mill himself in his notes on Villers,
that when a man threw off Catholicism, he had no available
standing ground between that and atheism. Hence, the free-
thinkers in Catholic countries have usually been atheists.†
Mill says, "the two most celebrated infidels we have had in

* " But if we presume that God wills anything, we must suppose that he
has a reason for so doing, a reason worthy of himself, which can only be the
greatest happiness of his creatures. In this point of view, therefore, the divine
will cannot require anything inconsistent with general utility.

" If it can be pretended that God can have any will not consistent with
utility, his will becomes a fantastic and delusive principle, in which the ravings
of enthusiasm, and the extravagancies of superstition, will find sanction and
authority."—*Principles of Penal Law*, Part II., Book I., Chap. X.

† See Leslie Stephen, *History of English Thought in the Eighteenth Century*, Vol. I., p. 89. "In Catholic France, a rigid and unbending system was
confronted by a thorough-going scepticism. Men of intellect could find no
half-way resting-place, and could disguise their true sentiments with no shreds
of orthodox belief."

this country, Hume and Gibbon, had spent a great part of their youth in France, and were intoxicated with the vanity of imitating Frenchmen ".

If we knew less of the facts, we might easily suppose that a mind of Mill's cast, finding in the Edinburgh book-shops Hume's *Dialogues on Natural Religion*, would have been carried away by the style of reasoning there employed, and have taken in the seeds of his ult:.nate scepticism.　But Mill, like his countrymen generally, was proof against Hume ; and possibly had not read the book, or, if he had, it would be for giving a refutation in his Latin discourse (" Num sit Dei cognitio naturalis ") before the Presbytery.

John Mill tells us that his father's greatest difficulty in regard to Religion was the moral one ; but he partly admits, and should have been still more express on the point, that, in the end, the whole question becomes intellectual.　If there be a difficulty felt in reconciling the moral character of the Deity with human misery, there are also endeavours to obviate it ; and to adjudicate upon the merits of these endeavours is clearly an intellectual function.

For some time after his marriage, Mill himself went to church ; and the children were all baptized.　The minister that baptized the eldest was Dr Grant, probably rector of the parish, who used to dine at the house, and meet General Miranda.　John, as a little boy, went to church ; his maiden aunt remembered taking him, and hearing him say in his enthusiastic way " that the two greatest books were Homer and the Bible ".　As regards father and son, the church-going did not last ; but the other members of the family continued the practice.

Negation, pure and simple, as Mill held it, was a rare thing in the cultivated society of the time in England.　It was more frequent a few years earlier ; but the beginning of the century, says Godwin, witnessed a change of feeling on religion.　Mill's doctrinal views were very strong meat even to the most liberal of the young men that became his disciples.　Grote told me that, though he had been quite familiar with negation carried as far as deism, he was a good deal distressed on first hearing Mill declare that we could know nothing whatever of the origin of the world.

On the subject of Christianity, Mill used in conversation to say that the history of the first centuries needed to be wholly re-written : and I am not sure that he did not at one time think of doing this himself.

After these preparatory surveys, I will follow the order of events from 1808 to 1818.

1808.

If Mill was one of the writers introduced into the *Edinburgh Review* after the 20th number, we ought to be able to trace his hand from October, 1807 (No. 21), onwards. Yet, it is not till October, 1808, that we can authentically specify his contributions. In that number is an article on Money and Exchange. The author reviewed is Thomas Smith ; Mill following up his pamphlet on Spence of the year before, and evidently full of the subject, which was a pressing one at the time. He laments the prevailing ignorance of the doctrines of political economy, and quotes as evidence thereof—" the late Orders in Council, respecting the trade of neutrals ; the popularity of Mr. Spence's doctrine in regard to commerce ; our laws concerning the corn trade ; a great part of our laws, in fact, respecting trade in general ; the speeches which are commonly delivered, the books which are often published, and the conversations which are constantly held". The last third of the article is on the Bank of England question, and controverts Henry Thornton's doctrines, then in vogue.

This is all that I can find of Mill's in the *Edinburgh* of this year. There are two previous articles on the Spence controversy (Jan., 1808, and April, 1809); but we cannot assign the authorship.

I have been furnished by Mr. Macvey Napier with an extract of a letter addressed to his father by Joseph Lowe, with reference to the character of Fox. We know already with what feelings Mill listened to Fox after his arrival in London. Speaking of Fox, Lowe says, "If you think this a deficient eulogy, pray cast your eye over the review of his historical fragment in the *Annual Review* for 1808. It was written by Mill, one of his warm admirers—as far as he can bring himself to admire any Minister."

This is a valuable indication for the time when Mill's contributions to periodicals are so difficult to trace. The article is so far illustrative of Mill's political tone, and so complimentary to Fox, that a short account of it will be of interest.

After some preliminary observations as to the commonplace character of politicians generally, the reviewer regards it as very much in Fox's favour that he challenges an estimate of his talents, by risking the publication of such a book. He thinks that Pitt would have lived long before he gave any such test of himself. "On the severest principles of criticism, the fragment now presented to us must be allowed to be a fine production, and to afford evidence that, had the work been completed, it would not have ranked low in the class of historical compositions."

The great merit of the work, in the reviewer's eyes, is its moral tone. On this point he compares it favourably with the Greek and Roman historians, to the disparagement of most modern historians. He allows that the moderns have given good examples of philosophical history; but their histories contain little more besides than a dry statement of vulgar historical facts. We read them, accordingly, with a species of cold interest, compounded of that with which we peruse a philosophical dissertation and a common chronicle. The perusal of them is a task. Even Robertson fails to impart the touches of nature to his pictures.

This moral part implies first the lessons of common morality, on which the ancients in their conception of history laid the greatest stress. The narrative should present in a clear and instructive light the natural rewards of virtue, and the punishment of vice; a point on which modern historians are shamefully defective. Most of all should public spirit be celebrated as a high virtue. It is well known how the ancient historians excel in this respect. Compare with these the work of Hume, or even Robertson's Charles the Fifth, which teaches us to admire the ambition of that cold-blooded and selfish destroyer; while Voltaire makes a hero of Louis the Fourteenth.

Another ingredient in history is the development of the human character. Here, too, Tacitus, Thucydides and Livy attain the highest success.

It is the moral element that shines in Fox's work. Of the speculative philosophy not much appears. Probably "his talents were not vigorous and cultivated enough to be very capable of generalisation and analysis Any reflections of this sort that he hazards are superficial and common. But in the moral department of the philosophy of history, we know no rival to him in the English Language. In every part of his valuable fragment, the moral qualities of his actors come home to the bosom of his readers, and call forth their love or their detestation. With regard to public virtue, the love of which it is so peculiarly the business of the historian to inspire, there is scarcely any praise to which he is not entitled. It is hardly possible, we think, to read his book, and to rise without a warmer love of one's country than before; without a stronger disposition to make for it every sacrifice: to risk all in resisting its oppressors, and to account life not worth preserving, where freedom, independence, liberty, are not enjoyed, where tyranny reigns, or oppression operates. Everywhere too are the keenest sympathies of his reader called forth, in the contemplation of the passions and emotions of his actors. The manners and feelings of the individuals who come forward in his pages, it seems to have peculiarly suited his genius to depict; and those

sympathetic pleasures, of which so rich a banquet is derived
from the ancient historians, and in which the modern historians
are so extremely barren, form one of the great charms which
distinguish the specimen before us, and which, no doubt,
would have continued to adorn his historic efforts."

The reviewer then goes on to quote special passages for
illustrative criticism, and points out in some detail the strength
on the moral side, and the weakness in the speculative; which
last feature he effectively contrasts with the wonderful subtlety
and penetration of Hume.

"There are three advantages which are derived from this
fragment, short as it is, of the projected history of Mr. Fox.
The first is, that he has drawn a picture of the practical tyranny
which was exercised over this nation under the reigns of Charles
the Second and James the Second, that he excites against it the
hatred and indignation of his readers, and clearly gives them to
see, that had affairs proceeded, for but a little time, in the same
course, the forlorn and desolate aspect of despotism must have
been permanently impressed upon this country.   The second
advantage is, that he draws a picture of that servile submission
which then seemed to form the character of the nation, and to
point them out as the willing and deserving victims of oppression, and rouses against the wretched sycophancy and debase-
ment of the times, the contempt and detestation of every manly
bosom.   The third advantage is, that he stigmatises those time-
serving and bigoted historians who have endeavoured to disguise the enormities of that period, to write the apology of
venality and despotism, to repress the virtuous emotions of
hatred and indignation which the scenes in question are calculated to excite, and who have contributed so largely to corrupt
the moral sentiments of our people, and extinguish among us
the love of country, independence of spirit, disinterestedness,
and courage in public affairs."

The remarks on Fox's composition are somewhat curious.
So great an orator ought to have come out better as a writer.

"The language or style of this history has no very remarkable characters of excellence. Mr. Fox, in fact, appears to be still only serving his apprenticeship to composition. He seems by no means at home in the business; though neither is it stiffness that is in any degree the defect of his style. His language is perspicuous, and flowing. It has no appearance of labour, though it is often incumbered. Like most beginners in composition, he is too circumstantial, too anxious to make out precisely his meaning, by qualifying clauses. The same want of experience has on various occasions led him to dwell too long on trivial circumstances; and it has not unfrequently betrayed him into awkward, and even into inaccurate expressions. Mr. Fox's genius, however, is diffuse, and with the greatest experience he would have always drawn out his details to too great a length."

Having been led to the discovery of Mill's hand in the *Annual Review* (a periodical published yearly from 1802 to 1809, by Longmans), I looked in the volume for other indications of his work. It was impossible to mistake an article on Bentham's "Scotch Reform," which must have been one of his first, if not his very first, exposition of Bentham's views on Law Reform. In the previous year, 1807, Lord Eldon laid on the table of the House of Lords, a bill for amending the constitution of the Scotch Court of Session, and Bentham seized the opportunity of trying to obtain a hearing for his plans of legal improvement. In a pamphlet published this year, in the form of three letters to Lord Granville, he criticized the proposed Bill for Scotland, and at the same time extended his criticism to the English system. In an article of six close pages, the reviewer gives an inkling of Bentham's way of looking at the existing practices of the law, together with his remedies. Nobody, so far as I know, except Mill, would at that time have written of Bentham in these terms :—

"Every thing which comes from the pen or from the mind of Mr. Bentham is entitled to profound regard. Of all the

men, in all ages, and in all countries, who have made th
philosophy of law their study, he has made the greatest progress
If the vast additions which the science of legislation owes t
him be hitherto little known to his countrymen, it is owing t
the indigence of instruction among them, and to the infinit
smallness of the number who take any interest in the mos
important inquiries.

"To a profound knowledge of the general principles of law
Mr. Bentham adds an intimate acquaintance with its practice
both in his own and other countries; and it abundantly appear
that his study of what law *ought to be*, has not made him a share
in the admiration, so common among its professors, of what la\
is.   As most of the articles of the reform proposed by Lor
Granville to be incorporated with the Scotch system of law o
of law procedure, were founded upon analogies with practice
and forms of the English courts, it was necessary for Mi
Bentham, in showing that these were not the reforms whicl
would be good in Scotland, to prove that they were not regula
tions which were advantageous in England.   From this he ha
been led into a criticism on the courts of law and the modes o
administering justice in England, which forms a piece of the mos
important instruction which was ever laid before any nation."

In the same volume, Mill's answer to Spence is criticize
thus :—

"Mr. Mill's answer is the work of a man who defines befor
he proceeds to argue, and who is thoroughly conversant witl
the doctrines of political economy.   The reader who wishes t
be amused with the contradictions of a superficial author, wil
find a fund of entertainment at Mr. Spence's cost in the note
subjoined to Commerce Defended; while the text affords
specimen of the perspicuity with which the most abstruse sut
jects may be treated by the writer who has thoroughly meditate
them."

I cannot tell who was the editor of this periodical, but h
evidently reposed complete confidence in Mill.

Seeing the close intimacy of Mill and Bentham for the years 1808 to 1818, Bentham's work becomes almost a part of our record. Occasionally, it rises to special prominence among the events that more strictly concern us. Whatever Bentham did, in that interval, he discussed with Mill. For the present year, supposed to be the first of their intimacy, Bentham seems to have been principally engrossed with the Scotch Reform publication, which, we have seen, was at once taken up by Mill, as a topic for his periodical contributions.

The public events of this year are notable in themselves, but do not aid us in our proper subject. There was a great deal of excitement in the cause of Spain. A strike among the cotton-weavers of Manchester assumed formidable dimensions, and led to serious tumults. In Parliament, Romilly works at his Sisyphus stone of reforming the Criminal Law.

1809.

In the January number of the *Edinburgh*, appears a very full article on the Emancipation of Spanish America (35 pages). It recounts the entire public career of General Miranda, and was no doubt inspired by him. A second article on the same subject is contained in the July number, where Miranda's 'coaching' is still more apparent; Mill could not of himself quote authorities in the Spanish language. The situation of South America was one of no little complication; it was in revolt against Spain, while we were assisting Spain at home. The fate of the mother country had first to be decided, either for independence or for subjection to Buonaparte. Under the first supposition, Mill enumerates five alternatives, under the second, three; the one most advantageous to this country, would be, for us, having secured the independence of Spain, to secure next the independence of the colonies.

In July there is an article on China, the occasion of which will be seen in a letter to be quoted presently. It is a review of the Travels of M. de Guignes, French Resident in China.

7

The article professes "to collect the scattered lights which he and others offered for illustrating the condition of the Chinese". The preparatory remark is made—"It is to be lamented that philosophers have not as yet laid down any very distinct canons for ascertaining the principal stages of civilization". Nevertheless, the reviewer does his best to estimate the actual stage reached by the Chinese. The general conclusion is—"China is very little advanced beyond the infancy of agricultural society". As to the higher politics—"the practical business of Government, through all its organs, is to plunder the people, and deceive the sovereign". The much vaunted stability of the empire is only "immobility". Even the number of the population is greatly exaggerated. The main art, agriculture, is proved to be in a very low state. Not one of the arts is advanced, except pottery, which is within the compass of a rude people. In building arches, and in laying out grounds, the people deserve some credit. The crowning evidence of the low state of the civilization as a whole is the utterly degraded condition of the women.

For this year, there is a great deal of interesting incident in the Memoirs of Bentham. First is a letter (July 25) on what was an anxious subject in the small Bentham circle, the publication of Bentham's *Elements of Packing.*

Bentham had been long contemplating a work on the Law of Libel, in which he took the ground that the "Libel law as it stands, or rather as it floats, is incompatible with English liberties".

A series of wholesale prosecutions instituted in the beginning of this year for libelling the Duke of York and the British Army, aroused his attention to the system of packing Juries in Government Prosecutions, and he wrote this treatise, in which he deals terrific blows upon the Government, and the Judges, and turns the system round and round with excruciating minuteness.

Here is the letter as given in the Life of Bentham.

"12 RODNEY STREET, PENTONVILLE,
"*July 25, 1809.*

" As to ' Elements,' for the outcoming of which I appear to be far more impatient than you, I have been to give the man a lesson in reading Benthamic copy, and he is far less frightened than he formerly was, or pretended to be—and I expect that his experience will soon prepare some other bold-hearted man to take your stuff in hand.   I have told Baldwin, that it must be, through thick or through thin, *published* in six weeks.   My motive for naming this time, was, that then it will be ready time enough for the *Edinburgh Review,* No. after the next— and I do not want it out much sooner, that no law *boa* may lick it over, and cover it with his slime, that it may glide the easier into his serpent's maw, and afterwards offer the excrement to Jeffrey, to the frustration and exclusion of an offering of my own.

" What is to be, will be ; what is not to be, will not be :— I hope I have here provided myself ground enough to stand upon.   You see I have not turned my eye to the *pastoral office* so long for nothing : had it been ever turned, like your own, to the equally reverend and pious office, the dispensation of law, the field of generalities would hardly have been more familiar to it."

An unpublished portion of the same letter gives, in some- what uncouth fashion, the particulars of the first visit of Mill to Barrow Green.   We cannot afford to suppress this portion, having so little means of enlivening the narrative with home- life pictures.

.   .   .   .

" Coming to Barrow Green on Wednesday, that is, to-mor- row—under which of the clauses does that fall ?   Alas ! under the latter.   The reason?   So it was in the womb of Providence. Who can command what is in the womb of Providence ?   As Jonah was three days and three nights in the whale's belly, so must we be three days and three nights in the darkness of

Pentonville before we can emerge into the light of Barrow Green. Saturday is the day decreed. The causes various. 'Flounces and furbelows,' if among them, are latent. Those set forward to view, if by the art of description I can give them dignity requisite, are as follows :—1. The duty of detersion— a great household abomination, of twelve times recurrence in the year, for which Monday before last was the regular day— but the wedding on the said day delayed, after the fashion of the great expedition which is now a-going, a-going, till Monday last. This, with all its appendages, goes for a great part of the week. Then there is another mischief—there are two aunts, one of whom is necessary to take charge of the brat to be left behind, and they have first to be pulled home from Margate. To pull women from their pleasures, you know too much not to know is not a trifling task. Saturday is the earliest day we can expect them. Another reason concerns myself. Having consented to review this book on China for Jeffrey, I had intended to carry it to Barrow Green, had we gone there on Monday—but now I am anxious, as there is so little time, to have done with it before I leave town. In the meantime, I hope the lilies and roses will be generous and delay their departure for a few days. It will be dreadful to lose them.

"By-the-bye, in a note I received from Mr. Koe on Saturday, he desires me to bring *Motive Table*, and *Evidence Exclusion Table*. *Motive Table* I have, and *Table des Délits*, but no such table as *Evidence Exclusion Table* did I ever see.

"When I received your letter on Monday, John, who is so desirous to be your inmate, was in the room, and observed me smiling as I read it. This excited his curiosity to know what it was about. I said it was Mr. Bentham asking us to go to Barrow Green. He desired to read that. I gave it him to see what he would say, when he began, as if reading—'Why have not you come to Barrow Green, and brought John with you?'

"The prospect of the pleasures to come keeps up our spirits under the vexation and delay of the days we must lose. The pleasures you are in the actual enjoyment of, ought to keep up yours.

"Mrs. Mill desires me to offer her very best respects, and to say that she promises to make up in good behaviour when she comes, for what of the delay in coming is layable at her door.

"I am, my dear Sir,

"With the highest regard,

"Yours, &c.

"Devil take them! Since writing the above, has the mother of these aunts come into the house, telling us she has heard from them—that they will be in town on Sunday, spite of fate, but not before. It will be Monday morning therefore, before we can be with you. We shall set off, however, before breakfast. We shall breakfast at Croydon, and be with you to the enjoyment of the day—not, however, to break in upon you, till your own dinner-hour—the intermediate time shall be spent in getting acquainted with the place. We shall come in a post chaise, by which means we shall avoid the trouble we should otherwise occasion in sending for us, as Mr. Koe had the goodness to mention, to Godstone. John asks if Monday is not to-morrow."

This was the first of the visits to Barrow Green. The exact duration of these visits is not certain, for want of references. The last was in 1813, and is authenticated by a letter that we shall have to produce. That they could have been only a few weeks at a time, is evident from the fact, that Mill does not seem to have ever had the whole of his family with him.

The paragraph alluding to a note received from Koe, Bentham's amanuensis or secretary, shows that Mill was revising for Bentham portions of his work—*Introduction to Rationale of Evidence.*

In exactly two months, we find another letter, showing that Mill was back in London. The book on Jury-Packing is getting printed, and Mill writes—

" I offer up my devotions to heaven every morning for the prosperity of Libel Law. After the feeble and timid talk on the subject of the freedom of the press in the House of Commons on Monday night, I am more impatient than ever. Pure fear of the lawyers seemed to tie up the tongues even of Sir F. Burdett and of Whitbread, who otherwise appeared willing to speak. They were afraid they should commit some blunder in regard to the requisite provisions of law, and, therefore, eat their words. Oh ! if they but knew what law is, and ought to be, as well as you can tell them, on this most interesting of all points, we should find the boldness, I trust, on the other side, equal to that of the lawyers."

It appears from Bowring that, while the book was going through the press, the publisher took alarm, and refused to proceed. To mitigate the offensiveness of the work, Bentham suggested a change of title—" Perils of the Press " ; but this was a very slight palliative. The opinion of Romilly was taken, and it was very strong indeed. He had not the least doubt that " Gibbs " (Sir Vicary) would prosecute both the author and the printer. "An attorney-general, the most friendly to you, would probably find himself under the necessity of prosecuting, from the representations which would be made to him by the Judges, but Gibbs would want no such representations, and would say, that not to prosecute such an attack upon the whole administration of justice, would be a dereliction of his duty."

The printing was proceeded with, but the book was not sold till 1821 ; copies being circulated privately. One wonders at Mill's temerity in urging the publication of such a work against the opinion of Romilly. I can fancy him supposing that Gibbs and his masters would be disinclined to send Jeremy Bentham to prison ; as Hume and Gibbon were allowed to pass unmolested, while humble scribblers had to suffer for holding their views. That the book escaped prosecution when it did appear, shows that Romilly was, after all, too apprehensive of danger. He made a similar mistake with a subsequent work of Bentham's. A prosecution of the Act of Packing would have been singular in another respect; it would have been an appeal to a Jury to say whether Juries were packed or not.

In the October number of the Review appeared one of Mill's important articles, a review of Bexon's *Code de la Législation Pénale.* The work itself he disposes of as vague, confused, and vacillating, and substitutes a short abstract of his own doctrines instead; but does not go far into detail. A considerable stir followed the publication of the article, and the irritant was a sentence on Bentham, as being " the only author who has attempted this most difficult and most important analysis; and imperfect as his success has necessarily been, we have no hesitation in saying he has done more to elucidate the true grounds of legislative interference than all the jurists who had gone before him ". On the Review coming out, Mill writes to Bentham—" Bexon sadly mangled. The mention of you struck out in all but one place, and there my words, every one of them, removed, and those of Jeffrey put in their place. What is to be done with this concern? I am indeed at a serious loss."

This was followed by a long exculpatory letter of the 27th Nov., which is not given. Allusion is made to it in a letter from Bentham, 5th December, enclosing one from Dumont, from which, he says, " you will see the sensation made by the *Bexon* at Holland House ".

"To preserve the person most immediately *injured*, it seemed to me that nothing better could be done than to send to Mr. Dumont a copy of so much of your letter of the 27th November as related to that subject. Under so serious a charge as that of a ' most *impudent plagiarism,*' it was no small satisfaction for me to have in my possession an anticipated exculpation, and that so complete a one for your defence; and it was an additionally fortunate circumstance that I was enabled to add the existence of at least one witness (meaning, though not mentioning), Mr. K. [Koe], by whom the groundlessness of the charge, in so far as you are concerned, could be attested."

Mill is evidently in a high state of excitement, and sits down immediately to pen a long letter, which is worth giving entire.

December 6, 1809.

" Your communication to me of Mr. Dumont's letter, though the intelligence imparted by it was not of the most agreeable sort, found it difficult to add to my anger, which was near its maximum before. Under this oddly generated surmise, I feel gratitude to Mr. Koe for his very lucky expression of his desire to read the article in MS. before it was sent off, and the very moment before it was sent off; for it came out of his hands, and was sealed up that very instant under his eye. The contradiction of this—not very measured accusation—would otherwise have rested on my self-serving testimony; for it was not my intention to have troubled Mr. K. with the reading of it, as I thought he would so much more easily satisfy himself with it when he could see it in print.

" It is no less satisfactory to me in respect to another of the said wisely conceived surmises, viz., *that of the article's being drawn up under your direction, &c.,* that you neither saw it nor heard it—a circumstance owing entirely to the same cause, viz., a reluctance to encroach with it upon your time, and the reflection that all you might desire to know about it, you would know, with most pleasure, when it should come to be read to you in print.

" Notwithstanding, however, the passage in which I endeavoured, not only to do justice to your merits, but to point you out, in as distinct a manner as I could, to the public, as the only man from whom light was to be got on legislative matters, I own that I, after knowing the dislike which Mr. Jeffrey had to praise, studiously made use of your doctrines, at the same time sinking your name; and in more places than one, as I dare say Mr. Koe remembers, I had originally named you as the author of what I was saying, and afterwards struck it out. This was done upon the exhortation of Mr. Lowe, who said, that from what he knew of Jeffrey—from what Mr. Jeffrey had said to him about what he called my propensity to *admire*, and in particular to admire you, as also what he said about his own (Jeffrey's) propensity *not to admire*—that he would not admit the mention of you in such terms to stand in so many places, and that it would be best to retain it in two or three of the places where I thought it of most importance, and strike it out in the rest, when the probability was, he would not meddle with it. As there appeared to be reason in this, I allowed myself to be governed by it—and after all this caution, we still see what has come of it.

"To come, however, to a more agreeable subject—after thanking you, as I most heartily do, for your zeal to exculpate me—I have this day got to the end of *Exclusion.** *Impossibility* then is all that remains; and I am at the end of the principal stage of my labours, viz., my operations upon your text—*i.e.*, among your various lections, the making choice of one—the completing of an expression, when, in the hurry of penmanship, it had been left incomplete, &c. Editorial notes, of which we have so often talked, are only thus far advanced, that a variety of rudiments are set down, with reference to the places of the work where they should be introduced. But it has often happened to me to find, what I thought might be added as a note in one place, was given admirably by yourself in another place, and a better place. And in truth, having surveyed the whole, the ground appears to me so completely trod, that I can hardly conceive anything wanting. It is not easy, coming after you, to find anything to pick up behind you. My memory, too, is so overmatched by the vast multiplicity of objects which the work involves, that I am afraid to trust myself in any kind of notes, save suggestions of cases, illustration by instances—lest

---

* In allusion to the Works on Evidence.

what I say should be an idea brought forward in some other part of the work. All this, however, is not intended to operate as an apology or pretext for indolence. Notes there shall be written, and very full ones—whether these notes shall be printed is another question. My feet are still lumber—still of no use. They seem slowly bringing themselves back to that state in which use may again be made of them. When they will accomplish that desirable object, it is not yet for me to say."

Bowring gives an extract of a letter from Brougham to Mill, on the same article: its being in his possession shows that Mill had forwarded it to Bentham.

.   .   .   "My observations on Bexon can easily keep till we meet. The principal objection is to the pains you have bestowed, or, I think I may say, thrown away, on the exposition of a man's blunders, who is obscure, and, apparently, only magnified into consideration for the sake of his mistakes. I also object to some attacks on Ellenborough, of which, perhaps, you are not aware. There are certain inverted commas which, in fact, mask quotations from his own words. The praise of Bentham seems to me excessive, and not very consistent with the tone of the former article, though perhaps less extravagant than a passage in your first South American article. The adoption of his neology, I must enter my decided protest against. It is possible you might not be aware that *forth-comingness* and *non-forthcomingness* are unknown in all writings on law, except his own; but such words as *semi-public* you must be convinced are of his mint."

The above extract was my clue to the South American articles. The reference to Bentham is in the first, and is slightly stronger than the present one. This "Bexon" article is, as we have seen, not quite the first of Mill's writings on Benthamic subjects; it is, however, apparently the first of any importance.

There follows in the Memoirs another letter of Mill to

Bentham, too interesting to be left out.   The occasion must be inferred.

" PENTONVILLE, 10th December, 1809.

"Though I hesitated at first whether the *fides literarum* permits me to shew to you the accompanying letter—a letter which would certainly not have been written, at least not as it is written, had it been supposed that it would be shewn to you —yet as I think there is real utility as between you and me that it should be shewn to you, and as no harm can thence arise either to the author or any other body, the reasons for shewing it to you appear to me to preponderate.   It appears to me at the same time to be proper that it should not be known to any other body that you have seen it; or if you think proper to communicate it to Mr. Koe, to which I have no objection, let this restriction be at the same time made known to him.

" The letter which is marked No. 1 was sent first.   I answered it by saying that I was unable to visit the gentleman as invited, but begged he would give me a foretaste of what he had to say by his pen, to stay my stomach, till we could meet.   I received in answer the letter I have marked No. 2.

" These two letters you had better here read, and the few words I have to add afterwards, as they will be in the nature of commentary upon the said letters.

" Forcibly did the reading of that last letter strike me with the truth of an observation, which you yourself have somewhere made—that the man who has anything of great importance for the good of mankind to propose, must be dead before his beneficent proposals have any tolerable chance for a favourable reception, or so much as a fair consideration.   The man who gets the start too much of his contemporaries, I see, must be an object of jealousy; and while he lives, must have eyes and ears purposely shut against him.   I own, in the present quarter, I am disappointed and grieved.   One of the most liberal-minded, and enlightened, and one of the most amiable men I know—

and yet, such is the letter he writes to me ! Let us not, however, be discouraged—let us go on cheering one another; and, as I shall find nobody when you are gone—why, you must, just for that reason, live for ever.

"When you have sufficiently perused the said notes, have the goodness to let me have them again.

"I have made a sort of discovery. In a piece of Voltaire's, the title of which caught my eye the other day, 'Essai sur les probabilités en fait de justice,' he makes use of figures (numerals) for expressing the different degrees of probative force in different articles of evidence. He applies it merely as an instrument for a particular purpose, and in a particular case; and seems to have had no idea of a scale for general use. But it may be useful for you to see it, and to say when and how you have seen it; as the fashion seems to be to impute plagiarisms where the imputation is not shut out by bolts and bars, and a guard of soldiers. The vol. is the 30th in my edition, and it is the second of those entitled Politique et Législation. If you have it not, I will send it you per first conveyance."

It was this year that Bentham wrote his Plan of Parliamentary Reform, published in 1817.

The public events of the year do not concern our narrative, except in the single allusion to the discussion on the Freedom of the Press. The Parliamentary enquiry into the conduct of the Duke of York, and the duel between Canning and Castlereagh (Sept. 22), helped to diversify the topics of general discussion.

1810.

The year of Mill's abortive attempt to live in Milton's house, and his migrating to Newington Green. Neither dates nor particulars are given. We can pretty well imagine the unsettlement and distraction of two "flittings" in one year; together with the aggravated disappointment to all parties from the necessity of giving up a promising and convenient residence. There would not apparently be the alleviation afforded by the summer visit to Barrow Green ; this being the one year that it did not take place, although Bentham himself went there.

Mill had now been at least three years engaged on India, and he would naturally endeavour to turn his researches to immediate account in the *Edinburgh*, Jeffrey permitting. It was in March that Brougham, in writing Jeffrey, urged him to find " a job for Mill ".

An article in April, 1810, is a slaying attack upon the Company's government, under the two heads—Commercial Monopoly, and Government. He first refutes all the pretences for granting the Company a monopoly of the trade ; and next reviews in minute detail the vices of the Company's Government. The remedy for the mis-government is curious, and is given only as a hint :—" Instead of sending out a Governor-General, to be recalled in a few years, why should we not constitute one of our Royal Family, Emperor of Hindostan, with hereditary succession ? "

The subject of a serious Disturbance and Mutiny in the Madras Army, was given to Sydney Smith, instead of to Mill.

The August number contains an article on Religious Toleration, based on an anonymous French work bearing on the state of religious liberty in France. The article displays Mill's usual energy on this question, and takes a wide scope, embracing among other things the Catholic disabilities.

He has two articles in the November number. One has come to our knowledge through a passage in Brougham's Autobiography, where he speaks of Jeffrey's Editorship. " As an instance of the care he (Jeffrey) took in revising and preparing contributions, I remember an article on the Memoirs of Prince Eugene was sent to Jeffrey by Mill : Jeffrey gave it to Dr. Ferrier of Manchester to revise ; and when he got it back from Dr. Ferrier, he himself corrected it, and added the moral reflections and the concluding observations in the new Paris Edition of the work !"—I., p. 265.

Jeffrey's unceremonious hashing of articles was very trying
to his contributors, and lost him several that he was unable to
replace.   Mill could not at this time afford to quarrel with his
means of livelihood.

The Eugene review need not detain us.   More important is
the other contribution to the same number ; a paper of twenty-
six pages on the part of the Code Napoléon referring to Criminal Procedure.   There is a full abstract given, and then a
series of criticisms from the more advanced position attained
through Bentham.   The faults found with the Code are pretty
numerous, and there is a sweeping remark as to the French
way of doing things : " if an end can be attained by an easy
but humble process, and by an operose but showy one, they
are sure to prefer the latter ".

In December, we find him corresponding with Brougham,
on a great constitutional question, connected with the private
patrimony of the King ; namely, the Droits of Admiralty.
Brougham had been pressing the subject in Parliament, and
Bentham is very much interested in it.

The year altogether is very meagre in recorded incidents.
One anecdote, given me on good authority, is worth introducing.
Mill's friend, David Barclay, made out a visit to London this
year.   He spent, of course, an evening at Mill's house, whether
in Pentonville or in Newington Green, would depend on the
time of the year, and is not known.   Mrs. Mill and a young
boy (John, four years old) were at dinner.   While they were
present, not a word was said of Scotland ; but, the moment
they left the room, Mill burst out in eager enquiry after everybody in Logie Pert.

Miranda's departure, in October, must have left a considerable blank in the small circle of Mill's intimacies.   I do not
know any one, except Bentham, that he was so much with for
the two or three years previous.

It is worth remembering, however, that this was the year
that John Black joined the staff of the *Morning Chronicle* as a

Parliamentary Reporter. We do not know when he first became acquainted with Mill, but it was probably soon after his arrival. He passed from the Reporters' gallery, to the Editor's desk, in 1817; and after Perry's death, in 1821, took the entire charge of the paper.

Bentham's work this year, was getting ready his Parliamentary Reform Catechism; also his Defence of Economy against Burke and Rose, being parts of his treatise "Official Aptitude maximised, Expense minimised". He farther gave Miranda the draft of a Law for establishing the Liberty of the Press, to take with him to South America.

The great political episode of the year was one that would influence the talk in Mill's circle; namely, the series of proceedings that ended in the committal of Sir Francis Burdett to the Tower. Sir Samuel Romilly never appeared to greater advantage than on this occasion; and the account given in his Life has a permanent historical value in connexion with the privileges of the House of Commons. Burdett's offence lay in publishing in Cobbett's Register a strong article denying the power of the House of Commons to send to prison, as they had done, John Galc Jones, and John Dean, printer, for discussing in a debating society, the exclusion of strangers from the debates of the House. Burdett was brought up for this article, and sent to the Tower. Romilly contended that it was a case for the Law Courts alone. The whole incident made the session one of unusual political excitement, especially in Westminster.

On the 21st May, Mr. Brand made a motion in the House of Commons for a Reform of Parliament. Lost by 234 to 115.

On the 24th February, Perry of the *Morning Chronicle*, was tried for a seditious libel, before Lord Ellenborough and a special jury. The Libel consisted in what we should think a very mild paragraph, in the *Examiner*, then recently started by the Hunts. Perry reprinted the paragraph. He was tried first; the Hunts were to follow. But Gibbs stopped after his first defeat.

1811.

In January, Jeffrey writes two letters. The first expects an article, and wishes it before the 7th Feb.; it also encloses a bill for £100, a balance being still due. Jeffrey's scale of payment, is explained by himself to have been a *minimum* of sixteen guineas a sheet " though two-thirds of the articles were paid much higher—averaging, I should think, from twenty to twenty-five guineas a sheet on the whole number". Mill's articles of the previous year, so far as I can trace them, amount to about eighty pages; so that great part of a year's contributions may have been unpaid for, showing that Mill did not press for his money. The second letter follows in two days; approves of a subject proposed by Mill, but urges him to be gentle, and something else that in Jeffrey's handwriting I cannot decipher. The two articles traceable for this year, are in February and May. The February article is twenty pages in review of a French pamphlet *Sur la Souveraineté*, by M. J. Chas. The pamphlet is considered to be a manifesto authorized by Napoleon, as an apology for his despotism; and is handled accordingly. The pamphleteer carries the war into the enemy's country and attacks the British Constitution itself, the better to strengthen his case. This only exposes him the more to Mill's batteries.

There is a letter from Jeffrey in March, declining a proposal to write on the Nepaul Embassy; the subject already bespoken by some one that he could not refuse, albeit not auguring well of the execution. The letter then refers to a coming article on the Liberty of the Press, and gives advice—to make allowance for difference of times, to take a candid view of the dangers of calumny, &c., &c. The article is in the May number, twenty-five pages. Its strongest point is the exposure of the utter uncertainty of our law as to what is allowed, or what forbidden;

it criticises very severely a saying of Burke's, "that the law would crush liberty, but juries save it". Mill follows Jeffrey's advice so far as to speak of the abuses of liberty; but the way of doing it is his own. "With regard to political subjects, the liberty of the press may be abused in two ways :—the one is, when good public measures, and good public men, are blamed; the other is, when bad public measures, and bad public men, are praised. Of these two, *we should consider the last as infinitely the worst.*" Jeffrey referred him to the French Revolution. On this he says :—"It was not the abuse of a *free* press which was witnessed during the French Revolution; it was the abuse of an *enslaved* press."

It was in this year that the *Philanthropist* began. Allen is represented as planning it in the previous summer. The title is— "The Philanthropist; or Repository for hints and suggestions calculated to promote the Comfort and Happiness of man".

From the first volume, we have a sufficient idea of the drift of the work. There is an introduction by Allen, on the Duty and the Pleasure of cultivating Benevolent Dispositions. The articles that follow are—On the most rational means of promoting Civilization in Barbarous States; Some successful attempts to civilize the Hottentots; Account of a Society to promote the Civilization of Africa, in connexion with the Abolition of the Slave Trade. Two articles are decisively Mill's—The Penal Law of England with respect to Capital Punishment, and as connected with the Transportation and Penitentiary Systems. A short article on Penitentiary Houses for Convicted Criminals, giving an account of Bentham's plan, is probably his too; he was a thorough convert to the Benthamic "Panopticon". An article on the General Education of the Poor soon launches out into Lancaster's system, not exactly in Mill's manner, and gives notice that the subject would be followed up—which indeed it is. The writing on this matter soon waxes to a furnace heat. The remaining articles

8

of the volume are—Penny Clubs for clothing Poor Children ; Employment of Poor Women in winter ; Refuge for the Destitute ; Considerations on War ; Sunday Schools.

A letter from Allen, on the 3rd of June, indicates the fervour on the Lancaster question. "We are much pleased with thy reply to the Bellites, it places the merit of the case upon strong grounds. We are now entrenched to the ears and shall fight with advantage—not with cannon balls, but with something far more powerful, when directed to those whose intellect has been cultivated : in such a warfare *even Quakers* will fight, and fight stoutly." I do not find anything in the numbers then published that answers to this outburst, although the matter in dispute had come up in several articles. What Allen must have been reading was part of the MS. of an article of fifty pages that appeared in January following.

Another letter from Allen shows that Mill was with Bentham at Barrow Green this autumn. It was on the 15th June of the previous year, that Brougham made his motion for the Abolition of the Slave Trade. I give this letter of Allen's entire.

LONDON, *22 of 8 month, 1811.*

"MY DEAR FRIEND,

"The first thing to be done in every mischance is to consider of the best possible way of getting out of the scrape. I shall therefore lose no time in lamentation, but beg leave to suggest whether we had not better give the substance of the Act making it Felony to carry on the Slave Trade, accompanying it with some appropriate remarks, and for this time sink the debates altogether ; we should, however, state that it was brought in by Brougham, who made an excellent speech, &c., upon the occasion, and as it passed triumphantly, and the arguments used by other speakers had been often employed before, &c., &c., we shall not weary our readers with them.

"Instruction, a Poem, should also be reviewed, and copious

extracts from it given—this I always designed to bring up the rear—and I think thou took charge of it for this purpose.

"As soon as ever this number is printed I wish us to concert measures for the next, which I think may open with an account of the labours of John Howard.

"Please to present me affectionately to our worthy Friend Bentham, and any of your *Corps* who may happen to know me. I do not know whether H. Koe is with you or not.

"Requesting to hear from thee by return of Post,

"I remain,

"Thine sincerely,

"W. ALLEN."

In the Memoirs of Bentham there is a long letter from Brougham to Mill, on Law Reform in America, meant for Bentham, and duly forwarded to him. This was the time when Mill was the medium of communication between Brougham and Bentham.

We are not to forget that this year was marked by Mill's introduction to Ricardo. It is also the year that he became acquainted with Place, and began to visit his shop, on the way to dine with Bentham. Place's topics of interest were limited to the strictly practical sphere: and, besides general politics, not very stimulating in those years, comprised Westminster Electioneering, and the Lancasterian education schemes. He was undoubtedly a good man of business, and was much deferred to by Mill in that particular capacity.

Bentham's work for the year was somewhat promiscuous. He makes notes on Nomography, or the Art of inditing Laws. He also worked at speculations in Logic, Language, and Universal Grammar, which he took up at different times of his life, but did not mature for publication. He brought out a second edition of the Scotch Reform pamphlet. This year Dumont published in Paris "Théorie des Peines et des Récompenses".

The Session of Parliament opened with a Regency Bill, the

King being laid aside. Sir Samuel Romilly, as usual, made farther attempts in the way of Reform of the Criminal Law; three of his Bills reached the Lords and were lost there. Lord Folkestone (in the Commons) moved for a return of prosecutions for libel by the Government since 1800; the object being to show that Gibbs's activity was unprecedented. Romilly supported the motion. It was lost by 199 to 36.

On the 24th January, there was a grand dinner at Glasgow, in celebration of the anniversary of Fox's birth. Jeffrey says of it:—" Our Whigs here are in great exultation, and had a fourth more at Fox's dinner yesterday than ever attended before".

In February, the Hunts were indicted for libel, on account of an article in the *Examiner* (copied from the *Stamford News*), denouncing military flogging *in toto*. Brougham appeared in the defence, and the verdict was—Not Guilty. Next month, however, Brougham's eloquence did not avail to save the printer of the *Stamford News*, who was convicted at Lincoln for the original publication of the article.

In November was established the " NATIONAL SOCIETY for promoting the Education of the Poor in the Principles of the Established Church".

1812.

This year there are two short articles in the *Edinburgh* on Indian subjects, known through Jeffrey's letters that have been saved. One, in July, reviews Malcolm's *Sketch of the Political History of India*, and is chiefly on the constitutional question, as to the best form of government for India; no very distinct solution being advanced. The other, in November, attacks the Commercial Monopoly; and urges farther inquiry, by a Committee of Parliament, into the whole system of Indian policy. Jeffrey apologizes for having made some retrenchments on this article. On one or other of the two contributions, Brougham writes—" I find the Indian article gives much satisfaction to the faithful ".

In the *Philanthropist*, Vol. II., is the long article above mentioned on the Lancasterian dispute. The Church of England organs had been denouncing Lancaster: "it has even been broadly and unblushingly asserted, in a high church quarter,* that Mr. Lancaster, as being a Quaker, is *no Christian* ". The cry " The Church is in danger ! " had been raised. " Unfortunately," the article says, "the name of the Church has been converted into an engine of war against us. In the use which is thus made of it, we are in self-defence constrained to resist it." "While bishops and archbishops, and deans and rectors, and lords and gentlemen, looked on in apathy, this individual (Lancaster) performed two things : he first proved that the education of the poor might be rendered incredibly cheap ; he next conceived the truly great and magnanimous idea of rousing by his own exertions a sufficient number of individuals in the nation to contribute the expense which the education of the whole body of the people would require. . . . While the Dr. Bells and the Dr. Marshes, the Bishop A's and the Bishop B's enjoyed their tranquillity and their ease, without an effort for the education of the poor, without a single school to which their exertions gave birth, Mr. Lancaster proved, &c., &c." Two main accusations had been brought against the system, and are dealt with in the article. First, " the teaching of the poor to read, and habituating them to read the Bible, without inculcating any particular creed, is the way to make them renounce Christianity ". In reply, Mill at once puts his finger on the sore, pointing out with remorseless plainness that "the *not inculcating some religious creed* is the mainspring of this objection"; and he meets opponents with an argument that he justly regards "as perfectly conclusive and unanswerable". The second accusation is "that teaching children to read and write, without teaching them the Church

* *Anti-jacobin Review*, Vol. XXIX. (Jan.-Apr., 1808), p. 292.

of England creed, is the way to make them renounce the
Church of England". No sooner has Mill stated this position
of his enemies than he declares vigorously : " We believe that
no sentence more condemnatory of the Church of England
ever was pronounced, or can be pronounced, by her most
declared enemies, than is thus pronounced by her professing
votaries". He then proceeds to discuss the charge at considerable length, being careful to meet numerous minor arguments more or less closely connected with this principal
accusation. Thus the larger part of the article deals with
general objections; the remainder in specific replies. Dr.
Herbert Marsh, afterwards Bishop Marsh, well known for his
criticism of the Gospels, had just published a sermon attacking
the Lancaster plans, and to this Mill replies with crushing
effect. He then overhauls the *Quarterly* for " an elaborate
and designing article against the Lancasterians ".

Besides making this grand effort to fight the Church, Mill
appears plainly, in the same volume, in two considerable
Toleration articles, in which he had always the warmest sympathy from Allen.

In Bentham's Memoirs there are two short letters for this
year. They are both addressed to Bentham.

" By what I learned from Sharp on Wednesday, at Ricardo's,
I look upon a Whig Ministry as certain. Marquis Wellesley,
having found it impossible to form an Administration, resigned
the task, when it was transferred to Lord Moira ; and on Wednesday, at five o'clock, Lords Grey, Grenville, and Wellesley,
met at Lord Moira's. Since that time, I know nothing, except
that there was no account of this in the papers yesterday. But
the certainty of the fact, that Lord Moira is the former, makes
an equal certainty, I think, of the Whigs being the material
with which the formation will be accomplished—Wellesley and
Canning to be included. This being the case, I cannot
imagine but that your proposal about Panopticon—namely,
along with their penitentiary house—will be immediately

assented to ; at least, after the reasons which you can so easily give them.   In truth, I suspect Panopticon will bar the way to Devonshire as a residence; and should the Whigs come in, as supposed, I suspect you will hardly feel easy at the idea of being away, till you know what is to be done with you.   It is a maxim in politics, says De Retz, '*que l'absent a toujours tort*'."

After quoting this letter, Bowring gives the following piece of information.

In conjunction with Mill, Bentham put forward various suggestions for the application of a Jury system to British India, with their *rationale* :—

" 1. To make the choice of jurors extend, as far as possible, not merely to half-castes of legitimate birth, but to half-castes of every kind.

" 2. Urge the reasons for admitting natives of all descriptions.   Whatever reasons are good for admitting half-castes, are good for admitting others, if no reason springing out of what peculiarly belongs to the other castes can be shown to exist.

" 3. Beginning with the half-castes discredits the institution in the eyes of the higher castes of natives.

" 4. The natives of all castes mix without difficulty, as sepoys in the ranks of our army."

The second letter is dated 28th July, 1812.   Young John (now six years old) had by this time become an object of interest to Bentham, from their being thrown together during the Barrow Green visits; and some illness of his father had led to this communication :

" I am not going to die, notwithstanding your zeal to come in for a legacy.   However, if I were to die any time before this poor boy is a man, one of the things that would pinch me most sorely, would be, the being obliged to leave his mind unmade to the degree of excellence of which I hope to make it.   But another thing is, that the only prospect which would lessen that pain, would be the leaving him in your hands.   I therefore take your offer quite seriously, and stipulate, merely, that it shall be made as good as possible ; and then we may perhaps leave him a successor worthy of both of us."

Bentham had prepared his work entitled *Introduction to the Rationale of Evidence*, but, as in the work on Jury Packing, still unpublished, he had been so unsparing with the critical rod, that one bookseller after another declined to take it, from fear of prosecution. Mill used his influence with some of them, and called their hesitation weakness; but did not succeed. The work was partly printed, but never published, until it found a place in the complete edition of Bentham's works.

A note from Brougham in July introduces a great friend of Indian questions, Mr. Bennett, son of Lord Tankerville, as having promised Mill the loan of his valuable journals and reports on India.

The only remaining scrap for this year is a letter from a warm friend of Mill's, the Rev. Dr. James Lindsay, an English Presbyterian minister, whose chapel was in Monkwell Street, in the east end of London.* He was a friend of Mill's next-

* Dr. James Lindsay was born, at or near Kirriemuir, Forfarshire, in 1753. Educated first at the parish school of Kirriemuir, and for a short time at Aberdeen Grammar School, he entered King's College, in 1769, and took his degree in 1773. He then went on to Divinity in Aberdeen, under the distinguished professors—Alexander Gerard of King's College, and George Campbell of Marischal College ; and was licensed to preach in 1776. From 1773 to 1778, he resided as tutor in the family of the Rev. Kenneth Macaulay, minister of Calder, by Nairn, Inverness-shire ; the Kenneth Macaulay that Johnson visited, and a near relative probably of Lord Macaulay's grandfather. Instead of looking out for a church in Scotland, he went to London, in 1781, on the invitation of a fellow-student, named Macleod, then curate of St. George's, Middlesex, and afterwards rector of St. Ann's, Soho. He first assisted the Rev. Mr. Smith, in an Academy at Camberwell, and preached for him occasionally at Silver Street Presbyterian meeting-house, City. In May, 1783, he was ordained to the charge of Monkwell Street meeting, as successor to Dr. James Fordyce (an Aberdonian, *b.* 1720, *d.* 1796). The ordainers on the occasion were all of the Arian section of the English Presbyterian church. He soon after took charge of Mrs. Cockburn's Academy in Newington Green, and married a niece of Mrs. Cockburn ; he was also for twelve years afternoon preacher at Newington Green meeting-house, as successor to the famous Dr. Richard Price. In

door neighbour, old Mr. Taylor, and may thus have been introduced to Mill. They had many points of sympathy. The letter is dated Dec. 4, and Lindsay is very excited over a trial just to come off ; which we discover to be the trial of the Hunts for the libel on the Prince Regent. He has not been able to get accurate information about the names (of the jurymen ?) ; but it grieves him to say that there is not a man among those in the eastern district that can be depended upon. Hunt has no chance except in the absence of special jurymen. The letter then passes to some point as to the signature of the Confession of Faith, which could not have arisen out of any part of the case between Leigh Hunt and the Prince Regent. Mill, apparently having forgotten the circumstances of his own signing the Confession, had desired information from Lindsay. Lindsay, however, had never signed it and could not tell what were the

1805, he removed his Academy to Bow. In the same year, he received the degree of D.D. from King's College. He became Evening Lecturer at Salters' Hall, with Worthington and Morgan. During the last two years of his life, he was afternoon preacher at Jewin Street.

Lindsay was a man of much force of character, and of great liberality of mind both in politics and in religion. His only publication is a selection of his sermons, which the Evangelical critics of the day declared to be tinctured with Arianism. Several single sermons of his on special occasions were also published. His death was very sudden ; it happened while he was at a meeting of the Ministers of the Three Denominations held for the purpose of opposing Brougham's Education Bill. The *Congregational Magazine*, in a review of his sermons, speaks of him as accustomed for half a century to subjects admitting of mathematical demonstration , which made him suspicious and slow in his theological deductions. Bentham, in writing to Richard Carlile while in prison, quoted Lindsay as an instance of a theologian that strongly condemned such prosecutions as Carlile had suffered from.

Being born in or near Kirriemuir, and educated there, he was probably intimate with the family of Mill's mother ; he was nearly of her age. The family of John Taylor would attend his ministrations at Newington Green ; they followed the Arian or Unitarian branch of the Presbyterian body, to which Lindsay attached himself from the beginning, so far departing from the creed of the church that had nurtured him.

There is a fine marble bust of Lindsay, in Dr. Williams's Library, Grafton Street : a large, massive head and face, with intellect and energy engraven on every lineament.

words, but he thought his friend Mr. Taylor might have a copy of the Confession.

This is strange.   For, although it was the glory of the English Presbyterian Church, by the famous decision at Salters' Hall in 1721, to have risen above the imposing of subscription to articles upon the clergy, yet Lindsay must have subscribed the Westminster Confession on being licensed by the Presbytery of Nairn, as Mill did before the Presbytery of Brechin.   It shows how very mechanically the act of subscription was gone through, when neither of the two could remember enough about it to say what it amounted to.

Mill's query is manifestly at Bentham's instance, in connexion with his pamphlet on Oaths, what he called a pre-detached portion of the *Introduction to the Rationale of Evidence,* which could not find a publisher.   We see in Bowring's Life a letter from Jeffrey, apparently on Brougham's solicitation, giving the Scotch law of subscription for ministers, professors, and parochial teachers, which Mill ought to have been able to furnish, but evidently could not.   The next year brought about the publication of this remarkable tract.   Even here he was running close upon danger, if we may judge from the advice given to him by Mackintosh, to disclaim any attack upon individuals.

This Essay seems to have been Bentham's chief work during the present year; coupled perhaps with additions to the main subject—the *Introduction to the Rationale.*

Brougham has at last made his way into the " hermitage ".*

The public events of the year were more than usually sensational.   The accession of the Prince Regent led to a ministerial crisis; and a Liberal administration, for a few moments,

* " The member by whom this letter is franked, is the famous Mr. *Brougham* —pronounce *Broom*—who, by getting the Orders in Council revoked, and peace and trade with America thereby restored, has just filled the whole country with joy, gladness, and returning plenty.   He has been dining with me to-day, and

appeared possible. Mill, we have seen, had formed hopes of a Wellesley and Moira combination; but Romilly, who had better opportunities of judging, saw through the whole sham. Perceval is assassinated. The Liverpool ministry resumes. In September, Parliament is dissolved. Westminster returns Lord Cochrane, along with Sir Francis; Brougham is out of a seat, but looks forward to Westminster when Cochrane's father, Lord Dundonald, dies. Romilly tries Bristol, but retires, and is nominated by the Duke of Norfolk to Arundel.

In the course of the session, the long-standing topics of Catholic Disabilities and Reform had been duly aired. Brougham got the famous "Orders in Council" repealed, although the news did not reach America in time to avert the declaration of war. Riots were abundant in the manufacturing towns; frame-breaking at Nottingham, and disturbances in Lancashire, Yorkshire, and other parts.

We have seen in Lindsay's letter a reference to the trial of the Hunts, which occurred on the 9th of December. The trial had aroused the sympathies of the Liberals; for the *Examiner* was now a well-recognized liberal paper. A letter of Bentham's of this year shows us the position it had gained. He says, speaking of weeklies, "the *Examiner* is the one that at present, especially among the high political men, is the one most in vogue. It sells already between 7000 and 8000." "The Editor, Hunt, has taken me under his protection, and trumpets me every now and then in his paper, along with Romilly. I hear so excellent a character of him, that I have commissioned Brougham to send him to me." I presume Mill

has but just gone. This little dinner of mine he has been intriguing for any time these five or six months; and what with one plague and another, never till this day could I find it in my heart to give him one—I mean this year for the last we were already intimate. He is already one of the first men in the House of Commons, and seems in a fair way of being very soon universally acknowledged to be the very first, even beyond my old and intimate friend, Sir Samuel Romilly: many, indeed, say he is so now."—Bentham to Mulford, July 6, 1812.

was also a reader of the paper; but I doubt if Leigh Hunt had got so far into his good graces.   He had latterly much the same dislike to Hunt as to Godwin : indeed the merits and defects of the two men were nearly parallel ; only Godwin was, of the two, by far the more robust and original.

The Hunts were defended by Brougham, on this occasion also : but the verdict was against them ; and they were heavily fined and imprisoned for two years.

1813.

A note from Jeffrey, 5th January, declines a proposal for another Indian article ; one was expected from Mackintosh, and it was well to change hands on so great a subject.   An article on Lancaster is accepted, with the caution to adopt a conciliatory tone toward the sceptical and misguided part of his opponents.   The words " I shall be very glad to have your South Sea Speculations," indicates the opening of a new view.   The note is followed in two days by another.   After apologising for retrenching the Indian article, Jeffrey asks " to hear for what other articles I am in your debt ; for I have formed a magnanimous resolution to get fairly out of debt ".   He considers that this last number beats the *Quarterly* this time ; and thanks Mill for remarks on it, and invites his free criticism at all times.   He then returns to the South Sea article, which " Brougham mentioned to me some time ago as engaging a share of your attention ".   He thinks that a very interesting article might be made, by bringing together all that has been made known of the South Sea Islands since the time of Captain Cook.   The letter finally hopes that Mill's health has been restored—probably from one of his periodic fits of gout.

I cannot find that he ever wrote the South Sea Article.   In February appeared the account of the Lancasterian System of Education.   The *Review*, we have seen, had already distinguished itself for its advocacy of the cause ; and the articles in 1810 and 1811, were not wanting in vigour. Mill, however, was capable of improving considerably upon them ; but the conciliatory tone is not very apparent. It is chiefly an attack upon the English Church for thwarting the education of the poor, with allusions to the progress effected by the Lancasterian schools ; in fact very much a repetition of the great *Philanthropist* performance. In July there is a short review of Malcolm's *Sketch of the Sikhs*. It is attested by a note from Jeffrey, but the handling of the religious creed of the Sikhs would be attestation enough ; he is utterly impatient of calling any of the barbaric creeds " pure deism ".

This is the last *Edinburgh Review* article of Mill's that I have been able to trace.

In the volume of the *Philanthropist* (III.) for this year, there is an elaborate paper on the Formation of Character with a view to the improvement of mankind ; which savours of his hand, but at present Psychology as a subject was in abeyance. A review of Owen's Schemes is probably his. An article on War is certainly not by an honest quaker. A long review of Dr. Thomson's *Travels in Sweden* is sure to be Mill's ; it is continued into the next volume. Clarkson's *Memoirs of Penn* is reviewed in the first of three articles ; Penn's views of toleration are quoted with strong approbation, and farther enforced by the writer.

" In 1813," says John Mill, in the *Autobiography*, " Bentham, my father, and I made an excursion, which included Oxford, Bath, and Bristol, Exeter, Plymouth, and Portsmouth. In this journey I saw many things which were instructive to me, and acquired my first taste for natural scenery, in the elementary form of fondness for a ' view '." This was an eventful excursion to all the three, and several scattered references to it occur. Probably Bentham had not been in Oxford, since he took his degree there fifty years before, but he may still have found old acquaintances among the easy-going, long-lived race of dons. He did some business with his tract on Oaths (now printed), causing a copy to be delivered to one of the Heads of Houses, and waiting to hear his opinion. (The Oxford tests had received a pretty severe handling). It was here that Mill was cautioned by Sir Francis Burdett against Place.

It would be the long coach or carriage journeys that would give John the opportunity of taking in "views". The interest of the elders would not be wanting, seeing that they so rarely indulged themselves in change of scene ; but the towns would still be the centres of their operations. Oxford at the one end and Portsmouth at the other presented the highest attractions to all. Bentham's brother, Sir Samuel, resided at Gospest as Constructor to the Navy, and could receive the party and shew them the war ships and all his newest designs.

The tour was made in the summer months. The annual visit to Barrow Green took place in autumn. Our documents make distinct reference to it this year, being the last.

There is a note from Allen, in September, to attend a meeting of the Lancaster Committee, for which he has secured the two Royal Dukes. In the end of October, Mill goes to a meeting in Kensington Palace ; the Dukes of Kent, Sussex, and Bedford being present. The *agenda* of this meeting may be found in Place's MS.; the details, not very pleasant, are unnecessary here.

This was the year of the great meeting at the Freemasons' Tavern.

On the 14th October, while Mill was still at Barrow Green with Bentham, Sir Samuel Romilly sends by Lady Romilly's hand an invitation to Bentham to visit him at Tanhurst, and to bring Mill, whom Romilly "has long wished to become acquainted with". Romilly's Diary shows that the visit took place.

In December there is a letter from Dr. Lindsay replying to a solicitation on the part of Mill to use his influence with some East Indian proprietors in favour of Joseph Hume, then aspiring to become a Director. This seems to have been

Hume's first object of ambition, on his return from India; and Mill would do everything to help his friend. Lindsay would like to see Hume appointed, but is reluctant to canvass. The letter also indicates that Lindsay had been got to work on the Lancaster Committee.

Bentham's "Swear not at all" is printed this year, but not published. His activity otherwise seems to have lain in the least profitable of all his speculations—Ontology and Logic. The collected writings contain many papers on these subjects. He sharpened his own logical faculty by such work, but did not contribute much to the general stock of knowledge. There is little evidence that Mill and he influenced each other in those matters.

From an entry in Mill's commonplace book, Sept. 11, it would appear that he was assisting in the revision of Bentham's *Table of Springs of Action*, then printing, but not published till 1817.

Among the public events of the year, was the Renewal of the East India Company's Charter. There is nothing of Mill's that we can trace in immediate connexion with the passing of the Act: he came to have plenty to do with the expiry of it. The conduct of the Princess of Wales led to an exciting Parliamentary discussion, in which Romilly took a leading part. As we were at war both with France, and with the United States, there was scope enough for criticizing the Administration. One step was made in the direction of religious liberty by relieving the Unitarians of their special disabilities, as deniers of the Doctrine of the Trinity.

There was a lull in the Government prosecutions for sedition. Sir Vicary Gibbs was now a judge. The Government was finding out the impolicy of prosecuting newspapers in particular. Very few prosecutions of any kind are recorded for the next three years.

1814.

This was the year of removal to Queen Square. A letter dates from it in May, but the family was kept out for some time, while the house was under repair. The fifth child, James, was born on the 9th of June, in the grandmother's house at Hackney. This is also the first year of the residence with Bentham at Ford Abbey.

This same year, Macvey Napier was employed by Constable to edit the celebrated Supplement to the *Encyclopædia Britannica*. He entered into communication with men of scientific and literary eminence, and went to London to seek contributors by personal solicitation. Mill was in his eye from the outset, and the following letter is an answer to the request for an interview.

"SIR,

"I am very much obliged to you for the flattering terms in which you have been pleased to request my assistance in the composition of the supplementary volumes to the 5th Ed. of the *Ency. Brit.*

"It could not fail to be agreeable to me to be called upon to contribute to a work in which I see so many respectable names united with your own. And besides, Mr. Constable has for so long a time been an acquaintance and friend of mine, and I should be sorry, if it were in my power to forward any object of his, to withold my assistance. It is, however, necessary to add, that my studies are now so directed as to make me desirous of contracting my engagements with all periodical publications of every sort; and that I shall not, I am afraid, be a large contributor.

"Excepting Saturday next, there is no forenoon on which I at present foresee a probability of my being out of the house; and any day which suits you, I shall be happy to hear the details respecting your important undertaking.

"I am, sir, your most obedt. st.,

"QUEEN SQUARE,   "J. MILL.
    "*17th May, 1814.*"

It is to be supposed that, at this interview, the chief topics to be handled by Mill were agreed upon.   The correspondence with Napier will aid us in reporting progress from time to time.

The expulsion of Lord Cochrane from the House of Commons led to a vacancy for Westminster, and Mill was strongly in favour of proposing Brougham : he wrote to Place to that effect.   At the same time, he guaranteed the soundness of Brougham's liberalism, by saying that he would make a declaration in favour of the three principles put forward in Parliament, in 1809, by Burdett.   Those principles were—Extension of the suffrage to " freeholders, householders, and others, subject to direct taxation in support of the Poor, the Church, and the State "; redistribution of seats, on the basis of " taxed male population," and "all the elections to be finished in one and the same day"; and "that Parliaments be brought back to a Constitutional Duration "   Brougham, in replying to Burdett's Resolutions of the 2nd June, 1818, made a pretty considerable retractation of what he now professed to Mill.

Bentham, having rented Ford Abbey, invited Mill and his family to take up their abode with him.   The party must have gone there in July.

As an aid to the narrative for the next four years, I feel called upon to give some description of Ford Abbey, which Bentham rented from its owner, and occupied, with short inter-missions, till 1818.   The structure of the Abbey has been considerably changed since it ceased to be a religious house.

The situation of Ford Abbey is in the valley of the river Axe, four miles from the market town of Chard in Somerset. The railway to Exeter passes through the grounds a mile east of Chard junction station, the passenger going west sees from the left window the back range of the building lying obliquely to the view.   The magnificent front is not visible except by entering the grounds.

It is not possible to convey by words an adequate represen-

tation of the vast pile in its extensive surroundings : a drawing
of the front would be an essential aid ; and such a drawing
should be given in the next Life of Jeremy Bentham.   Yet,
something may be done to make intelligible the repeated
allusions to the place that occur in our narrative.   The building dates from the twelfth century, and was begun in the
Norman style of architecture, carried on into the early Gothic ;
but only one interior now remains to show those styles, namely
the chapel, originally the chapter house of the Abbey.   The
last Abbot, Thomas Chard, built the most conspicuous and
ornamental part of the building in the Tudor style , and, as left
by him, the building would have had a certain unity of design.
But, in the following century, it came into the possession of
Edmund Prideaux, Attorney General to the Commonwealth,
who employed Inigo Jones to enlarge it, by additions in the
square domestic style, which renders the entire front an incon-
gruous mixture, and has mostly concealed or obliterated the
original conception.

The general plan of the structure is by no means complicated.
There is no quadrangle, or court enclosed by the buildings.
The greater part is one continuous mass of building nearly three
hundred feet in length, facing the south.   To the eastern end is
joined another building at right angles running south and north ;
and on the north side of the principal range, are the offices
irregularly attached to the building, which meet the view of
the railway traveller, as he passes through the grounds.   The
main front and the building at the east flank contain all that
we need to notice for the elucidation of our subject.

The original plan of the front, as altered by the additions of
Inigo Jones, compels us to divide the whole range into seven
portions.   The mass is not in perfect line, and yet it does not
deviate very far from the line : there is nothing of the nature of
wing projections.   The easiest way to conceive the whole, so far
as is possible without a drawing, is to start from the centre of the
seven portions.   This is the grand porch tower, formerly the

main entrance. It is wholly of Abbot Chard's work. Over the archway there are five distinct divisions. The lower, resting on the arch, is a surface decorated with coats of arms, and above this are two sets of windows with galleries between; the square top of the tower rising slightly above the adjoining buildings. The tower so far projects from the next portion on the left, as to leave room for a handsome window in keeping with the whole.

It is this adjoining building, on the left as we stand facing the front, or towards the west, that next calls for notice. It is purely of Tudor work. It is what was the Abbot's Hall, and is now the great Hall; it figures notably in every account of the Abbey. There are four great divisions of windows, with buttresses between, carried from near the ground to the roof. The interior will be noticed presently.

Next in order, westward, is a piece of Inigo Jones's work: a plain square front of two stories, three windows in each, the height the same as the Abbot's Hall, from which it has been cut off, in order to furnish modern apartments. The lower floor is the present dining room; what would have been the dais portion of the Refectory. The upper floor is part of the suite of bedrooms.

The fourth, or extreme west portion, is an exact repetition of the third, added on to strengthen the building. It differs only by a superadded top floor, much lower than the others, but having three windows to correspond.

Returning now to the centre building, or porch tower, and moving to the right or eastward, we have a projecting arcade, and over it a square face, with three fine windows, or rather two windows, and central glass door, leading to the balcony, over the arcade. This is the front of another notable apartment, the work of Inigo Jones.

The second remove from the porch is a long mixed building, of two storeys. The lower storey is the Cloister, fronted by six arches, into which perpendicular or Tudor work has been inserted: it reaches the height of one floor, the top being on a line with the top of the adjoining arcade. Over this is a front of plain wall, with six square windows, at unequal distances; these are windows of the upper range of rooms, connecting with the great saloon in the previously named portion.

Last of all, to the extreme right, is a plain front, not symmetrically placed with the previous portion. Its height is greater; and its upper windows, four in number, stand much higher. In this building is the chapel, which is an old interior, encased in a modern exterior.

Such is a rough sketch of the seven constituent parts of the great front. They are of unequal extent. The porch tower has the least frontage of all: the dimensions of the Abbot's Hall and of the Cloisters will be given presently.

We must now round the east corner, and view the long building (a hundred feet or more) at right angles to the main range, and nearly continuous with its east end. This is called the monk's walk. It was really the monk's dormitory, and had two storeys. The upper storey was originally one great hall, 97 feet in length, lighted by lancet-windows, where the monks slept as in a hospital ward. It is now divided into a long passage and a series of sleeping rooms, which are for the domestics of the house. The under storey is a double cloister or crypt, the whole length of the building.

The important apartments are next to be surveyed from the interior. The grand entrance is not now the gorgeous archway of the porch tower, but a door under the adjoining arcade. Passing by this entrance into a lobby, we open a door to the left and are in the great Hall, 55 feet in length, $27\frac{1}{2}$ feet wide, and 28 feet high. Bentham waxes eloquent over this room. It was lighted by the four great Tudor windows; the opposite side of the window is made to match; the walls are partly painted and partly wainscotted, the carved ceiling is gilded and painted, and studded with golden stars. Oaken benches surround the walls.

This leads into the dining room, which was cut off from the

original Abbot's Hall; a fine square room, with carved and gilded wainscot, and a gorgeous ceiling. From it we enter the drawing-room, the lower floor of the extreme east portion of the building: this is adorned with four pieces of tapestry, placed between carved and gilded pilasters. It was the winter work-room of Bentham.

Returning to the main entrance, our attention is called to the cloister. This is directly approached from its east or extreme end, there being two rooms at the other end, between them and the main doorway. The length of the cloister is 82 feet, the height 17 feet. It is used as a conservatory, and was so in Bentham's time: but there was a clear walk, which was his principal place for "vibrating," as he called his indoor exercise. The vaulting and tracery of the cloister are considered in keeping with its external front; and the inner side is also laid out in arches, filled up with solid masonry.

We now make the ascent to the upper floor. The grand stair case, erected by Jones, conducts from the Hall to the great Saloon, whose front surmounts the arcade. The balustrade is a work of art: and pictures adorn the walls, as we ascend. The great saloon, entered at the landing, is a room 50 feet long, 26 feet wide, 28 feet high. The ceiling is vaulted, and divided into compartments painted with historical subjects. It is also called the Cartoon room, from containing a set of fine Mortlake tapestries, after five of the Cartoons of Raphael. "About half the room," says Bentham, "was lined with settees of a kind of stuff, with tufts of the date of the Commonwealth. In that saloon, we used to sit and work—Mill in one place and I in another. This was in the summer." Bentham was very fond of tapestry, and there is a tradition in the house that he found some parts of the cartoon tapestry in a crumbling condition, and had it fresh lined.

A suite of fine apartments is entered from the east side of the saloon: they are the rooms over the cloister. At the end of these a flight of stairs leads up to a large apartment, on a higher level, being the floor over the chapel. Other rooms are on the north side of the great corridor.

The chapel itself exhibits the Norman style of the original structure, having a window to the east of the Tudor style, to make the exterior conform to the rest of the building.

The Kitchen and domestic offices are on a great scale: they make the projecting buildings seen from the railway behind.

There are not less than thirty bedrooms in the house, including those for domestics in the monks' building. According to a letter written by John Mill, as a boy, eight rooms in the western end of the house were occupied by Bentham and his father's family, and these did not amount to one quarter of the entire upper floor of the house.

A gravel walk nearly thirty feet wide runs by the house front and extends beyond it on each side, being more than a quarter of a mile in length.

The grounds and shrubbery are very magnificent. I can give no adequate idea of the view from the front. Fine walks are in every direction; splendid rows of chesnuts, beeches, limes, and firs; a very grand cedar of Lebanon. Two large pieces of ornamental water are in the lower part of the grounds. There is a gradual ascent to what is called the Park, which in Bentham's time contained deer, which he delighted in caressing. His walk before breakfast was round the park, and took three-quarters of an hour; at an ordinary pace, it is half-an-hour's walk. The general view from the house is an upward sloping expanse. Behind, northward, is the kitchen garden, and a flat grassy surface, in which the river Axe zigzags; a rather diminutive stream, scarcely more than ten or twelve feet wide, and running between upright muddy banks, at about two or three feet below the surface. A farm house and steading formerly abutted against the arch way at the west end of the abbey. It covered nearly an acre of ground, but was demolished about 1871. Two cottages standing a little to the west of the abbey are the only remains

GROUNDS AND SURROUNDINGS.

of the extensive farm buildings. Beyond the flat grassy portion,
the ground rises and presents an abrupt hill-side of seven or
eight hundred feet; here lies the boundary of the Ford Abbey
estate.

A more superb residence was never at the disposal of a
couple of literary men, one having a wife and a family of small
children. Their out-of-door walks need not pass beyond the
bounds of the domain. The principal excursion outside would
be to the town of Chard, the nearest place for supplies. According to Francis Horner, a visitor of Bentham's, "for three
or four miles round, the roads are so bad that the place is
almost inaccessible, and lies secluded in very green meadows".
Perhaps the road to Chard would be the best.

The country round is more than undulating; it is decidedly
hilly. There is a high point above the upward sloping town of
Chard that commands a very fine view of valley and rising
ground beyond; one ascent must be at least a thousand feet.
Here a finger post, "To Honiton," reminds us that we are in
the lace country. Not very far from Chard Junction is a large
newly-erected brick building, which is a lace factory.

I don't exactly understand how Bentham and Mill came to
work together in the cartoon room: in summer, when heating
was not required, they might easily have had a room a-piece.
Francis Horner gives a very particular description of Bentham's apartment and mode of working; but his language
might apply either to the upper saloon, or to the drawing-room
beneath, which was the winter room. There seemed to be no
one in the room but Bentham and his amanuensis. Bentham
himself speaks a great deal of his favourite cartoon room; and
visitors were shown in while he was at work, but he himself
was screened from view—a pile of books sometimes answered
this purpose.

Battledore and shuttlecock was provided among the amusements; and occasionally there were dances and balls. Bentham
brought three women servants with him: one was general

housekeeper; two more he engaged in the place; he kept, besides, three men at work, one a sort of indoor footman. He got into a quarrel with the farmer that rented the Park, and to keep him out of sight, planted a row of Hornbeams all round the upper part of the lawn, at the division of lawn and park.

Bentham says the works he wrote in Ford Abbey were, besides Papers on Logic, *Not Paul but Jesus*, and *Church of Englandism*, two out of his three chief sceptical books. We shall see presently, however, that the first year's occupation was chiefly the finishing of the *Chrestomathia*.

They had not been at the Abbey very long, when there occurred an incident that almost led to a rupture. It is recounted in the Life of Bentham. There, a few sentences of Bowring's own introduces a letter of Mill's, but the letter itself is given with an important omission, which I am happily able to fill in.

"In the course of Bentham's intercourse with Mill, little misunderstandings sometimes took place; and as the infirmities even of great minds may be instructive to mankind at large, I will introduce a passage or two from a letter of Mill, on an occasion when, after some years of intimate intercourse, they agreed that a temporary separation would be for the happiness of both."

JAMES MILL TO BENTHAM.

"*September 19, 1814.*

"MY DEAR SIR,—I think it is necessary we should come to some little explanation, and that, according to your most excellent rule, not with a view to the past but the future, that we may agree about what is best to be hereafter done.

"I see that you have extracted umbrage from some part of my behaviour; and have expressed it by deportment so strongly, that I have seriously debated with myself whether propriety permitted that I should remain any longer in your house. I considered, however, that I could not suddenly depart, without proclaiming to the world that there was a quarrel between us; and this, I think, for the sake of both of us, and more especially the cause which has been the great bond of connexion between us, we should carefully endeavour to avoid. The number of those is not small who wait for our halting. The infirmities in the temper of philosophers have always been a handle to deny their principles; and the infirmities we have will be represented as by no means small, if, in the relation in which we stand, we do not avoid showing to the world we cannot agree. Where two people disagree, each person tells his own story, as much to his own advantage, as much to the disadvantage of the other, at least as he conceives the circumstances to be, that is, in general, as much as the circumstances will permit. The rule of the world, I observe, on these occasions is, to believe much of the evil which each says of the other, and very little of the good which each says of himself. Both therefore suffer.

"In reflecting upon the restraint which the duty which we owe to our principles—to that system of important truths of which you have the immortal honour to be the author, but of which I am a most faithful and fervent disciple—and hitherto, I have fancied, my master's favourite disciple; in reflecting, I say, upon the restraint which regard for the interest of our system should lay upon the conduct of both of us, I have considered that there was nobody at all so likely to be your real successor as myself. Of talents it would be easy to find many superior. But, in the first place, I hardly know of anybody who has so completely taken up the principles, and is so thoroughly of the same way of thinking with yourself. In the next place, there are very few who have so much of the necessary previous discipline, my antecedent years having been wholly occupied in acquiring it. And in the last place, I am pretty sure you cannot think of any other person whose whole life will be devoted to the propagation of the system. It so rarely happens, or can happen, in the present state of society, that a man qualified for the propagation should not have some occupation, some call or another, to prevent his employing for that purpose much of his time, that, without any overweening conceit of himself, I have often reflected upon it as a very fortunate coincidence, that any man with views and propensities of such rare occurrence as mine, should happen to come in toward the close of your career to carry on the work without any intermission. No one is more aware than yourself of the obstacles which retard the propagation of your principles. And the occurrence of an interval, without any successor whose labours might press them on the public attention after you are gone, and permit no period of oblivion, might add, no one can foresee how much, to the causes of retardation. It is this relation, then, in which we stand to the grand cause—to your own cause—which makes it one of the strongest wishes of my heart that nothing should occur which may make other people believe there is any interruption to our friendship.

"For this purpose, I am of opinion that it will be necessary not to live so much together. I cannot help perceiving, either that you are growing more and more difficult to please, or that I am losing my power of pleasing; or perhaps there is something in being too much in one another's company, which often makes people stale to one another, and is often fatal, without any other cause, to the happiness of the most indissoluble connexions.

"I should contemplate, therefore, with great dread, the passing another summer with you, and think that we ought by no means to put our friendship to so severe a test. I am desirous of staying with you this season, as long as you yourself continue in the country, both for the sake of appearance, and because you have had no time to make any other arrangement for society : and I shall remain with so much the deeper an interest, that it is a pleasure not to be renewed. For I can most truly assure you, that at no moment were you ever more an object to me of reverence, and also of affection, than at the present ; and nothing on my part shall be left undone while I here remain, to render my presence agreeable to you : perhaps, I ought rather to say, as little disagreeable as possible."

The portion omitted, as being of a private nature, I here supply :—

" There is another circumstance which is of a nature that it is always painful to me to speak of it. My experience has led me to observe that there are two things which are peculiarly fatal to friendship, and these are great intimacy and pecuniary obligations. It has been one of the great purposes of my life to avoid pecuniary obligations, even in the solicitation or acceptance of ordinary advantages—hence the penury in which I live. To receive obligations of any sort from you was not a matter of humiliation to me, but of pride. And I only dreaded it from the danger to which I saw that it exposed our friendship. The only instances of this sort which have occurred are—first, that a part of my family, while with you in the country, have been for a small part of the year at your expense, this year the whole of them were destined to live a considerable part of it,—and secondly, that at your solicitation, that I might be near to you, I came to live in a house of which, as the expense of it was decidedly too great for my very small income, part of the expense was to be borne by you. The former of these obligations of course will now cease, and I reckon it still more necessary that the other should. And as it would be ruinous for me to bear the whole expense of the house, of course I must leave it. I shall explain to you the course which I have planned in my own mind, and hope that you will approve of it. Next summer I shall go to Scotland with my family on a visit to my relations and friends, which, for the sake of being with you, I have deferred till I have offended them all ; and as my friends have long been apprised of an intention I had formed of residing, as soon as peace should permit, for some time in France, I shall go there before the winter, which will not be a matter of surprise to anybody, both as I long ago declared the intention and because the growth of my family and the smallness of my means render a cheap place of residence more and more desirable for me, and even indispensable.   I shall therefore propose, if it is agreeable to you, that I should keep the house in Queen Square for the next half year after Christmas, which will both afford you time to dispose of it, and me to make my arrangements."

The conclusion, as already printed, stands thus :—

" As I propose all this most sincerely, with a view of preserving our friendship—and as the only means, in my opinion, of doing so—the explanation being thus made, I think we should begin to act towards one another without any allusion whatsoever towards the past ; talk together, and walk together, looking forward solely, never back ; and as if this arrangement had been the effect of the most amicable consultation, we can talk about our studies, and about everything else, as if no umbrage had ever existed : and thus we shall not only add to the comfort of each other during the limited time we shall be together, we shall also avoid the unpleasant observations which will be made upon us by other people.   For my part, I have been at pains to conceal even from my wife that there is any coldness between us.   I am strongly in hopes that the idea of the limitation will give an additional interest to our society, and overbalance the effects of a too long and uninterrupted intimacy, which I believe to be the great cause—for there is such a disparity between the apparent cause, my riding out a few times in the morning with Mr. Hume, to take advantage of his horses in seeing a little of the country, instead of walking with you, and the great umbrage which you have extracted— that the disposition must have been prepared by other causes, and only happened first to manifest itself on that occasion.

" I remain, with an esteem which can hardly be added to, and which, I am sure, will never be diminished, my dear Friend and Master, most affectionately yours."

Bowring thinks the citation of this letter a suitable opportunity for making some observations on Mill's general character, and especially his unamiability and weakness of temper. To my mind, the observations are wholly misplaced. Granting that there were occasions when some such criticism was applicable, the present was not one; nor could any part of Mill's intercourse with Bentham furnish a sufficient pretext. The loss of temper in the above incident was on Bentham's side; the moderation, the self-restraint, the gentlemanly feeling, were all on Mill's. At any rate, the dose so effectually purged Bentham's humours, that a full reconciliation followed, and the two lived together for four years, in the intimacy that Mill accounted so hazardous.

Bowring follows up his own criticism with some of Bentham's conversations about Mill's early history, which are not only at variance with the facts that we know, but contain contradictory statements. Thus, "He and his family lived with me a half of *every year* from 1808 to 1817, inclusive"; and again "only one summer was I there (at Barrow Green) without Mill". The first year of Barrow Green, was 1809; the "half year" is too long for Barrow Green, too short for Ford Abbey. It is likely that there was a year's intermission of the Barrow Green visits. For the year 1810, we have no documentary reference; we have John Mill's statement that he was there every one of the four years, but he admits that his memory is not to be relied upon for the duration of the visits. Bentham, one would think, might be trusted to remember a summer passed at Barrow Green alone; even although his memory was confused as to the other points.*

The passage omitted by Bowring, and here restored, is

* Probably when Mill first became familiar with Bentham, he told him more of his early history, than he had been accustomed to disclose to his most confidential friends of later years. If Bentham's memory had been exact, these memoranda of conversations given by Bowring would have been of great use. I quote the following additional particulars.

"Mill came in the train of Sir John Stuart, a man of good estate, married decisive authority in reference to Mill's family circumstances and intentions during the years embraced in this chapter. It is a more complete and authentic refutation of Bentham's reported statements, than John Mill was able to furnish in his letter in the *Edinburgh Review*.

I may here remind the reader that the scheming of the Chrestomathic school was in full operation this year, and that Bentham had turned aside from his juridical operations to work out a system of Education. He took his notes with him to Ford Abbey, and made them his chief occupation for the winter; getting, as Mill says, "hot" upon the subject. We may therefore put this down as a leading topic of conversation during those months. Mill having just been applied to by Napier, to contribute articles to the *Supplement*, must have already thought over some of the subjects, perhaps that on Education for one. At all events, he must have turned over in his mind the materials eventually worked up in that article, and must have felt some interest in discussing the whole subject with Bentham. If so, it is very curious to remark how few

---

to a lady of quality." What Sir John's "train" was, nobody knows. He was himself "a person of quality"

"Mill's father had been his tenant." Mill's father was tenant of Mr. Barclay, himself tenant of the Earl of Kinton.

"Sir John, finding Mill something different from other men, sent him to Edinburgh for education—there he became bearleader to a Marquis, who gave him an annuity." A strange jumble; yet a confirmation of the fact of the Marquis-of-Tweedale tutorship, which Bentham could not have invented

"Through Sir John, Mill got faculty of attending Parliament." Got admissions to the gallery, which he used freely, on first coming to town.

"His work (on India) got him the situation he now holds. Mill thought it was through Canning's suggestion, that they (the Directors) applied to him." This lends a probability to the supposition that Canning favoured his appointment to the India House.

"When I took up Mill he was in great distress, and on the point of migrating to Caen." The letter above quoted gives the truth on this matter the phrase "in great distress" was never correctly applicable.

"Our scheme, which we talked of for years, was to go to Caraccas, which, if Miranda had prospered, we should have undoubtedly done" There are references in Bentham's Life, showing that he thought of this, but there is no indication that Mill meant to go with him.

signs of action and re-action between the two minds their respective products bring to light; there is hardly any appearance in either treatise to show that the subject had undergone discussion between the two authors. I have often dipped into the very elaborate treatise of Bentham, with its enormous mechanism of tables : these tables, indeed, are the basis and almost the substance of the work ; the remainder taking the form of expository notes. One part of the work is an ambitious classification of all knowledge, modified from the French Encyclopædia. Very little value attaches to this now ; and I doubt if it was of much use at the time. Another table deals with Exercises, or Methods of tuition, in which Bentham took a start in advance, being inspired by the promise of the Lancasterian system, after it had a few years' trial. Here, as usual with him, although abounding in acute suggestions, he is minute to excess, and makes distinctions without adequate differences. In the other part of the same table—Principles of School Management—he appears to great advantage ; his discussion of Discipline, and especially Punishments, takes him into his own walk, where he reigned supreme. His highly elaborate proposals for superseding corporal punishment are worthy of the deepest attention ; and, it was principally in consequence of his views, that at least one great institution (University College School) excluded this form of punishment, and proved that it could be dispensed with.*

Bentham was not content with classifying knowledge, and suggesting the methods of teaching and Discipline ; he must needs throw in an enormous Logical dissertation on Nomenclature and Classification, with a view to improve upon D'Alembert's scheme of the Sciences. At one time or other he had devoted a good deal of study to General Science, Logic,

---

* Bentham's house adjoined a Barracks, which was built after he came to live there. He complained of being disturbed in his studies by the cries of the men under flogging. It grated both on his feelings and on his principles. He had made up his mind that it was unnecessary for the discipline of the army.

Language, and Grammar, and had amassed piles of notes, wh
were drawn upon for this occasion, although his full store was
to his posthumous Editors to bring to light.   Mill had larg
meditated in the same fields, but his exposition was always m
succinct, and more to the point in hand ; and, though Benth
could have profited by his criticisms, I am afraid he rarely did.
fact, Mill could have been little more than an approving lister
in all those numerous conversations : with his admirable ta
saying nothing, when he found that he could make no impressi
We have to look to his own article on Education to see that
pursued a distinct track ; agreeing with Bentham always
spirit, but not dwelling upon the same topics.   Bentham l
an extraordinarily ambitious mind : Aristotle was not more b
on being universally re-constructive.   He aspired to remo
the whole of human knowledge ; while it is very doubtful if
attainments were up to the level of his own time.   Mi
education was defective in physical science, and he was of li
use to Bentham here ; even if Bentham had been disposed
listen to any monitor.

In the *Philanthropist*, in the course of the year, Mill m
have done a good deal.   The second article on Penn is a l
discussion of the evils of Unwritten Law.   A review of Gilp
Lives of the Reformers is Mill's without a doubt ; the argum
for toleration is in his strain.   So is this sentence :—" All n
are governed by motives, and motives arise out of interes
interests are the source from which all inferences from
actions of men of former times to the actions of those of
present may safely be drawn"   An Appeal to the Allies a
the English Nation, in behalf of Poland, has for its text
good of mankind as the purpose of government ; " to behol
union of governments seriously concerning themselves with
happiness of the millions of human beings would be a r
scene in the world !"   The review of the *Life of Penn*
concluded in the strain of the previous articles.   " How

and admirable are the ideas thus distinctly expressed—nothing in the acts of government, or in the acts of one man towards another, should have any regard to anything in religious opinions except their morality." A short article dictated by the conclusion of peace, is probably Mill's ; it expounds the connexion of war with barbaric passions, and urges the need of restraint upon the powers of a monarch. An article on Schools for All, opens up the theory of education as a preface to the report of the great meeting in Freemasons' Hall. A Comparison of the Sixteenth Century with the Nineteenth, in regard to the Intellectual and Moral state of the public mind, is a review of the Memoirs of Sir James Melvil, and is shown to be Mill's by the terse and spirited remarks on human improvement.

The public events of this year were sufficiently exciting. Peace is concluded not only with France, but also with America. Ireland is a prominent subject in Parliament. The Nottingham Frame-breakers are still busy. On the 17th June, while the Allied Sovereigns are in London, a great meeting on the Slave Trade was held in Freemasons' Hall, and was immediately followed by a debate in Parliament, which it was intended the Sovereigns should hear. This was an epoch-making demonstration on Slavery, and a leading topic for the *Philanthropist.*

1815.

A fragment of a letter from Allen, addressed to Ford Abbey, and docketed March, showed that the return from Ford Abbey did not take place sooner than March. Bentham protracted the stay, to finish the *Chrestomathia*, which he brought with him for publication. " Mill," says Place, " was gouty, and intensely occupied on his *History of India*, and on other literary matters which his family made perpetually necessary." Meetings and conferences on the Chrestomathic school took place at various times during the next three months. On the 16th May, there

is, at Wakefield's house, a meeting of Managers of the Chrestomathic school, and a society is organized to carry on the work.

The *Chrestomathia* was printed in London, during the
residence there ; copies are in course of distribution in summer.

There was very hot work at the Borough Road Committee,
as we see from Place, who withdrew from it at this time, in
opposition to Mill's advice,

Early in July, Bentham and Mill return to Ford Abbey.
On the 6th July, Bentham writes to Koe, his amanuensis, who
seems to be still in London :—" Mill and I are mourning the
death of a free government in France. The name of a man
who has cut so many French throats as have been cut by
Wellington, will serve as an essential cover for the most flagrant violation of any of the most sacred and universally
beneficial engagements."

A communication to Bentham, in August, from Jean Bap-
tiste Say would add fuel to the flame. It has this passage :—

" They are trying to build up here a rotten throne. It
cannot stand. Your ministers are throwing dust in vulgar
eyes ; but in the eyes of the thoughtful they are playing a
miserable game. Out of this frightful chaos freedom will
spring. Meanwhile what sufferings and sins ! I write to you
in the midst of tears. There is no satisfaction anywhere but
in the newspapers, which are written by the police of the
Bourbons, and dictated by the Allied Powers."

The volume of the *Philanthropist* for this year is wanting in
the only copy that I have been able to procure access to, the
one in the British Museum. Fortunately one of Allen's letters,
the best of the set, reveals some interesting facts. It is a good
exhibition of this sterling and honest quaker.

"LONDON, *18th of 9th month, 1815.*

"MY DEAR FRIEND,

"We all arrived safe and well from Clifton on the 9th
instant, and I am certainly better and stronger for the excursion,
but I am not a little harassed by the crowd of things of all sorts,

which press upon me for attention. The best way, I believe, is, to make a sort of arrangement of the succession in which things are to be taken, set about doing one at a time calmly, and think as little as possible of the whole mass. I was much gratified with thy Letter of the 23rd ult., and with the few lines which came with the last manuscript—both have arrived safe, and I think we can pretty clearly see our way through this number. Thy remarks upon the mismanagement of the Prison under the jurisdiction of the Court of King's Bench are forcible and the castigation just; but I am at my wit's end to know what to do, for, as the writer in the *Spectator* says, "one does not like to be in the power of the creature," and farther I know that the exhibition we have made of the state of the Colony at Sierra Leone has stirred up so much gall in a certain quarter that it would be quite delightful to some persons to see Mr. Philanthropist peeping through the gates of a prison. Our friend Brougham told me more than a year ago that he had been applied to, to say whether there was not ground for a prosecution. Now it strikes me that in exposing flagrant abuses, the safest, and indeed the most effectual, course is, to place *facts* in a striking point of view, and leave the public to make their own comments; you may often safely show that a man is a knave, when it would be dangerous to call him so, and besides I think that by checking our feelings a little in the way of comment, we shall gain more ground than by expressing ourselves freely. To use one of Bentham's expressions, there must be a certain degree of 'preparedness' in the minds of those whom you wish to inform before you can hope for much success. Now this will be brought about in time by *facts* and *arguments*, and I confess that I would mainly trust to them, though it is certainly difficult, when you catch a confounded villain in the very act, to avoid giving him a kick in the breech. After all this *criticism*, I must say that I am quite pleased with the article, except as to the doubts above expressed. The proofs of the second article have not yet been sent me; by the way, shall they be forwarded to Ford Abbey? I have fully concluded to go on with another volume, and, on consulting with Longman & Co., they think that it may be done without any risk of loss. They have promised to examine their books as to the sales and give us their best advice. I am quite sure, however, that there exists in this country a sufficient number of persons, who would be interested in our lucubrations, to support the thing, if it were fairly brought before them, but I am constantly meeting with enlightened and benevolent characters who never heard of our little work. The necessity for advertising is therefore apparent, and if thou wilt contrive a short and pithy one, I will have it inserted in the newspapers. It should import that on the 1st of July was published No. 19, containing, among other things, some notices on the state of the Colony at Sierra Leone, with engravings, descriptive of the Free Town and the surrounding country, and, that No. 20, to be published on the 1st of October, will contain an account of the state of some of the Prisons in the metropolis, &c : also of an establishment in America, called Harmony, consisting of a number of religious characters, who have formed themselves into a sort of commonwealth, which seems to be in a very flourishing state. We shall also have an article from a member of the University of Cambridge, in terms of praise of the poem of Wordsworth entitled the *Recluse*. It was put into my hands by T. Clarkson, with the warmest recommendation, and, as it appears favourable to the cause of morality and virtue, though perhaps rather too sentimental, we must give it a place. There will also be a short notice of the prospect of recommencing the efforts for civilising the North American Indians. Before I quit this subject, I must request thee to set me at ease in one particular, and that is to let me know how our accounts stand— and not only so, but either tell me where to pay the money in London, or draw upon me at 7 days' sight, in which case I will make the Bill payable at my Bankers. I am much obliged by the present of Bentham's book, it is marked with his usual strong good sense, but before I can commit myself neck and crop in the concern, I must be assured that it contains nothing at variance with my religious feelings and prejudices (if you please)—but I feel with my dear friend the immense import-ance of imbuing the rising generation with right notions upon points in which the interest and happiness of every community are deeply concerned.   Depend upon my co-operation, such as it is, as far as I can conscientiously go, but I must dissent from assisting in teaching the art of war, &c.

"We have very gratifying letters of the progress of the schools at Paris.   T. Clarkson is there, and on his return, I expect to have very important intelligence.   Our invested subscription is now about £4300.   The Baptists have finally resolved to make education the basis of their missionary plans in the East Indies, and are about to send off Penny, one of our ablest Generals.

"I have not half got through what I wished to write, but the clock has struck 7, and I have only time to beg to be cordially remembered to our worthy friend Bentham, and to express a wish that thou wouldst write soon to

"Thy affectionate Friend,

"Wm. Allen."

All that remains of this year is a letter from Lindsay, on the 20th October.   It is in reply to a letter of Mill's.   The follow-ing is an extract :—

"I am happy to hear that Brougham means to take up two subjects so greatly important as the Law of Libel and the Education of the Poor.   To support a free press, and to give the whole mass of the people the capacity of profiting by it, is to prepare the triumph of truth and liberty; and it is indeed the only means by which such a triumph can be obtained. What Mr. Mortimer has already written will furnish him with powerful weapons, and no man knows better how to wield them.   God send him health and vigour.   The rest he will command from the energies of his mind: and though no immediate effect is to be expected, yet frequent returns to the charge will ultimately insure the victory.

"I was indeed alarmed for the safety of the Church when I found so orthodox a Bishop likely to trust himself in such heretical company. Pray tell me whose conversation was most edifying, that of Mr. Bentham or that of the Bishop; or whether you had the hardihood to put in a word occasionally for our guid auld Kirk. I hope we shall have the honour of seeing you and your most excellent Friend here at more leisure when you come to Town. Offer him my very respectful good wishes. Long may he live a pillar of the good cause."

I fancied at first that this was a visit of courtesy from the then Bishop of Exeter, in whose diocese, they were located; but as bishops' visits would be few, the following sentence from Bentham probably refers to the same occasion.

"The present Lord Harrowby I have seen at Mr. Wilberforce's: his father was once at my house. His brother, the bishop, was my guest, at the convivial hour, at Ford Abbey in Devonshire, in the year 1813, or thereabouts." Lord Harrowby's brother was Bishop of Lichfield; but not, so far as I know, a man of any public importance.

Bowring gives a scrap of Bentham's, for this autumn, on Ford Abbey.

"It is the theatre of great felicity to a number of people, and that not a very inconsiderable. Not an angry word is ever heard in it. Mrs. S. (the housekeeper) governs like an angel. Neighbours all highly cordial, even though not visited. Music and dancing, though I hate dancing. Gentle and simple mix. Crowds come and dance, and Mrs S. at the head of them."

Excepting the unfortunate farmer of the park, Bentham was on a good footing with all the neighbours. The church-going part of the household went to Thorncomb church, and the vicar and his family became friendly visitors. Several years afterwards, Mill received into his house, in London, the Vicar's widow and daughters, and shewed them every kindness.

The occupation of Bentham after the publication of the *Chrestomathia* is not easy to trace. The next work of importance published by him, and not written prior to this year, is the *Church-of-Englandism and its Catechism Examined.* This was printed in 1817, and published in 1818. He must, therefore, have been engaged upon it this or the following year. It grew out of the Bell and Lancaster controversy, and was his share in the general attack upon the Church.* It must be taken along with his other work, *Not Paul but Jesus*, published in 1823, but written, by his own account, in Ford Abbey. I have been told by Mr. Edwin Chadwick, who lived in Bentham's house some time before he died, that the commencing of this book was occasioned by one of his attacks of weakness of sight. He was living in Ford Abbey; and the only book that he could read was a large type Bible belonging to the house. He then fell upon what he conceived the discrepancies between the Gospels and the Acts of the Apostles. The conclusions that he came to were :—1. That Paul had no such commission as he professed to have : 2. That his enterprise was a scheme of

---

* Romilly gives us the following account of it.

"The work is written against the National School Society, whose aim is to proscribe all education of the poor, except that in which the religion of the Church of England forms an essential part ; and the work, therefore, undertakes to prove, that Church-of-Englandism is wholly different from true Christianity, as it is to be learned from the gospel. The subject, however, is treated with so much levity and irreverence that it cannot fail to shock all persons who have any sense of religion   I had prevailed on Bentham till now not to publish it. He desired me to strike out the passages I thought most likely to give offence ; but they were so numerous that I was obliged to decline the task , and I understood that he had given up all thoughts of publishing the work. To my astonishment, however, I learned yesterday that it had been advertised the day before with his name, and had been publicly sold   I have made a point of seeing him to-day, and, by the strong representation I have made to him of the extreme danger of his being prosecuted and convicted of a libel, I have prevailed on him to promise immediately to suspend, if not to stop altogether, any further sale of the book."

Not much would have been gained by a prosecution. It is a bulky volume, costing 20s., and not easy reading. Pitt would not prosecute Godwin's *Political Justice*, because it was sold at £3. We are safe in supposing, what Mill probably felt, that the Government would at all times be averse to prosecuting Bentham.

personal ambition and nothing more : 3. That his system of
doctrines is fraught with mischief in a variety of shapes, and, in
so far as it departs from, or adds to, those of Jesus, with good
in none : and, finally, that it has no warrant in anything that,
as far as appears from any of the four Gospels, was ever said
or done by Jesus. These conclusions are most elaborately
worked out, in the course of four hundred closely-printed pages.
The climax is reached when he declares Paul to be the real
Anti-Christ.

In the *Church-of-Englandism* this startling position is not
openly taken up, but is implied. Bentham's own scheme of Religious Instruction from the Bible consists in presenting, first, the
Discourses of Jesus, headed by the Sermon on the Mount, and
followed up by the Parables; and, next, the narrative of his Acts;
all to be selected from the four Gospels. He says nothing of
the remainder of the New Testament. The Old Testament, he
thinks, concerns the Jews alone ; and, in omitting it bodily, he
considers no apology necessary except to Jewish parents.

Although, in the composition of these two bulky volumes of
heterodoxy, Bentham was in daily intercourse with Mill, and
must have had his criticisms as he went along, there is no
record of the nature of their agreement or disagreement of
views, or as to the help rendered by Mill to Bentham's elabora-
tion. The interest, as far as we are here concerned, therefore,
would be purely in the effort to fill up, by imagination, the
blanks of our records of the Ford Abbey intercourse—were it
not that Mill himself, at a later period, came forward as an
ecclesiastical reformer, and the comparison of his proposals with
the foregone labours of Bentham attains relevance and importance.

The public events of this year are sufficiently notorious.
Besides the larger issues that led to Waterloo, and the Peace,
there were minor questions pregnant with future consequences.
A most injudicious Corn Bill was immediately productive of
riots, and was a link in the long chain of operations leading to

Free Trade. Catholic Disabilities was again discussed; but ground was lost. The Slave Trade is now a leading topic, the refusal of the Ministry to pass a law for the Registry of Slaves, offends some of their own supporters. The slave owners are now in arms in defence of their interests.

1816.

On the 16th of " 1st month," Allen writes anxiously expecting Mill's return to London; which took place in February. Allen needs for his next number an article of a sheet on a pamphlet respecting the Registry of Slaves in the West Indies: the author is "Stephen," who gave up his seat in Parliament because this was not made a Government measure. There occurs in the first number an article with that heading. Again Allen urges upon Mill the settlement of the accounts.

A letter, dated January, is from Ricardo, and still addressed to Ford Abbey. It is but an end-fragment, and opens—" fill 8 pages in the Appendix, will that be too much?" John Mill tells us that it was through his father's urgency and encouragement that Ricardo brought out his great work on Political Economy; and to that work we must refer this request. A long letter in February, from that voluminous correspondent, Major Cartwright, is occupied with Westminster electioneering.

Allen again, on the 3rd of March (a fragment); Mill now in town. He asks Mill to a meeting with Wilberforce, about St. Domingo, and forwards a bundle of papers from Hayti.

In a scrap of a letter, dated June, this year, an Irish gentleman, Mr. Ensor, greatly devoted to Mill, seeing much of him when in London, and often writing from Ireland, seems to reply to Mill's Savings Bank hobby, as proposed by him for Ireland; the tone of the reply is grim incredulity.

On the 2nd of July, a letter to Napier indicates that he is at work for the Supplement to the Encyclopædia.

" Upon turning the subject in my mind, which I had

not time to do just at first, I think it will be impossible to separate the matter of an article on the word "Beggar" from the subject of Pauperism in general. If you contemplate nothing more than a description of the artifices of the professional beggar, this is, properly speaking, a branch of the art of imposture and swindling, and really belongs to that head, not to that of Pauperism at all. If the persons who solicit charity from passengers in the highways, and from door to door, are to be considered as a class, and with reference to the operations of the legislator, you cannot separate the subject from that of pauperism in general. The first question is—What are you to do with beggars? If you suppress them, you must make a legal provision for those who fall into want, otherwise you inflict a capital punishment upon poverty, and in that case you enter upon all the difficult questions relating to a poor's rate. My own opinion therefore is, that the subject of mendicity should be treated under some title which would embrace the whole of the questions relating to pauperism.

"Under the title 'Beggar,' without anticipating the general subject, you can do nothing but address yourself, without any public utility, to the idle curiosity of those who wish to hear strange stories, and write an article fit for a catchpenny magazine, but by no means for your noble Supplement. Nevertheless, if you are of a contrary opinion, I will write the article as you desire, and give you the stories in the House of Commons Report, with my own commentaries, which will detract not a little from the marvellous with which some of them are seasoned. From this and other sources an entertaining article might no doubt be made, if not a scientific one. I am looking forward to your calls on the article *Government*, and shall, I trust, be well prepared for you by the time, as I am now drawing to a close with a heavy load which I have long had upon my shoulders."

I cannot say whether the topic "Beggar" was suggested by Napier in the first instance or by Mill. We can see that Napier had his own views as to the mode of handling, and that Mill was anxious to conform to these views. We shall find him equally accommodating all through. On the 12th, follows another letter.

"I readily submit my judgment to yours in a subject which you have looked at so much more closely—and will readily undertake an article BEGGAR, on the plan which you propose.

"With regard to Savings Banks and Benefit Societies, I should have been more willing to comply with your solicitation, had it been a month later; as just now, to my other occupations is added the trouble of moving to Devonshire for some months, with my family. However, I am extremely desirous to perform what you request of me; and as I think that none of the three articles needs be long, I think I may undertake for them within the time which you mention.

"I believe I have, or can easily command, all the publications required for the several articles, unless it be *Sinclair's Agricultural Report*. The simplest plan for procuring me here the books I may have occasion to use, would be to give an order to the publisher of the work here, or any other of Mr. Constable's correspondents to lend them to me, or procure me the loan of them. Any book not common in the shops, I can always, when in London, get access to in some channel or other. The only difficulty is when I am in the country. Mr. Constable, if you speak to him, will know best how this may be arranged.

"I have glorious accounts of your success—and the prospect of abundance of readers adds not a little to the inducement to write.

"The direction to me in the country is Ford Abbey, Chard, Somerset. But if you address your letter or anything else here—it will be immediately forwarded—I shall not, however, be gone before this day fortnight."

Another meeting of the Chrestomathic Managers took place at his house, just before he left; the last for the year.

A melancholy announcement reaches Bentham in midsummer. It is to this effect—

"This day, at five minutes past one in the morning, my beloved master, Don Francis de Miranda, resigned his spirit to the Creator ; the curates and monks would not allow me to give him any funeral rites, therefore, in the same state in which he expired, with mattress, sheets, and other bed-clothes, they seized hold of him and carried him away for interment ; they immediately afterwards came and took away his clothes, and everything belonging to him, to burn them."

Probably the bitterness of this ending had been partly gone through, when Miranda was known to be hopelessly immured in a Spanish dungeon.

On the 20th September, Mill writes from Ford Abbey to Dr. Thomson, who has just been married. By an arrangement with Mill, he has occupied part of the house with him for a year or more.

"MY DEAR DOCTOR,

"I received your letter last night, and derived from it very sincere satisfaction. I have no doubt whatever, that the change which you have made in your state of life will greatly add to your happiness. At home you were no doubt lonely before, and you justly remark that the case would have grown worse as you grew old. Besides, human happiness requires that the human heart should have something to love, that it should have one at least with whom it can enjoy sympathy, and in whom its confidence can be reposed. I am satisfied that you will have made a good choice, both because I know you are not easily deceived in persons, and because you are past that hey-day of the blood when the solid qualities are apt to be overlooked for the superficial. I am happy that she is an old acquaintance, because then people are more likely to know one another, and less likely to have any source of disappointment. I have no doubt that your lady will be a great acquisition not to you only, but to the circle of all your acquaintances. Mrs. Mill is highly delighted at the prospect of making her a friend, and of living under the same roof with her. There will be no doubt at all of our accommodating ourselves with her. The only doubt is about her liking us; and whether a great parcel of children will not be an annoyance which she will not admire. However, that experience will soon determine; and in the meantime she may count upon it that nothing shall be left undone that we can do to add to, or at anyrate not to diminish from, her comforts. Mrs. Mill is sorry that she did not know before leaving London, that she might have left our rooms in a usable state, in case Mrs. Thomson may for any purpose have occasion for any beyond her own. In the meantime, we beg she will use of our things whatever is within reach as if it was her own. John, who has read your *System of Chemistry* with vast ardour since he came here, is not the least pleased to think of an increase of your happiness; and we all join in hearty congratulations to you and your lady, to whom we beg to present our very best wishes and regards.

"So much for an agreeable, now for a disagreeable subject. I should have been under the necessity of writing to you this week. I have a half-year's rent to pay at Michaelmas, the 29th inst., and I meant to have written to you to say that Place, who performs all matters of business for me in my absence, and among other things pays my rent, would be directed to call upon you, to receive, if convenient, your rent for the last year. The sort of agreement that was between us was that we should divide the rent and taxes of the house in equal proportions. The particulars I cannot here mention; the whole is some little matter about 100 guineas. It will be enough, therefore, if you pay 50; and I shall shew you the receipts which vouch for the particulars when I return.

"Believe me, always most devotedly,

"Your

"J. MILL."

A letter to Napier of the 23rd Oct., has a special biographical value.

" On turning to your letter for the purpose of answering it, and observing the date, I see I have reason to be ashamed of myself.   I am not, however, so faulty as at first sight I may naturally appear ; for, seeing it would not be in my power to give you an article on Botany Bay, I endeavoured to find out a person who I thought would do it, and as well as anybody whom you had much chance of finding.   The person I mean is Major Torrens, who has written several very good pamphlets on different parts of Political Economy, and who I knew had been at pains to collect information respecting Botany Bay, having projects of being sent out to be its Governor.   Torrens, I find, is just now wandering about in Ireland, and I conclude has not received my letter, for I have not heard from him at all, though I have no doubt he would have liked much to have contributed the article.

" Of India I have undertaken to give no less than a complete history, in which I aim at comprising all the information in which we Europeans are very materially interested ; and, thank God, after having had it nearly ten years upon the carpet, I am now revising it for the press, and hope to begin to print as soon as I return to London.   It will make three 4to volumes, which, whatever else they may contain, will contain the fruits of a quantity of labour, of which nobody who shall not go over the same ground, and go over it without the assistance of my book, can form an adequate conception.   Had I foreseen that it would be one half or one third of what it has been, never should I have been the author of a *History of India*."

A fragment from Ricardo, in December, congratulates the family " in this day of rejoicing " : I suppose it was the birth of the sixth child.

In the volume of the *Philanthropist*, we find Savings Banks again ; also the Registry of Slaves and St. Domingo—the response to Allen's bundle of papers.   But for the indications of these subjects, I could not trace his hand in a marked way in this volume.

Bentham must have been principally occupied this year with *Church-of-Englandism*, if not also with *Not Paul*. His *Defence of Usury*, written in 1787, is now printed at full. His psychological notes are stated by himself as ranging from 1814 to 1816. He does a little more at his Constitutional Code, which he seems always to have executed by snatches.

Public affairs are now entering on the new groove after the Peace. The public discontent is compelling more serious criticism on the measures of Government. An amendment on the Address to the Regent's Speech is moved by Mr. Brand and seconded by Lord John Russell. The conduct of the Allies to France, in restoring the Bourbons, was brought up, and was also the subject of a distinct debate. Romilly spoke admirably on this topic. Brougham entered into this and other standing questions with his fiery energy; but was much censured for having overdone an attack on the Prince Regent. The Property Tax was vehemently opposed, and its renewal defeated. Ireland again. The Registry of Slaves Bill is now made to bear the blame of a great insurrection in Barbadoes. Great riots of colliers out of work. Meal riots in Dundee.

Two great meetings to petition the Regent on public distresses were held in Spa Fields, Islington. The chief speaker was the well-known radical orator Henry Hunt. He denounced all public men, except Burdett, Cobbett, and Cochrane. Watson, another well-known radical, headed a portion of the meeting in an assault upon the shops of the city, which the Lord Mayor got great credit for suppressing.

The summer of this year is described as wet to a degree. The harvest in consequence was very bad. The result was, to aggravate the political excitement of the following year.

1817.

This year, the *History of India* goes through the press. The *Philanthropist* is stopped, after the publication of two numbers. The first of the two is remarkable for a review of Dumont's edition of Bentham's *Treatise on Rewards and Punishments*. The article expounds and defends Bentham at some length, and is to be continued; but never was. In March, Allen sends notes of the Prison at Ghent, to be worked up by Mill into an article; which accordingly appears. In April, he writes to urge the publication of a paper on the Establishment for the Poor at Mannheim, and will " be glad to know how thou gets on with the Amsterdam article ". This also appears, headed "Charitable Institutions at Amsterdam". The concluding article of the last number is on the Report of a Committee of the House of Commons on the Police of the Metropolis.

Thus, for six years and a half, Allen and Mill carried on a most energetic agitation in favour of a wide range of works of philanthropy and usefulness. They were at the same time, Allen especially, on all the Committees for putting their numerous schemes into operation. The extent of Mill's contributions may be judged from the fact, that at one settlement, Allen accounted to him for 8½ sheets.

On the 14th April, he writes to Napier :—

" I received your letter with its enclosure, for which I beg leave to return you many thanks. With regard to the amount I am perfectly satisfied; for in fact the articles, which you wanted in a hurry, were got up without much labour, from the materials which were nearest at hand ; and assuredly I expected no fame from them, so that I am agreeably surprised to hear from you, that they receive some approbation.

" I will give you an article on *Caste*; though having just begun to print my book, and printing at the rate of seven sheets a week, with the business of revising not yet nearly performed, I have my hands more than usually full. But it will be very unnecessary to make the article long—to go into the wearisome details. If I describe the grand classes, and show the tendency of it as an institution, I suppose that will fulfil your expectation. It will be easy to show the woeful mistakes of poor Abbé Dubois, as well as the similar ones of a more celebrated man, your Dr. Robertson himself.

"I am very grateful for the copy you have ordered for me of the work. I have not time at present to tell you my opinion of the execution of it. I can shortly, however, say that nothing to compare with it has yet appeared ; and that I have no doubt it will do ample credit to the zeal and ability which you display in conducting it."

Again on the 22nd August, we have the following :—

"I thank you for my reward in both shapes, the praise you bestow upon me, as well as the money.

"Situated, however, as I yet am, I tremble to undertake your *Colonies*. I have printed two volumes and have begun the third. But the MS. of a great part of the third is still to revise, and Colonel Wilks, who was Resident in Mysore, is just about to publish, or has published, two volumes more of his historical sketches, of which I have received the sheets ; and they, having been written by a man with peculiar opportunities of obtaining knowledge, lay me under the obligation of making a very close comparison of my own narrative with his , and afford me here and there a few facts which render fresh writing necessary. I can hardly expect to get through the drudgery of this preparation before the end of next month ; and unless you can give me some more time, I must pray you to put the subject into the hand of some other contributor ; though I confess, it is a subject on which I should have been glad to throw a little light, of which, after all that has been said upon it, I think it stands a little in need.

"By the *end* of October, if none of those rubs, which are very usual in such cases, interpose, I shall be ready with my three volumes, and shall be very anxious for your opinion of me."

The commencement of the printing of the *History* is marked by a letter, July 22, from the Secretary of the Post Office, Freeling, to Lord Auckland, conferring upon Mill the privilege of sending his proof-sheets through the Post Office free. I was not aware that such a privilege had ever been accorded. The letter shows that such applications were not always successful.* Mill was at Ford Abbey the whole time of the printing.

Two letters to Dr. Thomson (Sept. 13 and Oct. 5) refer to his being appointed Professor of Chemistry in Glasgow. There are congratulations, and also regrets, at the breaking up of the Queen's Square connexion, which seems to have been very harmonious; all the children lamented the departure. Both Mrs. Thomson and a maiden sister, Miss Colquhoun, were popular; and John had fulfilled a promise to write to Miss Colquhoun. No wonder, when his father styles her " dear Miss Colquhoun ".

The letter intimates that the printing of the *History* would be finished in November In point of fact, it was published about the new year. The family left Ford Abbey, for the last time, in January. The correspondence shows that the residence there was as much as ten months in the third and fourth of the four years. I cannot doubt that the finishing of the *History* would have been protracted considerably, if Mill had not enjoyed the advantages that Ford Abbey gave him. Mrs. Mill told the children that, while there, he got up at four in the morning, and worked till twelve at night. This, of course, would only be during the final stage of the work, perhaps for a few months; but his application all through must have been much beyond what would have been possible in London.

It is now quite evident that John Mill overstated his father's

* In the correspondence with Thomson, in 1802, on the starting of the *Literary Journal*, he says that Baldwin had applied to Freeling to frank the articles transmitted from Edinburgh. The result of the application does not appear.

exertions, wonderful as they were, in saying that he maintained
his family by Review and Magazine contributions, while himself
their sole teacher, all the time of writing the *History*.   I was
very much staggered by this assertion, when I first heard it,
many years ago, from John Mill in conversation.   Two doubts
occurred to me at once, although I did not venture to press
them.   The one was the enormous quantity of his very compact writing that would be required to realise what was absolutely necessary.   The still greater difficulty was to point to
the articles.   Ten or twelve considerable review articles a-year
for eleven years would be the least that would suffice; about
three or four a-year is, however, the utmost we can trace.
Mill may have realized about £150 a-year, but certainly not
more, from his literary work, during those years: so that he
must have had other ways of meeting his wants.   The four
years' residence at Ford Abbey, although more of Bentham's
seeking than of his, must have been a great assistance.   Moreover, I have heard from very good authority that Francis Place,
who took charge of Mill's money affairs, made him advances
while he was writing the *History:* these, of course, were all
repaid; but Place would have cheerfully allowed the loan to
lapse into a gift, had that been necessary.

Bentham's activity for the year appears chiefly in printing.
His Papers relative to Codification and Public Instruction,
written at various intervals since 1814, are now brought out;
and Romilly reviews the work in the *Edinburgh Review*.   The
Table of the Springs of Action, in which Mill assisted him, is
published.   " Swear not at all," printed for some time, is now
published.   The Plan of Parliamentary Reform is printed and
published.   Church-of-Englandism is printed, but publication
is suspended at Romilly's instance.

This year, the war between the Government and the rising
spirit of the country had become formidable.   Societies, meetings, unions, clubs, were starting up everywhere.   The Govern-

ment (24th Feb.) introduced in the Lords a Bill for Suspension of Habeas Corpus, and in the Commons a Bill for preventing seditious meetings: both were ultimately passed. A Peace Preservation Bill for Ireland was soon after introduced. As if this were not enough, Lord Sidmouth issued a circular letter to the Lords Lieutenants of Counties in England and Wales on preventing the circulation of blasphemous and seditious writings; Lord Grey and Romilly strongly remonstrated, but to no purpose. A motion, by Grattan, on the Roman Catholic Claims was lost, although supported by Castlereagh and Canning.

Sir Francis Burdett moved for a Committee on the Representation: lost by 265 to 77.

The death of the Princess Royal was treated as a great public calamity. Among other supposed effects was the indefinite postponement of the return of the Whigs to power, and a consequent thinning of the ranks of the Opposition.

The fires of prosecution were stirred anew. For the Spa-Fields affair of December, the Government brought Watson and three others to trial for High Treason, but failed to get a verdict. On this Romilly remarks.—"If they had been committed to Newgate (instead of being sent to the Tower), tried at the Old Bailey, and indicted merely for an aggravated riot, they would, without doubt, have been convicted."

The trials for libel and blasphemy were resumed with vigour. One—the trial of Hone the bookseller—became celebrated from the crushing defeat of the Government on three successive attempts; Lord Ellenborough (the presiding judge) himself getting a sharp lesson.

Two incidents occurring this year in the newspaper world, are closely interwoven with our immediate subject. The first is John Black's becoming principal Editor of the *Morning Chronicle*. He had not as yet the entire management of the paper, which he acquired on the death of Perry in 1823. But he could now make a beginning in the useful work that he carried on with such vigour and success.

The other incident, no less important in its own sphere, is the starting of the *Scotsman* in Edinburgh. The first number came out on the 25th January, under the editorship of Charles Maclaren. Partly by popularising Liberalism, as represented by the *Edinburgh Review*, and partly by keeping a steady hold of the popular side, which the Review often failed to do, the *Scotsman* was a powerful impulse to progress. The immediate occasion of its being started, was a crying local abuse; and it never ceased to carry on the fight against abuses. Before Maclaren assumed the full editorship, during the years 1818 and 1819, M'Culloch the political economist acted as editor, Maclaren merely assisting, as he was still a clerk in the Custom House. M'Culloch being now, or very soon after, one of Mill's Scotch chums, Mill soon began to take an interest in the paper, although M'Culloch was far below his mark as a liberal politician, and never got beyond Whiggism. Maclaren was more a man after Mill's own heart; and, if the two had been thrown together, Mill would, I believe, have found him as open as Black was to his suggestions and advice.

1818.

Notwithstanding the cessation of the *Philanthropist*, Friend Allen is the first to salute the year. Opens (16th of 2nd month) with a lament—" I have not heard a single line from thee since my return to England." Always doing business: Prison Discipline pressing now. *Inter alia*, " Owen has made a fool of himself ". Hopes that the poor *Philanthropist* may be soon revived. To his great relief, Mill writes, and forthwith is pressed to dine at Plough Court—" a great deal to communicate ".

A letter from Mill to Dr. Thomson on the 22nd February, brings out a forgotten episode of his life. In Hunt's *History of the Fourth Estate*, there is an anecdote to the effect, that Mill, from his singleness of devotion to the Philosophy of Mind, would have resigned his lucrative post in the India House, for the Moral Philosophy chair in Edinburgh; but was advised by his friends there that he had no chance. This anecdote is not discredited by the circumstance that his family knew nothing of the transaction; and it has a certain air of plausibility. The chair was vacated in 1820, when Mill had got his foot upon the first step of the ladder of the India House (£800 a year, with the certainty of promotion). It was just possible, I should hardly have said probable, that he would have surrendered his future for the chair. However, we shall soon see his own opinion on that very contingency. The present letter shows us all that was now in the wind. His ever watchful friend, now the professor of chemistry in Glasgow, informed him of a vacancy in the Greek chair of that University, and set forth the temptations of the chair.

"WESTMINSTER, *22nd Feb., 1818.*

" MY DEAR DOCTOR,

"You cannot doubt the sentiments with which I received the strong mark of your friendship manifested in the letter which I last received from you. The subject was of too much importance not to engage my serious consideration. But I was still in the country when I received your letter, and thought, as nothing was pressing immediately, I might defer my answer till I arrived in town, and would write to you free from the expense of postage. We have now been here for a few days, and I hope this will reach you, before any inconvenience can have arisen from delay.

" The amount of the emolument, and the respectable rank of the professor of Greek in your University, cannot fail to have abundance of charms to a man in my situation, though at the same time they would be attended with drawbacks which make me set a less value on them than would be set by most other people. The great question, however, is about the means of getting the object; and as to that I must be guided in a great measure by you. I must be known chiefly

by my book.   Your University is divided between Whigs and
Tories, and the Tories predominate.   Now, though I am any
thing in the world rather than a Whig, I am quite as far from
being a Tory ; and if there be as much illiberality in your
politics at Glasgow as I know there is about Edinburgh, both
parties are likely to join in keeping me out.   If, however, they
can bear with the *opinions* of a man, whose *politics* will give
them no disturbance, and who would despise himself if he
cared one farthing which was uppermost of two individual
factions who are only contending with one another for the
privilege of preying upon the rest of their countrymen, it might
not be difficult to afford them means of satisfaction.   You will
soon have the means, I think, of forming something of a judgment upon this subject.   You have, I hope, long before this
time, the copy of my book which I desired Mr. Baldwin to
send to you, and will be able to form some idea of the manner
in which your professors are likely to regard the author of
some of the opinions which are there delivered.   You may
have an opportunity of hearing what those of them who have
curiosity enough to read the book, may say ; and if, after all
this, you think there is any chance, you can then do what
appears to you to be advisable for paving the way, and I shall
be guided by you in what you tell me it is fit that I should be
doing to help you.   Upon Sir W. Forbes, and Sir John Stuart,
I think I may count, and the influence of Sir W. F. cannot be
small.   [The professors were the electors, but always subject
to pressure from the gentry.]   One thing, however, of course
you will bear in mind, that I should by no means wish to
appear in the thing unless there were tolerable probabilities of
success.   It is fit also I should mention to you (though at
present it is a secret which is to be kept very close) that there
are some friends of mine among the East India Directors, who
have views in my favour of considerable importance in the
East India House.   The probabilities of success they reckon
strong, but yet the uncertainties are such that I think we

should not overlook any of the chances in favour of so important a thing as your professorship. Mrs. Mill, which rather surprised me, would be delighted to go to live in Glasgow, to which her friendship with Mrs. Thomson seems naturally to contribute. She is highly delighted, and so am I, to hear such good accounts of her and her fine boy, notwithstanding that tormenting malady of the suppuration which prevented her from suckling him. She will be more fortunate, I hope, next time.

" There is one thing which I must yet mention to you with regard to the professorship. I am afraid you must sign the Confession of Faith. Now, though an overscrupulousness in things of form, is rather a sign of wanting than of possessing virtue, I should by no means wish to do any act by which I was really to be *understood* as declaring, or binding myself to, a belief in that book.

" We are all well ; excepting that the children have all got cold as usual, upon coming to London. John has fastened with great greediness upon your book, and gives me an account of the new knowledge he gets out of it. He would have a great passion for the science, if he had the opportunity of seeing a course of experiments.

" I am very anxious to hear your opinion upon my book ; and hope you will let me know it as fully as your time will admit, immediately after perusal. The first going off has been successful, greatly beyond my expectation. You will hear more of it shortly.

" Ever faithfully yours,

" J. MILL."

This is our first inkling of the India Office appointment Next year we shall see the consummation.

The following interesting letter (Apr. 30) to Napier refers to a criticism of Professor Playfair's opinions on the Hindu Astronomy, which occurred in the *History of India*.

" I will lose no time in acknowledging your letter, more especially on account of what you mention as to any expressions of mine* in relation to your 'revered friend' and ornament of our country, Mr. Playfair, whose talents I revere as much as it is possible for any man to revere them, who is so little capable of appreciating their exertions in the line in which they have displayed themselves, and whose character, so far as I am acquainted with it, I regard as even a model. I shall be extremely happy if you will carefully attend to the passage, and give me your honest opinion, for nothing will give me greater pain than to think that I have used any other language than that of esteem towards a man whose approbation I should be so proud to enjoy. If you should really think that my language is faulty (for, as I had not only an opinion of his to controvert, but was also under the necessity of guarding my readers against what I knew was great—the weight of his authority—and as I am but too apt, in my eagerness to give the *matter* of my reasons, to think too little of the language in which they are clothed, I am not insensible to my peccability in this respect), I shall account it a particular act of friendship if you will stand my friend with him, and endeavour to explain the want of coincidence between my sentiments and expressions, if in this instance they are anything but expressions of respect. It will also be an act of kindness (as, like other authors, I live in hopes of a second edition at no wonderfully distant period), if you will suggest to me any alteration of the expressions, or of the entire passage (not inconsistent with the object), which will render it agreeable to yourself and the other friends of Mr. Playfair ; for as to himself, it must be a matter of too little consequence to him to merit his regard.

" I wish you had found time to read my heavy volumes, because it would have been a great gratification to me to hear your opinion of them. I have had but one opinion from

* *History of India,* 1., 395-7, where he criticises Playfair's opinions on the subject of Hindu Astronomy.

Edinburgh about them, which, being from a very Tory quarter, was fully as favourable as I could expect. When you do write again, which I hope will be soon, it will be a favour if you will tell me a little of what you may have heard about them ; for as I reckon the best judges to be among you, I am proportionately anxious to know what I am thought of among you. I am truly obliged to you, not only for sending me your paper on Bacon, but for writing it. His is a battle which I have often to fight—in conversation at least ; for Englishly-educated people are all hostile to him, as they (at least the greater part of them) are hostile to everybody who seeks to advance the boundaries of human knowledge, which they have sworn to keep where they are. Your learned and valuable collection of facts will make me triumphant."

On the 10th of June, Parliament is dissolved. Westminster was astir in anticipation. Mill and Place are leaders in the Radical Committee. First, it has to be seen whether Cochrane will stand : he having recently announced his intention of going abroad for 18 months. At a meeting, on the 1st June, at Mr. Brooks's, 110 Strand, Messrs. Adams, Brooks, Mill, and Place are named as the Committee to make this enquiry. Mill declines to serve on this errand, for want of time   He is present, however, at Brooks's house next day, Tuesday, the 2nd, and is one of four (with Place, Adams, and Sturch) named to draw up resolutions for the general meeting, fixed for Thursday, at the Crown and Anchor Tavern, to receive Lord Cochrane's answer, and to decide on the candidates to be nominated. On Thursday, the public meeting makes choice of Sir F. Burdett and the Hon. D. Kinnaird. Mill is on the Committee for securing their return. Joseph Hume and Hobhouse are also on the Committee. Their first difficulty is to deal with two small noisy factions, one for proposing Henry Hunt, the other for Cartwright. Place is led into consultation with Mill, as to the proper answer to a bill denouncing their Committee. This, however, was only preparatory skirmishing ; the real fight came to lie with a different enemy. On Saturday the 6th, an independent body of the electors adopt a Requisition to Sir Samuel Romilly; this he receives on Monday following, the 8th; and thereupon consents to stand, if he can be returned without personal solicitation or canvass. He is strongly backed in the *Chronicle*, by Perry. His friends set to work, and are soon confident of his success. Place's Committee regard the nomination as an act of hostility, and persist with their own candidates. The facile pen of Hobhouse produces a squib, ridiculing Perry as the sole author of Romilly's candidature. Abusive squibs and placards were contrary to Place's principle of conducting elections, but he could not control other people. Place pronounces Romilly a really formidable candidate; and so he is. Joseph Hume, having fallen from his horse, is confined to the house, and writes Place that Romilly is "a very proper man". Place replies that he does not think so. The supporters of Romilly must have drawn off many of the electors that formerly stood by Place. Romilly goes so far as to say that Kinnaird "is set up by a little committee of tradesmen, who persuade themselves that they are all-powerful in Westminster".* This was simply to adopt one of the stock sneers of their political opponents; true in form, with an insinuation not justified by the facts. There can be no doubt whatever that the Mill and Place party was very powerful, although, on this occasion, deserted by many of its usual allies. Mill appears at two meetings of the general committee on the 17th. He informs Place, who forthwith communicates to Brooks, that "after having accepted nearly £400 from the personal friends of Kinnaird, those who had taken and ex-

---

* Brougham echoes this sentiment in a speech made at Kendal, in connexion with the election for the county of Westmoreland. Referring to what was going on at Westminster, he said "it was precisely the same in principle with the Westmoreland election, with this only difference, that the usurpation of the people's rights was attempted by an oligarchy, a junto of themselves in the Metropolis; whereas, in the province, it would be effected by a single family". Brougham retained the soreness of his disappointment in 1814.

pended it were going to abandon him". Place is intensely
disgusted.

The poll commences: Romilly at the head; Kinnaird
nowhere. "Burdett and Kinnaird's Committee appear," says
Romilly, "to be very angry at my being named as a candidate,
and have published some violent hand-bills against me, in
which they accuse me of being a lawyer, one of the Whig
faction, &c. This nonsense seems to have had very little
effect." Jeremy Bentham took a line of his own, and wrote
and signed a hand-bill, representing Romilly to be an unfit
member for Westminster, as being a lawyer, a whig, and a friend
only to moderate reform. He sends this to the Burdett Committee, but they decline to publish it. The *Examiner*, however,
taking much the same line, very fairly states the objections to
Romilly: the strongest being that he was certain of a seat
elsewhere, and was merely weakening the stand that the Westminster electors had so long made for thorough-going Reform
principles.

After the fourth day, Kinnaird's friends are obliged to withdraw him, in order to secure Burdett against the Government
candidate, and, if possible, to place him at the head of the poll.
In spite of all their exertions, Romilly keeps the head; but
Burdett comes in second, and the ministerial candidate third.

In a few weeks after the election, Romilly records "a small
but very pleasant dinner party" at Bentham's, with Brougham,
Dumont, Mill, and Rush the American minister. So ended
the mighty strife for the present: another end is not far off.

Whatever Mill might think of the Romilly election, he would
be highly gratified by the return of his dear Ricardo, who, by
pocket power, secured the Irish borough of Portarlington. Of
yet greater importance was the election of Joseph Hume, who
found honour in his own country (thanks probably to Lord
Panmure), and was returned for the Montrose burghs, keeping
his seat, till he was chosen for Middlesex, in the Reform Bill
times. Brougham also is in the House.

In the beginning (5th) of August, there is a farther letter to
Napier, which, among other things, lets us know Mill's projects
for the future.

"My delay in writing did not arise from what you mis-
name your 'scold about Playfair'. I take all that you said for
sound and proper remonstrance; and shall doubtless attend
to it, in a manner, I hope, to give you satisfaction, when I
come to a second edition, of which you will be glad to hear
that there is a near prospect.

"I was anxious to say, if I could, something useful on the
subject of Conveyancing. I have looked into the subject with
a good deal of care, and have often conversed upon it with
Bentham. There is nothing in any book beyond the practice
of the different systems of actual law. Principles on the
subject nobody has thought of exhibiting. As far as it has
been touched upon in any of Bentham's MSS, it is under the
head of Evidence, where it falls into the chapter on what he
calls 'Preappointed Evidence,' or those articles of Evidence,
consisting chiefly of writings brought into existence at the
present moment, for ascertaining at some future period a
matter of fact which had its existence now, or at some antecedent period. I believe you will find this the general
characteristic of all the branches of Conveyancing. The act of
transferring is the volition of the parties; the writings are the
mode of providing evidence of that volition. To discuss the
subject, you must work out this general idea by the force of
your own philosophy. You will get no assistance from law-
books or from lawyers. You do not know, perhaps, what is
my presumption on the subject of Law. The next work which
I meditate is a History of English Law, in which I mean to
trace, as far as possible, the expedients of the several ages to
the state of the human mind, and the circumstances of society
in those ages, and to show their concord or discord with the
standard of perfection; and I am not without hopes of
making a book readable by all, and if so, a book capable of

teaching law to all. And, after this, I will do what I can to
exhibit in full a system of Jurisprudence to the world. This
at any rate stands far forward among the several projects which
float in my head.

"I had a letter from Mr. Ricardo only two or three days
ago, in which he expresses himself in terms of unbounded
gratitude for your more than politeness. I beg you will accept
my warmest acknowledgments. I know not a better man than
him on whom you have laid your obligations, or who will be
more desirous of returning them. I feel myself in such good
humour with you just now, that I know not well how to refuse
you anything. One thing comforts me in undertaking *Economists*, that I see not at present any reason for a long article.
However, at your leisure, I shall be glad of as minute an
explanation as you can afford, of your views with regard to
both articles."

One thing surprises and disappoints me here, namely, that
he should be so close upon his notable article " Education,"
and not advert to that article, which must have taken up a
large portion of this autumn's work. Although the subject was
congenial to him, as partaking of pure Psychology, yet it was
completely outside of all his lines of occupation for the last
few years.

The melancholy death of Romilly, on the 2nd of Nov., took
Mill down to Worthing, to render his sympathy and aid to the
family in their double bereavement. A new election for Westminster was thus precipitated, and no time was to be lost in
searching for a candidate. Place is the first to move. He
concocts a hand-bill putting forward Kinnaird. He obtains
the concurrence of Bentham and Henry Bickersteth. Still,
there was a question as between Kinnaird and Hobhouse.
There were the usual troubles and complications with Hunt and
Cartwright. In the end, Hobhouse was put forward, and was
opposed on the Whig interest by the Hon. George Lamb, son
of Lord Melbourne.

On the 5th Nov., Place wrote a long letter to Mill at Worthing, describing the initial operations and the deplorable want of agreement among the liberals. Mill's reply, dated the 6th, is as follows :—

"I do not wonder at the disgust you express on so capital a blunder, about which there can be no doubt that you judge correctly. I look upon the thing as marred. Not that I am so sanguine as you about the returning of Kinnaird, had the best course been pursued. The people will be lukewarm about him, in spite of all that could have been done ; and the ministry will be active and powerful, and have plenty of time. The desirable thing would be that Reformers and Whigs should agree about some one man, and unite their efforts, when there would be no contest. But who that man can be I own I do not see. If Lord Folkestone would consent, he would be the man, without any declaration ; or if Bennet would only declare for household suffrage and the ballot. About all this, however, it is useless to talk here—as I shall soon see you. It was not worth your while to write all the particulars of the miserable blunder. I shall hear them when I come.

"I cannot tell you how much I have been affected by the dreadful tragedy in this family. When you and I saw them last year at Ford Abbey, and admired and loved them all, we should have declared that there were more elements of happiness mixed up in their lot than in that of almost any other human beings we knew—and yet how sudden the reverse !

"I do believe the gloom has affected my health—I have been obliged again to have recourse to medicines."

Mill did not act on the Committee on this occasion, and his hand is no longer apparent. The contest ended in the return of Lamb, by a majority of 604 over Hobhouse.

Mill's struggles may now be considered as ended. The *History* was a great and speedy success. The first edition was almost sold off; and he was entitled to a large sum as sharer in the profits. This, and the income of the subsequent editions, he left in Baldwin's hands, as an investment bearing interest; the proceeds would have been a good provision for his family. Unfortunately, Baldwin came to grief, and the money was not recovered. The crash did not come till after Mill's death, so that he was spared the mortification of witnessing the downfall of a house that he had implicitly trusted, as well as the loss of his twelve years' earnings.

At this time of day, I am not called upon to criticize the *History of India.* It has exercised its influence, and found its place. Any observations that are needful are such as will aid us in appreciating the character of the author. Coming to the subject with his peculiar powers and his acquired knowledge, and expending upon it such an amount of labour, he could not but produce a work of originality and grasp. If the whole of his time for twelve years was not literally devoted to the task, it was, we may say, substantially devoted; for his diversions consisted mostly in discussing topics allied to the problems that the History had to deal with. In a long Preface, he sets forth his design, and the difficulties he had to encounter; and makes his well-known apology for writing on India without having seen the country.

The first Book narrates the commencement of the British intercourse with India, and carries it on to the establishment of the Company on a durable basis by the Act of the sixth of Queen Anne. The second Book is what arrests our attention as the most characteristic, bold, and original portion of the work. It undertakes to exhibit the character, the history, the manners, religion, arts, literature, and laws of the people of India; together with the physical influences arising out of the climate, the soil, and the productions of the country. This last part, however, has no chapter expressly allotted to it, and is hardly perceptible anywhere. The first-named part is the best product of the author's genius. Here he exerted all his powers to make a grand sociological display—valuable in itself, and a most important accessory to the narrative of events. The analysis of the Hindoo institutions is methodical and exhaustive, and is accompanied with a severe criticism of their merits and their rank in the scale of development. To the student of forty years ago, the reading of this book was an intellectual turning-point. The best ideas of the sociological writers of the eighteenth century were combined with the Bentham philosophy of law, and the author's own independent reflections, to make a dissertation of startling novelty to the generation that first perused it. Subsequent research and criticism found various mistakes and shortcomings. Being written while the public was prepossessed by an excessive admiration for Hindoo institutions and literature, due to Sir W. Jones and others, the review was too disparaging—the bow bent too far in the opposite direction.

The annotator employed to edit and continue the History, Mr. H. H. Wilson, does not scruple to charge his author with a hostile *animus* both here and in other parts of the work: of this the reader of the text and notes together will be the best judge. He also complains that the undue disparagement tended to increase the difficulties of the British rule in India, and to pre-occupy the minds of officials with an undue contempt for the Hindoo people. If this effect really happened, it was more than compensated by the unsparing severity of the criticism bestowed upon all those that had borne a part in founding and extending our Indian Empire.

The third Book is devoted to the narrative of the transactions of the ninety-eight years from 1707 to 1805—the critical period of the consolidation of the East India Company This was the eventful century that saw the extension of their dominions by all kinds of accidents and arts; that was wound up by the administrations of Clive and Hastings, and the first military glory of Wellington.

The concluding paragraph of the Introduction is comprehensive and short.

" The subject forms an entire, and highly interesting, portion of the British History ; and it is hardly possible that the matter should have been brought together, for the first time, without being instructive, how unskilfully soever the task may have been performed. If the success corresponded with the wishes of the author, he would throw light upon a state of society, curious, and commonly misunderstood ; upon the history of society, which in the compass of his work presents itself in almost all its stages and all its shapes ; upon the principles of legislation, in which he has so many important experiments to describe ; and upon interests of his country, of which, to a great degree, his countrymen have remained in ignorance, while prejudice usurped the prerogatives of understanding."

The author's *forte* in the mere narrative is lucidity of statement. His higher function is to criticize, and to apportion praise and blame. His impartiality in this respect may not be unquestionable ; but it is as great as could be expected of any man in such a subject. His judgment errs in pitching his standard somewhat too high.

The arrangement, or method of the narrative, in the point of view of composition, is far from perfect ; but must be reckoned probably as good as the author's situation would allow. The work being new, the materials had to be sought out, and presented in tolerable fulness. This, with the other aims that the author entertained, was enough to engross his powers as the first historian of India. We can now, however, see that the great complexity of the details, the plurality of concurring events over an immense area, makes up an enormous problem of narrative art, soluble only by concentrating attention upon that one effort Mill's power of political generalizing helps him here ; he discerns and sets forth comprehensive views that reduce the chaotic mass into a happy simplicity. Thus, take the opening sentence of his chapter on the conquests of Timur :—

" The birth of Timur, or Tamerlane, was cast at one of those recurring periods, in the history of Asiatic sovereignties, when the enjoyment of power for several generations, having extinguished all manly virtues in the degenerate descendants of some active usurper, prepares the governors of the provinces for revolt, dissolves the power of the state, and opens the way for the elevation of some new and daring adventurer."

Still, there are wanted in addition, some of the highest devices of narrative composition to make the *History of India* take any distinct shape in the memory. What these are, I do not here enquire: they are probably far from perfection even in the latest historians; yet a great advancement may be traced in such examples as Carlyle's Friedrich, and Kinglake's Crimean War. Both these writers appear to be alive to the class of difficulties that attach, in a still greater degree, to any narrative of the events that make up the history of British India; I mean, more particularly, multiplication and complexity of transactions.

The style of the *History* was always spoken of by Bentham in terms of general condemnation. The friendly reviewer in the *Edinburgh Review* is more specific in pointing out what he considers its defects.

"We cannot speak as favourably of Mr. Mill's style as of his matter. It has many marks of carelessness, and some of bad taste; and the narration, in a few instances, is not free from that greatest of all defects—obscurity; which has arisen from an inattention to the use of the tenses of the verbs. In his disquisitions, it is vigorous, though not always pure or dignified: and violations of the usage of the language with respect to particular words, are not unfrequently to be met with. But of all these faults our readers will be able to judge from the extracts more severely than we can ourselves—who rise from the reading of the work, grateful for the vast body of information which it conveys, and impressed with respect, not only for the intellectual qualities of the author, but for his high and rare virtues as an historian."

CHAPTER IV.

APPOINTMENT TO THE INDIA HOUSE.

1819-1823

THE present chapter includes the appointment to the India House, and the writings carried on during the five years subsequent to that event. The break is made after the finishing of the articles for the *Encyclopædia*, and before the starting of the *Westminster Review.*

This period saw a great augmentation of Mill's influence in general society. The four years at Ford Abbey, and the engrossment with the History, had kept him within a very select circle of friends and acquaintances. He is now fixed in London, and, although carrying on literary work as well as the business of his office, he is in every way a freer man, and can afford to spend more time in company. The circle of his intimate friends is enlarged. The new accessions include some very important names.

It was in the year 1818, that he became acquainted with GEORGE GROTE: the introduction being effected through Ricardo. The following extract of a letter written in May, 1819, gives Grote's first impressions of Mill :—

"I have breakfasted and dined several times with Ricardo, who has been uncommonly civil and kind to me. I have met Mill often at his house, and hope to derive great pleasure and instruction from his acquaintance, as he is a very profound thinking man, and seems well disposed to communicate, as well as clear and intelligible in his manner. His mind has, indeed, all that cynicism and asperity which belong to the Benthamian school, and what I chiefly dislike in him is, the readiness and seeming preference with which he dwells on the *faults and defects* of others—even of the greatest men! But it is so very rarely that a man of any depth comes across my path, that I shall most assuredly cultivate his acquaintance a good deal farther."*

This contains perhaps the strongest language Grote ever employed in describing Mill's censorial tendency. His mode of speaking in after life was in terms of almost unexceptional eulogy; as may be seen in his Review article on John Mill's *Hamilton*. Mrs. Grote, in her *Personal Life of Grote*, while speaking in terms of highest admiration of Mill's powers and his influence for good, greatly exaggerated the strength of his antipathies to the Aristocratical Class. She also couples with his dislike to Established churches a corresponding dislike to the ministers, which was not the fact; he never ceased to have friends among the clergy of the church. She is equally guilty of overstraining, when she says that Mill, while possessing the faculty of kindling in his auditors the generous impulses towards the popular side, led them, at the same time, "to regard the cultivation of individual affections and sympathies as destructive of lofty aims, and indubitably hurtful to the mental character".

It was fortunate for Grote that Mrs. Grote came herself

* His Diary for March, contains, at an interval of five days, two of these meetings with Mill, Thus: "*Tuesday*, March, 23rd. Rose at 6. Read Kant, and ate a little bread and butter, till ½ past 8, when I went up to Brook Street to breakfast with Mr. Ricardo; was very politely received by him; walked with him and Mr. Mill in St. James's Park until near 12" "*Sunday, March, 28th.* Rose at ½ past 5. Studied Kant until ½ past 8, when I set off to breakfast with Mr. Ricardo. Met Mr Mill there, and enjoyed some most interesting and instructive discourse with them, indoors and out (walking in Kensington Gardens), until ½ past 3, when I mounted my horse and set off to Beckenham Was extremely exhausted with fatigue and hunger when I arrived there, and ate and drank plentifully, which quenched my intellectual vigour for the night."

under the spell of Mill's conversation, and was always ready to meet him in society ; so that he became one of their most frequent guests, and in return received them at his own house. The occasions of their intimacy both on private and on public affairs, will come up in the course of our narrative, chiefly through the aid of Mrs. Grote's reminiscences.

No other notable accession to the list of friends is recorded for the next two years. The India House post brought him into contact with many superior men, both among the officials, and among the Directors. It is enough to name Peacock, who was just beneath him in position, and came to be head at his death.

It was in 1821 that he became acquainted with JOHN AUSTIN. Soon after this, Charles Austin arrived in town fresh from Cambridge, and was introduced at once to Mill, and became one of John Mill's associates. He was the medium of introducing a number of his Cambridge contemporaries, young men of ability, then also commencing their career in London : these were Edward Strutt (Lord Belper), Hyde and Charles Villiers, and Macaulay. Strutt and the Villierses became zealous disciples of the elder Mill, and remained his admirers to the last. Of Macaulay we shall hear afterwards. John Romilly (Lord Romilly) was, of course, known to Mill in his father's life-time : he was a youth of sixteen when Mill went down to the family on their affliction.

About the same date, 1822-3, William Ellis was introduced to Mill, and through him to his son, and was very much with them both, till his marriage took him to reside at a distance from town. He had two brothers who also came to see Mill.*

---

* In a letter to the *Times* in 1873, Ellis wrote :—" Fifty years ago it was my good fortune to be introduced to Mr. James Mill, and through him to his son, John Stuart Mill, to both of whom I am indebted for more than I can find words to express They set me thinking for myself. One result of my studies and reflections has been the deep conviction that the elementary truths of Social Science—founded long before I was born—ought to be taught in all our schools, and for more than 25 years I have employed the greater part of the time which

Roebuck and George John Graham, were for a long time John Mill's inseparable companions, but they did not enjoy his father's regards in any great degree ; they are not to be counted among visitors at the house. Walter Coulson, in 1822, was Editor of the *Traveller* newspaper, an important Liberal organ. He had been, says John Mill, an amanuensis of Bentham, then a reporter, then an editor, before settling down in the profession of the law. He was one of Mill's most intimate companions, especially in the last years of his life. Albany Fonblanque began to write in the *Chronicle*, under Black, in 1823, and became one of the Mill circle.

I cannot point to the beginning of the intimacy between Mill and HENRY BICKERSTETH, who became Master of the Rolls, as Lord Langdale.

Their strong mutual attachment will be manifested as we go on. Bickersteth first appears in the Bentham circle, in 1818, when he writes a long letter to Burdett, with a view to bring about a common action between him and Bentham, in the cause of Reform (Bentham's Works, x. 492).

The well-known Richard Sharp, commonly called Conversation-Sharp, has been for some time one of Mill's acquaintances. A year or two hence, they are much thrown together.

I must not forget in the list, for this period, John Ramsay M'Culloch, the political economist, whose genial and hearty ways got him numerous friends, although he never abated one whit of the roughness of his native speech. John Mill, Mrs. Grote, and everybody, delighted in mimicking M'Culloch.

1819.

It was in the early months of this year, that the canvass for the India House appointment was going on. There is a letter to Thomson explaining the situation in the beginning of April.

I could spare from business to promote such teaching, both as a teacher and a writer of little books intended chiefly for children and their teachers."

"I was much pleased with your felicitation upon the success of my book. We are now busy preparing for a second edition. What you tell me about some of the Edinburgh Reviewers was not altogether a secret to me; and was by no means unexpected, as I know something of the spirit which reigns in that quarter. There has been an account of it in the *Journal des Savans;* and its reputation is higher than I expected it to be for several years; knowing that it had nothing to recommend it in respect to those superficial decorations, on which ephemeral reputation is built. I am fully aware at the same time of the force of your observations about style, and shall profit by them as much as may be in preparing for the 2nd Edition.

"I had heard something of the Edinburgh Journal set up in rivalship of yours; and thought the conduct not very handsome on the part of some of the individuals. I shall hear from Baldwin the results, but hope you will send me as much as possible of the secret history.

"I am now going to mention to you an affair which is in agitation, and for which your interest may be of good service to me. A place in the India House of (I am told) £700 a year, requiring attendance from 10 to 4, is about to be vacated. It is the place held by Mr Halhed in the Examiner's Office. I have been encouraged to apply for it. My letter has been laid before the Court of Directors; and I think I have considerable chance of success. Several of the Directors are my declared friends, and a good deal of application of considerable weight has been made to others of them. The reputation of my book, too, I am told is even a strong recommendation. You can do a great deal, I doubt not, with Thornhill, and I could wish you to write both to him and to Col. Beaufort, in as strong terms as your conscience will allow; Mr. Thornhill may not only have his own vote, but may be able to influence others. The thing is of more importance than it seems; as it may lead to more. I have been told by my friends in the Direction, *entre nous,* "Accept of any thing, however small, in

the first instance : if once in, we shall be able to push you on."
As the affair will be decided shortly, you cannot make your
application too soon.   These are all the circumstances which I
think are necessary to let you know what is in the wind; and
with you, I know, nothing more is wanted."

Mill's friends spared no pains to secure this appointment.
Hume and Ricardo made great exertions in the city.   Mr.
Grote remembered being asked by Ricardo (who had then
recently introduced him to Mill) to use his influence with India
proprietors.   The " chairs " (Chairman and Deputy-Chairman)
were in his favour, solely on the ground of his ability and
knowledge of India.   There was of course a considerable mass
of Tory opposition to be got over.   Canning, however, who
was then President of the India Board, is credited with being in
Mill's favour.   This is rendered highly probable by Bentham's
remark already quoted, and by an expression in one of Mill's
letters (to be given presently), which seems to show that he
made the personal acquaintance of Canning soon after.

It was on the 12th of May, that he was appointed "an
Assistant to the Examiner of India Correspondence," salary
£800.   The subsequent steps of his promotion were as
follows :—On the 10th April, 1821, he was appointed second
Assistant to the Examiner, Edward Strachey being first Assistant; salary £1000.   He was now fourth in the office.   On the
9th April, 1823, he was put ahead of Strachey, and appointed
Assistant Examiner at £1200; he was now second.   This rise
created the vacancy that led to John's being taken in as a junior
clerk.   On the 1st Dec., 1830, he became Examiner; salary
£1900.   He was now chief.   On the 17th Feb., 1836, his
salary was fixed at £2000.   This he enjoyed only four months.

It appears that the business of the office was greatly in
arrears, when Mill joined.   I shall have to quote a letter of
his own containing a passage to this effect.   A still stronger
statement occurs in a letter of Bentham to Lord Colchester.
After speaking in a very slighting manner of the action of the

Directors, Bentham says :—" Of the four Examiners, all of
them very well disposed men, Mill almost alone finds appropriate active talent, in addition to intellectual aptitude.   When
he came in, there had been, in relation to the financial department, not to speak of others, more than a twelvemonth's
despatches of which no notice had been taken .   .   .   . ."

From the time of his entering the India House, till he
became chief Examiner, in 1830, his occupation was the
Revenue Department ; which was, therefore, the only branch
where he exercised direct control.   It was his duty to draft the
whole despatches relating to that department.   When he became
Examiner, he superintended all the departments ; he did not
necessarily draft despatches in any one, but read those that
were prepared by the Assistants.

John Mill speaks in general terms of the improvements
introduced by his father into the Indian Administration, but
unfortunately does not specify any precise heads.   No one is
now left that can speak of the details of his official career.
It is certain that he made the first drafts of the despatches in
his own department, but he is not answerable for their final
form ; they had to pass through the superior authorities in the
office, and then be submitted to the Board of Control.   Our
best, and indeed our only, opportunity of obtaining an insight
into his official work, will occur in the course of the discussions
on the renewal of the India charter (1831-33), when he came
before a succession of Committees of the House of Commons,
and was examined at great length on all matters coming within
the sphere of his duties.

At the India House, the highest officials, in common with
the lowest, observed the office hours, from 10 to 4.   In the
government offices, at Whitehall and Downing Street, the
chiefs of departments and the upper officials usually take a
margin, and appear some time between eleven and one.   They
may have their despatch boxes conveyed to their own houses in
the afternoon, and do a little work in the morning at home ;

but nobody asks any questions, provided they get through the business somehow. In those six hours at the India House, strictly kept by the Mills, father and son, to the last, they found time for a good deal of their philosophical and other writing; while doing full justice to the demands of the Court of the Directors upon their time and attention. Their business did not flow in a stream, but came by gushes.

In the Bentham Memoirs, there are scattered allusions as to what Mill might induce the Indian Government to do, in the way of Judicial Reforms: the subject was often mooted between Mill and Bentham. The wide influence that John Mill alludes to must have been apart from the routine of his office.

It appears from two notes that have been preserved, that John Murray the publisher, sought and obtained, through Ricardo, Mill's assistance in connexion with some of his publications. The notes are civil and deferential in the extreme, and might have led to closer relations, had Mill been so disposed. Well would it have been for his family, if he had committed to Murray's hands the publication of the *History*.

The only remaining scrap of information for 1819 is a letter to Napier (10th Sept.), which I give entire :—

"I wrote immediately to Ricardo, telling him you counted upon his half promise as a whole one. I received from him a parcel of excuses, but as there was none of them good for anything, I wrote to him that I should send you word of his having undertaken the task. It is unaffected diffidence which is the cause of his unwillingness, for he is as modest as he is able. He will put down his thoughts, he says, and send them to you, but that you will have to write the article [Funding System] for yourself. But of this there is no fear except his own. As for *Foundation*, I have no doubt you ought to make it an article, and a great many very absurd prejudices standing in the way of good might be removed by it. I should like to do it, but am afraid to overload my time. I am preparing the second edition of my *History of India*, and I have loads of East India despatches with their enclosures to read, of a size which would frighten you. When I have got up the arrears, which had accumulated in this department before my admission, I shall be more at my ease. You need be under no alarm about my article *Government.* I shall say nothing capable of alarming even a Whig, and he is more terrified at the principles of good government than the worst of Tories. I would undertake to make Mr. Canning a convert to the principles of good government sooner than your Lord Grey and your Sir James Mackintosh ; and I have now an opportunity of speaking with some knowledge of Canning. You have at any rate seen what has been in the newspapers with regard to the health of Mr. Brougham, which struck me with much alarm, the moment I saw it, and all I have since heard has only added to my fears."

This was a year of great commercial distress, of riots, demonstrations, and uprisings ever increasing ; with unflinching resistance on the part of the Government. In January, Henry Hunt presides over a great Reform meeting in Manchester. In July, Birmingham elects Sir Charles Wolseley as its representative. He is very soon arrested, and becomes long a popular hero. In August, took place the Manchester demonstration that led to the Peterloo affair, for which Hunt and many others were apprehended. In December, Parliament passed the famous Six Acts of Castlereagh, against sedition and libels. The last of the six was specially directed against the unstamped political periodicals, and was more prolific of prosecutions and imprisonments than all the rest. The provisions were such as to keep up a perpetual war between the government and the cheap press, which lasted into the Reform times, and became the opprobrium of the Liberal Ministry till the reduction of the stamp duty in 1836.

The Fox Dinner at Newcastle, on the 6th January, was

memorable for a powerful speech of Earl Grey, given at full in the *Morning Chronicle*. In December, Lord John Russell brought in a motion on Parliamentary Reform.

1820.

For this year, the extant indications are few. There are pressing notes of invitation from Brougham to Sunday breakfasts. Here is the only sentence that touches a point of interest :—"In these times of Queens and Kings [Queen's trial going on], there is hardly any rational talk with any one, &c."

A letter to Napier on the 11th May, is a milestone in the progress of the more important articles of the Supplement, and has some interesting matter besides :—

"The article *Government* will make about three sheets, and that on *Jurisprudence* I will endeavour to confine within the same limits. I agree with you that nothing but a comprehensive outline should for such a work as yours be attempted. The difficulty, however, is to give as much of the reasons on which your framework is erected, as not to leave it wholly unsupported ; for the giving of reasons requires words, and sometimes not a few. Both articles are already on paper, and need only some curtailing and filling to be ready for you. Both, however, will need transcription, which is a devil of a task. You will grieve me by what you predict respecting the Professorship of Moral Philosophy. From what I had heard, I rejoiced to think that you would be the man. I reckon the appointment of a proper person a matter of first-rate importance, and the one to whom you allude (John Wilson) makes one sick to think of him. Instead of the delightful exhortations to mental enterprise, and to press forward unceasingly to new attainments, to which I listened with rapture from the lips of Mr. Stewart, the unfortunate youth will hear from the man in question nothing but exhortations to the implicit adoption of opinions already received, and to hate and persecute every man who shows a disposition to go beyond them. You flatter me highly by telling me you thought of me. If it were offered to me—notwithstanding the degree in which I think I am useful here, notwithstanding both the power and the income which may in time be connected with my situation, and notwithstanding London, the centre of intelligence, out of which I should not willingly take up my residence—I should be puzzled what to do. So it is better, perhaps, as it is. You have no chance for Mackintosh, and I cannot imagine he was ever serious of thinking of it. He lives but for London display, *parler et faire parler de soi*, in certain circles, in his heaven "*

We have here that very contingency which Hunt mistook for the vacancy in the Glasgow chair of Greek. My surmise, expressed before I saw this letter, as to how he would feel if the Edinburgh chair had been put in his view, is almost exactly confirmed from his own mouth.

Four days after this letter was written, John leaves for France, where he stays fourteen months. His father's home-occupations are so far changed; he has now to take charge of the education of the younger children himself, and to correspond with John as to his doings in France.

The next letter is on the 20th Nov., and also tells its own tale. It would appear that Ricardo, in the plenitude of his wealth, had scruples about taking payment for his contributions to the Supplement.

"I received your very liberal enclosure for the article *Government*, for which please to accept my best thanks. I had been spending a month with Ricardo in Glostershire, and I and your letter arrived at home on the same day. As I felt no difficulty in talking to Ricardo himself about the point which you have referred to me, I transcribed what you had

---

* See in *Cockburn's Memoirs*, p. 370, the account of the election to the Moral Philosophy chair

said. I have his answer in which he says he would have no pride in refusing, but rather a pride in receiving such remuneration, if it is customary for amateurs in such circumstances to do so. Ricardo adds that his scruples are of two kinds—first on account of the article, which he says is not worth payment; secondly, because, payment having formed no part of the motive which induced him to write the article, he reckons himself not entitled to payment. He then prays me to decide for him, but says he will on no accout receive more than at the rate of your most ordinary allowance.

"I see no reason to doubt my being ready for you with *Jurisprudence*. My object is to describe exactly what a complete *corpus juris* ought to be, and to afford some specimens, if possible, of the mode of composing it.

"I have yet to speak to you about an application which has been made to me as to the article on *Government*, from certain persons, who think it calculated to disseminate very useful notions, and wish to give a stimulus to the circulation of them. Their proposal is, to print (not for sale, but gratis distribution) a thousand copies. I have refused my consent till I should learn from you, whether this would be considered an impropriety with respect to the Supplement. To me it appears the reverse, as the distribution would in some degree operate as an advertisement." . . . .

Napier must have given consent to the re-printing of the article "Government" Hume, Grote, and I don't know how many others, subscribed for this reprint; and there were ultimately included all Mill's greater articles, which were bound in a volume, and privately disseminated. Once when Hume came to Aberdeen, on an electioneering occasion, he gave a copy to our then-commencing Mechanics' Institution; which is the one I have been in the habit of referring to.

It is of importance to mark the date of the publication of the article *Government*, as constituting an epoch in the political history of the time.

The first great public event of the year, is the death of George III., and the accession of his son. Then come the exciting months of the Queen's trial, damaging alike to the King and to the Ministry. The Cato-Street Conspiracy (Feb.) gives rise to a very sensational Trial for High Treason, where all the antique forms were preserved. Glasgow takes its turn in popular disquiet.

In Parliament, May 8, there is presented by Mr. Alexander Baring (Lord Ashburton), a Petition from the Merchants of London in favour of Free Trade. This led to important consequences. In June, Brougham introduces his Plan for the Education of the Poor, about which he soon gets into hot water with his allies in the Liberal camp. Hume is already conspicuous in overhauling the Revenue machinery. Lord John Russell creeps on in the path of Reform. He brings in a Bill to suspend the issue of Writs to Grampound, and three other places, with an ultimate view to their disfranchisement.

In the beginning of this year came out a remarkable work that played a great part in the next ten years' Reform struggle. It is entitled—The BLACK BOOK, or CORRUPTION UNMASKED, being an account of the Places, Pensions, and Sinecures, and the Revenues of the Clergy and the Landed Aristocracy. It provided the data for the statement so often made in the course of the Reform agitation, that less than two hundred persons (members of the Aristocracy) returned two thirds of the House of Commons. The exact numbers are, according to the book, 471 members, returned by 144 Peers and 123 Commoners. To these add 16 members nominated by Government; and the remainder independent of nomination is 171. I can well recollect often hearing the name of the *Black Book* in the exciting months of 1831-2; but I never saw the volume itself till lately; and I was not aware that it had been so long published.

1821.

The record of the present year is considerably fuller.

On the 3rd of January, there is a letter to Napier.

"I believe I have now fulfilled all the obligations, in the way of articles, which I am under to you. There is one article more, however, which, if you have not otherwise provided for it, I shall be very glad to undertake. That is, Liberty of the Press, or Libel Law, whichever title you chose to range it under. I think on that subject I could throw a good deal of light. I have also a hankering for *Logic*, but they come too near each other; and I am afraid to undertake for too much.

"By the by, there is a friend of mine who has written a very learned, and, what is more, a truly philosophical discourse on the subject of Magic, which he would be very happy to have printed in your work. From the specimen I have seen, it will prove, I think, not only instructive, but amusing. I am not at liberty to mention the name of the author. He is a young City banker, and the son of a man who is an eminent banker, and is a very extraordinary person, in his circumstances, both for knowledge and clear vigorous thinking.

"As to public matters, the question of a change of Ministers is still very doubtful. If the present people are not faint-hearted, they may remain in. I am told, however, and by people who have opportunities of knowing, that they are faint-hearted, in which case the Whigs may have another six months, which I think is as long a purchase as their Ministry will be worth. They will neither please the people nor the harpies. They cannot do good, even if they would, without reforming the Parliament, for the harpies (forming a majority of the House) must be satisfied, and reform the Parliament they will not. They are fools both in the public and selfish sense of the word."

The city banker was Grote. The article did not appear, and

13

was probably destroyed or transferred by its author; I am not aware of any trace of it in his subsequent works.

It is worth while to note that the proposal to write on the Liberty of the Press came from Mill himself. He had discussed the subject so often, from the days of the *Literary Journal* down to the last year of the *Philanthropist*, that he could not but feel himself pregnant and anxious to arrange his thoughts into a more systematic and permanent form; and it was fortunate that Napier gave his consent.

On the 24th February occurred Lindsay's sudden death at a public meeting for thwarting Brougham's Education Scheme. As may be supposed, the opposition was grounded on Brougham's trimming to the Church

On the 10th April, Mill gains a step in his office; being "confirmed in appointment as Second Assistant to the Examiner," Salary £1000. The head of the department, called "the Examiner," is William M'Culloch; the first Assistant, Edward Strachey; then Mill, followed by Peacock. This arrangement continues for two years.

Again progress is reported for the *Encylopædia*, on the 10th of July, in a letter otherwise interesting.

"I have been hard at work upon the article Liberty of the Press, and for that purpose suspended the printing of my book on Political Economy. I have refused to pay my annual visit to Ricardo, that I may work for you, so that you must not blame me if there is a little delay. I will see what I can do for "Law of Nations". I have no expectation of being able to satisfy myself; for it is a wide subject, to which little has been done, the study of which I have reserved for some period of leisure. But it is better I should say what I can say, than that the subject should be omitted. I must not omit to express the great satisfaction I received from your telling me that Professor Stewart expresses some curiosity respecting me. You say he wishes he could recollect my being at his class. I doubt not he would know me if he saw me. He must at least have been perfectly familiar with my face." (Here follows the passage already quoted, p. 16.)

Among incidental scraps of this year that have been preserved are three letters from the Rev. William Mills, Fellow of Magdalen College, Oxford, and Professor of Moral Philosophy. The last is this.

MAGD. COLL., OXFORD, *July 30th, 1821.*

"MY DEAR SIR,

"I was much disappointed that your engagements were of such a nature as to prevent your visiting me. I had promised myself much pleasure from receiving you among us. The fates seem indeed to have interfered to oppose our meeting; but I will hope better things next year. I am glad to hear that John is returned—it would have given me sincere pleasure to have seen him here, but I am obliged to set off for Lausanne to-morrow morning. A letter from him will always be a gratification, and need I add from yourself. My address is, Rev. W. Mills, Poste restante, Lausanne.

"Believe me, my dear sir,

"Very truly yours,

"WM. MILLS."

On the 27th July, indefatigable Allen wrote about re-commencing the *Philanthropist*—a new series; the first number to to be out in October. He asks a sheet from Mill on Education, the terms being as before. "I am encouraged to hope from what passed between us when we conversed on the subject at the India House, that they (his friends the promoters) may be favoured with thy assistance in this way—the work is to be kept quite clear from all politicks, if thou canst make it convenient. I will write again and state my views as to the principal points to be insisted upon." This letter of Allen's is addressed to Mill, at "Great Marlow, Buckinghamshire". I do not know who he was now visiting at Great Marlow.

A letter to Napier on the 21st Aug., relates to *Liberty of the Press*, which, it seems, was considered too long.

"I had not an idea that you wished less than three sheets. I set however about curtailing, and that, without doing more than there was time for doing, was no easy matter. It is easy to compress when you write anew; but to cut out, without destroying the continuity of the discourse, and weakening the evidence of your doctrines, is not, if your discourse has any continuity, without its difficulties.

"I was not pleased with this article (*Liberty of the Press*) before, and I am less pleased with it now—but I have, I think, brought the size of it within your limits, and still think my doctrines are made out.

"I meant to have written a long letter, but I have continued nibbling at the article till I have left myself no time. It goes by the mail addressed to Constable & Co., this evening. I am sorry for the inconvenience to which I fear you have been put by the delay of it. I could not however do more.

"Let me know, with your first convenience, as near about the time as you can when you will want the article 'Law of Nations,' and how much space you should like to bestow upon it."

There is an interesting letter on the 28th of December, from Zachary Macaulay, with whom Mill had long been on terms of intimacy, in connexion with the philanthropic schemes that both had laboured at.

BRIGHTON, *28th Dec., 1821.*

"MY DEAR SIR,

"You will recollect my mentioning to you some time back, a paper of the Court of Directors on the Sugar Trade of India, which was likely to prove of great use in the discussions likely soon to arise on the subject of the West Indian Monopoly. The paper to which I allude, is thus referred to by the West Indian Planters in 1804, in order to shew how impossible it would be for them to enter into competition in the growth of Sugar with the free labourers of Hindostan. 'We refer to the reports made in the year 1801, on the subject of private trade, by a special Committee to the Directors of the East India Company, and approved by them, and by a General Court of Proprietors, to establish these positions, &c.' If you should be able to trace the paper from this allusion to it, so as to give me the dates, or other distinguishing circumstances by which on applying to some Director it may be easily and certainly got at, you will do me a very great favour. You may address the particulars hither.

" I have lately been applied to to find an intelligent person, capable of writing well and quickly on general political subjects; some such person, for example, as Spankie was when imported from the North—some alumnus of a Scotch University, who can turn his hand readily to any common topic of public interest, and who is in want of employment, and to whom a moderate salary would be an object of desire. Do you know any such man? You might do him as well as my friend a service by pointing him out.

" I ought not to close this letter without telling you that I have read your book with much interest, and that I owe to it a great accession of information. It will prove, I have no doubt, a most valuable elementary work. I will not venture to say that I agree with you in all your positions until I shall have given it a second perusal. On one point, and one point only at present, I am disposed to question the correctness of your reasoning, and that is the same which was questioned by Mr. Tooke when we last met. I doubt, that is to say, whether the tendency of taxation be to increase the price of articles. The currency and productions being given quantities.,

" With sincere esteem, I remain,
" My dear sir,
" Yours very faithfully,
"ZACHARY MACAULAY."

Mill adds this in Pencil. " Mr. Mudie—was educated at Aberdeen—co-conductor of the *Dundee Advertiser*—Reference to Dr. Barclay—and to Mr. Ross of the *Times* Office—Editor and principal writer in the *Caledonian*, a sort of collection of essays."

The work alluded to in the letter is of course the *Elements of Political Economy*, which was published this year. It is the summing up and methodizing of all Mill's reflections, discussions, and writings upon the subject for nearly twenty years. John Mill *(Autobiography)* says that the book first took shape in a course of verbal instructions to him by his father, during their walks. Each day after returning home John committed to paper what his father had expounded, and in this way the book was gradually developed. This must have been before John went to France. For several years, the discussions with Ricardo may have been instrumental in bringing the plan of the work to maturity.

With the publication of this work, we may associate the founding of the *Political Economy Club*, which also took place this year. The projector of the Club was Thomas Tooke ; the same who drafted the Petition to Parliament, of 8th May last year, from the Merchants of London, in favour of Free Trade. The nucleus of the Society was a small knot of Political Economists (Mill included) who had for some time held evening meetings at Ricardo's house, for the discussion of Economical questions. The furthering of the Free Trade movement, inaugurated by the Merchants' Petition, was the foremost object in the view of the projectors of the Club. Mill was specially named to draft the Rules, the original of which is still preserved in his hand. To the strictly regulative portion, he appended the following paragraphs, by way of recommendation or exhortation.

"The Members of this Society will regard their mutual instruction, and the diffusion amongst others of first principles of Political Economy, as a real and important obligation.

"As the Press is the grand instrument for the diffusion of knowledge or of error, all the Members of this Society will regard it as incumbent upon them to watch carefully the proceedings of the Press, and to ascertain if any doctrines hostile to sound views on Political Economy have been propagated; to contribute whatever may be in their power to refute such erroneous doctrines, and controvert their influence; and to avail themselves of every favourable opportunity for the publication of seasonable truths within the province of this Science.

"It shall be considered the duty of the Society, individually and collectively, to aid the circulation of all publications which they deem useful to the Science, by making the merits of them known as widely as possible, and to limit the influence of hurtful publications by the same means."

The Society soon embraced a large body, including the most eminent political economists and politicians of the time. It has continued to the present hour, and has been maintained from the same sources. All the men of political eminence have been enrolled in it. Every one of our Chancellors of the Exchequer has passed through the ordeal of its debates. John Mill was eventually introduced, and was most assiduous in attendance for the remainder of his life; for a very long time, it was the only society that he frequented.

Mill was of course a prominent member from the first; and always appeared to advantage in the discussions. The renowned Malthus, who made such a success in dealing with the one subject of Population, was by no means regarded as a steady light on Political Economy at large. His manual of the general subject is certainly not a satisfactory performance. The survivors among the early members of the Club well remember Mill's crushing criticisms of Malthus' speeches.

The article on *Government* was already bearing fruit. Sir James Mackintosh had propounded in the *Edinburgh Review* a scheme of Parliamentary Reform, that was much in vogue for a time, founded on the representation of Classes. Grote brought out a pamphlet in reply, in which he went over the

whole ground of Parliamentary Reform very much from Mill's
point of view.   He disposed of the Class system and handled
with vigour the Reviewer's objections to Universal Suffrage
and the Ballot.

In public events, the year was very stirring.   The Parliamentary Session was an unusually busy one.   The omission of
the Queen's name from the Liturgy made the first topic of
attack on the Ministry.   Petitions for Reform are pouring in :
various motions are made on the subject.   Lord John Russell
repeats his Bill for the Disfranchisement of Grampound.
Burdett is in trouble for reflecting on the Manchester (Peterlooo)
massacre, and is convicted (in a Court of Law) for the Libel,
and fined and imprisoned.   His constituents hold a demonstration ; Hobhouse in the chair.   The Roman Catholic claims
are brought up.   Joseph Hume attacks the Army Estimates,
and has a general motion for retrenchment of the Public
Expenditure.   Sir James Mackintosh is doing himself credit
by following in the footsteps of Romilly, with an equal amount
of rebuffs.   Free Trade is discussed.

This year Sir John Stuart died.   Just before his death, he
sent a silver cup to his godson, with an inscription testifying
his respect both to his father and to him.   He also made John
a present of £500 (such is the family tradition) with the
ostensible aim of sending him to Cambridge.   His father is
reported to have said that John already knew more than he
would learn at Cambridge.

Mill's correspondence with Sir John and Lady Jane is not
preserved.   The death of their only daughter in 1812, must
have drawn forth from him a strong expression of condolence.
A letter of Lady Jane to him, probably after the publication
of his History, was long kept among his papers, but is not now
in existence.   The substance of it I have heard repeated from
memory.   She addresses him as of old, " My Dear James ".

She congratulates him on having become a great man, but hopes that he has not slackened his interest in the great end of life (religion). She further informs him that she has been delighted with Chalmers's Astronomical Sermons, and gives her opinion of the Doctor, then in the blaze of his preaching fame.

1822.

A letter to Napier on the 14th January, describes his condition at the beginning of this year. His fits of gout were almost of a periodic nature, and seem to have been growing in severity.

"I have been disabled for work for upwards of a month by a severe fit of the gout, of which I have still so much in my right hand that I am obliged to use the penmanship of another to write to you.

"This has thrown me so far back in all my operations that it will not be in my power to undertake your three proposed articles, *Penitentiaries*, *Police*, and *Prisons*. Besides, I question whether I should have had anything to say upon any of these subjects, which would have answered your purpose. With respect to two of them, *Penitentiaries* and *Prisons*, I should have done little more than describe Jeremy Bentham's Panopticon, and his plan of Panopticon Management, which appear to me to approach perfection. And with respect to *Police* if you have an efficient Penal Law, such as I described in the article *Jurisprudence*, I hardly see anything which remains for Police to perform; unless it be to guard against certain nuisances and calamities, arising not from moral but from physical sources. I have of course been retarded in my work on the *Law of Nations*, as well as in my other undertakings. In that, however, you shall not be disappointed, at least in respect to time, for of the matter I cannot speak with so much confidence. My principal object will be to shew that there is hardly any such thing as a law of nations : that hardly any thing deserving the name of law between nation and nation, has existed, or ever can exist.

"Thanks for your congratulations on the appearance of the *Elements of Political Economy*. It will flatter me much to learn that you approve of it. I have considerable curiosity to know what you the Scotch Economists think of it.

" It gratifies me exceedingly to hear that a copy of Sir Dudley North's *Discourses on Trade*, is in existence. I have been on the look-out for it for years : and you will confer on me a great favour by securing for me a copy of the impression which is to be made by your friend."

On the 13th May, Bentham sends to Brougham one of his *jeu d' esprit* epistles :—

"*13th May, 1822.*

"Get together a gang, and bring them to the Hermitage, to devour such eatables and drinkables as are to be found in it.

"I. From Honourable House :—

   " 1. Brougham, Henry.

   " 2. Denman.

   " 3. Hume, Joseph.

   " 4. Mackintosh, James.

   " 5. Ricardo, David.

"II. From Lincoln's Inn Fields ·—

   " 6. Whishaw, John.

"III. From India House :—

   " 7. Mill, James."

" Witness matchless Constitution."

On the 21st of May, Mill writes again to Napier.

"I have at last sent to Hurst & Robinson the article on *Law of Nations* which has been a heavy weight on my conscience for the last fortnight.

"I had postponed, as you relaxed the time, the performance

of the last things required for it, till I had left myself too little time for them, and fifty things, when the push came, happened to break in upon me, and day after day permitted me to make little progress.

"I shall be extremely sorry, if I find that I have put you to inconvenience.

"I hope that what I have said will help to circumscribe the vagueness of men's ideas on the subject, a vagueness which here, perhaps, has hitherto been more remarkable than on any other part of the field of legislation.

"I shall be much obliged to you to let me have a few copies of the article, which I know I can dispose of in such a manner as to be serviceable to the Supplement. Pray, also, remember your promise about a copy of Sir Dudley North's pamphlet."

After John returned from France, in the preceding year, his father had written a letter of thanks to Sir Samuel and Lady Bentham, for their great kindness in taking charge of him. The letter, it appears, had been put aside by mistake, and was not received for a year afterwards. On 7th September, Sir Samuel writes in reply. A short extract is enough for our purpose.—"His wife and family often express to one another great desire of learning how far your son continues to pursue his studies with the same extraordinary success which we witnessed, and what line of life he seems likely to take to."

In one of Mrs. Grote's letters, to which I have had access, dated 14th October, there are a few references to Mill and his friends :—

"I read, a few days ago, an interesting and long letter from Mr. Ricardo to Mr. Mill, a good part of which related to the conversations he had maintained with the great men at Geneva " . . . .

"Mill is very well, and is much occupied by the interest which he feels in the chance of a new Governor (-general) for India, Lord Hastings being about to return. Lord William Bentinck is the man among the candidates whom he thinks most fit, as indeed I believe every one else thinks ; but I fear he has no chance."

A postscript to the same letter says :—"Mr. Mill and Mr. Black dined here yesterday, and the former acquainted us that Lord Amherst certainly goes out Governor-general of India."

Zachary Macaulay writes on the 18th Nov., respecting some important election then pending. I cannot say what it was, but the note has an interest as bearing on Mill's friendships.

" 18th November, 1822.

"MY DEAR SIR,

NB   "I cannot find that G. Townsend of Trinity has yet declared himself.   May I beg you therefore to write to him ?

"Malthus is with us, and Whishaw will be with us if Scadell retires.   We have pursued the policy of asking for second votes, in the event of the candidate withdrawing for whom the vote is first engaged.   Perhaps you could secure the reversionary vote of Bickersteth, and of Townsend should he be against us.

"Yours ever truly,

"Z. MACAULAY."

It was this year that Mill began to compose his *Analysis of the Human Mind.* He had taken a summer residence at Dorking, where the family stayed six months in the year ; he remaining there throughout his six weeks' holiday, and going down from Friday to Monday, during the rest of the time. To the end of his life, he kept up this arrangement, shifting his quarters from year to year ; but finally settling in the small rural village of Mickleham, on the Dorking road, not far from Leatherhead and Epsom.   The *Analysis* cost him six of these holidays, being published in 1829.

John's reading had this year advanced to Psychology, and

his exercises and conversations would no doubt chime in with his father's own studies preparatory to his work.*

The business of Parliament for the year opens with discussions on Agricultural Distress. Next come bills for Irish Insurrection, and Suspension of *Habeas Corpus* in that unhappy country. On the 25th April, there is a long debate on Lord John Russell's motion—"That the present state of the representation of the people in Parliament requires the most serious consideration of this House". Canning delivers an elaborate oration, which is the subject of a scathing letter by Grote in the *Morning Chronicle*. Motion lost by 269 to 164. Hume has a motion on Irish Tithes, and, a few weeks later, proposes a string of Thirty-eight Resolutions relative to our Financial System.

1823.

This was an eventful year, and documents have been preserved on all the leading incidents.

In the month of March, Prof. Townsend of Cambridge writes urgently to induce Mill to send John to Cambridge. "When you have decided what to do with your son, pray let me know. I cannot but still adhere to my first opinion, that he ought to form acquaintances with his contemporaries at the commencement of his life, at an English University."

On the 27th May, he writes again to entreat that he may be allowed to enter John's name at Trinity College. "Whatever you may wish his eventual destiny to be, his prosperity in life cannot be retarded, but must, on the contrary, be increased by making an acquaintance at an English University with his Patrician contemporaries. I have not forgotten your wish for

* The list of books given in the *Autobiography* comprises—Locke, Helvetius, Hartley, Berkeley, Hume (Essays only), Reid, Stewart, Brown (Cause and Effect).

the books I promised you, and you may depend upon their being sent; but the work I have now in hand compels me to proceed slowly, and to keep by me whatever profitable authorities I may be required to consult. The *Michaelis*, however, I will bring to town with me, and send it by my brother's servant to your house."

John's destiny had been settled a fortnight previous to this letter.

There is no clue so far as I know to Mill's object in borrowing Theological treatises at this particular time. Townsend had a fine library, and is pressing in his invitations to Mill to come and look through it. Mill never lost his interest in Theology, even when he took the negative side; and his articles in the *Westminster Review*, to be afterwards referred to, contain plenty of matter bearing on the ecclesiastical relations of the churches.

A long letter from Major Cartwright, on the 26th May, entreats Mill's intervention in getting up a meeting for aiding the Spaniards to maintain their independence against France. The meeting took place on the 14th June, at the London Tavern; Hobhouse in the chair. Burdett sent a letter of apology, being ill with gout, but spoke of Reform in very enthusiastic terms. Hume gave "Liberty of the Press. There was a good subscription at the meeting."

Bentham had recommended trying Ricardo. "The others thought of, are Lord Folkestone, Sir F. Burdett, Messrs. G. Bennet, Hobhouse, Peter Moore, as well as Messrs. Knight & James (M.P. for Carlisle) of which two we consider ourselves as sure.

"It is wished that you would undertake to speak with Sir Francis, who, after his well-remembered resolutions of 1817, and his letter of *Friday last*, cannot be supposed to hang back. He ought indeed, and perhaps he will, take the lead. I mean to speak with Lord Folkestone, Messrs. Bennet &

Moore. Should you succeed with Mr. Ricardo, we must not despair of Mr. Hume."

A letter to Thomson on the 22nd May, contains important intelligence.

" Good health, and our usual occupations have been pretty invariable with us. Mrs. Mill and the children are all down at Dorking, very happy, and where they will be for the rest of the summer, I going down pretty regularly on the Friday evening, and remaining till Monday morning.

" You will be glad to hear that I have been appointed 1st Assistant Examiner, that is next to M'Culloch (who is at the head of the office), and of course his successor, and that I have had £200 a year added to my salary, which is now £1200 a year. The court of Directors have also appointed John to this office, on a footing on which he will in all probability be in the receipt of a larger income at an early age than he would be in any profession ; and as he can still keep his hours as a student of law, his way to the legal profession is not barred, if he should afterwards prefer it.

" I shall have occasion to write you a line in a day or two, by M. Louis Say, the brother of the author of the famous French work on *Political Economy*. He is a manufacturer of eminence, and is here with a desire to see what he can of our manufacturing establishments. John lived in his brother's house when he was in Paris, and I am anxious to make some return. I hope therefore you will do what you can to forward his views."

We now see what Mill's friends among the Directors meant by saying that they would push him on. He is made to change positions with Strachey, who falls from the second to the third place in the office.

For May and June, there are a few memoranda from Mrs. Grote's correspondence. Ricardo, with Mill and Maberly, dined at " Threddle," as she called their house in Threadneedle Street, over the banking house. She and Grote breakfasted some

days afterwards at Ricardo's.   It was the morning of a grand
Westminster political dinner, and Grote prompted him for his
speech on the occasion, which was much looked forward to.
The dinner was to celebrate the 16th anniversary of the triumph
of the Westminster electors, in taking the elections into their
own hand at Place's instigation.   Ricardo proposed : " The
only remedy for our natural grievances is a full, free, fair and
equal representation of the people in the Commons House of
Parliament "

Another dinner at " Threddle " brings together Ricardo,
Mill, and M'Culloch (on a visit to London, he being now
editor of the *Scotsman*).   In her chaffing way, Mrs. G. tells
us that they had a controversy on the measure of value,
and gives M'Culloch's winding up, in his incurable broad
Scotch.

Mrs. Grote next intimates that she has fixed a breakfast for
Lord W. Bentinck to meet Mill, and talk over Ireland, whither
Lord W. is going.

We now come to the harrowing incident of the year, the
unexpected and painful death of Ricardo.   Several letters have
been preserved sufficient to tell the sad story.

I give first a portion of a letter to Napier, dated 11th September.

" I am very much flattered with the favourable opinion which
you tell me Mr. M'Culloch has formed of me.   I certainly
very much desire it, for few men have ever made a more
favourable impression upon me.   I like, and I admire him
exceedingly.   Please to offer my kindest remembrance to him.
He will be grieved to hear that we have been on the very point
of losing our inestimable friend Ricardo.   I had the first
intimation of it by a letter from poor Mrs. Ricardo yesterday.
An abscess in the ear, deep in the head, was the malady.   It
has been got the better of; and I trust, from her representation, that danger is over.   But his constitution, which is not
strong, must have received a dreadful shock.   I tremble to

think of the risk we have run. M'Culloch and I would have been inconsolable.

"As to Logic, we must talk of that another time: but you must not expect the book too soon: though my expositions are pretty well down upon paper.

"Mr. M'Culloch is a man with abundance of leisure. Tell him he ought to think of an old friend in Leadenhall Street; and not to be too long in letting him know how the work of grace goes on within him."

The reference to Logic can hardly be for the Supplement. There was talk of an article on the subject, in a former communication, but the letter L has now been long passed. Mill is busy on the studies for the *Analysis*, which contains a considerable "screed" of Logic; and he may have been proposing to himself a separate treatise.

Now comes the catastrophe. This is given in a long letter to M'Culloch on the 19th.

"EAST INDIA HOUSE, *19th Sept., 1823.*

"My dear Sir,

"You and I need not tell to one another how much we grieve on this deplorable occasion. With an estimate of his value in the cause of mankind, which to most men would appear to be mere extravagance, I have the recollection of a dozen years of the most delightful intercourse, during the greater part of which time he had hardly a thought or a purpose, respecting either public or his private affairs, in which I was not his confidant and adviser.

"My chief purpose in writing is the relief I shall find in communicating with the man who of all men in the world estimated my lamented friend most exactly as I did; and also, in case you should not have received the particulars of his illness from any other quarter, to give you a few details which will be interesting to you.

"The malady commenced with a pain in the ear, which resembled a common ear-ache and which they treated as the effect of some small cold.   He suffered somewhat on the Sunday night, but had little pain remaining after he got up the next day; and the same symptoms were repeated for several nights and days.   Towards the end of the week the suffering increased, and became dreadful, when the strongest applications were deemed necessary.   On the Saturday night the imposthume broke, and the pain abated : but so much was he reduced, and the whole frame affected, that they continued in considerable alarm.   On Tuesday morning, however, he seemed decidedly better, and Mrs. Ricardo wrote to me describing what had happened, and urging me to make a run down to Gatcomb, as likely to help in cheering the dear sufferer, and accelerating his convalescence.   This letter I received on the Wednesday morning and on the Friday morning I received a few lines from poor Mary, written at twelve o'clock on Thursday, and stating that they were all assembled in the adjoining room, waiting every moment for the dissolution of her beloved father.   The pain in the head had returned, and after a period of unspeakable agony, pressure on the brain ensued, which produced first delirium, and then stupor, which continued till death.

"I have had several communications from the family since, one from Mr. Moses Ricardo yesterday.   Their sufferings you who know how he was loved and how he was valued can easily conceive.   Of Mrs. Ricardo he says that "though she is looking shockingly, she does not complain, and bears her loss with resignation and fortitude".   The health of those who are younger is less likely to be seriously invaded.

"There is a point which I must mention though I shall probably have to write to you about it more at length hereafter.   Some of us have been talking of the desirableness of some appropriate testimony of respect for his memory : and the foundation of a lectureship of political economy, to be marked by his name, has suggested itself.   The thing will be seriously considered, and you shall hear.

"I have only room to add, that as you and I are his two and only genuine disciples, his memory must be a bond of connexion between us. In your friendship I look for compensation for the loss of his.

"Most truly yours,

"J. MILL.

"Excuse me for addressing this to the *Scotsman* Newspaper Office, as I know not but there will be another of your name in Edinburgh, and am anxious that this letter should certainly reach you."

A note from Brougham touches on the event, and informs us what business of a public kind was up at the moment.

"MY DEAR SIR,

"I have hardly had the heart to write to you since the fatal event of last Wednesday. I had seen our most excellent friend on the day before and in the very place where he died, having attended the Deputation there. I trust you will be able to meet the directors of our Infant Asylum on Tuesday next at four, at J. Smith's, No. 13 New Street, Spring Gardens, which is a central situation and chosen as convenient for all.

"Yours ever most truly,

"H. BROUGHAM."

Here are a few sentences from Mrs. Grote.

"As to Mr. Ricardo's death, it is useless to commence any observations on the irreparable loss to the country and to his friends. I never saw George so oppressed by any event before. Mill was terribly affected—far more so than you would have supposed it likely. The heart of him was touched, and his nature revealed more tenderness on this occasion than I had believed to reside within his philosophic frame. I am woman enough to feel greater admiration for him than before, on this account."

The following letter by Mill was inserted in the *Morning Chronicle*.

" Permit me to pay a tribute, in the name of my country, to the memory of one of the most valuable men whose loss she has ever had to deplore.

" Perhaps no man was ever taken from his friends, leaving in their minds a more unmixed sensation of having been deprived of one of the greatest blessings which it was possible for them to possess. His gentleness united with firmness, his indulgence tempered with prudence, rendered him an object of affection and confidence to all connected with him, beyond what those who have not witnessed an equally perfect character can easily conceive.

" The history of Mr. Ricardo holds out a bright and inspiring example. Mr. Ricardo had everything to do for himself, and he did everything. Let not the generous youth whose aspirations are higher than his circumstances despair of attaining either the highest intellectual excellence, or the highest influence on the welfare of his species, when he recollects in what circumstances Mr. Ricardo opened, and in what he closed, his memorable life. He had his fortune to make, he had his mind to form, he had even his education to commence and to conduct. In a field of the most intense competition, he realised a large fortune, with the universal esteem and affection of those who could best judge of the honour and purity of his acts. Amid this scene of active exertion and practical detail, he cultivated and he acquired habits of intense, and patient, and comprehensive thinking, such as have been rarely equalled, and never excelled.

" The lights which Mr. Ricardo shed upon the science of Political Economy may be compared, either for difficulty or for importance, with those which have given renown to the very greatest names in the history of moral and political science.

" A new field of exertion was opened to him in the House of Commons; and when one reflects on what he had done, and what he was capable of doing, to accelerate the progress of enlightened legislation, it is difficult to point out another life the loss of which could be regarded as such an evil to his country.

"It is universally known how signal a change has taken place in the tone of the House of Commons, on subjects of Political Economy, during his short Parliamentary career ; and though he had the advantage of a Ministry, some of whom were sufficiently enlightened to be warm in the same beneficent course, yet they will not be among the most backward to acknowledge how much his calm and clear exposition of principles, his acute detection of sophistry, and unwearied industry, contributed to the great result ; and they will not be among those who will be the most insensible to his loss.

" Mr. Ricardo had given indications that his mind was not confined to the department of Political Economy, but embraced the science of Legislation in its most extensive sense. When one reflects on the decisive exposition he had made of what is essentially demanded as security for good Government ; on his intrepid and ever memorable declaration in favour of un-limited freedom of thought, and freedom of speech, on subjects of religion ; on the perseverance with which he pursued his objects ; on the growing influence inseparable from his moral and intellectual character ; on his total exemption from the vulgar trammels of party and from all those weaknesses of which so many men of considerable parts render themselves the voluntary slaves of the interests and prejudices of the great, it is impossible to estimate the amount of obligation under which we might have been laid to that truly great man, had his life been prolonged some years for our service.

" By affording insertion to this simple statement, you will gratify the feelings of one who, in the death of Mr. Ricardo, has sustained a loss which can never be repaired, and who will cherish the recollection of his friendship while sense and memory remain."

On the Lectureship mentioned in the letter to M'Culloch, Mrs. Grote gives some farther notices. " There have been two meetings at our house, about the P.E. chair. I believe if Mr. John Smith had not exerted himself as he did, at the last, it would have dropped. Mr. Lefevre, Mr. Mill, George Grote, and Mr. J. Smith, were the only strenuous supporters." A little later she writes, "The resolutions adopted are, to raise subscriptions of £1200, which is to support a Lecture on Political Economy for ten years—£100 per annum for the lecturer, £20 for the use of a room. The committee (Mill, Tooke, John Lefevre, Grote, and Warburton) to choose the lecturer. George says, M'Culloch will in all probability be the lecturer." M'Culloch was chosen.

This year saw the starting of the London Mechanics' Institution; Dr. Birkbeck, President. According to Mrs. Grote's account, in the letter just quoted, " Place is the main promoter, and is devoting his whole time just now to its establishment ". Mill gives a donation of £5.

The last memorandum of the year is a letter to Dr. Thomson, the interest of which has been anticipated ; being the letter where he declines becoming a security, on the ground of the misfortunes that his father had brought upon himself from that cause.

I postpone for a little the notice of the starting of the *Westminster Review*, which fell within the present year.

It is worth repeating that John Black has now his full swing in the *Morning Chronicle*.

In Parliament, the rush of Reform Petitions is steadily increasing. Lord John Russell moots the subject twice in the House. Agricultural Distress still continues. Free Trade is discussed once. Hume attacks first the Colonial Expenditure, and then the Church Establishment in Ireland. Maberly has a motion for reducing Taxation to the extent of 7 millions. The Roman Catholic Question is again debated. There is another Irish Insurrection Bill. Brougham reviews the administration of the Law in Ireland.

CHAPTER V.

ARTICLES IN THE SUPPLEMENT TO THE ENCYCLOPÆDIA BRITANNICA.

1816—1823.

GOVERNMENT.

I SHALL commence with this, as being out of sight the most important of the series. In the train of events culminating in the Reform Bill of 1832, this article counted as a principal factor. It was both an impelling and a guiding force ; and, taken along with the other disquisitions of the author, and his influence with those that came into personal contact with him, it, in all probability, made our political history very different from what it might otherwise have been.

A farther point of interest attaches to the present article,— namely, its being attacked by Macaulay, in a series of articles, in the *Edinburgh Review* ; an attack made in the interest of Whiggism, as against the Radical school. There was much superficiality, as well as flippancy, in Macaulay's articles ; yet, they exposed weak points in the statement, if not in the sub- stance, of our author's theories ; and they are memorable for having created an epoch in the intellectual history of his son, so far as concerned the Logic of Politics.

Previous to the composition of the article, in 1820, Mill had little or no opportunity for explaining his views on the theory of Government. Jeffrey would not trust the subject to him, in the *Edinburgh ;* and it did not come within the scope of the *Philanthropist.*

Although Bentham and he were very much at one in the general doctrines of Politics, Bentham was late in approaching the problem of the best Form of Government ; he was content with elaborating those portions of Jurisprudence, that were equally applicable under every form.   His Constitutional Code was occupied more with the distribution of functions, and the mode of administration, than with the choice of rulers ; although he never doubted that for the more advanced nations, the representative principle was the best.   In the years after the Peace, when parliamentary reform became a question, he produced his *Catechism of Parliamentary Reform,* in which he advocated universal suffrage, annual parliaments, and vote by ballot, and thus became the head centre of radicalism in Westminster politics.   He was cheered to the echo by Burdett, Cartwright, and the extreme men, while very impatient with Romilly and Ricardo, for stopping short * of his positions.

All this time, Mill, so far as we know, was silent.   At last his opportunity came, and he set forth the whole theory of Government in a compact shape, which bore the impress of his own thinking, although powerfully backed by Bentham's searching criticisms, and fertile constructiveness.   The form of expressing the foundation of Ethics—the greatest happiness of the greatest number—was clung to for its political bearings ; it asserted the rights of the many against the few.   In this advocacy, as we shall see, Mill stood supreme.

It will shorten the account of the article itself, to preface a remark or two regarding the points in dispute as to the logic of

---

* We have seen his opposition to Romilly's election for Westminster, in 1818.   To Ricardo, he wrote a few months previously, to this effect ·—

"I told Burdett you had got down to *triennality,* and were wavering between that and annuality, where I could not help flattering myself you would fix ; also, in respect of extent, down to *householders,* for which, though I should prefer universality on account of its simplicity and unexclusiveness, I myself should be glad to compound."

the question. Whoever has read John Mill's chapters
Logic, on the Logic of Politics, will understand the e.
nature of the difficulties attending a Science of Government.
It is enough here, to indicate the two grounds of the Science
—namely, the Deductive, or *a priori* method, and the
Inductive or Historical method. As John Mill effectually
shows, no trustworthy conclusions can be drawn without at
least a concurrence of these two methods. James Mill was
regarded as exclusively reposing on Deduction; Macaulay
ostentatiously avowed his sole reliance on Induction or
Historical experience. I will endeavour to show briefly how
the case stood as between the two.

The article begins by stating the end of Government; the
union of a certain number of men to protect one another.
Then comes the means: namely, to entrust certain persons
with power to protect the rest. One leap farther brings us to
the gist of the whole question—how to prevent the power
given for protection from being abused. The author reviews
the simple forms of Government—Democratical, Aristocratical,
and Monarchical and shows that in no one of these, are the
requisite securities to be found. The Democratical, in its
primitive form, being the assembling of the whole community,
is unwieldy and impracticable. In an Aristocracy, there is
the defect of want of motive to intellectual application, on the
part of the members, and, farther, the natural disposition of
men to prey upon those that are within their power. Monarchy is liable to much the same objections.

At this point, however, comes in the ingenious argument of
Hobbes, that the Monarch, being one man, will be sooner
satiated with good things than an Aristocracy, and will thus
cease at a much earlier stage to make his community his prey.
In examining this question, Mill shows his views of the method
or logic of politics. First, he refers to History, or the experience test. This he soon finds to be so divided as not to
yield any certain conclusion. Absolute monarchs have been

...tly the scourges of human nature. Then, again, the ple of Denmark, tired of an oppressive Aristocracy, resolved that their monarch should be absolute, and are now as well governed as any people in Europe. In Greece, in spite of the defects of Democracy, human nature rose to a pitch of brilliancy never equalled. In short, "As the *surface of history* affords no certain principle of decision, we must go beyond the surface, and penetrate to the springs within" This means that we are to proceed to deduce from the laws of human nature the conduct of human beings entrusted with absolute power. The deduction is, that there is not in the mind of a King, or in the minds of an Aristocracy, any point of saturation with the objects of desire And an appeal is made to corroborative facts, such as the treatment of slaves in the West Indies, by that most favourable specimen of civilization, knowledge, and humanity—the English Gentleman.

Next is his examination of the celebrated balance of the three forms in our British Constitution. Bentham had pretty well exposed the absurdity of the supposed balance ; and it does not cost any acute man much labour to see that there cannot be three co-equal powers working in mutual antagonism ; two would soon swallow up the third, and, if one of these could not be master of the second, they would agree to some division of the spoil.

The author is now brought to the Representative System, as the only security for good government; and the remainder of the essay is occupied with the principles of a good Representative body. First, the duration of their power is to be limited : he does not fix upon a year, or any number of years; there are counter disadvantages of too frequent elections. Then, the representation must be so wide as that the interests of the choosing body shall be the same with the interests of the whole community. When we come to limit the suffrage, we may strike off those individuals whose interests are indisputably included in the interests of others. This disposes of children :

the question. Whoever has read John Mill's chapters may be *Logic*, on the Logic of Politics, will understand the either nature of the difficulties attending a Science of Government. It is enough here, to indicate the two grounds of the Science —namely, the Deductive, or *a priori* method, and the Inductive or Historical method. As John Mill effectually shows, no trustworthy conclusions can be drawn without at least a concurrence of these two methods. James Mill was regarded as exclusively reposing on Deduction; Macaulay ostentatiously avowed his sole reliance on Induction or Historical experience. I will endeavour to show briefly how the case stood as between the two.

The article begins by stating the end of Government; the union of a certain number of men to protect one another. Then comes the means: namely, to entrust certain persons with power to protect the rest. One leap farther brings us to the gist of the whole question—how to prevent the power given for protection from being abused. The author reviews the simple forms of Government—Democratical, Aristocratical, and Monarchical and shows that in no one of these, are the requisite securities to be found. The Democratical, in its primitive form, being the assembling of the whole community, is unwieldy and impracticable. In an Aristocracy, there is the defect of want of motive to intellectual application, on the part of the members; and, farther, the natural disposition of men to prey upon those that are within their power. Monarchy is liable to much the same objections.

At this point, however, comes in the ingenious argument of Hobbes, that the Monarch, being one man, will be sooner satiated with good things than an Aristocracy, and will thus cease at a much earlier stage to make his community his prey. In examining this question, Mill shows his views of the method or logic of politics. First, he refers to History, or the experience test. This he soon finds to be so divided as not to yield any certain conclusion. Absolute monarchs have been thus a question between an elective and a hereditary chief of the administration ; one or other there must be. Then as to the House of Lords. If for the perfect performance of the business of Legislation a second chamber is necessary, and if hereditary landowners are the class best fitted for making up that chamber, then a body of Representatives, whose interests were identified with those of the nation, would establish such a chamber. Cold comfort to the House of Lords.

Objection second—That the people are not capable of acting agreeably to their interests. This allegation is the stronghold of the Aristocratical party. The answer is, if the community at large, or that portion of it whose interest is identified with the whole, will not act according to its interest, but the contrary, the prospect of mankind is indeed deplorable. But, in reality, all that can be maintained is, that the community may very readily mistake its interest. The Aristocracy may be more knowing, but then it is sure to act for itself ; its acts will be consistent ; and its interest is adverse to the community. But, in short, this brings us at once to the point, where all political philosophy centres:—Enlighten your people.

The present possessors of power, and all that share in the profits of the abuse of that power, have an interest in making out the community incapable of acting according to their own interest ; just as it was the interest of the priesthood to withhold the Bible from the laity, who, they said, would make a bad use of it.

After pushing the contrasts between the conduct of an Aristocratical body and a popular body, he winds up with a reference to the power that would be exerted by the middle class under a popular representation. " There can be no doubt that the middle rank, which gives to science, to art, and to legislation itself, their most distinguished ornaments, and is the chief source of all that has exalted and refined human nature, is that portion of the community of which, if the basis of Representation were ever so far extended, the opinion would ultimately decide.   Of the people beneath them, a vast majority would be sure to be guided by their advice and example."

The whole contribution occupies only 32 closely printed pages.   It is hardly more than notes for a theory of Government at large, although the principles are wide enough for any application, being those fundamental laws of the human mind that come into play in the relations of governor and governed. Neither can it be said that there is an absence of corroborative appeals to history.

Short as the article is, it was the starting point of the radical reformers.   It was the first opportunity that Mill had of addressing himself to the great problem of Parliamentary Reform.   In the *Westminster Review*, he had fuller swing, and carried on the battering of the Aristocratical system, with an impetus that soon opened a breach in the walls.   We shall see presently the nature of that attack ; but meanwhile, it will be convenient to take, along with the above abstract, the criticisms that the original article has been subjected to, considered as a general theory of Government.

Macaulay's reply did not appear till 1829, when the article may be said to have done its work.   The author's thorough-going views had come into open conflict with a qualified liberalism as represented by the *Edinburgh*; and Macaulay in his youthful vigour entered the lists against the veteran radical. It may seem surprising that the attack was so long deferred. The volume of collected articles was printed in 1828, and that collection is the work ostensibly reviewed ; but I do not see why the obnoxious article might not have been taken up on appearing in the *Encyclopædia*, except that the authorship was not there avowed.

The reviewer begins thus :—" Of those philosophers who call themselves Utilitarians, and whom others generally call Benthamites, Mr. Mill is, with the exception of the illustrious founder of the sect, by far the most distinguished." This will seem a high encomium, until we see how the sect is made up: "These people, whom some regard as the lights of the world, and others as incarnate demons, are in general ordinary men, with narrow understandings, and little information. The contempt which they express for elegant literature, is evidently the contempt of ignorance." "Mingled with these smatterers . . . . there are, we well know, many well-meaning men, who have really read and thought much; but whose reading and meditation have been almost exclusively confined to the class of subjects, &c." This is pretty well for such men as the two Mills, John and Charles Austin, and Grote.

As to Mr. Mill himself, his style is generally as dry as that of Euclid's Elements; he has inherited the spirit and the style of the Schoolmen; he is an Aristotelian of the fifteenth century, born out of due season. "We have here an elaborate treatise on Government, from which, but for two or three passing allusions, it would not appear that the author was aware that any governments existed among men." The reason for not appealing to historical experience seems most extraordinary; namely, that experience appears to be divided as to which form of government is best. On this the reviewer remarks—"Experience can never be divided, or even appear to be divided, except with reference to some hypothesis." The writer of the article "reasons *a priori*, because the phenomena are not what, by reasoning *a priori*, he will prove them to be".

After reciting the positions of the article, as to the ends of Government, and the respective merits of the three different forms, the reviewer gives the following summary criticism :—

"Now, no man who has the least knowledge of the real state of the world, either in former ages or at the present moment, can possibly be convinced, though he may perhaps be bewildered, by arguments like these. During the last two centuries, some hundreds of absolute princes have reigned in

Europe. Is it true, that their cruelty has kept in existence the most intense degree of terror; that their rapacity has left no more than the bare means of subsistence to any of their subjects, their ministers and soldiers excepted? Is this true of all of them? Of one half of them? Of one tenth part of them? Of a single one? Is it true, in the full extent, even of Philip the Second, of Louis the Fifteenth, or of the Emperor Paul? But it is scarcely necessary to quote history. No man of common sense, however ignorant he may be of books, can be imposed on by Mr. Mill's argument; because no man of common sense can live among his fellow-creatures for a day without seeing innumerable facts which contradict it. It is our business, however, to point out its fallacy; and happily the fallacy is not very recondite."

The exposure of the fallacy consists in pointing out that the author overlooks, in his statement of human motives, the desire of the good opinion of others, and the pain of public hatred and contempt. In the manner of Mr Mill, a syllogism might be constructed, to prove that no rulers will do anything which may hurt the people; we have only to select their fear of unpopularity as a middle term, and the reasoning is complete. In short, Mr. Mill has chosen to look only at one half of human nature.

Then comes a discussion of the balance of the three powers in our constitution, in which the reviewer has a long argument to show that it is not an absurdity, that they do not, in point of fact, swallow one another up, and come at last to a single power. He expends a quantity of historical knowledge on this point, but we need not dwell upon it. "When there are three parties, every one of which has much to fear from the others, it is not found that two of them combine to plunder the third."

Then comes the author's theory of Representation, as the check to mis-government. On this subject, the reviewer is rather weak, making out that a Representative body as soon as elected is an aristocracy, with an interest opposed to the interest of the community. Although sent up (he says) in the first instance, under a law that provides for frequency of election, they may repeal that law, and declare themselves senators for life. "We know well that there is no real danger in such a case. But there is no danger only because there is no truth in Mr. Mill's principles. If men were what he represents them to be, the letter of the very constitution which he recommends would afford no safeguard against bad government. The real security is this, that legislators will be deterred by the fear of resistance and of infamy from acting in the manner which we have described. But restraints, exactly the same in kind, and differing only in degree, exist in all forms of government. That broad line of distinction which Mr. Mill tries to point out between monarchies and aristocracies on the one side, and democracies on the other, has in fact no existence. In no form of government is there an absolute identity of interest between the people and their rulers. In every form of government, the rulers stand in some awe of the people. The fear of resistance and the sense of shame operate in a certain degree, on the most absolute kings and the most illiberal oligarchies. And nothing but the fear of resistance and the sense of shame preserves the freedom of the most democratic communities from the encroachments of their annual and biennial delegates."

When the reviewer comes to the composition of the constituent body, he makes a very successful hit. Seizing hold of Mill's proposal to purge the electoral roll of all those individuals whose interests are involved in those of other individuals, and thereupon to omit women, he retorts, in his best style of lofty phraseology, and telling citations from history, and shows what a miserable protection this principle affords.

The next branch of the argument relates to the extent of the suffrage. There is not much to detain us here; the reviewer's argument being grounded on the danger, that the poor, as being in the majority, might plunder the rich. One passage foreshadows some of the most renowned strokes of his later rhetoric. The civilized part of the world, he says, has now nothing to fear from the hostility of savage nations. The deluge of barbarism will no more return to cover the earth. "But is it possible that, in the bosom of civilization itself, may be engendered the malady which shall destroy it ?" "Is it possible, that in two or three hundred years, a few lean and half-naked fishermen may divide with owls and foxes the ruins of the greatest European cities—may wash their nets amidst the relics of her gigantic docks, and build their huts out of the capitals of her stately cathedrals ?" The possibility is to be a reality, if Mill's principles are adopted ; that is, if we make even an approach to Universal Suffrage.

One more criticism remains. Mill's appeal to the middle ranks, as the effective control of the democracy, which he conveys in a passage of real eloquence, notwithstanding Macaulay's comparison of his style to Euclid, is given as a "delicious *bonne bouche* of wisdom, which he has kept for the last moment". The reviewer thinks that this alone is enough to dispose of Mill's whole theory of Representation. A few pungent alternative interrogations are given as settlers. "Will the people act against their own interest ? Or will the middle class act against its own interest ? Or is the interest of the middle rank identical with the interest of the people ? If any one of the three be answered in the affirmative, his whole system falls to the ground. If the interest of the middle rank be identical with that of the people, why should not the powers of government be trusted to that rank," and so on. In short, the reviewer brings Mill round to his own settlement of the question :—"The system of universal suffrage, according to Mr. Mill's own account, is only a device for doing circuitously, what a representative system, with a pretty high qualification would do directly." Did it never occur to the reviewer, that the suffrage, once extended to the middle class, must go on extending till it became universal ; and that Mill's view of the restraining power of the middle class, would then be all that was between us and the lean fishermen anchoring their boats in the docks of London and Liverpool ?

The article has still several pages of highly seasoned rhetoric, in which the writer amplifies the absurdities of Mill's theory of motives. We must, however, confine ourselves to one paragraph which contains his own Political Logic.

" How, then, are we to arrive at just conclusions on a subject so important to the happiness of mankind ? Surely by that method which, in every experimental science to which it has been applied, has signally increased the power and knowledge of our species,—by that method for which our new philosophers would substitute quibbles scarcely worthy of the barbarous respondents and opponents of the middle ages,—by the method of Induction ;—by observing the present state of the world,—by assiduously studying the history of past ages,— by sifting the evidence of facts,—by carefully combining and contrasting those which are authentic,—by generalising with judgment and diffidence,—by perpetually bringing the theory which we have constructed to the test of new facts,—by correcting, or altogether abandoning it, according as those new facts prove it to be partially or fundamentally unsound. Proceeding thus,—patiently,—diligently,—candidly,—we may hope to form a system as far inferior in pretension to that which we have been examining and as far superior to it in real utility as the prescriptions of a great physician, varying with every stage of every malady and with the constitution of every patient, are to the pill of the advertising quack which is to cure all human beings, in all climates, of all diseases."

The writer is sorry and surprised when he sees men of good intentions and good natural abilities abandon this healthful and generous study, to pore over speculations like those which he has been examining ? As for the greater part of the sect, it is of little consequence what they study, or under whom. On the whole, they might have chosen worse. They may as well be Utilitarians as jockeys or dandies. Their quibbling about self-interest and motives, hurts the health less than hard drinking, and the fortune less than high play; it is not much more laughable than phrenology, and is immeasurably more humane than cock-fighting.

Such is the first of the three articles. We have to regret that it did not appear before the *Westminster Review* passed out of the hands of the original circle; the reply, in that case, would no doubt have been Mill's own. The actual reply made a stand for the author's original positions, but it was no match for Macaulay, and enabled him to produce a second, and a third article, even more unsparing than the first. These are almost exclusively occupied with a dissection of the Greatest Happiness Principle, which, the writer tells us, in one place, is important if true, but unhappily is not true. The only interest of the articles is the conclusion, which iterates the idea of middle-class representation; and states the whole controversy between him and Mill to lie " in the success [he should have also said, and the *finality*] of the experiment which we propose ".*

It so happened that Mill did himself reply to these articles. In the " Fragment on Mackintosh," he has to encounter an onslaught on his " Government," in which Mackintosh avows that his mode of reasoning is the same as that adopted in the

* In his speech on the People's Charter in 1842, Macaulay disavows finality, and does not consider that the settlement made by the Reform Bill can last for ever. Yet, he adds :—" My firm conviction is that, in our country, universal suffrage is incompatible, not with this or that form of government, but with *all forms of government* and with everything for the sake of which forms of government exist ; that it is incompatible with property, and that it is consequently incompatible with civilisation ". Events have shown whether he or Mill reasoned best.

Wilberforce writing to Macaulay's relative, Mr. Babington, speaks of his first article thus :—" I am much pleased with a review of Tom Macaulay's in the *Edinburgh*; it is not merely the superior talent which it indicates, but its being on the right side. The *Westminster Review*, of which Mill is a principal support, is a very mischievous publication; and this review will be a death-blow to Mill as a reasoner."

Review articles.* With an evident chuckle, Mill says this is convenient, because the answer which does for Sir James, will do for the *Edinburgh Review*.

The main argument against Mill's *a priori* reasoning is that men do not always act in conformity with their true interest, sometimes mistaking it, and sometimes impelled by passion to disregard it. This, say the two critics, overthrows the whole fabric of Mr. Mill's political reasoning. The reply is, " that Mr. Mill's political reasoning is in perfect conformity with it, as will now be shown ". With a view to the principles of government, it was indispensable to ask, what is that within a man which has the principal influence in determining his actions. The answer of Mr. Mill was,—" the man's view of his own interest ". " Would Sir James have had him return any other answer? Sir James abstains from saying so." " It is very obvious to any one who has read Mr. Mill's Treatise, in what sense he uses the word 'interest' He uses it neither in the refined sense of a man's best interest, or what is conducive to his happiness on the whole , nor to signify every object which he desires, although that is a very intelligible meaning too. He uses it, in its rough and common acceptation, to denote the leading objects of human desire ; Wealth, Power, Dignity, Ease ; including escape from the contraries of these " " In deliberating on the best means for the government of men in society, it is the business of philosophers and legislators to look to the more general laws of human nature, rather than the exceptions."

He then adduces a number of quotations from great authorities to the effect that, in political matters, the paramount

* In a letter to Napier, Mackintosh has this remark. ''I think the articles 'Government' and 'Education' in the *Supplement*, though very ably written, remarkable examples of one of the erroneous modes of philosophising from experience which are condemned by Bacon in the passage to which I have above adverted." The passage is one where Bacon charges the ancient philosophers with having consulted experience, but with having consulted her either partially or superficially.

determining fact is always self-love or self-interest.   Thus says Hume—" Political writers have established it as a maxim, that in contriving any system of government, and fixing the several checks and controls of the constitution, every man ought to be supposed a knave, and to have no other end, in all his actions, than private interest."   " It appears somewhat strange, that a maxim should be true in politics which is false in fact.   But to satisfy us on this head, we may consider, that men are generally more honest in their private than in their public capacity, and will go greater lengths to serve a party, than when their own private interest is concerned.   Honour is a great check upon mankind ; but when a considerable body of men act together, this check is in a great measure removed ; since a man is sure to be approved of by his own party for what promotes the common interest ; and he soon learns to despise the clamours of adversaries."   " In any plan of government, continues Hume, where the power is distributed among several courts and several orders of men, we should always consider the separate interest of each court and each order ; and if we find that, by the skilful division of power, this interest must necessarily, in its operation, concur with the public, we may pronounce that government to be wise and happy."   " In this opinion I am justified by experience, as well as by the authority of all philosophers and politicians, both ancient and modern."

He next quotes, from Blackstone, a passage invoking the Creator's view of the subject, and treating it as a part of Divine wisdom and benevolence, to reduce the rule of obedience to one paternal precept, *each man should pursue his own happiness.* He next produces a number of striking expressions of the same view from the *Republic* of Plato, such as this :—" Without identity of interest with those they rule, the rulers, instead of being the guardians of the flock, become wolves and its devourers."

He winds up by taking the sting out of the reproach of falsifying human nature, in a very few words.   " Mr. Mill, it is necessary to observe, confines his enquiry to one department of government." "Sir James says, it is a wrong thing to attempt to explain the immense variety of political facts, by the simple element of a contest of interests. Be it so, but Mr. Mill has not sought to explain the immense variety of political facts at all. What he attempted was to show how a community could obtain the best security for good legislation." As to referring "the immense variety of political facts to that variety of passions, habits, opinions, and prejudices, which we discover only by experience, Sir James's enumeration, far as he thinks it goes beyond Mr. Mill, is by no means complete. Sir James, for example, does not include reason among the principles in human nature, which account for historical facts. I, on the contrary, am of opinion that the whole nature of man must be taken into account, for explaining the 'immense variety' of historical facts."

We can see now how much more edifying it would have been if Mill and Macaulay had encountered one another directly in the controversy. I will here add a remark of my own, as regards the charge of leaving out of account men's sympathies and disinterested affections, in framing a theory of government. It is quite true that our nature is endowed to a certain degree with such motives, and when they are in operation, they restrain the outgoings of pure selfishness. But even this does not complete the compass of human motives. We are constituted farther with a high susceptibility to the pleasures of malevolence, which also play a part in the relations of government. The worst miseries that have been inflicted by rulers have been dictated not simply by the love of aggrandisement, but by positive delight in cruelty. In savage life, the pleasure is habitual; in civilized nations, it is more rare, but not wanting.

It is now time to finish this survey by referring to the last and best criticism on the article, in the political chapters of John Mill's *Logic*.

In recounting the imperfect or one-sided methods of reasoning in the Social Science, John Mill devotes a chapter to the Experimental or Chemical method, to which Macaulay exclusively trusted, and another to the Geometrical or Abstract Method, of which his grand example is the "interest-philosophy of the Bentham School". He gives the doctrine the benefit of those liberal qualifications that its supporters claimed for it, by which it is reduced to such a statement as this:—Any succession of persons, or the majority of any body of persons, will be governed in the bulk of their conduct by their personal interests. The theory goes on to infer, he says, quite correctly, that the only rulers who will govern according to the interest of the governed, are those whose selfish interests are in accordance with theirs. And to this is added a third proposition, namely, that no rulers have their selfish interest identical with that of the governed, unless it be rendered so by accountability, that is, by dependence on the will of the governed.

Now, says John Mill, no one of these propositions is true; the last is extremely wide of the truth. In refuting them he insists only on what is true of all rulers, viz., that the character and course of their actions is largely influenced by the habitual sentiments and feelings of the community, and also by the maxims and traditions which have descended to them from other rulers, their predecessors. Although, therefore, private interest is a very powerful force, even the particulars constituting the goodness or badness of their government are in no small degree influenced by those other circumstances.

Turning now to the proposition that responsibility to the governed is the only thing capable of producing in the rulers a sense of identity of interest with the community; this is still less admissible as a universal truth. Even identity in essentials is not confined to this cause. The suppression of anarchy and of resistance to law, the complete establishment of the central authority in a state of society like that of Europe in the middle ages, is one of the strongest interests of the people, as well as of the rulers ; and the responsibility of the rulers to the people, instead of strengthening might even weaken this motive.   He quotes Queen Elizabeth and Peter the Great as cases in point.

He goes on :—I am not here attempting to establish a theory of government, nor to determine the proportional weight to be given to the circumstances left out by this school of politicians, I am only concerned to show that their method was unscientific.   To do them justice, he adds that their mistake was not so much one of substance, as of form ; they set forth as a great philosophical question what should have passed for what it really was, the mere polemics of the day. The constitutional checks that they stood up for, were those that England, and the leading nations of modern Europe, actually stood in want of.   He expresses his regret, however, that the small portion of the philosophy of government wanted for the immediate purpose of serving the cause of parliamentary reform, should have been held forth by thinkers of such eminence as a complete theory.   No doubt they would have applied, and did apply, their principles with innumerable allowances.   But it is not allowances that are wanted, but breadth of foundation.   The phenomena of society do not depend, in essentials, on some one agency or law of human nature, with only inconsiderable modifications from the others. A deductive politics should be a deduction from the whole, and not only from a part of the laws of nature that are concerned.

Such is John Mill's criticism of his father's Method of Politics.   Were it not for the very ample concessions he makes, I should feel disposed to object to his taking the article on Government as a nearly pure specimen of *à priori* reasoning, unbalanced by the application of the supplemental method of experience, that is, reference to political facts as given in history.   His father knew as much history as any man of his time ; he had pondered its lessons, and would not have propounded any doctrine at variance therewith.   But in such a very synoptical article, the citation of historical instances would have been impossible, or, if possible, illusory. What was wanted was a formal and exhaustive setting forth of the generalizations of historical facts, widely examined, sifted and compared; a process that John Mill would have been the first to do homage to, as the only complete and satisfactory supplement to his deductive positions.

For a pure specimen of the *à priori* method, I should refer to the political systems of Owen and Fourier, men who trusted in their theories without any historical reference whatever. Or if John Mill wished a good specimen from a higher source, he might have quoted his father's paper on Education, where the *à priori* method is worked to the nearly total exclusion of experience; the writer's mind in this case, being almost wholly unprovided with the materials of such experience.

JURISPRUDENCE.

This was one of the author's special studies. He had made progress in it, when he first came to London; he had imbibed all that Bentham had given forth upon the subject; and we have seen what were his projects of future work in regard to it.

The word "Jurisprudence" does not always cover the same field. The definition given of it in the article is the protection of rights. It belongs to Legislation to establish rights, to Jurisprudence to protect them. In the protection of rights, however, there are various operations that need not all be taken in connexion. Rights have to be carefully defined, for one thing : this relates to the Wording of the Law, and is a department by itself. Then comes the means of settling disputed rights, involving Judicial Procedure and Evidence ; a subject so far cognate to the previous, that it may properly fall within the same treatise. When rights are wilfully set at nought, the offenders are subject to penalties ; which introduces the doctrine of Punishments, their choice, and their gradation according to the offence. But the discussion of Punishment is so peculiar that it admits of an isolated treatment, and needs not be handled in the same science that embraces the previous departments. Bentham was one of the first to give a complete theory of Punishments;[*] and he made it into a separate branch of study.

Mill introduced the subject into the present article; but he might have done better to exclude it entirely from the circle of subjects connected with the expression and the interpretation of the law. Even in this limited circle, there is a useful subdivision of heads that need an isolated discussion, although more closely connected with one another than the theory of Punishment is with any.

"The definition of rights constitutes that part of law which has been generally denominated the *Civil Code*. The definition of offences and punishments constitutes that other part of law which has been generally denominated the criminal or *Penal Code*.

"When rights are distributed, and the acts by which they may be violated are forbidden, an agency is required, by which that distribution may be maintained, and the violators of it punished. That agency is denominated Judicature. The powers by which this agency is constituted, require to be accurately defined; and the mode in which the agency itself is to be carried on must be fixed and pointed out by clear and determinate rules. These rules and definitions prescribe the form and practice of the courts, or mode in which the judicial functions are performed; and constitute that branch of law which has been called the *Code of Procedure*."

These three codes—the civil code, the penal code, and the code of procedure—form the whole subject of jurisprudence (in the widest sense). Of the three, the last exists only for the sake of the first and the second. Courts and their operations

---

[*] The treatise of Beccaria was almost the only work of any mark before Bentham. It has great value, and Bentham testifies to its merits.

are provided in order that the provisions of the civil and penal codes may not be without their effect.

First, then, comes the peculiarly logical operation of defining rights. For example, to define the rights to Land, is to enumerate all the services that a man is allowed to derive from his land—cultivating it, letting it, building on it, and so forth. [I may remark, in passing, that the use of negative or exclusive definition has not yet been fully appreciated in legal definitions]. Another essential part of the definition of a right is the description of the fact that gave birth to it; as first occupancy, labour gift, contract, succession, the will of the legislative. To this has to be added a description of the facts that put an end to a right; as gift, contract, death, &c. When a right becomes matter of judicial enquiry, therefore, what has to be seen is—(1) whether there happened any of the events that give a right, and (2) whether there happened any of the events that put an end to the right.

The definition of rights in these ways makes up the Civil Code, as a matter of form, the legislature having previously determined the substance. [The word " Codification " expresses the highest refinement of the civil code, the classifying and arranging of rights in the most natural and illustrative connexion, like the classification of Plants in Botany.]

The Penal Code has to declare what acts are meet for punishment. This is to make out *offences ;* and these ought to be as rigorously defined as rights under the Civil Code. Here, the author summarizes Bentham.

He next devotes a chapter to the nature of Punishment, or Penalties, which, as I have said, might be excluded from the present connexion, without impairing the discussion of the other subjects. The chapter is a good epitome of Bentham's elaborate and almost exhaustive treatment.

Then comes what must always be a principal part of Jurisprudence as limited to a group of kindred and mutually dependent topics ; that is to say Procedure in the Courts, or the Judicial Business. This was the topic of Bentham's life-long fight with English Law as he found it, and Mill gives a few of Bentham's leading suggestions, such as that the parties in a dispute should meet at the very outset in the presence of the judge. He contrasts the effect of such a proceeding with the complicacy and chicanery of the English Law. This is the first stage of judicial business. The next is the taking of Evidence, on which also Bentham is the authority *par excellence*, and is here strictly followed.

The last topic is the Judicial Establishment; the appointment and qualifications of judges, the check upon their proceedings, and the constituting of Courts of Appeal. Here the grand safeguard is Publicity and a Free Press. A favourite idea with Bentham was that judges should decide singly, so that there might be no divided responsibility.

In discussing the expediency and the constitution of Courts of Appeal, another has a fling at the aristocracy, who, he says, monopolize this luxury. "It is the aristocratical class who have made the laws; they have accordingly declared that the suits which were important to them should have the benefit of appeal; the suits not important to them should not have the benefit of appeal."

The judgment seat should never be empty; there should be deputies to take the place of the judges in their absence. Moreover, besides the judge and his deputy, there are two adjuncts to every tribunal, which are of the utmost importance; indispensable, indeed, to the due administration of justice. These are, a *pursuer-general*, and a *defender-general*. Their business can easily be gathered from their designations. Neither has yet found his way into the English courts.

My chief purpose in giving this outline is to show that Mill was an apt disciple of any man that had thoroughly worked a subject. He was a good learner, and did not affect originality by making changes upon other people's views for the mere sake of change.

LIBERTY OF THE PRESS.

The articles in the reprinted volume are not given alphabetically, as they were published, and the arrangement may therefore be supposed to be according to the author's view of their natural sequence. The third in order is the LIBERTY OF THE PRESS, which Mill, in common with Bentham, considered bound up with Law and Politics alike. There is scarcely a right that may not be violated by the instrumentality of the press, scarcely an operation of government that may not be disturbed by it. If the employment of the press has the effect of depriving any one of his rights, or of producing disobedience to government, the offence is to be treated, not as something new, but as any other mode of producing the same amount of interference with rights would be treated. If the press is made an instrument of causing murder, the person so employing it is guilty of murder.

In point of fact, however, the Press is an instrument particularly adapted for the commission of injuries against Reputation, and for effecting disturbance to the operations of Government, while it has no particular adaptation for the commission of other offences. The enquiry then is twofold—how far the press needs to be restrained with respect to *private reputation*, and how far with respect to *Government.*

The right of Reputation means that every man is considered as having a right to the character that he deserves ; that is, to be spoken of according to his actions. The author sees no difficulty in defining this offence so that it can be made the occasion of an action at law. The law can say such and such actions are not to be imputed ; and the court decides as a question of fact whether words have been used that impute them.

The remedy for offences of this kind includes compensation to the injured individual. Whenever a money value can be put upon the injury, the reparation should take that form. In most cases, it is enough that the man that has propagated calumny should contradict it as openly and as widely as the calumny has spread.

' The farther question arises—how shall we create sufficient motives to prevent the commission of slander ; ought there to be specific penalties, in addition to the redress provided above ? This, the author thinks, is a question of the perfection or imperfection of the laws. If the machinery were so perfect as to secure compensation to the injured party, the certainty of that compensation would be a deterring motive without other penalty.

It is a farther question, whether the rights of reputation should extend beyond the boundaries of truth. On this ticklish matter, the author puts forth his usual nicety of discrimination. In cases where people commit offences against the law, information should never be withheld by any one. If the offence alleged is one to draw down public censure, without legal penalty, there should, in like manner, be no concealment either ; provided always that public approbation and disapprobation were rightly dispensed. In the present state of society, in most countries, this cannot be said ; and the press should not be justified in awakening up antipathies that happen to prevail on matters of religious or other sentiment. Where the good or evil of actions is beyond dispute, it is of great consequence that they should be stated in their true colours. This is the rule ; the other case is the exception.

The second question regarding the Press, the relation to Government, is by far the more important of the two, and receives a searching investigation. Both before and after the writing of this article, the author was often engaged in the polemic in favour of freedom of speech ; here, he gives his judicial handling of the question.

First, then, exhortations to obstruct the operations of government *in detail*, should be considered as offences ; while directed against government generally, they should not be so considered. As the application of force to resist any single act of the government is pernicious and punishable, so should be an incitement through the press to such resistance. But to punish general disapprobation of the government is to destroy all the securities of the people against misgovernment ; and the objectionable point is reached only when it amounts to civil commotion for no end.

In apportioning punishment for this class of offences, the thing to avoid is *vengeance*. So long as there are abuses in government, so long will the men that profit by these, exert themselves to multiply offences against government, and to apply punishments with the greatest severity. Hence punishments for contempt ; for vindicating the honour of the court, the government, or the magistracy ; all intended to gratify vengeance, and to protect abuses.

In treating as offences all exhortations to obstruct government in detail, a distinction has to be drawn between those exhortations that are direct or explicit, and those that are implied or constructive. The last ought not to be punished. Of course, to blame the government at all, is to bring it into hatred or contempt ; and if this is to be punished, all freedom of criticism is at an end. Without the liberty of censure, there can be no wakening up of the public mind to overthrow a bad government. Especially in a government of popular origin, is the freest speech necessary for directing the people's choice. The press imparts knowledge of the character of the candidates to begin with, and when they are chosen, it informs the public as to their conduct and behaviour. The proceedings of the Legislative Body should be reported ; and there should be a perfect liberty to comment upon them. This may seem to open a very wide door ; just and unjust criticism being equally permitted. But who is to draw the line ? If not every censure, but only some censures, are to be forbidden, which are to come under the law ? The answer to this disposes of every difficulty connected with the liberty of the press.

There is no one that can be permitted to judge what censures are just, and what are unjust.   Whence the path of practical wisdom must be—permit all alike.   The author supports this conclusion on the ground, that where all opinions are presented and argued fully, the true must prevail.   He adduces a long array of authorities in favour of the same view.

He next gives the question an unexpected turn.   The press is abused, when a government receives undeserved praise.   This is quite as mischievous, and quite as usual, as undeserved censure.   Still, the liberty of the press must include the licence of over-praise, as well as of under-praise.   We must not permit either, without also permitting the other.   The same remark was made by Bentham, and was characteristic of him and Mill alike ; either was capable of originating it, and I am not aware that it was made by any previous defender of a free press.

A special chapter is devoted to showing that Freedom of Censure in the Institutions of Government is necessary for the good of the people ; and the illustration contains a variety of vigorous home-thrusts.   The concluding chapter—Limitations to Freedom of Discussion, which involve its destruction—deals with " decency " and " indecency " as applied to discussions, and as contributing a ground for permitting or not permitting freedom.   This brings up the use of vehement, passionate, or intemperate language, in which he lays it down, that you cannot forbid passionate language, without giving a power of obstructing the use of censorial language altogether.   The application is made to Religious opinions.   These may include anything : passive obedience was treated as a religious doctrine.   Without perfect freedom to express religious opinions, the press is not free even for political opinions.

PRISONS AND PRISON DISCIPLINE.

The reform of Prisons was one of the chief labours under-taken by the philanthropists of the early part of the century. Howard had begun his labours previously. Bentham took up the subject and spent several vexatious years upon the intro-duction of his Panopticon arrangement. It was a leading topic with William Allen's band, and occupied many pages of his *Philanthropist ;* Mill frequently contributing to the expositions and urging the Panopticon plan. In this article, he presents a reasoned view of the entire subject, dealing with all the pre-valent errors and abuses, and expounding first principles at every stage. He discriminates between the means of safe custody and the means of punishments ; insists strongly on taking care of the prisoners' health ; examines and appraises all the devices for punishment, and considers how best to combine punishment with reformatory discipline. This last involves some kind of labour, which should be productive, both to the public and to the prisoner. He concludes the article thus :—" In the delineation presented, the only merit we have to claim is that (if our endeavour has been successful) of adding perspicuity to compactness. There is not, we believe, an idea which did not originate with Mr. Bentham, whose work ought to be the manual of all those who are concerned in this material department of public administration."

COLONY.

Here the author's breadth of knowledge appears to great advantage. He surveys all the colonizing operations known to history, discriminates their kinds, and assigns to each its benefits and its evils. The Greek and Roman colonies took off a redundant population ; a circumstance that in Greece was visible to vulgar eyes, although in modern Europe it is visible only to enlightened eyes. The author makes this a text for a discussion of the population question, with the view of

16

assigning the precise conditions wherein a remedy for excessive numbers at home is provided by emigration. The chief conditions are—the existence of good land to go to, and the distance moderate.

For penal colonies, he has nothing but unqualified condemnation.

Another leading class of colonies is those where the predominating idea is Territory as such. There are two ways of making profit of increased territory. One is by Tribute ; which the author soon disposes of. "We may affirm it, as a deduction from the experienced laws of human society, that there is, if not an absolute, at least, a moral impossibility, that a colony should ever benefit the mother country, by yielding it a permanent tribute." The other mode of making profit is by Trade. This involves monopoly ; and it was denied by Adam Smith that monopoly could ever be of any advantage ; on the contrary, it must be a source of disadvantage to the mother country. The author supports this position at length.

He then exposes the fallacy of increasing our maritime strength by colonies. A more plausible case in favour of colonial possessions is the occurrence of rich mines. Even this would do a government little good, unless it worked them on its own account.

What then is the good of Colonies? Chiefly to give places to members of the ruling class. They are a grand source of war, and of additional expense in war ; but they create and increase patronage and the means of corruption to the government at home.

Mill was thus early in the field with those home truths on Colonies, that have since been expressed by G. Cornewall Lewis and Goldwin Smith. Bentham had likewise gone over the ground and come to much the same conclusions.

LAW OF NATIONS.

This subject was still in a vague condition when the present article was written.   Bentham had discussed it, but not at all with the same minuteness and exhaustion that he had bestowed upon the other parts of law.   He invented the present designation for it—" International " Law.   In a conversation, near the end of his life, he is reported to have spoken thus of the text-book then in use.   " Few things are more wanting than a code of international law.   Vattel's propositions are most old-womanish and tautological.   They come to this : Law is nature—Nature is law.   He builds upon a cloud.   When he means anything, it is from a vague perception of the principle of utility ; but more frequently no meaning can be found. Many of his dicta amount to this : It is not just to do that which is unjust."

Mill begins by recurring to the definition of law in general —a Command, with a Sanction, enforced by Authority ; which shows at once that the Laws of Nations are not law in the proper sense of the word.   They want the power of enforcement.   Still, " it is of use, that the ordinary intercourse of nations should be conducted according to certain forms, generally known und approved ; because they will be observed on all occasions when there is no particular motive to violate them, and will often prevent disputes that might arise on frivolous occasions.   They resemble, in this respect, the ceremonial of a court, or the established forms of polished society". He should have carried his comparison farther, by including private ethics, or the rules of morality that are enforced, not by law, but by opinion, honour, or approbation and disapprobation. He does, in fact, expend several pages in showing the influence of public opinion upon the conduct of men in all ranks ; only that it is liable to be perverted in an Aristocratical country, where the code of morality is swayed to suit the interests of the wealthy and the powerful.

In framing a Code of International Law, we fall back upon the forms of Jurisprudence, and enquire what things, as between nations, ought to be constituted Rights.   There are two states

that have to be considered—the State of Peace, and the State
of War.

In time of Peace, questions arise between conterminous
countries, by the inhabitants of one country infringing the
property of the other.   Here, the party sued should be amen-
able only to the tribunals of his own country, but the definition
of right should be taken from the country of the plaintiff.   For
such a case, it would be convenient to have a common judicature, to consist of two judges, one from each country, with
power to choose a third when they could not agree.

There is more difficulty in applying redress when the rights
of the person are violated.   It is desirable that each man should
receive protection according to the laws of his own country ;
and it is also desirable that each man should be punished
according to the laws of his own country ; which objects are
to a certain degree incompatible.   In many cases, the tribunals
of both countries will act much in the same way ; in some
cases, they may not.   An inhabitant of Persia that forced cow-
broth down the throat of a Hindoo, would not be punished
in his own country as the Hindoo would consider sufficient

The rules applicable to individual property should apply to
what belongs to the government.   Portions of Land may give
rise to disputes as to boundaries ; and these involve the whole of
the questions respecting the acquisition of dominion or territory.
Now, as with individual rights to property in land, so here—
there ought to be a clear definition in the form of a statement
of the events that confer domain, and of the events that take
away domain ; and the question for a judicature would be the
question of fact, whether such events had taken place.   For
the most part, these events are agreed upon among civilized
nations ; as, for example, Occupancy, Transfer, and Conquest
in a lawful war.

As regards Waters, there are peculiar rights and privileges,
as between nations.   The sea is equally open to all nations as
a passage for their ships.   The most flagrant violation of this

right is piracy.   There is no general tribunal for this offence, as there might be ; the nation suffering punishes at its own hands.   The portion of sea adjoining each country has a more special value with regard to that country, as, for example, for fishing ; and special rights are allowed on this head.   But the practice of levying tolls at narrow inlets should be condemned.

When two countries are bounded by a river, navigable or otherwise, the mutual rights should be a matter of agreement between themselves.

Rights in time of War are those tnat give rise to the more serious difficulties.   What should be considered as necessary to render just the Commencement of a War ?   What should be regarded as just and unjust in the modes of Carrying on a War ?   It would be impossible, even if it were within my purpose, to epitomise the masterly handling of the delicate questions connected with this greatest of all political problems. Nothing, it seems to me, is wanted but fuller illustration to make it a perfect treatise on the thesis *De jure belli.*   The thorough regard to human well-being at all points, the careful weighing of the whole of the considerations on both sides of every emergency, the judicious suggestions for accomplishing the ends in view—are beyond praise.   I am not aware that the author's treatment has since been improved upon.   He starts with the position that, before going to war in order to redress a supposed injury, compensation should first be demanded.   He then considers the limitations that ought to be imposed on the destruction of property and of life.   He argues against the devastation of a country, and the destruction of commerce. He considers in what light the desertion of sailors should be viewed.   He thinks that a free march through neutral territories should be allowed to both parties.

So much for the scope of an International Code.   The framing of such a Code ought to be entrusted to delegates from all civilized nations.   Such a body of delegates would be the proper judicature to interpret the code in each particular case. They would choose a judge, with whom the final decision should lie. It would be their duty to be present during the whole of the proceedings, and each of them to record separately his opinion upon the case, after the decision of the acting judge had been pronounced.

The author enters somewhat minutely into the procedure suitable for such a tribunal, and descants upon its value as a great school of political morality (he might have added private morality as well). The code once formed should be promulgated. "Not only that, but the best means should be in full operation for diffusing a knowledge of the proceedings of the tribunal; a knowledge of the cases investigated, the allegations made, the evidence adduced, the sentence pronounced, and the reasons upon which it is grounded."

"The book of the law of nations, and selections from the book of the trials before the international tribunal, should form a subject of study in every school, and a knowledge of them a necessary part of every man's education. In this manner a moral sentiment would grow up, which would, in time, act as a powerful restraining force upon the injustice of nations, and give a wonderful efficacy to the international jurisdiction. No nation would like to be the object of the contempt and hatred of all other nations; to be spoken of by them on all occasions with disgust and indignation. On the other hand, there is no nation, which does not value highly the favourable sentiments of other nations; which is not elevated and delighted with the knowledge that its justice, generosity, and magnanimity, are the theme of general applause."

It might even be possible to attach something of the nature of penalties to the smaller violations of the code. Marks of dishonour and disrespect, such as operate powerfully in private life, would have an efficacy as between nations. A number of cases might be found where certain benefits of the law, granted to other foreigners, might be refused to a delinquent state.

"By the application of the principles, which we have thus expounded, an application which implies no peculiar difficulty, and requires nothing more than care in the detail, we are satisfied that all might be done, which is capable of being done, toward securing the benefits of international law."

EDUCATION.

This article must have been written in 1818, after the publication of the *History*. The correspondence is silent upon it; yet, it must have cost a great deal of labour.

The plan of it is comprehensive to a degree, indeed too comprehensive, except as a survey of the whole field of influences bearing on the formation of character; to be partitioned among several workers. No one person could overtake all that is here sketched; there would be even a disadvantage in including all subjects in one treatment.

I have already remarked that the *a priori*, or deductive handling is here exclusively carried out. The author hardly ever cites an actual experience in education; far less has he a body of experience summed up in empirical laws, to confront and compare with the deductions from the theory of the human mind. One would think he had never been either a learner or a teacher, so little does he avail himself of the facts or maxims of the work of the school.

Still, the essay has an interest of its own, and that interest I will endeavour briefly to set forth.

"The end of Education, is to render the individual, as much as possible, an instrument of happiness, first to himself, and next to other beings."

All circumstances bearing upon this end are proper to be taken into account. The primary division of them is into physical and moral, or rather psychological.

To act upon the mind, we must know the nature of the mind. In particular, we must enquire what are the qualities of mind that chiefly conduce to happiness, and how to produce those qualities.

Having laid out the ground, he enters at once into a dissertation on Psychology; he reviews the history of the doctrine of Association of Ideas, which he traces through Hobbes, Locke, Hume, and Condillac : drawing a few practical inferences therefrom; such as the importance of attaching trains of thought to starting points that often recur in life. Thus the sagacity of priests discovered that religious thoughts and feelings could be best sustained by being connected with rising in the morning, going to bed at night, and meals.

Again, as a train commences in some present sensation, so it may be conceived as terminating in the idea of some future pleasure or pain, as in our desires to attain good and to ward off evil. Now, everything depends on how the interval is filled up; the intermediate trains may be either beneficial or hurtful. Suppose wealth and its adjuncts the end; the enchained ideas terminating in the idea of wealth may be honest labour, or they may be vicious modes of acquiring riches. Education determines which.

Next comes the more specific enquiry, what are the Qualities of mind that should be fostered by education. There is, first, Intelligence, or Knowledge, with the sagacity of adapting means to ends. In the second place, there must be a power of restraining the hurtful appetites, commonly expressed by Temperance, which is, however, to be distinguished from ascetic self-denial. Thirdly, for promoting the happiness of others, there must be benevolent impulses, under the two forms—Justice and Generosity.

The objects now stated suffer at present from the want of any clear definition of Happiness. This deficiency is illustrated by the antagonism of philosophers in settling the Ethical End; which state of uncertainty is incompatible with precision in the means.

The remainder of the essay is headed—" Instruments, and

practical Expedients, of Education," and may be expected to supply such guidance as the present condition of the subject will allow. At the threshold stands a question of theory, as to how far the useful qualities of our nature are subject to the power of education. On this the author goes nearly all lengths with the extreme view of Helvetius, namely, that the mass of mankind are equal as to their susceptibility of mental excellence. " People," he says, "form a very inadequate conception of all the circumstances that act during the first months, perhaps the first moments of existence, and of the power of these circumstances in giving permanent qualities to the mind. The works of Helvetius would have been invaluable, if they had done nothing more than prove the vast importance of these circumstances in giving permanent qualities to the mind."

On this subject, the author is the victim of a theory that grossly misrepresents the facts. The power of education is great, but it does not account for all the differences of character of men and of races.

The curious thing is that, in the next section, he enters into the influence of physical causes, in which he is obliged to advert to the natural differences of corporeal constitution; admitting, that in this respect, people are very unequally constituted by nature. He attributes great credit to the works of Dr. Erasmus Darwin, and M. Cabanis, for illustrating the power of physical circumstances in the production of mental modifications, and quotes largely from both. All this was in advance of his age, but it is now superseded by statements of much greater precision. Dwelling upon the importance of Aliment, or nutrition, he puts admirably a truth that mankind have been very reluctant to receive. " The physical causes must go along with the moral; and nature herself forbids, that you shall make a wise and virtuous people out of a starving one. Men must be happy themselves, before they can rejoice in the happiness of others; they must have a certain vigour of mind, before they can, in the midst of habitual suffering, resist a presented pleasure; their own lives, and means of well-being, must be worth something, before they can value, so as to respect, the life, or well-being, of any other person. This or that individual may be an extraordinary individual, and exhibit mental excellence in the midst of wretchedness; but a wretched and excellent people never yet has been seen on the face of the earth."

He proceeds to the circumstances of a moral kind that operate in education The first is Domestic Education. This he expresses under his general formula, adopted throughout, of placing in the mind those mental trains that conduce to happiness and good conduct. "Children ought to be made to see, and hear, and feel, and taste, in the order of the most invariable and comprehensive sequences, in order that the ideas which correspond to their impressions, and follow the same order of succession, may be an exact transcript of nature, and always lead to just anticipations of events. Especially, the pains and pleasures of the infant, the deepest impressions which he receives, ought, from the first moment of sensation, to be made as much as possible to correspond to the real order of nature. The moral procedure of parents is directly the reverse; they strive to defeat the order of nature, in accumulating pleasures for their children, and preventing the arrival of pains, when the children's own conduct would have had very different effects."

One of the commonest examples of perversion of the early training is to allow children to connect terrific images with being in the dark. Another is to connect admiration with the rich and powerful, and contempt with the poor and weak; and to couple disgust and hatred with people that differ from us in country or religion. Again as regards the virtue of Temperance. The grand object evidently is, to connect with each pain and pleasure those trains of ideas which, according to the order established among events, tend most effectually to increase the sum of pleasures upon the whole, and diminish the sum of pains. In regard to Benevolence the primary experience is this. The pleasures of those that surround the child are usually causes of pleasure to him ; their pains, pains to him. Now, it should be systematically arranged, that children should share in the pleasures of others, and thus, by connecting their own pleasures with those of others, have an inducement to do good to others. In this manner would be laid a foundation for a life of beneficence.

The author has next some very pertinent remarks upon the love of power. The right way to command the wills of others is to do them good ; the wrong way is to do them harm. " When a command over the wills of other men is pursued by the instrumentality of pain, it leads to all the several degrees of vexation, injustice, cruelty, oppression, and tyranny. It is, in truth, the grand source of all wickedness, of all the evil which man brings upon man. When the education is so deplorably bad as to allow an association to be formed in the mind of the child between the grand object of desire, the command over the wills of other men, and the fears and pains of other men, as the means ; the foundation is laid of the bad character—the bad son, the bad brother, the bad husband, the bad father, the bad neighbour, the bad magistrate, the bad citizen—to sum up all in one word, the bad man. Yet, true it is, a great part of education is still so conducted as to form that association. The child, while it yet hangs at the breast, is often allowed to find out by experience, that crying, and the annoyance which it gives, is that by which chiefly it can command the services of its nurse, and obtain the pleasures which it desires." To this illustration he adds another from the fagging of boys at the great schools ; where, he says, it was found that the objections to its abolition came from the boys themselves ; they submitted to the pain of being tyrannized over for a time, that they might have the counterbalancing pleasure of being tyrants in turn.

The next head is termed Technical Education, a wide

phrase for all the qualities necessary to make a man a good member of society in every way. They include, first and foremost, Intelligence. Under this branch the author dwells principally on the kind and amount of knowledge requisite for the different classes of society, and puts especial stress upon educating the lowest class. He disposes of the remark that intelligence does not necessarily conduce to virtue, by the counter-statement (which has the authority of Hume) " that knowledge and its accompaniments, morality and happiness, may not be strictly conjoined in every individual, but that they are infallibly so (in the mass) in every age, and in every country ". He has, as we might expect, some very strong remarks on the deficient education of our higher classes, and on the vices that impair the utility of old and opulent establishments for their education.

A separate handling is given to Social Education ; but it does not evolve any new line of thought ; the main topic being our enormous susceptibility to the good and the evil regards of society. The Political Education is the last branch. This is the key-stone of the arch ; the strength of the whole depends upon it. The play of the political machine acts on the mind immediately, and with extraordinary power. " When the political machine is such, that the grand objects of desire are seen to be the natural prizes of great and virtuous conduct— of high services to mankind, and of the generous and amiable sentiments from which great endeavours in the service of mankind naturally proceed—it is natural to see diffused among mankind a generous ardour in the acquisition of all those admirable qualities which prepare a man for admirable actions; great intelligence, perfect self-command, and over-ruling benevolence. When the political machine is such that the grand objects of desire are seen to be the reward, not of virtue, not of talent, but of subservience to the will, and command over the affections of the ruling few ; interest with the *man above* to be the only sure means to the next step in wealth, or power, or consideration, and so on ; the means of pleasing the man above become, in that case, the great object of pursuit."

Such is a feeble outline of this remarkable essay. The line of thought is highly original, and most instructive on the points chiefly embraced. There is no possibility of palliating the defects of a too exclusive deductive handling ; but the study of the educator is repaid by the suggestiveness of the theories. Unfortunately, there was no one but the author himself capable of giving the full application to his principles ; and his most fruitful openings were not pursued.

Sir James Mackintosh having ventured on a criticism of the Essay, the author took the opportunity of introducing into the " Fragment " a biting reply. Sir James made some plausible enough objections, but fenced them so badly, that the author trips him up at every turn. He says, with an air of justice, that the essay shows the inconvenience of leaping at once from the most general laws, to a multiplicity of minute appearances. This is one point. The other remark is directed against the author's theory that the intellectual and moral character is entirely formed by circumstances ; and might have been a formidable criticism in stronger hands.

In addition to the articles now reviewed, there were others not included with these in the reprint : namely, *Caste, Economists, Beggar, Benefit Societies, Banks for Savings.* The article " Caste " is, of course, a historical account of the institution of that name, with the author's reflections upon it. " Economists " refers to the early French school of Political Economy, of which it gives a historical and critical account. The three last may be briefly noticed as giving the author's mode of viewing the great social problems connected with indigence.

BEGGAR.

It is difficult to define and classify beggars. Yet it is necessary to distinguish the classes before applying measures for curing the evil. One great distinction is between such as beg from necessity, and such as beg from choice; there being great varieties of both sorts. For a description of the field of mendicity, the author refers to the Report of a Committee of the House of Commons, in 1815, with reference to mendicity in the metropolis. The inquiry was very imperfect; the interrogation of witnesses superficial and unskilful; but the facts and conjectures given in the Report are still the best information available.

There is great difference of opinion as to the proportion of the two kinds. Some say, half beg from necessity; others, all, or nearly all, from choice. Mill inclines to the second view as regards the journeymen in the metropolis, being confirmed in this view from private knowledge (meaning, no doubt, information supplied by Place). Begging is all but unknown in that class; and, considering the fluctuations in their means of subsistence, "the resolution by which they abstain from begging should be regarded as one of the most remarkable phenomena in the history of the human mind ".

Adverting to the number of beggars, he remarks that this is little ascertained; yet, according to the experience of every attentive man, it is gradually diminishing.

As to the deceptions practised by beggars, he holds in great contempt their alleged inventive ingenuity. The supposed gains of beggars are liable to great exaggeration. With regard to the allegation of their being violent and abusive when refused alms, he says :—

" The writer of this article may give his own evidence. He has lived above fifteen years in the metropolis; he has walked more than most people, both in the streets of London and in the roads and fields immediately surrounding it; he never gives anything to a casual beggar; he cannot at this moment recollect that, in the whole course of his experience, he ever met with one abusive word; but he has a hundred times received a ' Thank you, sir,' with a bow and a curtsey from the little boys and girls whom he has refused and repulsed, and to whom it is evident that such a lesson is taught by those on whom their conduct depends. The impostrous beggar, in fact, knows his art too well to lose his temper; and the spirit of the age, so much improved, renders a mild deportment necessary to the success even of the worst employment."

I am not aware of any parallel instance of such obduracy on principle, except Archbishop Whately, who remarks somewhere to the effect, that he had given away large sums for benevolent purposes, but he could not reproach his conscience with having ever given one halfpenny to a beggar.

The author then proceeds to review the causes of Mendicity. They include—(1) Soldiering; (2) The State Lottery; (3) Drink; (4) Local demands for temporary labour; (5) Gratuity-taking, or Tipping—a degrading practice, which brings down the mind to the mendicity level; (6) Want of Education; (7) The Poor Laws, on which he passes a lengthened condemnation; (8) Early and improvident marriages; (9) Ireland—"supplies more than one-third of all the beggars of the metropolis"; (10) War; (11) Bad Legislation.

I do not think that this enumeration shows the discrimination of the author at its best. Soldiering and War come to nearly the same thing. Poor Laws is but a case of Bad Legislation. Want of Education he himself regards as a primal cause, of which Drink and Improvidence may be but effects.

His remedies correspond with the causes, but are somewhat better arranged. They are :—

Review and amend the existing laws relating to beggary. This, of course, is equivalent to Poor Law Reform.

Make provision for the efficient education of the whole mass of the people, down to the lowest individual.

Take all means for preventing the too rapid multiplication of human beings.

Reform the mode of governing Ireland.

Make a law to prohibit all modes of paying the people that

have an affinity with yielding to the cravings of a beggar—*i.e.*, abolish Tips. Here also he seems at fault. The most stringent laws made (as by Railway Companies) for this purpose have proved a dead letter. The improvement has consisted in substituting fixed payments, to servants and others, in place of gratuities. But, indeed, I doubt if his view of tips is perfectly logical; they are often a form of wages for work done or expected, and sometimes a form of gift or free-will offering.

Cultivate the moral sensibility that prefers death to begging. (Clearly a department of Education.)

Provide an asylum for rearing to virtue the children of beggars.

Provide a system of Reformatories or Penitentiaries.

Organise the visitation of the mendicant class; and make a complete Registration of the whole.

Set up voluntary societies for the suppression of Beggary. These are valuable adjuncts of the State machinery.

In these recommendations we have a forecast of what has actually been achieved in dealing with our indigent population. The English Poor Law of 1834 was the first great legislative advance; and Mill and his friends in Parliament were strenuous in their advocacy of that measure. Indeed, the principal author of the law, Edwin Chadwick, although a man of great independence and originality of mind, came under the immediate influence of Bentham and Mill.

BENEFIT SOCIETIES.

The institution of Benefit Societies had been in existence for a good many years, and had been productive of admirable results. Mill reviews the history of the institution, and brings his philosophy to bear on its ramified workings. Taking into account the poverty and the ignorance of the people, the striking feature in these societies is the self-command and foresight that make provision in the present for the future. Having perused the rules and regulations of a number of societies in the metropolis and elsewhere, the writer pronounces some of them to be in a very remarkable manner favourable to virtue. He traces the general effects of the societies, first, on the individual, and next on the public.   They diminish intemperance, and help to keep alive sensibility to disgrace; and so far "contribute greatly to all that virtue and good conduct of which the labouring classes of this country are day by day displaying a greater and greater share".   The main reason why the benefits of these clubs have not been fully realized is the unhappy state of the law in England.   For a long time, they had no means of redress against being cheated; and the cost of law-suits prevented appeals to the courts.   This evil has been only partially redressed.

BANKS FOR SAVINGS.

The objects of this class of banks are first stated.

"If human happiness is prodigiously improved by reserving for future use a proportion of the command which, over and above the necessaries of life, a man may possess over the means of enjoyment, it is surely desirable that this great instrument of happiness should, in the greatest degree possible, be provided for the most numerous, and in the same degree in which the most numerous, the most important portion of the race."

The chief merit of the institution lies in creating the disposition to accumulate; out of this will spring industry and frugality, which will imply temperance.   The upshot of the whole is a provision against the miseries of want.

In enquiring how far Savings Banks have these consequences, the author is led to consider the principle of population. "Though no part of the doctrine of Mr. Malthus has been left uncontested, it is now, among thinking men, pretty generally allowed that, excepting certain favourable situations, as in new countries, where there is unoccupied land of sufficient productiveness, which may be placed under cultivation as fast as men are multiplied, a greater number of human beings is produced than there is food to support. This, it is understood, is the habitual condition of human nature." . . . "What is wanted, then, is, the means of preventing mankind from increasing so fast; from increasing faster than food can be increased to support them. To the discovery of these means, the resources of the human mind should be intensely applied. This is the foundation of all improvement."

Now the disposition to accumulate is the foundation stone. But people in a state of starvation, or on the very brink of it, have nothing to accumulate. It is only the unmarried, and those that have no families or very small families, that can take advantage of savings banks. In this part of the population the disposition to accumulate will to a certain extent be increased, but experience alone can say how far. Single persons, being mostly young, are exposed to the temptations of youth, to sacrifice the future to the present. "The training of the human mind must be more skilful, and more moral to a vast degree, before this salutary power will belong to any considerable portion of the youth in any class of the population, especially in the least instructed of all."

"The greater part of those that have written on Savings Banks have left altogether out of view the principle of population. They have, therefore, left out of view that circumstance on which the condition of the most numerous class of mankind radically, and irremediably, and almost wholly depends. Of course, their observations and conclusions are of little importance."

Others, more philosophical, expect the institution to "have a salutary effect upon the principle of population, and ameliorate the condition of mankind, by lessening the rapidity with which they multiply. This is a speculation of the deepest interest. If this be an effect of savings banks, they will, indeed, deserve the attention and patronage of the philanthropist and the sage."

The first public suggestion of an institution corresponding to Savings Banks occurred in a scheme of Bentham's for the management of paupers, which appeared, in 1797, in Arthur Young's *Annals of Agriculture*. These " frugality banks " of Bentham were confined to the purchase of annuities for old age ; an unnecessary limitation of their functions.

In the article on Benefit Societies, there is an elaborate comparison of these with Savings Banks, showing their superior applicability in many respects to the situation of the poorest.

Chapter VI.

WESTMINSTER REVIEW: ANALYSIS OF THE MIND.

1824—1829.

TO the six years, from 1824 to 1829 inclusive, we have to refer, as leading events, the starting of the *Westminster Review* and the completion of the *Analysis of the Mind*. To the same period belongs the founding of the University of London.

The history of the *Westminster Review* is given briefly by John Mill in the *Autobiography*, and by Bowring in the *Life of Bentham*. Neither account is very specific. According to John Mill, the need of a Radical organ, to make head against the *Edinburgh* and the *Quarterly*, had been a topic of conversation between his father and Bentham *many years* earlier, and it was a part of the plan that his father should be editor. The "many years" would probably go back to the Ford Abbey intercourse, when there was the most abundant opportunity of discussing all manner of projects. It would be a not unlikely supposition that Mill should resolve to finish his History before entering on the task of editor. When that time arrived, Bentham was implicated in money losses, which might indispose him to risk a new venture; while Mill's speedy appointment to the India House would be accepted as a disqualification for the editorial post. This last supposition, however, did not seem to be present to Bentham's mind, for John Mill tells us that when the *Review* came to be started, Bentham made a formal offer of the editorship to his father, and had to be then told of the incompatibility of the post with his official work.

There is no very distinct statement of the amount of Bentham's pecuniary contribution to the scheme. From a phrase employed by John Mill, when it changed hands, in 1828—"the original funds were nearly or quite exhausted"—we might infer that Bentham set aside a particular sum to carry it on until it should be able to maintain itself; but what that sum was we have never been informed.* Indeed, both our sources of information leave Bentham himself entirely in the background. Even his opinion of the management and writing of the several numbers is never alluded to. Nevertheless, although not so successful in all respects as its promoters could have wished, it gave the first opening for the promulgation of advanced views; while the occasion that detached the Mills from its staff in less than four years was much to be regretted. It went on as a Benthamite organ when it passed into Colonel Thompson's hands, Bowring being still editor, till it was acquired by Molesworth in 1836, and amalgamated with his *London Review*.†

---

* "The *Review* had fallen into difficulties. Though the sale of the first number had been very encouraging, the permanent sale had never, I believe, been sufficient to pay the expenses, on the scale on which the *Review* was carried on. Those expenses had been considerably, but not sufficiently reduced. One of the editors, Southern, had resigned; and several of the writers, including my father and me, who had been paid like other contributors for our earlier articles, had latterly written without payment."

† The account given by Bowring is to the following effect:—"In 1823, the *Westminster Review* was started. The funds were all furnished by Bentham. The editors, for some years, were Mr. Southern in the literary, and myself for the political department. It afterwards passed into my hands alone; and next was carried on by me in connexion with Colonel Perronet Thompson. Its appearance excited no small fluttering among the two sections of the aristocracy, which it attacked with equal, though not undiscriminating ardour. The sale, for some time, was nearly 3000; and as its readers were, to a large extent, among the unopulent and democratic classes, whose access to books is principally by associations of various sorts, the number of its readers was very great." Contributions were paid ten guineas a sheet.

Bowring gives Bentham's own account of it, in a letter to a correspondent, but no new fact is added. Both Bowring and Bentham mention that the

The articles contributed by Mill will be noticed, in the narrative, according to date.

Coincident with the third and fourth years of the *Westminster Review*, was the appearance of the *Parliamentary History and Review*, started by the elder Mr. Marshall of Leeds.

The composition of the "Analysis of the Mind" went on, by John Mill's account, chiefly in the autumn holidays of those six years. It must have occupied his thoughts during many leisure moments besides. His other writing would not be sufficient to engross his spare time even when engaged in his office routine.

The failure of the Chrestomathic School must have had a discouraging effect. Nothing was done towards a scheme of higher education on an enlightened basis until 1825. The credit of projecting the University of London is due to the poet, Thomas Campbell. The most detailed account of the proceedings is found in Place's MSS. Campbell's published letter to Lord Brougham (*Times*, Feb. 9, 1825) was the first public intimation of the scheme.

In an entry in Place's MS., dated 12th Feb., 1825, he says Campbell had often talked to him, for three years back, on the project of a London University. In the previous June, he told Place the results of his enquiries into the German Universities. It was after a conversation with Joseph Hume, that he wrote his letter to Brougham. Place talked in favour of the project in his wide circle. "Thus the matter became known to a great many persons. On the 29th of January last, he urged the matter very strongly upon me, and I had a long conversation with Mill respecting it. Mill discountenanced it, as

Longmans undertook the publishing of the *Review*, and then declined, whereupon Baldwin became the publisher; but neither of them states what we learn from John Mill, that it was the sight of his father's article in the *Edinburgh Review* that deterred the Longmans, and that it was his father's instigation that Baldwin took their place.

he thought it was unattainable.   On the following day, Brougham gave a calves'-head dinner; among others who dined there were Lord King, Joseph Hume, Thomas Campbell, and James Mill.   After dinner, Campbell's project was talked of, and, as I am informed, Campbell . . . was countenanced in his project by the whole company, every one of whom had probably heard of it before . . . ."

At a dinner at Mr. John Smith's, a few days later, Mill, Brougham, and Campbell were present, and measures were resolved on.   Hume undertook to procure subscribers to the amount of a hundred thousand pounds.

Mill, once embarked in the scheme, was a powerful ally. It was frequently remarked by Grote, that Mill's personal ascendancy with men of wealth among the dissenters and among liberal politicians generally, and the trust that they placed in his judgment, had a great deal to do with the obtaining of the requisite funds.   There are frequent notes to him from Brougham, consulting on the progress of the scheme. Here is one:—"I wish you could look in on your way to the city, as I have a talk to hold with you, on our liberal ministers having refused a charter as not daring to face Oxford bigotry, &c."

At a public meeting (the third that had been held) on 19th Dec., 1825, Mill is one of a number of "Noblemen and Gentlemen selected by ballot to compose the first Council". The foundation stone of the building (now University College) was laid on 30th April, 1827; followed by a dinner at Freemasons' Tavern.   Mill present.

In 1826, the arrangements were so far advanced, that they began to look out for professors; and, in October, Mill wrote to Dr. Thomson begging him to accept the chemistry chair, on the supposition that it could be made worth his while.

The appointment that gave the Council most trouble was the philosophy chair.   Mill and his allies put forward Charles Hay Cameron, who is only recently deceased.   He was then a barrister, but afterwards held high appointments in India, being one of the Commission of three, presided over by Macaulay, for preparing the Criminal Code.   He was one of Grote's friends, and may have been brought forward by him.   But as his orthodoxy was doubtful, the Evangelical Dissenters were hostile, and he could not be carried : Brougham staid away at the final push.   Another candidate, a dissenting clergyman, conciliated Mill's support by professing to follow Hartley, and Mill took him up as a *pis aller*, and got him elected; not without the opposition of Mr. Grote, who then, as afterwards, held strongly the incompatibility of clerical vows with the *libertas philosophandi*.

1824.

The Supplement to the *Encyclopædia* is now finished, and a letter from Mill to Napier, on the 7th of May, winds up our extant references to the undertaking.

"EAST INDIA HOUSE, *May 7, 1824.*

"MY DEAR SIR,

"I ought to have replied to your kind letter before this time; but the fact is, the number of the *Supplement* was not sent to me till the other day, and I deferred writing till I saw it, though I ought to have sent for it, but have the apology of having been both very busy and very ill.   As to what you have said of me, I have but two feelings; one is, fear that you have said much more good of me than I deserve; the next is, great delight, which I am not so modest as to seek to disguise, that I am so highly estimated by you, who, I am persuaded, would not, on such an occasion, utter any but your real sentiments. I am happy to say that both Mr. M'Culloch and I are greatly pleased with the execution of your preface.   I am happy also to say that nothing can be more complete than the success of his lectures, and the estimation in which M'Culloch is held among us is such as to satisfy the most affectionate of his friends, of whom I reckon myself one of the foremost."

M'Culloch had been brought from Edinburgh to deliver the Riccardo Memorial Lectures, and they seem to have been a great success. His own account of them is given in the *Napier Correspondence*, p. 39. The following sentences occur in his letter ·—" I have seen Mill frequently, and find him extremely kind and friendly. It is a pity he is so incorrigible a Radical. A new number of the *Westminster* has been published, and it contains the sequel of the attack on the *Edinburgh*, and a more contemptible and pettifogging one never was published. I do not believe Mill wrote it."

It remains to complete the record of this year, by a full account of the articles that appeared in the first and third numbers of the *Westminster Review*—one dealing with the *Edinburgh* and the other with the *Quarterly*. It had been a cherished object in the scheme of the *Westminster*, John Mill tells us, that a part should be devoted to reviewing the other Reviews; and for the first of the articles by his father, he himself read through the volumes of the *Edinburgh* from the commencement, making notes of the articles that seemed suited to his father's purpose, on account of either their good or their bad qualities.

This paper, John Mill tells us farther, was the chief cause of the sensation that the *Westminster Review* produced at its first appearance. He gives a short outline of the contents. I shall here abstract it more fully. It was the first occasion when Mill had full swing in the expression of his political views. For he was not allowed to express these when writing for Jeffrey; and, although he was not fettered in the *Philanthropist*, that periodical dealt with the fundamental questions of politics only in an indirect way.

The introduction of the article consists of remarks on the peculiarities of periodical literature. One peculiarity is, that it must have immediate success in order to secure its existence. The good result of this is that writers are induced to make knowledge palatable, and thereby increase its diffusion. There is another side, however. "The most effectual mode of doing good to mankind by reading, is, to correct their errors; to expose their prejudices; to refute opinions which are generated only by partial interests, but to which men are, for that reason, so much the more attached; to censure whatever is mean and selfish in their behaviour, and attach honour to actions solely in proportion to their tendency to increase the sum of happiness, lessen the sum of misery." But this is just the course that the periodical writer cannot pursue. To please the great mass of men, he must flatter their prejudices and pander to their errors. Now, of all opinions the most mischievous are those that lead to the injury of the larger number of men for the benefit of the smaller number. These, however, are the opinions that periodical literature is under the strongest inducements to promote; and why? Because they are the opinions of the people in power, who are able to set the fashion. There is a tendency in the opinions of the wise to prevail at last; but then these must be diffused and brought fully under the attention of mankind; and periodical literature endeavours to thwart this operation. Its success depends upon finding plausible reasons for maintaining the favourite opinions of the powerful classes. After the mass of the people have become a reading people, a reward is held out for writings addressed particularly to them. They too have their erroneous opinions, but it is not by the periodical press depending on their support, that these are likely to be corrected. The cheap publications of the day addressed to the more numerous class, are productive of more evil than good.

The two great Reviews—*Edinburgh* and *Quarterly*—are addressed to the aristocratical class; and it is to be seen by the evidence what is the amount of their subservience to that class. As they are conducted on opposite principles, it would seem that both cannot follow the same ends. This is a nice point, the elucidation of which goes far into the philosophy

of British history; and it is the main strain of the present
article.

The term "aristocracy" has to be carefully explained. In the
author's view it means, not simply the titled nobility, nor even
the families possessed of large fortunes; these are the nucleus,
but not the whole. "The comparatively small number possessing political power are the real aristocracy, by whatever
circumstances—birth, or riches, or other accident—the different
portions of them become possessed of it." In our own country,
the aristocracy is a motley body; and if we assent to the doctrine of the *Edinburgh Review*, that the powers of government
are centred in the House of Commons, we need only enquire
who they are that compose that house, and who send them
there. The broad facts are enough. The owners of the great
landed estates have the principal influence; they have all the
counties, and a large proportion of the boroughs. In some of
these, the electors sell their votes to the highest bidders—a very
culpable thing, in the code of aristocratic morality, although
there is nothing wrong in a rich lord of the soil selling his vote
in parliament.

The author next reviews what he calls the props to the
aristocracy—the Church and the Law. The influence of religion on men's minds is necessarily great, and to secure this to
the side of the governing few, it is requisite merely to influence
the teachers of religion. For this purpose they are formed
into a corporate and dependent body, with gradation of
emoluments and power; the nomination to these emoluments is
kept in the hands of the governing class; and the holders are
admitted to a share of the power and profits of the aristocracy.

Then as to the Law. From the complexity of our English
law, the class of lawyers come to have a great influence with
the community. It is important to the aristocracy to use the
influence of the lawyers for its own purposes. Hence it is
requisite to admit them also to a share of the aristocratic
privileges.

In this way, then, is the aristocracy made up: the landed families (not two hundred in all) and their partners—the monied interest, the church, and the law. Men of talent, as such, are erroneously said to have a share; their true position is as servants in office.

One more preliminary explanation is needed. The aristocracy, in this country, is divided into two sections: the *Quarterly* follows one, the *Edinburgh* the other. These are called respectively ministerial and opposition.

All that part of the aristocracy that think themselves better off under the King's present advisers than they would be otherwise, lend their influence to the ministry. The author is careful to explain that he is speaking of classes as a whole, and not of the exceptional individuals that are found in every class. The theory of government must repose upon class tendencies; and, that these are governed by class interests any man would only make himself contemptible to deny.

Next, as to the Opposition. Their object is to change the hands that distribute the advantages of power. To drive a minister from office, it is necessary to deprive him of support in the House of Commons. Now, putting aside minor expedients, such as court intrigues, we come upon one great means, namely, to operate upon the middling and lower classes. Public opinion is still a force in the country, in proportion to the mass operated on. It is the interest of the Opposition to speak so as to gain favour both from the few (the aristocracy themselves) and from the many. This they are obliged to endeavour by a perpetual trimming between the two interests. In their speeches and writings, therefore, we commonly find them playing at *see-saw*. If a portion of the discourse has been employed in recommending the interests of the people, another must be employed in recommending the interests of the aristocracy. In this game, it is sufficiently evident on which side, at last, remain the winnings. For one thing, it is the aristocracy that must, in the House, vote down the ministry For

another thing, the Opposition is itself a section of the aristoc
racy, and one that hopes to be the leading section ; it cannot
therefore, seek to diminish its own advantages.

This preamble brings us to the line of action pursued by th
organs of the respective parties. The organ of the ministr
has its course clear ; its writers advocate the interests of th
aristocracy with enthusiasm, affected, or real. The people ar
represented as altogether vile ; any desires that they may hav
for securities against the abuse of power by the aristocracy ar
inconceivably wicked. The Opposition is blamed, first, fc
attaching blame to ministers, and, secondly, and far worse, fc
holding forth to the people pretensions about good governmer
that lead to the overthrow of the church and the state.

The Opposition organs, again, must work the see-saw ; to b
called the middle course and moderation. Bad names mu'
be given to both sets of opinions, which the party is in realit
putting forward by turns. The opinions on the side of arist
cratical power, are called despotical. Those that deman
securities in favour of the people are declared anarchical ; i
the slang of the day they are jacobinical, and radical. Th
wise course is the middle one. When the writers are blame
as tending to the aristocratical side, they declare their languag
to be misinterpreted, and point to other declarations of opinio
in favour of the popular demands. They do not allow th;
two contradictory opinions, on one and the same point, destr
one another, and should be regarded as no opinion at all.

" It is essential, in writing upon this plan, to deal as muc
as possible in vague language, and cultivate the skilful use
it. Words which appear to mean much, and may by those
whom they are addressed be interpreted to mean much, bi
which may also, when it suits the convenience of those wh
have used them, be shown to mean little or nothing, are
singular importance to those whose business it is to play th
game of compromise, to trim between irreconcileable interest
to see-saw between contradictory opinions."

Language of this description is particularly needed in making declarations that are to gain favour with the people. Nothing is risked by speaking explicitly in favour of the aristocracy. What is requisite is to have vague terms at command, when it is necessary to speak in opposition to these privileges. The people may be warned against aristocratical domination in the abstract, but great care must be used not to lift any part of the veil that conceals the real amount of aristocratical power there is in this country. When any specific measure is proposed that would operate to diminish that power, as the ballot, it must be loudly decried, and everything done to attach to it the apprehension of evil consequences. If, on the other hand, anything is proposed having the appearance of diminishing aristocratic power, although it has no such tendency, perhaps the reverse—as the disfranchisement of the rotten boroughs, to give the seats to the counties—then the epithets of praise must be collected. The invention of such schemes is a part of the business of the writers. A farther example is the doctrine of the representation by Classes.

Before citing his examples, the author interposes a personal explanation. Is the new periodical now started, people will ask, to rise superior to the inducements that others have succumbed to? The answer is—We claim to be tried. Men have diversities of taste; and it is not impossible but some men may exist having really a taste for endeavouring to obtain the securities of good government. Moreover, there is a growing class in the country that may perhaps prove sufficiently numerous to reward our endeavours.

When the *Edinburgh Review* first appeared, it was not decidedly attached to the opposition section of the aristocracy. At that time, the terrors of the French Revolution still overwhelmed that party. The see-saw was at first performed between opinions necessary to obtain the favour of the aristocracy, and opinions that had obtained the sanction of philosophy. Examples of this had already appeared in Blackstone and in Paley. The first article of the first number, is a review of *Mounier de l'Influence des Philosophes*. For the aristocrats, a great part of it is in the anti-jacobin tone ; concurring with the fashionable opinion—namely, that the cause of the Revolution and all its imputed evils, is in a great measure to be ascribed to the philosophers. For the philosophical part of the public, again, a portion of it is employed in representing philosophy as perhaps the foremost among the causes of good. Then follows a long passage in point. The gems are resumed thus :—" That Raynal should be enumerated among the soberminded writers, Condorcet among the inflammatory, must surprise any one who has read them. Observe, however, the real doctrine. It is laudable to put forth such writings as those of Montesquieu, Turgot, and Raynal ; this is for the philosophers. It is wicked to put forth such writings as those of Rousseau, Mably, and Condorcet ; this is for the aristocrats. Observe also the covert recommendation of restraining freedom of discussion." The presumptuous theories of the last-named class " have a necessary tendency to do harm ".

In the same number, Godwin is praised for setting the doctrine of the particular and the general affections in a light superior to Dr. Parr's sermon on the same topic. This is going a great way for philosophy. But the writer had " no sooner entered upon his remarks on population, than the pleasing delusion was expelled, and we were convinced it was a case for life ". A suitable offering at the throne of aristocratical bigotry and insolence.

It is a favourite doctrine of the Review that irregular and tumultuary ebullitions of the people in favour of liberty are of singular importance. By this both aristocracy and people are pleased. It is not from such irrational effervescence that the aristocracy have anything to fear ; while it is expected that the vanity of the people will be piqued. Already, in the first volume, the doctrine appears. For example, " The uproar even, and the confusion and the clamour of a popular election in England, have their use; they give a stamp to the names *Liberty, Constitution,* and *People,* they infuse sentiments which nothing but violent passions and gross objects of sense *could* infuse," &c.

The first article in the second volume is almost wholly anti-jacobin; the other side being remembered only by a pointed condemnation of that popular object of attack, the partition of Poland.

The ethical doctrines of the *Review* come in for a share of notice. In one article, the benefits of falsehood are rather strongly put: "we may assume as *established and undeniable,* that there is nothing in the nature of truth which makes it *necessarily* good". In another department, the ancients are considered very immoral for not including all the conditions included by us, in the marriage contract. The *Delphine* of Madame de Staël is singled out for ferocious condemnation; so different from the tone employed respecting her ten years afterwards, when, in England, she was in fashion with the opposition aristocracy.

The second volume is distinguished by its contributions to the aristocratical politics and morality. In an article on Belsham's *Memoirs of George III.,* there is much indignation at the writing of party pamphlets in the name of history. "We presume it will not be reckoned much more laudable to write party pamphlets under the guise of reviews." A certain petition of the "Society of the Friends of the People," is called a libellous oracle, for setting forth that a majority of the House of Commons is chosen by less than two hundred great families; that is to say, the authors should be treated with fine and imprisonment.

This being the period when the aristocratical tide was running high, when the war was just renewed with France, when fear of invasion and the courage of volunteering were the passions of the day, the only marketable commodity was aristocratical opinions; and the popular side is entirely unrepresented in the volume.

At this time much respect was professed for the old government of the Bourbons. To call it tyranny and despotism is revolutionary verbiage.

The fourth and fifth volumes are much the same as the second and third, except that there seems "a disposition to avoid grappling with any important and tender subject. Political economy, indeed, obtains a due share of attention; and the abolition of the slave trade begins to be recommended—two subjects upon which the *Edinburgh Review* has rendered important service. And upon these subjects, as well as upon that of Catholic emancipation, which has been laboriously handled, a remark is required."

These are the subjects well suited to the purpose of the *Review.* The position of the aristocracy would not be weakened by better opinions on political economy, or on the slave trade. Even Catholic emancipation would only raise a clamour among the priest-ridden party, but would do no harm otherwise. Such subjects would gain for the *Review* a reputation with the liberal, the enlightened, and the disinterested part of the public, without risking much with the aristocratical class.

Even political economy is occasionally prostituted. "A nation situated like ours, is much more likely to suffer from increasing wealth, than from increasing numbers of people," and, in such circumstances, the expenses of war are a blessing.

In the sixth volume (1805), a counterpoise begins to be applied to the popular scale. A paragraph is introduced in favour of what the few by whom the powers of government are usurped, have so much occasion to dread; the prevalence of enlightened principles, persecuted, under the name of theory, by the said few, the patrons of practice, and eulogisers of "things as they are".

The article on Bailly's *Memoirs* is more opposed to the anti-jacobin spirit, than anything occurring before. "Occasion had been taken from the Revolution, it says, to involve in discredit the principles of political philosophy, to give strength

18

to prejudices, and to sanction abuses, &c." Two classes of
men had received injustice ; the philosophers, who inculcated a
love of liberty and a spirit of reform, and the virtuous and
moderate, who attempted, at the outset, to act upon these
principles. To balance all this, these parties should have foreseen the dangers arising from their exasperated opposition to
the court, the clergy, and the nobility ; from their parade of
popularity ; from their alliance with the mob of Paris, and
so on.

The next passage produced is a laboured panegyric upon
the actual composition of the House of Commons, with a
fancy picture of the harmonious relations between the legislature and the people.

Belsham's continuation of his *History* again flourishes the
red rag ; the consequence is a strain of remark which "seems
as if a page of a ministerial daily paper had slipped into our
hands". On the famous expedition to Holland in 1799, we
are told of the disaffected newspapers, and the military talents
of the British commander-in-chief.

From the sixth to the ninth volume, there is nearly a blank
on the securities of good government. In the ninth volume
occurs "one of the most remarkable specimens of the use of
words without ideas, and of forms of expression covering
ignorance with the semblance of knowledge, that we could at
present point out, fashionable, and popular, and of course
prevalent, as this mode of composition is". The passage is
long and desultory ; and the author's sentences of comment
will be enough. The see-saw here is so rapid, that, as in the
swift succession of the prismatic colours, the mixture becomes
confusion. The ancient republics are "beautiful fabrics of
civil polity," but nevertheless such wretched fabrics, that "they
might be swept away by the surge of a moment, whenever the
factions who loved sedition, or the ambitious who aimed at
tyranny, should rouse the madness of the multitude". There
is a class of writers who love change, and a class who hate it,

seemingly for its own sake. We are sorry the writer did not inform us where they are to be found. From habit, and from the love of ease, all men are averse to change, where the prospect of some considerable good is not presented to them.

In one passage, the influence of the House of Peers is real and effective; in another, the House of Commons possesses nearly the whole of the legislative authority. In a farther passage, a writer dilates on the great mischiefs likely to arise from the growing inability of the other branches to thwart the House of Commons.

He passes on to a period when the *Review* thought expedient a much higher utterance on the side of the people than it had ventured on before. The whole of the article entitled " On the Rights and Duties of the People," in the twentieth volume, though much of the language is still vague and slippery, may be given as a specimen of the new lengths to which it was not scrupled, at this particular time, to go, in opposition to aristocratical interests.

According to one passage, though it had, in the previous paragraph, been allowed, that the principle of representation is the grand secret for good government, yet it is maintained, that for the people to let the powers of government out of their own hands, even to real representatives, is attended with imminent danger. It seems, according to the reviewer, that the plan of delegated authority necessarily implies a surrender of the function itself. How is this to be prevented? By mass meetings of the people, to declare their opinions on public measures and public men. Pitt is severely censured for being the first minister to abridge the rights of Englishmen to discuss their own affairs. When a writer is in this vein, he is naturally led to expose the weakness of the representative system as it then stood—the exclusive power of the aristocracy, the nullity of the large manufacturing towns, and so forth. On the other hand, there is a passage in the same number, which, though somewhat misty and oracular, nevertheless contains a view of the *beau idéal* of government, well calculated to administer consolation to the holders of aristocratical power. " The main end of government, to be sure, is, that wise laws be enacted and enforced." The best government, however, is a government that has an end more highly valued than its main end. " A representative legislature is incomparably of more value when it truly represents the efficient force of the nation in controlling the executive, than when it merely enacts wholesome statutes in its legislative capacity."

Such is a feeble attempt to summarize this scathing article. I cannot tell exactly how it affected Jeffrey and his contributors ; but no one had the courage to reply, or to retaliate in any form, until Macaulay took up the cudgels, in 1829, against the author's article on Government. Although the main charges could not easily be rebutted, several things could be said in palliation of the conduct of the *Review.* Few of the writers had studied Government in a very thorough manner ; unvarying clearness of thought, precision in the use of terms, and rigid consistency of statement, had never been exacted of any periodical , still less was it thought necessary that the different writers should be always at one. I cannot but think that the dependence of the *Review* on the Whig Aristocracy is too strongly stated. It was surely read extensively by the middle classes, and by that portion of them (in the towns, for instance) which was as yet unrepresented, and which must have felt its interests bound up with some extension of the suffrage, such, at least, as Pitt and the Whig leaders of the last century had more than once brought forward. As the fulness of the time drew near, the *Review* did advocate such an extension, and assisted in bringing it about ; not perhaps seeing that the end must be the destruction of aristocratical power.

The continuation of the attack in the second number is by John Mill, who had assisted his father in selecting his passages. Good points are made here too, especially on the Liberty of the Press and Libel Law, on which the younger Mill was already well primed.   But a more particular reference is here unnecessary.

In the fourth number of the *Westminster*, for October, the *Quarterly* receives its share of attention.

While both organs, it is here said, depend upon the aristocratical class, the line of the *Quarterly* is rendered distinctive by its subservience to the ministerial party.   Besides this principal difference, however, there are others that deserve to be noticed in advance.   For one thing, the *Quarterly* has always been more of a bookseller's catch-penny than the *Edinburgh*.   We are surprised to observe to what a degree it renounces the character of being a vehicle of instruction, and aims at nothing higher than furnishing amusement and subjects of prattle to loungers and gossips.   Its main resources have been books of travels, and books of poetry and amusement.

Another difference is that a much higher kind of intellect has always appeared in the *Edinburgh*.   A majority of its articles are from men of stored and cultivated minds ; such an article being very rare in the *Quarterly*.   There is something in the more distinguished of the *Edinburgh* reviewers to show that they have a leaning to better things, even when they are lending themselves to the sinister interest of their patrons. When they perceive a turning in the public mind towards anything that is good, they are ready to fall in with the happy current ; to which they have often lent additional velocity and force.   The writers in the *Quarterly* take the directly opposite course.   Watching the earliest symptoms of a tendency to improvement, they decry it, render it ridiculous and odious, and do everything to thwart it.   They play the part of the cold-blooded, remorseless enemies of mankind.

While the operation of see-saw needs skill, the task of writing for the party in power may be performed by coarser instruments.   Strictly speaking, that party does not need to argue or persuade people ; it can command and strike.   This affects the position of the advocate, who knows that he has power on his side.   He does the nearest to commanding and striking that his situation admits ; he employs the two weapons—Assumption and Abuse.   These are the logical arms of power ; as may be testified by all history, civil and ecclesiastical.   The advocates of the Catholic church, in their arguments with the reformers, employed the instrument of Assumption.   Universal consent, and the will of heaven, they said, were in their favour.   The supporters of the Stuarts took for granted that king's reigned by divine right ; that the people were incurably stupid and inclined to mischief ; whence it followed that arbitrary power is at once divine and indispensable.

The second ingredient in the logic of power is Abuse.   To illustrate the employment of this by the *Quarterly*, which is the author's chief purpose, he resuscitates a discourse from the Logic of the celebrated Le Clerc.   It is on that one source of delusion—*argumentum ab invidia ductum*, named by him *Argumentum Theologicum*, which name Mill finds fault with as too narrow (at least for our day) ; it should be *argumentum imperiosum*, the argument of power, in whatever hands it is placed. This branch of the Logic of Power is really all-including; it presupposes the assumption that the opinion attached is wrong.

The *argumentum ab invidia ductum* (rendered the *Dirt-flinging argument*) is divided by Le Clerc into sixteen species. There is a good deal of repetition, such as we find in the men of that age, who were fond of subdivisions.   Several of the species come under one head—Misrepresentation (*male explicare*).   Several are forms of suppression of evidence.   Others are—connecting the opinions with those of men already odious; imputation of bad consequences and wicked designs ; differing in opinion from great men ; dirt-flinging irrelevancies ; exciting the prejudices of the ignorant; accusation of subverting institutions.

" What do the men become who drink from these poisoned fountains of the Logic of Power? Wolves, says Le Clerc; and seldom has issued from human lips a truth of greater moment."

The grand question between the *Quarterly* and its opponents being whether there is anything in our constitution detrimental to the people, and that ought to be changed, its affirmation is—little or nothing. This position it maintains by begging questions, and venting calumny.

The production of illustrative extracts is rendered difficult by the prevailing verbosity of the composition. The first produced is a passage from an article on Parliamentary Reform. A few of the author's comments will sufficiently indicate what it is composed of. There is in one place a triplet of assumptions : that (1) the call for reform, (2) the use of a free press, (3) the power of holding meetings—all lead, by natural consequence, to insurrectionary violence, to the loss of all security for person and property, figured by the reviewer under the names—broken heads and broken windows. This is both assumption and abuse. Again, there is assumed the perpetual existence, in the people of England, of unreasonable discontent and a fondness for revolt. Once more, " radical reform " supposes universal insurrection, that is, not only all the evils that man can inflict upon man, but all the evils and crimes that aristocratical eloquence can find language to express. Such is aristocratical logic near its perfection ; its essence, its elixir. There is, farther, the assumption that the mass of the nation are contented ; the contradiction of a previous sentence. "True ; but this was necessary for the purpose of the Reviewer. And contradictions, though they are contrary to the rules of ordinary logic, are by no means contrary to the logic of power. The advocate of the ' old-fashioned government ' wanted to make the friends of an amended government appear both odious and contemptible. He could not make them appear so odious as he wished, without making them appear formidable. He could not make them appear so contemptible

as he wished, without making them appear to be not formidable.
And he knew well the sort of people whom he wished to please.
If he spoke strongly enough for their interests, in the way
which they deemed according to their interest, they would little
care for the congruity or incongruity of his ideas."

The next notable assumption is that all who desire Parliamentary Reform avow a love of Revolution, by which is meant
a horrible aggregate of the worst of crimes.   The closing
sentence applauds one of the articles on Parliamentary Reform
in the *Edinburgh ;* a striking illustration of the devotedness
of that organ to the aristocratical cause.

A second passage is given on the topic of Reform.   It is a
very curious specimen.   In the time of Charles I., the people
respected the decencies and the duties of life, deluded as they
were.   But now that popular knowledge has gained a footing,
men have come into a state to confound right and wrong.   Of
all men, the smatterer in philosophy is the most intolerable and
the most dangerous ; he begins by unlearning his Creed and
his Commandments.   While he confines himself to private
practice, his neighbour's wife may be in some danger, and his
neighbour's property also, but when he commences professor
of moral and political philosophy, his very breath becomes
venomous, &c.

The third extract is a very long characteristic passage, also
on Parliamentary Reform.   Of course, we count upon such
expressions as these :—The three possible forms of government,
each liable to abuses when existing alone, are with us blended
in one harmonious system, working for the safety, welfare, and
happiness of all.   Then, again, it is the influence of the democracy that has increased, is increasing, and ought to be
diminished.   All the additional influence of the crown, by the
increased establishments, is but a feather as compared with the
weight given to the democracy by the publication of the
debates.   But now what is meant by Parliamentary Reform ?
When this question is put at the meetings of reformers, the

confusion of Babel has been renewed. One is for triennial parliaments, another for annual. Orator Hunt is for vote by ballot; one of the Penny Orators is for Magna Charta. They talk of restoring the constitution—what constitution? The British constitution, says the reviewer, is not the creature of theory. The radical reformers, retorts Mill, do not say that it is. "Under it we are free as our thoughts." This is the aristocratical logic, without reserve, and without shame. Freedom there is in abundance to applaud the aristocracy and abuse the people. The want of freedom is all on the other side. All the reformers, says the reviewer, have offered to prove that the House of Commons merely represents the powerful families. But would any fool suppose it possible or desirable, in this country, to deprive wealth and power of their influence? In fine, reformers are defied to show in any age of history, or in any part of the world, a body of representatives better constituted than the British House of Commons.

The next extract is to show the application of the characteristic logic to the two peoples most distinguished for their efforts to throw off the yoke of aristocracy—France and America.

As to France, it seems, according to the Reviewer, "the lower and middling classes had latterly made progress in knowledge and intelligence, *unaccompanied by a corresponding improvement in morals*". How does the Reviewer know that? The Revolution is defined as sudden development of malignant power. It would be an equally correct, and a much more intelligible definition, to say a sudden destruction of malignant power. The object being to get a horror-raising and hatred-inspiring phrase, to apply to the Revolution, "a malignant power" appeared to be delightfully suited to the purpose. The occasion leads the reviewer to indulge in many similar outbursts of tawdry rhetoric. "Through all the utter and the middle darkness of the reign of regicide." "The jerky tongues of the popular leaders were systematically and incessantly employed in hissing forth the cant of *philanthropy* and *cosmopolitanism."* " Of what consequence can it be to ask, at whose bidding, or of what materials, the bridge was constructed, that opened an access to Europe from the pandæmonium of robbery and murder."

To take now a sample of the treatment of the people and government of the United States. In the first place, it is a crime in them to leave England and transfer their allegiance and their affections to another government. " The endearing charities of life are all sacrificed to one sordid passion ; while, rudely trampling over the graves of their forefathers, they rush in crowds to deposit their wealth where it may be safe from the claims of their native land." Sentimental trash, applied to a mischievous purpose ! The reviewer makes the gigantic blunder of contrasting the *amor patriæ* of the Greeks with that of the English, as if the patriotism of the Greeks displayed itself by staying at home. But power cares not what it says. Passion is proverbially short-sighted. The hatred of the reviewers in the *Quarterly* to a people that set a dangerous example to Europe carries them into another egregious blunder. They begin by describing the author of the work reviewed, as a person wholly unfit to be trusted for an observation or an opinion ; but finding him afterwards very much disposed to find fault with what he saw in America, they treat him as an oracle. On the other hand, Miss Wright, to whom we are indebted for a very interesting work, and who delighted in holding up the favourable aspect of things in the United States, is not only treated as at once wicked and contemptible, but wholly unworthy of belief. Whoever speaks against the Americans, is to receive implicit credit, and no questions asked. Whoever says anything in their favour, is to be told that he or she is a liar, and a knave, and a fool ; agreeably to the most approved rules of the aristocratical logic. It is needless to quote specimens of the Billingsgate poured forth upon Miss Wright. Enough that she is the abandoned prostitutor of the name and character of an " Englishwoman ".

The next specimen is the *Quarterly's* view of the perfection of English law—one of the numerous institutions to which England is indebted for its comforts, its security, and its prosperity. In tracing the causes that have forwarded the prosperity of the United States, we shall find *the foundation of them all to be laid in the English constitution and the English laws.*

Finally, as to Religion. There are two kinds of assumptions; the one set regarding the Ecclesiastical Establishment; the other, the Creed of the Church of England. Whoever questions the goodness of the Establishment is an enemy to the constitution, and a lover of anarchy. Whoever disputes the creed is an atheist, and being so, is exempt from all moral obligation, and ready for any and every crime. The Bible is an inspired test, to which all are willing to conform themselves. But without articles, a belief in the Bible would be equivalent to none, and end, perhaps, in general infidelity. This the Romanists hold in perfect consistency. To go the full length of the Romanists in condemning the Bible, and to take the composition of fallible men in its stead, can be nothing, says the author, but rank infidelity. Then follows a condemnation of the Church of England itself that, coming from any other quarter, would have been a proof of atheism and sedition. Her exorbitantly paid clergy is the only class of men that have not improved; they have even retrograded! No wonder, then, they are the enemies of improvement.

The tone respecting the Church is illustrated by the treatment of Mr. Hone for a work on the apocryphal gospels and epistles, written in a perfectly temperate spirit. His "sole aim is to destroy the credit of the New Testament, and to show that the most silly and drivelling forgeries can be supported by the same evidence which we use to establish the authority of the Scriptures". But, supposing such to be his opinion, as it was not, has he not as good a right to declare that opinion, as any other man has to declare a different opinion? The cause

of religion is disgraced by such a sentence as this, upon Mr.
Hone's reply :—" Having said that the pamphlet before us is
published by this notorious person, and put together by himself, or one of his party, we need not add that it is written in a
spirit of the most vulgar and contemptible ferocity." Again,
" He is a bold, bad man ; the wretched book by which he
attempts to pervert the faith, and destroy the happiness of
countless thousands " ; " that monstrous compound of ignorance, sophistry, and falsehood," &c.

The *Quarterly*, on such occasions, comes up nearly to the
mark of St. Jerome, who seems to be a favourite with its
reviewers. A few specimens of the Saint are given by way of
parallel.

On the matter of purity of mouth, the writer reverts to the
political articles for a few more instances. Cobbett, of course,
comes in for a liberal share of abuse—" a miscreant, a brutal
ruffian," " vulgar and ferocious spirit". The *Scotsman* newspaper, to which Mill pays a high compliment, in passing—not
merely for knowledge and talent, but for dignity and decorum
is delineated thus. " Even Cobbett (its admired prototype)
occasionally contrives to diversify the savage growl of the tiger
with the mop and mowe of the ape ; but the *Scotsman* never
lays aside the sulky ferociousness of the bear."

The only remaining topic is the Liberty of the Press, on
which the author quotes four pages of raving abuse ; winding
up with the demand for effectual suppression of the liberal
press. " It is only necessary to enforce the laws and to stop
the progress of sedition by such punishment as shall prevent
a repetition of the offence—any other is absurdly inappropriate."

The public events of this year need not be greatly pressed
into our service. The most notable aspect of the parliamentary
proceedings is the increasing extent and variety of topics
brought up for discussion. The old subjects, as Reform, State
of Ireland, Catholic Claims, Slavery, &c., are reproduced.

Education is coming more into the foreground. Hume attacks the Irish Church. Criminal Law Reform moves slowly. There are incidental discussions respecting various Import duties.

1825.

In the January number of the *Westminster*, appeared the review of Southey's *Book of the Church*.

Regarding the Church of England as a principal prop of our aristocratical system, the Radical reformers felt bound to include it in their onslaught upon that system. Mill had carefully prepared himself for this part of the campaign; and I am now to give a specimen of his manner of carrying on the attack. The fifth number of the *Review* contains his article on Southey's *Book of the Church*. This is the opening of the article.

"Misled by the name, we originally intended to place Mr. Bentham's *Book of the Church*, side by side with Dr. Southey's *Book of the Church;* that readers might have the 'bane and antidote' both before them. This idea was necessarily renounced as soon as we had read the volumes before us. What they furnish is not a Book of the Church, in any respectful sense of the word. It is an old woman's story-book; containing tales about the changes of religion, and the lives of the workers of wonders, in Great Britain, from the time of the people who set up rocking stones, and venerated the misletoe, to the time of those who sent our legitimate sovereign to count his beads at Rome."

The book, however, has put on the mask of history, and this needs to be torn off. It is the duty of the historian to state the evidence on both sides.

There are indications that the Church is falling into her dotage. The present book is one symptom. It is a poor imitation of a stale trick of the Romish church, in compiling the lives of her saints. A passage is then quoted giving the writer's design ; namely, to set forth at what a dear price the advantages of the Church Establishment were procured : " by what religious exertions, what heroic devotion, what precious lives consumed in pious labours, wasted away in dungeons, or offered up amid the flames ".

The writer of the article reduces the reasoning of the fore-going passage to a syllogism :—Every Church which can enumerate votaries who have suffered and lived in such a manner is an excellent church : Church of England can exhibit such votaries, witness the contents of the present pages : Church of England is an excellent church.

It is not what arguments are good, but what arguments will answer the purpose, that sometimes is the main look-out of an author. In this point of view, the reasoning of Mr. Southey may not be the worse for being absurd. The dignitaries of the church are active in circulating the book, hoping to get the same benefit that the Romanists have derived to their church from stories of the saints.

The author then shows what a vulgar fact in the history of human nature is the pride of voluntary endurance of suffering. But the martyrs of the Church of England were, according to Southey, not merely sufferers, but saints. Now saintship, says the writer of the article, hardly ever means anything else than a wonderful attention to the ceremonials of religion, with a superiority to the pleasures of sense. The fact is, however, the Church of England is remarkably ill supplied with the orna-ments of martyrdom and saintship. It is one of the remarkable things about her that she has produced so few men eminent for anything, even the priestly virtues, leaving altogether out of the question those moral and intellectual qualities by which the interests of the species are promoted. This book is the strongest proof of the assertion, seeing it is obliged to choose for the most distinguished ornament of the church such a man as Laud. The early part of the History, down to the com-mencement of Non-conformity can do no good, and will do little harm. The only exception taken by the reviewer is to Southey's determination in favour of Arminianism against Calvinism, which last he condemns as injurious in its consequences. The reviewer spends a page in putting him right upon this, and farther exposes his incapability to state the doctrine of the Manichæans.

An incautious attack upon the Romish Church for setting aside "the eternal standard of right and wrong, on which the unsophisticated heart unerringly pronounces" and for abusing the credulity of mankind, is retorted by the reviewer. Credulity is a delicate subject for a Church-of-Englandist to handle.

Mr. Southey imagined he had two things to do : one, to pull down the Church of Rome ; the other, to pull down the Dissenters. The Catholic critics are able to expose his rashness, ignorance, and groundless abuse, in dealing with their church. The present article is intended to expose the attack on Dissent : "to show to the friends of religious liberty, that they have a very zealous, at least, if not a very formidable adversary ".

The first thing is to exemplify his abusive language, of which two pages of choice expressions are given. One reflection is unavoidably suggested ; namely, such is not the style that naturally flows from the pure love of truth. If it is not assumed to answer a purpose, the author is most unfortunate in his taste, or else in his disposition.

A well-known Frenchman, Maimbourg, wrote a history of the Calvinists—the Non-Conformists, or Puritans, as Southey would call them, of France. One of these non-conformists, the celebrated Bayle, wrote a *Critique* upon this History. The resemblance of Maimbourg to Southey is so close, that Bayle's criticism is a valuable aid to Southey's critic ; who is glad to make use of a few passages from so great a master.

Mill then proceeds, in his own person, thus : When two parties in a state proceed to such extremities as to take up arms against one another ; there is superadded the utmost

endeavour to blacken the character of one another.   When the
Restoration placed all power in the hands of Charles II., the
arts of blackening character were exhausted against the vanquished Puritans.   What Mr. Southey has now done, is to
rake the filth thus arising, and to throw upon the memory of
the Puritans as much of it as he thought would stick.   The
reviewer, in exposing his arts, takes up first a part of the
pathetic story of Laud's confinement to the Tower, and quotes,
against Southey's version, Laud's own account of the situation
—a very different story.   He then takes note of Southey's
neglect to quote his authorities, and of his odd apology, namely,
his not wanting to make a display of research.

Executions and death-scenes are great things for vulgar
minds.   Southey knew this, and the dying scenes of Cranmer,
and Charles, and Wentworth, and Laud, have been mines to
him.

We might have thought we had lived to an era when the life
and deeds of Laud would no longer be held up to admiration.
But the Church of England seems to stand still ; yet she has
not sworn to retrograde.   The time certainly was, when her
leading men gave up Laud.   Warburton has nothing for him
but the severest condemnation.

The reviewer's own estimate of Laud brings to the foreground
by contrast his conception of the highest human virtue.   If
only for this reason, the following passage deserves to be given.

" Of all the crimes which it is possible for a human being to
commit against his fellow-creatures, that of corrupting the
springs of government is beyond all comparison the worst.
Other crimes strike at the well-being of one, or at most, of a
few individuals.   This strikes at the well-being of all the myriads, of whom the great body of the community is composed,
from generation to generation.   As no human being ever exerted
himself more strenuously, or with more persevering purpose to
corrupt the principles of government in any country, than did
Laud to corrupt to the heart the principles of government in

England, to strip the people of every security for the righteous administration of their affairs, by consequence to establish a perfectly infallible security for the mischievous administration of them, to place his countrymen in the condition of slaves, living only for the benefit of a master, a master, who both would desire to cultivate in them only the qualities which fit them the best for being slaves, the qualities of the spaniel, on the one hand, and the serpent on the other, and would have the power of preventing them from cultivating in themselves any other, of placing them, accordingly, in a condition resembling that of the worst of brutes—on the other hand, as of all the acts of virtue of which a human being is capable, that of ameliorating the institutions of government, of providing the community with more perfect securities for the right administration of their affairs, when all the facilities and all the motives for acquiring the highest intellectual and moral endowments and elevating their condition as men and as citizens to the highest possible degree, are enjoyed in the greatest perfection, is undeniably the highest, and every exertion and every sacrifice which is made by an individual for this noblest of all earthly purposes, acquires incomparable value, and entitles the maker to a correspondent share of moral and intellectual approbation, love, and esteem—as it is, moreover, an undoubted fact, that of all the men who, during his time, showed any portion of this virtue, Laud was the bitter and remorseless enemy, and with intensity proportional to the degree in which the virtue was displayed, as there was no punishment which he was not eager to inflict upon it, as he uniformly branded it with the names of the greatest vices, and endeavoured by all the arts by which characters are blackened to make the men who distinguished themselves by acts of this virtue be regarded as the greatest criminals and the most hateful of mankind ; as there was no suffering and no ignominy to which he was not eager to expose them, acting uniformly as if he wished to extinguish in their blood every spark of the virtue by which

19

they were distinguished—if all this, and more than this, be true, to the letter, then, of all the criminals on record, in the annals of the human species, Laud is one of the greatest."

A copious citation of facts follows this fearful denunciation. The article goes on : " The four names, in English history, which the Church, as a corporation of priests, have been most assiduous in their endeavours to hold up to admiration, are Charles I., Wentworth, Laud, and Clarendon ". An article in the preceding number of the *Review*, had given the means of estimating Charles and Wentworth. " We must, in order not to neglect any of these worthies, add a few particulars in regard to Clarendon, whom Mr. Southey declares to be the wisest, because the most upright of all statesmen." He here chiefly follows Brodie, in showing that Clarendon studiously sets himself " to pervert the materials of history, to suppress and mis-interpret evidence, to assert facts without any evidence at all, nay, in the very teeth of evidence ". His own pen records one of the most disgusting scenes of cant and hypocrisy ever acted. He was an approver, and a suborner of assassination. " The grand purposes of his life were those of a besotted, or intentional enemy of mankind ; to fix a despotical government upon the necks of his countrymen ; and to give vast wealth and power to a corporation of dependent priests, to enable them to act as the janisaries of that government." All these charges, which, in the intensity of the language, seem to resemble the style of abuse that the author reprobates in Southey, are supported at length by historical testimonies.

Next we have an exposure of Southey's misrepresentations of Neal, who wrote on the side of the Puritans. The article concludes with general reflections, very unfavourable to Ecclesiastical establishments in general, and to the Church of England in particular. The small number of eminent men produced by a church so highly favoured, is strongly commented on. Moreover, a corporation of priests is unfortunately situated with regard to all the highest moralities. They have

an interest in degrading the human mind.   Having the
powers of government in league with them, they have the
prospect of an extensive command over the minds of their
countrymen ; and thence a motive to strive to make that
command as irresistible and complete as possible.   For these,
and for many other reasons, the article concludes, it is intended
to show on a future occasion that a corporation of priests,
dependent on the government, is entirely Antichristian.   The
fulfilment of this intention, we shall presently see.

Two interesting letters in the *Life of Constable* are a help to
us for this year.   One is a long letter addressed to M'Culloch.
Some paragraphs omitted in the *Life* have been furnished to
me by Mr. Archibald Constable.

"CROYDON COMMON,
"*18th August, 1825.*

" MY DEAR FRIEND,
        " Your kind and gratifying epistle found me here,
commencing my holidays ; which I was prevented from taking,
as heretofore, in July.   I trust you feel yourself fully restored
from that too serious attack on your lungs, which seem to be
the only weak part about you.   You must be careful.   That
claret and champagne, which Napier mentions, must not
seduce.   You are also more tasked in London.   You must
therefore get up an abundance of health for that occasion.   *A
propos* of your London task, I conclude that you have received
by this time your letter from Mr. Bell.   He lamented, when I
last saw him, the delay ; which was owing to the difficulty of
coming at people, when dispersed, to get their signatures.
        " I am very much pleased indeed with that project of
Constable's, of which you speak.   Diffusion is now the
most important thing to be done for knowledge.   The two
essays to be written by you, especially that on Wages, will
render giant service.   By-the-bye, the second will include the
Corn Laws, and strong things on that subject, thus diffused,

will be invaluable. There was an excellent paragraph the other day in the *Scotsman*, stating the effect of the Corn-Laws in setting the rest of the community against the landlords, and showing the indispensable necessity of taking the monopoly of legislation out of their hands. The terror rising out of this view is the only thing which will work upon them. They must therefore be plied with it. I am gratified to learn that my essays are to be included. The information came in time to prevent another reprint, the second being all gone, and great demand remaining. It is much better they should be on sale. As I have made several corrections and little amendments for these reprints, Constable should print from the last; and I should like, if there is time, to go over them once more with care; if I can make a little more perfect that which was originally very imperfect, being all of them written against time, I shall be anxious to do it for this occasion, which is an admirable one. As they are the text-books of the young men of the Union at Cambridge, their appearing early will contribute to advertise Constable's project in a quarter not very accessible to hawkers, though of first-rate importance. Speaking of the Union—that Society, which owes its origin chiefly to you and John, is in a most flourishing way—upwards of a hundred names, several members of Parliament, some Lords, all among the young men likely to have the leading influence in the affairs of the next fifty years of their country. The effects cannot but be important. Good principles and talents will be equally advanced.

"Does your article in the Supplement make part of this cheap publication? or do you still retain your design of making it a book? I suppose you have seen by this time the review of your Discourse in the *Westminster*? John expresses great dissatisfaction with the behaviour of the editors. The whole was the joint production of him and Ellis : but they say that several important things were left out, and the article, by that and other editorial operations, disfigured. I sent an extract of that part of your letter which related to the strange delay in transmitting that review to Edinburgh to Bowring, for the purpose of belabouring Baldwin. By-the-bye, I suppose (indeed I hear) your *Edinburgh Review* people are in great wrath on the subject of the Parliamentary Reform article. On that subject, however, you deserve no quarter. It is of too great importance to let either puerilities or sophisms be there taken for wisdom. Oh, Party! Party! what a corrupter thou art!

"I have two weeks more of holidays. The Grotes are to be here all next week, when the memory of you will be frequently revived. Mr. J. Smith's family are again all well; it was Martin alone who was in danger. By the way, Cameron is the author of the article on Duelling in the last *Westminster*, which I mention because I think you will be pleased, as I was, with such a proof of his talent. You promised me a prospectus of Constable's proposed adventure : will you have the goodness to write to me with it, or following it, what I may or may not do, as to correcting and amending my articles ? "

"I have not been able to think of my Political Economy reprint. I am now absorbed by the phenomena of the human mind. If you were here, I would talk to you of nothing, but what you do when you think. I think I shall be able to tell you, to your satisfaction. Black desires to be remembered to you. He was here last Saturday and Sunday; and I told him the news of your letter. He is a great admirer of yours, though he says, it is hard, you will hold some opinions. He was running on precisely in the old way. Never was a man more *semper idem* than he. Best regards to Napier."

In Constable's List of publications for his Miscellany, Mill's articles in the reprint from the Supplement to the *Encyclopædia* were at first included, but were afterwards withdrawn. The reason for their withdrawal is not known. It is interesting to be told in the above letter that the articles had become text-

books in the Union at Cambridge.   We may presume that
Macaulay and Charles Austin had fought over them there.
There is a letter soon after to Constable himself.

"EAST INDIA HOUSE, *18th Oct., 1825.*

"MY DEAR SIR,

"I have just received, and with much satisfaction, your
kind communication.   Your project I think an admirable one,
and I shall be very glad to converse with you about it, because
I think it may receive important extension ; and after publication of works which are your own, may reproduce many things
which are of great interest, and are now to a great degree
inaccessible.   I even do not see why it may not become a
vehicle of essays and fugitive pieces in general, which have
never been published, and which it would draw out from the
portfolio of your literary friends, with profit to you and great
advantage to the public.

"It will give me great pleasure to take you by the hand once
more ; for I have never ceased to feel a deep interest in your
successful career, both for 'auld lang syne,' and because you
are the prince of booksellers.—With the most sincere regard,
yours, &c."

On the 9th December, Bentham writes a long letter to
Dumont, on the mode of designating his two functionaries—
Pursuer-general and Defender-general—which Dumont seemed
to have difficulty in rendering into French.   He introduces a
reference to Mill.   "Last night being Mill's visiting night
(Thursday), I put your letter into his hands.   He is in perfect agreement with everything you see here."

Allusion has already been made to one great event of this
year, the founding of the University of London.   The known
particulars, for the year, as regards Mill, have been anticipated.
From the record of Parliament, we find that on the 26th of
May, Brougham moved for leave to bring in a Bill for the
Incorporation of "London College".   It was, doubtless, at

this date that he wrote to Mill complaining of the refusal of the Ministry to grant a charter, from fear of the hostility of Oxford.

To summarize the Parliamentary discussions of this year would be to repeat the remarks on the year previous. We are now approaching the end of the existing Parliament; and, as one of Mill's most elaborate political articles consists in reviewing the transactions of that Parliament, I need say nothing farther until I come to the account of said article.

1826.

In the April number of the *Review* is the grand onslaught on *Ecclesiastical Establishments*.

The opening paragraphs present the theses to be maintained.

"We intend, on the present occasion, as far as our limits will permit, to examine to the bottom the question of an Ecclesiastical Establishment, and more especially of the Church of England, in its effect on religion, on morality, on the character and actions of the clergy, on learning, on education, and on government.

"We think it proper to begin by distinctly stating our opinion, that an ecclesiastical establishment is essentially antichristian; that religion can never be safe or sound, unless where it is left free to every man's choice, wholly uninfluenced by the operation either of punishment or reward on the part of the magistrate. We think it proper to go even further; and declare that it is not religion only to which an ecclesiastical establishment is hostile : in our opinion, there is not one of the great interests of humanity, on which it does not exercise a baneful influence.

"We know well to what we expose ourselves, by the promulgation of these great truths, for such they appear to us, and such we trust we shall establish them to be, by evidence which cannot be resisted. The clergy have, by a long course of usurpation, established a sort of right to call themselves and their interests by the most sacred names. In ecclesiastical language, the wealth and power of the clergy are religion. Be as treacherous, be as dishonest, be as unfeeling and cruel, be as profligate as you please, you may still be religious. But breathe on the interests of the clergy, make them surmise discredit at your hands, and you are the enemy of religion directly; nay, the enemy of your God; and all the mischief which religious prejudice and antipathy, the poisoned deadly weapon of the clergy, can bring down upon its victims, is the sure and necessary consequence of your sacrilegious audacity.

"For protection against this spirit of persecution, strong and formidable to the present hour, we look to public opinion, daily approaching to the condition of a match for this once gigantic foe; and the strong line which we trust we shall be able to draw between the interests of a corporation of priests, and those interests of religion about which alone good men can feel any concern.

"We desire also to be understood as disapproving an injustice of which clergymen have often great reason to complain, that of confounding the character of individuals with the corporation to which they belong. We have very many bad corporations, in which excellent men are included, and such is the case of the priestly corporation. But the question is not how many clergymen, from the influence of education, and the spirit of the community to which they belong, are, in their private relation, and taken individually, estimable men. You may take a number of men, one by one, all virtuous and honourable, who yet, if you club them together, and enable them to act in a body, will appear to have renounced every principle of virtue, and in pursuit of their own objects will trample, without shame or remorse, upon everything valuable to their fellow men."

He starts, as usual, from men's insatiable love of power. The ministers of religion are proverbially not less subject to this passion than other men. Acting singly, each confined to his own congregation, a minister's share of power is too small to prompt him to hazard much for its acquisition. It is on the large scale that the motive works to a mischievous degree. When the clerical class is aided by the magistrate in forming themselves into a body, to operate with united energy, they act under leaders possessed of the spirit to increase their powers without limit.

The clergy are peculiar in possessing an influence over men's minds, prior to, and irrespective of, their political position. Their power is the result of that peculiar influence.

He proceeds to trace the results. The first is, to enjoy a monopoly of influence; to allow no rivals. Rivalry requires vigilance; and the natural wish is to combine power with security, indolence, and repose. Nay more, as the competitors for spiritual influence resort to abstinence, self-denial, and mortification; so the corporate clergy, to maintain themselves, must use the same painful expedients.

How steadily they have pursued the impulse to extinguish rivals, history declares. The first and most conspicuous device has been, to apply to the magistrate for the powers of persecution. The author here reviews the early history of the church in illustration of this text.

"No time was lost. The first sovereign who protected the Christians was scarcely seated on his throne, when a fiery contest arose between the clergy of the Arian and the Athanasian creeds, for the possession of his ear. The Council of Nice, a memorable event, was summoned to determine the point, in other words, to satisfy the sovereign fully, which party, by its numbers and powers, it was most for his interest to join. The question was doubtful, and the balance for some time wavered. When the decision at last was made, and the Athanasian clergy became a distinguished body, with the power of government engaged for their support, what were the consequences? Even the cold narrative of Mosheim conveys a pungent sense of the zeal with which they proceeded to deliver themselves from all competition, in obtaining influence over the human mind ; their rage to establish a monopoly of spiritual dominion ; to accomplish the extermination of rivals.   Persecution flamed ; blood was spilt ; the non-conforming clergy, that is, non-conforming to the will of the leading divines, who now shared in the powers of government, were forbidden to teach : as often as they hazarded disobedience, they were thrown into prison, and subjected to other cruelties, not stopping short even of death.

"And above all things, great pains were taken to destroy their books.

"This was a capital point.   Books were the most dangerous, and of course the most hated enemies, of a monopolising clergy.   No truths, not for their advantage ; no exposure of lies which were ; therefore no books but their own."

Their strong and persevering purpose proved fatally effectual, as regarded the destruction of the very numerous writings of the early Christian sects.   Not only so, but the memory of these sects was handed down to execration, by general accusations of the most disgusting vices, and the most atrocious crimes.

The word "heretic" shows the bent of the clerical mind. Exactly rendered, this word means *choice*.   The crime of heresy was the crime of making a choice.

The author makes a passing allusion to the progressive assumptions of the church, the giving and taking away of crowns, the accumulation of wealth by extorting gifts ; and then, by a series of extracts from Campbell's Ecclesiastical History, he proceeds to show the growth of persecution, down to the setting up of the Inquisition.   "These are specimens of the evidence with which history teems of the persecuting spirit of the first great incorporation of priests.   The priestly incorporation called the Church of England stands next in power ; and, as a natural consequence, next, also, in the ranks of persecution."

He then reviews the leading epochs of the English church. It is astonishing how soon this church lost sight, or lost regard, of the inevitable conclusion, that, if she had a right, on the inference of error, to separate from the church of Rome, others had as good a right, on the same inference, to separate from her.

Hardly was the authority of the church of Rome renounced, when diversity of opinion began to give uneasiness to the leaders of the clergy. The primacy of Whitgift sets going the machinery of persecution, by the new ecclesiastical court, which he induced the queen to create ; a court, characterized by Hume, as a real *inquisition*, attended with all the injustice, as well as cruelties, inseparable from that tribunal.

The author then passes to Laud, but, having previously set forth his career, he is now content with a summary remark, " That he was a relentless persecutor, is saying little. With such an impetuous rage of persecution was he driven, that, undeterred by all that opposition which public opinion now obviously presented to him, he went on, recklessly, to raise the storm, in which the church and the monarchy were both levelled with the ground."

The Act of Uniformity is the next scene in the drama. The author is sufficiently satisfied with Hume's judgment upon this measure. The reign of the last two Stuarts was farther marked by the persecutions, hardly surpassed for savage barbarity by any with which the page of history is stained, carried on for the establishment of episcopacy in Scotland.

The epoch of the Revolution gave birth to a new order of things. From that day the people assumed the right of thinking, and of delivering their thoughts, both respecting government and respecting religion. The spirit was nourished by the new regime, which, when assailed by the adherents of the old, had to assume for the people the right to decide for themselves on the goodness or badness of every institution. To this situation, we owe the sober and manly views on government given forth by Locke and other eminent writers. In such a state of the public mind, the clergy had to proceed with caution. Yet, as the History of Burnet shows, their hand was still at work. But for the fortunate accident, that the king was able to nominate a sufficient number of bishops to give the crown a majority in the upper House of Convocation, and secure Burnet both for that house and for the house of Peers, the government of William and Mary might have been over-thrown; and a return to the former slavery of the nation, or else a new civil war, would have been the consequence. The author gives copious extracts from Burnet as illustrative of the clerical proceedings.

" It is well known in what manner the feeble and disjointed ministry, maintained by Queen Anne at the close of her reign, were dependent upon the church, and tools in its hands. It is also well known what measures were in progress, and would have been successful, but for the premature death of the queen and the insane squabbles among her ministers, for the restora-tion of the Pretender, and the barter of the liberties of England, for privileges, *alias* persecuting powers, to the church."

In those circumstances, the accession of the House of Hanover was a great relief. Walpole so long repressed the efforts of the church that the nation was familiarized to a mode of thinking inconsistent with a monopoly of the religious influence. The church manifested itself in clinging to the portion of power still left. One great example of this is furnished by the history of the Test and Corporation Acts, and the obstinate resistance to Catholic Emancipation. But the author devotes his remaining pages chiefly to illustrate the proceedings against heretics. He first adduces Blackstone, because, as a lecturer in Oxford, he had to look to his popula-rity in the University, and his interest with the church, for his promotion. Certain passages are quoted from the first edition of the Commentaries, with the remark, that, finding the spirit of the age would not bear what the spirit of the clergy had suggested, he materially altered his phraseology in the succeeding editions. The language used by Blackstone is severely commented on as deceptive and fraudulent; insinuating, without plainly declaring, the necessity of punishing diversity of opinion or of worship to any extent short of the old plan, no longer permissible, of extermination and destruction. It is indecent, according to Blackstone, to set up private judgment in public: that is, simply to have private judgment. Besides being indecent, private judgment is arrogant. Finally, it is an act of ingratitude; for, says this bold champion, it desires "that indulgence and liberty of conscience to the natural church, which the retainers to every petty conventicle enjoy". That is to say, nobody, not even the members of the church, may speak against the tenets set forth in the conventicles!

The Liberty of the Press gives the final illustration, as shown in connexion with heresy and dissent. When the enemies of this great instrument were unable to prevent its existence, they could equally show their enmity, in endeavouring to cramp its operation. When the system of licensing was abolished in England, severe punishment was provided against free discussion in matters of religion and of government, the two sources of greatest evil to mankind when made subservient to the purposes of the few against the many. The hateful powers thus conferred, the clergy have, until the present hour, shown the greatest disposition to employ. Having already alluded to the position of the English law regarding heresy, as expounded by Blackstone, the author briefly touches on the memorable prosecutions of the last century. The first is the case of William Whiston, the friend and successor of Newton, who underwent a merciless persecution for dissenting from the Athanasian creed.

The next case is discussed at some length, as being a leading case with the lawyers. It implicated poor unfortunate Woolston, who got into deeper mire than Whiston, by allegorizing the miracles of the New Testament. The government "fell upon him," says the narrator, and had him indicted for

blasphemy and profaneness.   It was moved, in arrest of judgment, that the offence was not punishable in the temporal
courts.   But the judges declared, they would not allow this to
be argued—" for the Christian religion is established in this
kingdom ; and therefore they would not allow any books to be
written which should tend to alter that establishment ".   That
is to say, it does not matter whether what is established be true
or false, good or evil.   The Court added—" Christianity was
part of the law ; that whoever derided Christianity, derided
therefore the law ".   On this the author remarks—we have
here a case of the fraudulent use of language, already seen in
Blackstone.   The "law" in its proper acceptation means the
whole body of the securities provided for all that is dear to us.
To weaken the force of these securities is highly criminal.
"Law" has another meaning, namely, any part or parcel of
the whole body of enactments ; and, it may be, a noxious part,
tending to impair our security.   To cut off such parts is to
improve the law.   If nothing that is part and parcel of the law
is to be free to the press, nothing is free.* .

The Court gave no attention to Woolston's plea that he did
not mean to attack Christianity.   Such profession on his part
was not to be credited, as being opposed to the fact.   What
fact?   Writing a certain opinion about miracles.   This fact
Woolston allowed ; he denied that he did injury to Christianity.
The Court said he did ; but that was matter, not of fact, but
of opinion.

The Chief Justice said—" We do not meddle with differences
of opinion : we interfere only when the very root of Christianity
was struck at ".   Wholly untrue, they meddle with nothing
but differences of opinion, in the case of religious libels.
Which is the root, and which is a branch of Christianity is
purely a matter of opinion.

* Bentham's comment on the doctrine that Christianity is a part of the law
of the land, is still more incisive.   If that be so, he says, any violation of a
precept of the New Testament is an indictable offence.

The author comments severely upon the existence of contradictory maxims in our law, by which the judges can be as despotic as they please. It is important for the sake of appearances to say, " Let the liberty of the press be sacred ". Under this everything is free. It is important to have another maxim—" Let the licentiousness of the press be prevented ". By this everything may be punished.

From the time of Woolston's prosecution to the French Revolution, there was little scope for using the powers of the law to crush the freedom of the press in religion. The spirit of the age would not allow dissenting religious sects to be meddled with : and with respect to infidelity, the situation of the clergy was perplexing. It was chiefly men of rank, or writers of very high reputation, that called Christianity in question—Lord Shaftesbury, Lord Chesterfield, Lord Kaimes, Hume, Gibbon, Adam Smith ; and with a formidable enemy, the clergy are inclined to avoid a dispute. Moreover, infidelity was a fashion in Europe, for the fifty years preceding the French Revolution. Prosecutions were then too hazardous to be insisted on. Nevertheless, the unabated rancour of the clergy towards the liberty of the press is shown in their sermons and other writings. This applies to the most illustrious of them ; to men of great powers, and of great virtues, as Berke-ley, Clarke, Tillotson, and Barrow.

From Barrow, our author gives examples of " mendacious calumny " applied to unbelievers ; representing them as capable of every private vice, as well as of revolutionary practices against government. He indicates, without quoting, passages from Tillotson, Barrow, and Clarke, of a like tendency ; and finishes with a few morsels from Warburton, which it is unnecessary to cite.

In conclusion, the author intimates that he has yet to overtake the further effects of an Established Church in depraving both religion and morality, in corrupting education and government, in retarding the progress of the human mind, and in degrading the character, intellectual and moral, of the clergy, and promises to do so on some future occasion. The occasion never came.

In the number of the *Westminster* for July, there is an article entitled *Formation of Opinions*, ostensibly a review of the second edition of Samuel Bailey's book on that subject, but more strictly an examination of a work by the eminent congregationalist preacher, Dr. Ralph Wardlaw of Glasgow, in reply to a famous utterance of Brougham—that man is not responsible to man for his belief, over which he has himself no control. A great deal of controversy grew out of this declaration, which to many seemed to open up the floodgates of universal scepticism It was a good opportunity to Mill, whose mind was always in a state of surcharge upon the question of free enquiry. He had at his command an endless store of quotations, as material for the argument from authority; and his own subtlity of mind provided him with nice distinctions. He is easily able to show that if evidence is laid fully before the mind, the impression produced by it is independent of the will, just as a man must see what is before his open eyes. It is not at this point, that we can evade the force of legitimate proof. We can, however, refuse admittance to an object of sight, by looking elsewhere, or by keeping the eyes shut; so we can blind ourselves to the influence of reasoning and evidence by withdrawing the attention. After disposing of Wardlaw, our author mounts the pulpit himself, and delivers a lay sermon on the Sin of Believing without Evidence. Seeing that he has had few followers or imitators, the topic is not yet thread-bare, like so many others; and a few short quotations may not be unwelcome to the reader. At all events, they contribute to our purpose of setting forth the man.

" There are two propositions, therefore, of the greatest certainty, and the greatest importance.

" The first is this, that, as the mind is passive in belief, and the will, to use the words of Dr. Clarke, has nothing at all to do with it, neither merit nor demerit can ever be ascribed to belief, without the utmost confusion of ideas, and the risk of a deplorable train of the most immoral consequences.

" The second is, that, as the mind is not passive in what it does relating to evidence, but has all the activity which is implied in its most voluntary exertions, merit or demerit may be justly ascribed to it.

" On his mode of dealing with evidence, the good or evil application of the powers of the man, in other words, the greatest possible degree either of virtue or of vice, almost wholly depends."

Proper dealing with evidence consists of two things. First, the full collection of it ; secondly, the equal reception of it.

The first point, fulness of collection, does not need a lengthened demonstration. The second, equality of reception, brings up the influence of bias, partiality, and the affections, and several pages are occupied with explaining and expressing it. In the first place, it requires that we have no affection to the one side more than to the other. On this head, the author adduces a few of the strong cases of the operation of self-interest and affection in swaying belief ; and urges upon us to begin the examination of every question by asking ourselves —Have I an affection on either side ? If so, as we cannot get rid of the affection, we must endeavour to allow for it. This was what Locke recommended so strongly under the name " Indifferency ".

The next thing is, that equal evidence, on the different ideas, should be treated as equal, that is, have equal effects. This is substantially the same thing in another aspect ; and is rendered difficult solely by the malign bias of the affections.

The author's strain of exhortation is shown in the following energetic passage :—

" This habit of forming opinions, and acting upon them without evidence, is one of the most immoral habits of the

20

mind. Only observe what it imports. As our opinions are the fathers of our actions, to be indifferent about the evidence of our opinions is to be indifferent about the consequences of our actions. But the consequences of our actions are the good and evil of our fellow-creatures. The habit of the neglect of evidence, therefore, is the habit of disregarding the good and evil of our fellow-creatures. It is the habit of hard-heartedness, and cruelty, on the largest scale, and rooted in the deepest part of the mind. This habit is the foundation of most of what is vicious and degraded in human character. The habit of disregarding the evidence of our opinions, with the habit necessarily involved, of disregarding the consequences to our fellow-creatures, of the actions founded upon those opinions, are the elements of a character, in which the general temptations to vice operate without any counteracting motive ; and as such a man is essentially without virtue, so it must be by a rare concurrence of accidents, if he is not deep in vice.

" Seeing the malignant nature of this habit, it is a melancholy reflection, that it is the general habit of mankind, and of none more than of our dear countrymen. How rare is it to meet with a man, who has almost ever concerned himself about evidence ; who has not adopted opinions, as he has adopted words, solely because they were used by other people ? This is a dreadful vice of education. One of the grand objects of education should be, to generate a constant and anxious concern about evidence ; to accustom the mind to run immediately from the idea of the opinion to the idea of its evidence, and to feel dissatisfaction till it is known that the evidence has been all before the mind, and fairly weighed. When the case is directly the reverse, when the habit is almost universal, of stopping at the opinion, without going on to a thought of the evidence, without an association of any the smallest feeling of dissatisfaction with an opinion the evidence of which has not been explored, we may be perfectly sure that education in that country is in the wrong hands, and that it is nearly in its most deplorable state.

"The effects are dreadful. How, but for the habit, almost general, of neglecting and disregarding evidence, could the progress of mankind in improvement be so very slow! How else could errors, of the grossest as well as most pernicious kind, be propagated, and the abominable actions which are grounded upon them, be repeated, from generation to generation? How could institutions, at variance with the interests of the community, which are a mockery of human nature, and act as a pestilential atmosphere upon the race, hold their endless existence, if the human mind was not ruined by the habit of adopting opinions, without evidence?"

He has various flings at the clergy in general. "Why is their praise and blame bestowed upon that which has neither merit nor demerit, belief and disbelief; and withheld from that which may possess the greatest, full and impartial enquiry, or the opposite?

"Not only do they attach a merit and demerit to mere belief, they attach consequences of unspeakable importance to the holding or not holding certain opinions; the favour or disfavour of Almighty God, and pains, or pleasures, infinite and eternal. Is it possible, that a mind, with these impressions upon it, can come to the examination of any question, touching those opinions, without affection, so much on one side, that no evidence on the other can have any effect?

"Instilling opinions, without the evidence, and at an age when the parties into whom the opinions are instilled, are incapable of understanding the evidence, is a practice which necessarily engenders habits of complicated misconduct towards evidence."

Besides dilating upon this topic, he brings to his aid "the sincere and honest mind of Locke," who fully understood "the rank misconduct of the clergy in this respect, and its direful consequences".

In conclusion, he remarks that " Wardlaw is prodigiously in earnest to convince the world, that the scripture attaches the greatest merit to faith, and the greatest demerit to the want of it. We know not that so much effort, on this subject, was necessary : but, be that as it may, this at least is certain, that the scripture can inculcate nothing that is absurd in point of reason, or mischievous in point of morality." " It is not belief which is called, in the scripture, faith, but the proper dealing with evidence." " Faith, in short, has nothing to do with creeds. Of two men, the one even an atheist, the other a sound believer, it may be that the atheist is the man who has faith, according to the scripture ; that the sound believer is the man who is destitute of faith, according to the scripture ; that the atheist is possessed of all the merit, the sound believer of all the demerit, which the scripture ascribes to the possession, or the want, of that saving grace."

In the number following, October, is a political article, entitled—State of the Nation.

The article takes a wide sweep. In adverting to the questions more immediately pressing, it takes a historical view of the situation, and never loses an opportunity of commenting upon the aristocratical constitution of the Legislature.

The first few pages are occupied with the policy of the French war. " This nation has enjoyed, if it can be called enjoyment, some years of peace since the termination of one of the most wasteful wars that ever nation waged, since nations existed on the earth : a war not begun in self-defence, for where were we attacked ? a war not begun for conquest, for we had no desire to add to our territory : a war, then, for what ? A war against ideas ! Whose ideas ? The supposed, the imputed ideas of a part of the population of a neighbouring nation."

France had got possession of horrid ideas ! What had we to do with the horrid ideas of the people of France ? If horrid

to themselves they would soon have had to bear the consequences. But then, this country might adopt them. That is,
we in this country abominated the ideas so much, that we
went to war to prevent ourselves from adopting them! In
point of fact, the ideas were horrid to our Aristocracy; they
suggested popular ascendency, and had to be stifled by every
possible machination. A new power had arisen, that of public
opinion. "The legislating class did not well understand it;
but they guessed that it boded them no good. The strength
of their endeavours, therefore, was directed against it. Everything was done to crush public opinion. Law after law was
enacted to punish assemblies of the people, and to prevent the
expression of their opinions in large bodies. Law after law
was passed to restrict the liberty of the press, to render the
dissemination of opinions in general difficult and costly, the
dissemination of some opinions, those called dangerous, that is,
unfavourable to the monopoly of power in the hands of a
particular class, in a high degree penal."

He then traces the numerous ramifications of the enormous
debt. Among the items in the state of the country may be
enumerated, as standing in the first rank, prodigal expensive-
ness on the part of the government; and, consequent upon
this, and inseparable from it, the vice, in the aristocratical
class, of living upon the labour of others. An enormous
enhancement of both evils we owe to the war waged against
the horrid ideas of the leading party in France, the war for
quieting aristocratical apprehensions, and consolidating aristocratical power. Enormous fleets and armies during the war
paved the way for enormous establishments during peace; the
nation was inured to such a state—the aristocracy to hold the
lucrative posts, the nation to pay the expense. The ministers
had to keep up the system for the sake of their partisans.

The next topic in the survey—the fluctuations in the state
of industry—introduces the alterations in the currency, the
corn laws and the usury law: which are all touched with the

author's usual vigour. He then notices the low condition of the labouring classes. "The condition of the people is low, and their numbers superabundant, because they are stupid, because no pains have been taken with their understandings, and because a bad morality is propagated through the nation. Why is it not felt by the labouring men to be infamous to live upon the labour of others? If it were so, a numerous brood, sprung from the engendering of a base couple unable to support them, would be as rare a phenomenon in the immoral world as robbery and murder. It is true that the progress of civilization has not been without its influence on the lower classes. Their deportment has improved, riot and drunkenness have diminished, and reading is more diffused. But here occurs a serious difficulty. An Irish population, wretched and degraded, is pouring into the country. If this is unchecked, it may keep wages down to the starving degree, whatever the prudence and morality of the English population. A wise and beneficent legislature would lose no time in seeking a remedy."

The author next reverts to his old subject, the composition of the House of Commons. The symptoms of coming change now began to be traceable. Obedience to government, in the last resort, depends on opinion. But, whereas, in the former times, governments fashioned opinions, the people of England at present form opinions for themselves; a novelty that existing governments naturally under-estimate. The legislature is often puzzled to know what is the matter with it. The ministry, more particularly, feels its stability affected by its popularity. The inherent incompetency of the House of Commons, as a result of its composition, is beginning to be better understood; the efforts for improving it have almost ceased. "What are we to augur from this? Are the wise men of practice satisfied that the silence of the people is the indifference of the people? Are they fully assured that there is not a spirit collecting, which, like a fixed air, will issue with unexpected force, when the moment of disengagement arrives?

What if the people have ceased to importune the legislature from something more deep-rooted than the want of prospect of success? Their present repose is rather an indication of confidence than of despair, and of strength, if strength consists in wisdom, rather than of weakness. The people can afford to wait, and they know it." "Yes; the people must wait the birth of events. The womb of time will not be found barren. The petitions of the people for reform of parliament will not be met with laughter by-and-bye."

After remarking on the diffusion of Literature and Education, and the growth of Mechanics' Institutes, he has some telling remarks upon the improvement of upper and middle-class education (describing, as he usually does, the middle class as the strength of the country). He adverts to the recent start of the University of London, and to the jealousy manifested towards it by the old universities: the effect in the end will be that Oxford and Cambridge will themselves be improved.

He next devotes himself to a celebrated topic of the time, the so-called "Equitable Adjustment" of the National Debt. After the suspension of cash payments in 1797, paper was issued in such quantity as materially to reduce the value of the currency. The interest of the then debt was paid in the degraded currency; the national creditor getting less than his due. While the depreciation lasted, new debt was contracted in the depreciated currency. On the return to cash payments, the interest was paid in a currency more valuable than when the loans were made. On this account, said the landlords, 30 per cent. should be deducted from the interest of the national debt. The whole transaction is strongly condemned as confiscation, and leads to a train of remarks upon the necessity of having regard to the rights of property, in a time of pending revolutionary change. "The insecurity of property, in times of transit from one state of government to another, constitute almost wholly the evils that attend them." "If the aristocracy commit an act of confiscation upon a class of their fellow-citizens, they may be assured that it will suggest the idea of another confiscation when the monopoly of the powers of government is made to quit their hands."

In a few remarks on the improvement of the Law, he praises the efforts of Peel. "Let us give our assistance to Mr. Peel, and believe that his timidity will give other men courage; perhaps, in the end, will give it to himself."

Ireland supplies the peroration. It is the great drawback upon the energy and resources of England; the foremost among our mountainous burdens. There is the genuine picture, the *beau idéal* of an aristocratic government. Had the Irish aristocracy rested on its own strength, it would have carried misrule only as far as the Irish people would bear. Being sure of English soldiers, it had no motive to set any limit to its oppressions. How one detestable thing grows out of another, and another out of that, and so on, without end! It would go a great way to a remedy, if we would withdraw the English soldiers, and leave the parties there to settle their quarrels among themselves. The expedient thing for England would be, at once to dissolve her connexion with Ireland, and to live with her as good neighbours only. It could never be the interest of Ireland, unless by some very gross misconduct of ours, to join with our enemies in war; and, if she did, she would add to their dangers, not to ours.

So ends the connexion with the *Westminster Review;* and the more the pity. The *Review* was still carried on, on the same principles; but there was great mismanagement in separating from it its most powerful writers. Bowring, as editor, kept up the connexion with Bentham; and the new proprietor is said to have expended upon it a thousand a-year, for the seven years that it was in his hands.

According to John Mill, his father gave way to pressure and wrote an article about three years after withdrawing; he himself, the more unyielding of the two, absolutely refused. The father's article will be noticed in course.

His holiday this autumn was spent at Dorking. We have no particulars of his occupation there, except from a letter to Dr. Thomson, of date 30th October, with special reference to the filling up of the Chemistry chair in University College. I give the extract on that subject.

"I would give a good deal of money out of my own pocket to have you in the projected University; and I have no doubt that the acquisition of you would be reckoned invaluable by the whole of the Council. I cannot, however, venture to predict that the situation will be such as to indemnify you for the honourable and important station which you now hold. I can have no doubt that your reputation and the popularity of the science would ensure you a very numerous audience from the beginning. The funds of the Institution, however, will allow but little in the way of salary, and it is not proposed to make the admission fee more than moderate. I shall, however, send you more full particulars as soon as the subject comes under discussion, which I hope will now be soon; and I am sure it will be reckoned a proud circumstance by the Council when they are told that you would become chemical professor, if the situation were made such as to be a compensation for that which you must relinquish to obtain it. Your suggestions respecting the class are most important, and together with any other with which you may favour us, will meet with the greatest attention."

A few scraps of personalities are added. "Black busy with his *Morning Chronicle*, and cheerful and happy as usual." Poor Lowe not prosperous.

1827.

The principal event to be recorded for this year is the appearance of an important political article in the periodical called *The Parliamentary History and Review;* of which John Mill gives the following account.

" Mr. Marshall, of Leeds, father of the present generation of Marshalls, the same who was brought into Parliament for Yorkshire, when the representation forfeited by Grampound was transferred to it, an earnest Parliamentary reformer, and a man of large fortune, of which he made a liberal use, had been much struck with Bentham's Book of Fallacies : and the thought had occurred to him that it would be useful to publish annually the Parliamentary Debates, not in the chronological order of Hansard, but classified according to subjects, and accompanied by a commentary pointing out the fallacies of the speakers.   With this intention, he very naturally addressed himself to the editor of the Book of Fallacies ; and Bingham, with the assistance of Charles Austin, undertook the editorship.   The work was called *Parliamentary History and Review*.   Its sale was not sufficient to keep it in existence, and it only lasted three years.   It excited, however, some attention among parliamentary and political people.   The best strength of the party was put forth in it ; and its execution did them much more credit than that of the *Westminster Review* had ever done.   Bingham and Charles Austin wrote much in it ; as did Strutt, Romilly, and several other Liberal lawyers.   My father wrote one article in his best style ; the elder Austin another.   Coulson wrote one of great merit."

It was in the second volume of the series that the article appeared.   Instead of a survey limited to the previous session of Parliament, the dissolution gave occasion to take a wider sweep and to review the outcome of the legislation of the six years—1820-1826.

There had been, during the recent sesssion (1826), two important debates in the House of Commons, relative to Parliamentary Reform ; one, on the motion of Mr. Abercrombie, to bring in a bill to amend the representation of Edinburgh, by substituting the householders for the Town Council, in whom the suffrage was vested : this was defeated by 122 to 97.   The other was, on the motion of Lord John

Russell—"That the present state of the representation of the people of England requires the serious consideration of this house ". The debates were comparatively short ; Canning spoke in the first, while the speech of Hobhouse in the second was a masterpiece. In the same session, Lord John Russell brought in a bill, and moved resolutions, for the prevention of Bribery at Elections.

Mill's contribution to the volume for 1826 is divided into two parts. The first part relates to the three proposals just named.

As usual he starts from his theory of representation based on the responsibility of the governing body to the people at large, and reviews the House of Commons in the light of this principle. Alluding to the influence of public opinion through the press, he says—"it is plain, from the continued evidence of jobbing and depredation, that public opinion, even aided by a partially free press, is not a sufficient safeguard for the interests of all ". Hence no adequate remedy can be expected till the power of choosing the representatives is vested in a considerable portion of the people.

He then considers Lord John Russell's plan—to take, say, a hundred of the decayed boroughs, returning two members, and transfer one of these to the counties and to the large towns of recent growth. This he considers would make matters worse, by playing directly into the hands of the great landowners. So long as bribery and intimidation are possible, the number of real electors would not be increased. We should still have all the disadvantages of landlord legislation ; both the sinister interest and the intellectual incapacity of men born in a position that deprives them of all motives to the acquirement of knowledge. He then urges the adoption of the Ballot, as the only means of securing a broader basis of election whether in county or in town. He denounces the riot and tumult of elections, which some theorists were so fond of eulogizing. " The plan for keeping up public spirit, or a love of liberty, as it is sometimes called, by periodical saturnalia, it is past our faculties to comprehend."

After disposing of the influence-of-property argument, which is, in other words the influence of landed proprietors, he criticizes the curious argument that Lord John Russell thought necessary to adduce for Reform, as being a restoration of our ancient rights.   So Hobhouse talked of *restoring the House of Commons to its original purity.*   He answers Hobhouse's remark as to the necessity of an aristocratical opposition to the Crown, by showing that there is no such opposition.   On a few trifling questions, the opposition part of the House of Commons harass ministers, in order to get into their places ; but let the question be one of principle, to give the people the choice of their representatives, or to stop extravagance in the gross, where is the eloquence, and what are the divisions ? There is talk about the evils of bribery, but upon the evils of intimidation, Lord J. Russell says not a word.   He has a fling at his friend Brougham for trying to support bribery by declaring it illegal to pay the electors *after* the election, and recommends him to propose the experiment of the ballot.   He touches slightly upon Canning's speech in the debate on Edinburgh, but reserves a thorough handling for his next part. To the hackneyed argument—Where are you to stop? he replies with a smartness that would bear reproduction in a newspaper at the present hour.   It says to the House—you must reject this measure, although unobjectionable, because you are so stupid, that if you permit this to pass, you would not have the sense to reject others, however objectionable.

The second part of the contribution is entitled "Summary Review of the Conduct and Measures of the Seventh Imperial Parliament": (elected April 23, 1820, and dissolved June 2, 1826).

His exordium is still the theme of our aristocratical constitution, with ever-varied illustrations.   After this he notes one improvement in the practice of government in recent times.

The governing class has renounced interference with personal protection. They have found the machinery of taxation the most commodious instrument for getting an undue share of the property of the people. For taxation, pretexts are necessary. The war of the French Revolution came conveniently.

He then introduces the efforts of Joseph Hume to expose the system of extravagance : a man had at last appeared, upon whom the ill usage of the House had little effect.

He next passes to the improvement of the Law, which again brings up reflections on the intellectual inaptitude of our governing class. Beyond the sphere of ordinary talk, and a very narrow and superficial observation, they are conscious of mere mental vacuity. A comprehensive view of the great subject of law, they find a task as little suited to their ability, as it is to their inclination. The end of the late Parliament saw the state of the law, with some trifling alterations, the same as at the beginning. Sir James Mackintosh brought in six bills, founded on the report of a Committee of the preceding Parliament for applying milder punishments than death to certain crimes. Only a part was carried, and the whole would have been trifling. Minute alterations are to be deprecated ; working in the small way is apt to be taken as a substitute for working in the great. To overcome reluctance and opposition the object must be large enough to give an interest. Lord Liverpool had adverted to the defect in our system arising from a want of secondary punishments of sufficient efficacy. Here was an opportunity for trying Bentham's Penitentiary.

The fate of Lord Althorp's bill for the county courts was sufficiently illustrative, being rejected by large majorities. The question—whether counsel should be allowed to prisoners on trials for felony, offers occasion for critical remarks. The lawyers, headed by the Attorney-General, Sir John Copley, refused this permission.

He then comes to the proposals for Parliamentary Reform, on which the last Parliament witnessed four debates, besides

the disfranchisement of Grampound.   Two schemes were propounded; one by Mr. Lambton, one by Lord John Russell.
Mr. Lambton would substitute for the cities and boroughs
election districts, and admit all householders to the suffrage;
the counties to remain, with the admission of lease-holders and
copyholders; the duration of Parliaments to be reduced to
three years.   All this would be nugatory without the ballot.
The scheme was disposed of in a house of not more than one
hundred present.

The Chancellor of the Exchequer (F. J. Robinson) had
advanced the stock argument, that public opinion governs the
house   The reply is—government must of course observe
public opinion; it must study the arts of misleading and
eluding, and, for the purpose of eluding, must occasionally
obey it.   But if public opinion be all-sufficient to secure good
government, what need have we of a House of Commons at
all?   Would not a House of Lords answer our purpose as
well?

Lord John Russell brought forward his motion four times.
The first was on the 9th of May, 1821, when he had the
speaking all to himself.   On the second occasion (1822),
Canning and Peel spoke, among others.   The third time was
in April, 1823; and the fourth, in the present session, a few
weeks before the general election.

The author's remarks on these debates are sufficiently
pungent.   His first point is that Lambton and Lord John were
left to fight their battle almost alone.   Brougham, Mackintosh,
and Tierney were silent.   Their motives can only be conjectured.   It is not easy to conceive that such men should not
have made the calculation how much it must affect the reputation of themselves individually, and of the party they lead, if a
Parliament of seven years' duration should begin and end,
without their having once unlocked their lips on the subject of
Parliamentary Reform.   Canning, with his accustomed alacrity
of attack, presented them with something to do.   And Sir

Francis Burdett—why had he not a word to say for his own "good old.cause"? What has he now to recommend him to the people of Westminster?

So much importance is attached to the exquisite fencing of Canning, in defence of the predominant interest in the House, and to the stabs and slashes that he deals upon those that draw their weapons against it, that some notice of his speech is thought necessary.

"At an early age, Mr. Canning proclaimed himself the champion of the power of the aristocracy; and sedulously and successfully did he cultivate the talents which were best adapted to the task he had undertaken. As a man of ambition, he chose his walk with skill. By what other career could he have attained the power and consequence to which he has ascended? This is one of the evils attached to the predominance of a particular interest in the legislature. The rewards it has to bestow pervert, and draw off, to the service of a part, some of the finest spirits which the country breeds."

One thing remarkable is that, on this occasion, Canning entirely renounced the tone of mockery and insult that he had been accustomed to, when the popular interests were put forward. Possibly he found that this no longer aided the cause; probably also he had become ashamed of so mean an exercise of his talents. His speech consisted, first, of objections to the specific plans of reform, and, second, of his usual display against reform itself. The first was an easy task; in the second, there is mighty little matter, but that little exceedingly well managed.

He makes good use of the influence of public opinion argument. It was assumed that the House of Commons ought to resist public opinion when wrong; and this it would not do if the aristocratical interest did not predominate. The author's reply to this may now be left to the reader's imagination. Let us attend to the analysis of Canning's rhetorical method. Of all the orators of modern times, Canning is

perhaps the man that has carried to perfection the art of insinuation.   Instead of repeating twenty times in one speech the
stock arguments—The Constitution is excellent, Alteration is
dangerous—he insinuates them twenty times in twenty different
forms of language.

The author then examines the meaning of these bulwarks of
anti-reform.   Canning affirms that under the English government, the English people have not only continued a people,
but also been happy and prosperous.   *Ergo*, the English
government is an excellent government.   Reply :—That the
English people have continued a people is true ; it is a dreadful
government that suffices to destroy a people.   Then, what is
the degree of happiness and prosperity that is the test of the
goodness of a government ?   The English people are the most
productive in the world ; and the government has not taken
everything from them.

The cry of the danger of change will not always frighten
people.   A civil war would create evil in abundance, but the
aristocracy of England will have wisdom to avoid that ex-
tremity.   As Earl Grey happily said, "The voice of the nation,
growing louder and stronger, will work upon the prudence of
the House".

He gives special praise to Ricardo for going simply, modestly,
but manfully to the point, by requiring protection to the voter.

The disfranchisement of Grampound, he treats as a display
of virtue, costing nothing.   When Grampound was to be had
for money, a competition among rich men determined the
election, and the man returned might act with the aristocracy
or against them.   When the seat was given to Yorkshire, in
which the permanent aristocratic influence is established, the
sphere of that influence is enlarged.   The aristocracy leave to
their competitors the giving of money directly ; they call that
by a bad name "Bribery," and denounce it.   The indirect
mode they call "Legitimate influence of Property," which is
everything that is good.   If at each election the whole of the

six hundred and odd seats were set up to sale and knocked down to the highest bidder, the advantage in favour of good government would not be inconsiderable.

A short paragraph on education brings up Brougham again, who had introduced a measure in the first session of the late parliament. Brougham's merit on this subject has redeemed many of the sins he commits by his connexions with a party, in whose trammels, had he known the true interest of his own glory, he never would have consented to draw.

Ireland comes up next, and, on this occasion, with fuller details. Its state is not better at the end of the Parliament than it was at the beginning. Yet its evils are such as might unquestionably be removed. Its condition would disgrace the legislation of barbarians. It is one of the rarer cases where misgovernment is without a check. The aristocratical workings in Ireland, traced through their channels, small as well as great, exhibit human nature in one of the states physically the most deplorable, morally the most detestable, in which it is possible to appear. Of the Catholic question, says the author, the view is shallow that takes it in whole, or in the greatest part, as a religious question; it is an aristocratic question. The aristocracy, wholly Protestant, have found it a convenient instrument of their ascendency of religion, to convert the mass of the people, on the score of religion, into a sort of outcasts. They labour under a mistake; for with emancipation, they would still have their present privileges. The habits of the people place them entirely at the mercy of the landlord.

The author then takes up at length the topic of Equitable Adjustment, noticed in the *Westminster*. He denounces with all his energy the pretexts for defrauding the national creditors under this plausible name. He is especially indignant at the suggestion that the nation might cease to be able to pay its creditors. He runs over the retrenchments that ought to be made before such a pretence should be hinted at. He makes

21

the matter a handle for exposing our aristocratic legislature, whose account in the taxation does not apply to the interest of the debt. He finally reviews the whole transaction in connexion with the sacredness of property. " That a class of men, who, possessing power by a firm tenure, find little occasion for intellect, should be short-sighted and inconsistent, is in the natural order of things. The Aristocracy of England, in order to frighten every man who possesses a little property into an enemy of improvement, have, with a prodigious display of fear and ardour, taught, that all attempts at improvement lead to revolution, and all revolutions to the confiscation of property. Both propositions are false. But they, by defrauding the national creditors, and thereby committing one of the most enormous acts of confiscation that ever was perpetrated on earth, would set an example of disregard to the laws of property, the bitter fruits of which they would deserve to be the first to feel. Why should the rest of the community, they to whom the interests of the fundholding class, and the interests of the landholding class are equal, be more willing to sacrifice the fundholders to the landholders, than the landholders to the fundholders ? If it be very inconvenient to the nation to pay the interest of the national debt, why not take the land to discharge the principal ? This would be spoliation and injustice, most assuredly : but not one atom worse than taking the property of the national creditors."

The next subject is our foreign relations. A great improvement had recently been made, not by Parliament, but by Mr. Canning and his associates, in disengaging the nation from the Holy Alliance ; on which, nevertheless, the author expends a portion of his indignation. Then comes the doubtful point— whether in permitting the occupation of Spain by French troops—one of the most impudent proceedings in the history of modern Europe, and an act directly insulting to the government of England, we avoided a war. The author reviews the precarious situation of the French government, in its own unpopularity at home, and declares that it rested its security on the fears of our government in regard to internal revolution, as the consequence of a new war with France.

Before concluding, he turns to the subject of our bloated establishments, and analyzes the brag of our high rank among the nations. Of all the curses that ever befel a nation, this said high rank is one of the greatest. Of all successful pretences for unnecessary wars, for exorbitant establishments, for the waste and ruin of the substance of the people, this, beyond comparison, is the most fertile in mischief.

The concluding remark is on the conduct of the Opposition party, and on their influence in qualifying the aristocratical preponderance. He reiterates the delusiveness of this influence. When the people became sufficiently clear-sighted to distinguish appearance from reality, the promises of one section of the aristocracy trying to turn the other out of office, will lose their effect. Things have already come nearly to this pass; the out-section of the aristocracy, " His Majesty's opposition," cease to have any hopes to the people, and are hardly less hostile to them than their opponents. Accordingly, the party is melting away. Until an adequate reform of Parliament take place, the ministry will be the *best* part of the legislature, with the exception of a small number of independent, enlightened men, hated by both parties, and persecuted by both, as far as it can be done quietly and by stealth.

With this remarkable piece of energetic writing, ends the author's contributions to party politics, for a number of years.

From the high, and not undeserved encomium passed by John Mill upon the execution of the *Parliamentary History and Review*, we cannot but be sorry that the opulent projector took such a purely business view of its success. At such a critical juncture of politics a little longer continuation of its support would have been valuable, if only to secure the services of the phalanx that had been got together to work for it.

In a long letter, dated 28th Dec., from Bentham to Col. Young, is an account of several interviews that Mill had with Lord William Bentinck, just appointed Governor-general to India, at which Mill and Grote together explained to him Bentham's Panopticon. " Mill paid me a morning visit, a very unusual thing with him ; for, in general, he waits for summons from me. He said he came as the harbinger of good news. For the purpose of bringing him in contact with Lord William, Douglas Kinnaird had made a dinner ; but, as his custom was, instead of a *tête-à-tête*, it was a mob dinner—mob composed of between thirty and forty individuals. However, some way or other, they two were brought into more special contact, and a conversation ensued—the particular import of which I do not remember, except that it ended in the expression of a desire of renewal of acquaintance on the part of Lord William." It appears that Mrs. Grote had arranged a dinner for again bringing Lord William and Mill together. " Mill has, at all times, been a declared, and, I have every reason to think, in this instance, a sincere trumpeter of Panopticon, recommending it within the field of his dominion, and, in particular, Bombay, during the vice-royalty of Elphinstone.

"He said he had trumpeted once, and should, on that occasion, trumpet again the said Panopticon. If so, said I, you may as well have a copy to give him, for your text or subject-matter. Yes, said he, but in that case, your name and his should be inscribed in it. Agreed, said I—and so it was. After this day, I saw Mill again, and in general terms he reported to me the result. At the nick of time, comes out a number of the *Scotsman*, Edinbro' newspaper, which you cannot but be more or less acquainted with, taking for its subject not only an immense Evidence work (a copy of which, you will receive along with these presents), but also the author thereof—a transprint of which, in a number of the *Examiner*, is likewise destined to accompany them. Mill said—Grote having, I forget how, in hand a copy of the original, made

Lord William hear it from beginning to end. . . . Another piece of information, was, that Lord William was, in his judgment, a well-intentioned, but not a very well-instructed man; but something more particular and proportionably instructive, on this head, was, that he said to Mill—'I must confess to you, that what I have ever read amounts to very little, and that it is not without pain that I can read anything'! Quoth Mill—'As to this book, it is not only a preeminently useful, but an amusing book; and so much so, that I could venture to recommend it for Lady William's reading in that view'. Well said, James Mill!—if it was so said; but that is more than the author himself would take upon himself to say of it."

This year saw the formation of the Society for the Diffusion of Useful Knowledge. Mill's name appears in the list of the Committee.

The public events of the year were in themselves momentous, but they can only in imagination be brought into our story. Lord Liverpool's Government gave place in March to Canning's famous Coalition Administration, on which were suspended for a time both hopes and fears; to be all extinguished in a few months.

The session wore away, says Roebuck, in personal recrimination (the Whigs that took office were twitted upon their former professions on Reform, &c.). Abroad, indeed, a powerful sensation followed the break-up of the old administration, and the coming of Mr. Canning into office. The oppressed of all nations rejoiced; expecting that some benefit, but what they knew not, was to result from the new order of things in England.

Canning died on the 8th August. The abortive attempt of Lord Goderich to form a ministry, left the king no option but to send for the Duke of Wellington.

The *Westminster* had not yet passed out of the hands of the original set. John Mill was writing for it this year and the beginning of the next; but not on any of the political questions of the day. The fact was that he or his father had in the two or three previous years exhausted nearly every topic of leading interest—Reform, Ireland, Liberty of the Press, Free Trade; and the present session was no doubt big with events, but brought forth as yet nothing. Of course, the political talk in the home circle would be earnest and energetic as usual: Black went either to Queen's Square or to the India House every two or three days, to get help for his leading articles in the *Chronicle;* and any one taking the trouble to turn over its pages, would find how Mill looked at the successive scenes of the parliamentary drama.

1828.

The documents for this year are very scanty; consisting of three references in the Bentham Memoirs.

In February, Bentham writes a long letter to Rammohun Roy, on the subject of legal reforms for India. I make a few extracts.

"With Mr Mill's work on British India you can scarcely fail to be more or less acquainted. For these three or four-and-twenty years he has numbered himself among my disciples; for upwards of twenty years he has been receiving my instructions; for about the half of each of five years, he and his family have been my guests. If not adequately known already, his situation in the East India Company's service can be explained to you by Colonel Young. My papers on *Evidence,*— those papers which you now see in print—were in his hands, and read through by him, while occupied in his above-noticed great work; a work from which more practically applicable information on the subject of government and policy may be derived (I think I can venture to say) than from any other as yet extant; though, as to style, I wish I could, with truth and sincerity, pronounce it equal to yours.

"For these many years a grand object of his ambition has been to provide for British India, in the room of the abominable existing system, a good system of judicial procedure, with a judicial establishment adequate to the administration of it; and for the composition of it his reliance has all along been, and continues to be, on me. What I have written on these subjects wants little of being complete; so little that, were I to die to-morrow, there are those that would be able to put it in order and carry it through the press.

"What he aims at above all things is,—the giving stability and security to landed property in the hands of the greatest number throughout British India; and, for this purpose, to ascertain by judicial inquiry, the state of the *customs* of the people in that respect. For this same purpose, a great *increase* in the number of *judicatories*, together with the *oral examination* of all parties concerned, and *recordation* of the result will be absolutely necessary: the mode of proceeding as simple as possible, unexpensive and prompt, forming in these respects as complete a contrast as possible with the abominable system of the great Calcutta Judicatory: natives of unmixed blood and half-caste, both of whom could serve on moderate salaries, being, on my system, as much employed as possible.

"Though but very lately known to your new Governor-general, Mr. Mill is in high favour with him; and (I have reason to believe) will have a good deal of influence, which, in that case, he will employ for the purpose above-mentioned.

"He has assured his lordship that there can be no good penal judicature without an apt *prison* and prison-management; and no apt prison or prison-management, without the plan which we call the *Panopticon* plan."

In a short note, dated August, addressed to "Chamberlain Clark," Bentham writes—

"The bearer is Mr. Mill, author of the celebrated *History*

of British India, which, if you have not read, you cannot but have heard more or less of. Under the obscure title of *Examiner,* he bears no inconsiderable part in the government of the threescore or fourscore millions, which form the population of that country. On the death of the chief of the four Examiners, which is expected to take place ere long, he will succeed him, with a salary of £2000 a-year.

" He was one of the earliest and most influential of my disciples. The house he lives in looks into my garden.

" Hearing of the two spots in your neighbourhood, in both of which I several times took up my summer quarters, he expressed a desire to make a pilgrimage to them, as he did once to my birth-place in Red Lion Street, Houndsditch, and the unfortunate half-burnt-down residence in Crutched Friars."

Under date 2nd November is a long letter from Bentham to Daniel O'Connell, with whom he has a constant correspondence at this time; the Liberator professing himself an ardent admirer and follower. The letter is chiefly occupied in characterizing Mill's Irish friend Ensor, whom probably O'Connell had designs upon.

" Received yesterday, yours dated Dublin, 27th. . . . Presently after, dropped in British-India and Political-Economy Mill, one of the earliest of my disciples. He had been seeing a man of the name of Glyn, who, I believe, is a somebody; he had been over a good part of Ireland lately, and was all praise and admiration of you, more especially on account of your prudence—*that* was the word. Mill knows Ensor extremely well: still better than I do. Good intentions, prodigious learning, sharp wit, poignant satire—all this Ensor has. Close and consistent reasoning? Alas, not; unless his attack upon your wings, which I admired at the time, but which is now out of my head, be an exception. Mill says he is impracticable, and in Parliament he sees not very well what particular use he would be of."

On the 1st October, the London University (now designated

University College) was opened, for its first session. In the staff of professors not the least was John Austin, whose Course of Lectures had perhaps the most distinguished attendance that ever honoured any lecturer. John Mill was a hearer, both this session and next.

This year is known to history, politically, as the year of the Duke's "No Surrender"—to Catholics or anything else : there being ominous indications of the vanity of the boast. The Government was defeated on Lord John Russell's motion on the Test and Corporation Acts, which had to be adopted and passed into law. It was again defeated, in the Commons, by a narrow majority of six, on Burdett's motion in favour of Catholic Emancipation O'Connell's renewal of his Catholic Association, which during Canning's ministry he had dropt, was followed by the decisive event of his election for Clare.

The Session was notable for Brougham's great speech on Law Reform, on a motion (Feb. 7) respecting the State of the Courts of Common Law. With all his ostentatious professions of being guided by Bentham, and with his dependence on Mill, he gave little satisfaction to his masters. The following is the opening paragraph of a memorandum by Bentham, entitled "On Brougham's Law Reform" :—

"Mr. Brougham's mountain is delivered, and behold !—the mouse. The wisdom of the reformer could not overcome the craft of the lawyer. Mr. Brougham, after all, is not the man to set up a simple, natural, and rational administration of justice against the entanglements and technicalities of our English law proceedings."

The date of the collected volume of the *Encyclopædia* Essays, judging from the copy that I am acquainted with, is 1828. This may have been a third reprint; as we saw a second alluded to in 1825.

This was the first summer of his residence at Mickleham,

where he spent his holidays for the remaining years of his life.
He first took a small house, opposite the church, but not
facing it, there being another house in front. He afterwards
took a second house, joined with the first, and occupied the
two. The family remained here, for six months in the year.
He staid continuously during his six weeks' holiday, and for
the remaining months, came down by coach from Friday or
Saturday to Monday. I understand that the head of the office
could skip Saturday; none of the Directors appeared on that
day. John had always to be at his post on Saturday till about
two; he went down on Saturday afternoon; the Sunday visitors
generally taking their places in the coach with him.

1829.

For this year, I am without any private reminiscences whatever. The great event to be recorded is the publication of
the *Analysis of the Mind*.

Although the Analysis has now its well-defined place in the
history of Psychological speculation, I am unable to state anything as to its immediate reception. Philosophy was then at
low water mark in this country. Dugald Stewart was dead, and
Hamilton was just beginning to show his hand in the *Edinburgh Review*; but it took him several more years to resuscitate
the interest in metaphysical speculation. He soon got hold of
Mill's book and included it in his multifarious reading; the
unfinished Note in the "Collected Works of Reid," curiously
enough, stopping short in the middle of remarks on Mill. The
first effect of the book was naturally felt in the author's own
circle. The reading society at Grote's house, which had ceased
for some time, renewed its meetings for the purpose of discussing the work *seriatim*, in the same fashion as their
previous readings in other subjects. Their last occupation
had been with Hartley.

It was this year that Macaulay wrote his articles in the

Edinburgh on Mill and Utilitarianism.   I have already indi-
cated their drift.   The Napier correspondence contains some
interesting incidental references to them.   Thus, on the
3rd October, Macaulay writes to Napier :—"The *Westminster
Review* has put forth another attack on us, and both Empson
and I think that, as the controversy has certainly attracted
much notice in London, and as this new article of the Benthamites is more absurd than anything that they have yet
published, one more paper ought to appear on our side.   I
hope and trust that this will be the last blow."   Again on the
23rd, Macaulay writes :—"By the mail of to-morrow I shall
despatch the proofs.   I have re-written the two first paragraphs,
which were, I must own, indecorously violent.   I have softened
some other passages.   If you think any further mitigation desirable, I hope that you will not scruple to exercise your prerogative.
You will not find me a refractory subject."   On the 28th,
Napier, writing to M'Culloch, says—"Do not blame me for
inserting another blow at the *Utilitarians*.   I have softened its
severity, and I am bound to say that Macaulay has behaved
handsomely."

It is commonly represented that Macaulay owed his seat in
Parliament to the attack on Mill.   It appears from a passage
in his *Life* that Lord Lansdowne "had been much struck by
the articles".   It is added, however, that Macaulay's "high
moral and private character" had determined Lord Lansdowne
to offer him the seat.   Viewed from one side, the promotion
has been regarded as a Whig tribute to his having vanquished
obnoxious Radicalism   Notwithstanding, Lord Houghton, in
the *Academy* (April 29, 1876), gives another side of the affair.
"His College intimacy with Charles Austin may not improbably
have had something to do with this important change in his
destiny, for with Charles and John Austin, and Sarah the
beautiful and accomplished translator of Ranke's *History*, Lord
Lansdowne long held the most friendly relations."   This brings

the wheel completely round, for the Austins (including Sarah) were the closest of Mill's own friends.

In the Life of Lord Ellenborough, published lately, occurs a passage that the newspaper reviewers referred to James Mill. "Goulbourn spoke against a Mr. Mill, who is a very clever man, and a good man, but a controversialist." Ellenborough was then (Jan 21, 1829) President of the Board of Control, and the remark would seem to be pointed at James Mill, as an India House official. In point of fact, however, the President of the Board knew nothing of the officials of the India House. He would read despatches drafted by them, in the first instance, but he had only to deal with the Court of Directors.

The connexion of the passage shows that the reference to James Mill is a mistake What was under discussion between Goulbourn and Ellenborough was the appointment of a bishop, and the " Mill " alluded to was of course a clergyman of the church.

The year 1829 owes its historical reputation to the concession of Catholic Emancipation. The bearings on ulterior questions are well sketched by Roebuck, in his *History of the Whig Ministry*. The events and discussions of the year " attracted attention to, and rivetted it upon parliamentary reform, which was evidently destined to be, together with the condition of the industrious classes, the grand topic of the coming session. The notice-book of the House of Commons consequently contained many notices of motion, propounding various schemes for a reform in the popular representation, and for relieving the burdens of the people."

We have now given the record of events to the end of 1829. As this is near the date of the removal from Queen's Square, I may introduce here a few of the domestic incidents of the sixteen years spent in that residence.

We saw that Bentham gave Mill the house, in the first in-

stance, at about half its value. We also found that, when Dr
Thomson shared it with him, he paid the full rent, showing his
determination to clear his way to the full as soon as possible.

When he went to Queen's Square, he had five children, the
eldest, eight, the youngest, just born. In 1830, he had a
family of nine, the eldest, twenty-four, the youngest, six. Their
education, up to this time, had been conducted wholly in the
house; partly, by himself, and, gradually more and more, by
the elder ones teaching the younger. He never entirely ceased
to take a part; either, in the early morning, in his dressing
room, or in the evening, he heard their lessons, in a summary
fashion; treating their deficiencies with sternness and severity.

Having been in his youth, a full-trained volunteer, he had a
due appreciation of army discipline, in giving bodily carriage.
He, accordingly, engaged a sergeant from the adjoining barracks,
to put them through a course of marching drill, while John
was practised in sword exercise. Very little came of this, as
far as John in particular was concerned; he was, to the end
backward in all that regarded bodily accomplishments, saving
the one point of persistence as a walker. The fact, no doubt,
was, that his nervous energy was so completely absorbed in his
unremitted intellectual application, as to be unavailable for
establishing the co-ordinations of muscular dexerity.

After John, the next elder children seem to have disappointed him, and he never looked upon them with any com-
placency. James, the second son, was destined for the India
Service abroad: he was an assiduous student, and appears to
have given his father tolerable satisfaction; but there was
nothing in his career to show that he had much intellectual
gift. The next brother, Henry, was everybody's favourite; I
have heard Mrs. Grote describe him as a "heavenly boy".
Personal beauty and charms, great faculty not merely for study
but for anything that he had to do, unselfishness in the extreme, were the traits that made his popularity. He died of
consumption, in his 20th year; aware that overstrain had

crushed him.   John watched his deathbed at Falmouth, and, in writing of the event, pronounced him " the noblest and worthiest of us all ".   The youngest son, George, I knew personally : he too possessed the family talent, but succumbed to the same malady.   It is apparent enough that while the father's fine quality of brain was not wanting in the children generally, John, besides other advantages, was single in possessing the physical endurance that was needed for maturing a first-class intellect.

The *Autobiography* expresses with sufficient frankness the defective side of Mill's demeanour to his children.   Such a phrase as " the most impatient of men " speaks a volume, and we have only to turn the leaves to realize the particulars.   He could exercise perfect self-control in his intercourse with the world, and his social and commanding qualities gained and kept friends, but at home he did not care to restrain the irritability of his temperament.   In his advancing years, as often happens, he courted the affection of the younger children, but their love to him was never wholly unmingled with fear , for, even in his most amiable moods, he was not to be trifled with.   His entering the room where the family was assembled was observed by strangers to operate as an immediate damper. This was not the worst.   The one really disagreeable trait in Mill's character, and the thing that has left the most painful memories, was the way that he allowed himself to speak and behave to his wife and children before visitors.   When we read his letters to friends, we see him acting the family man with the utmost propriety, putting forward his wife and children into their due place ; but he seemed unable to observe this part in daily intercourse.

Long before leaving Queen's Square, he had passed through the parent's inevitable hour of filial self-assertion.   His first check, he got, naturally, from John ; the particulars I will notice elsewhere.   The elder daughters, who were the greatest sufferers from his imperious rule, and between whom and their

father, John often acted the part of mediator, next read him a
sharp lesson.   Indeed, we are now close upon the time when
John came under another influence, with which all the world
is well acquainted.

It is not to be inferred that the children were made entirely
unhappy by their father's system.   John himself testifies that
his childhood was not unhappy; and we shall be able to
produce similar testimony from the younger ones.   Besides
having a fond, indulgent mother, they were very much attached
to each other; and for many hours every day, they were their
own masters.   They had a comfortable home.   The house
itself was roomy; it had its own garden, which was in direct
connexion with Bentham's more extensive grounds, of which
they had the full use.   Bentham had naturally a certain kindly
feeling towards the "brats," as he called them; their per
sonal charms, vivacious ways, and good breeding must have
interested him from the Ford Abbey time, when all but the
two or three youngest were domesticated with him.   His
amanuensis, Doane, was their playfellow.

CHAPTER VII.

CLOSING YEARS.—INDIA CHARTER: LONDON
REVIEW: FRAGMENT ON MACKINTOSH.

1830—1836.

THE year 1830 is the culmination of Mill's career. Before the end of the year, he is at the head of his office. Soon after, he quits Queen's Square for a large villa in Vicarage Place, Church Street, Kensington. Here in opulence and fame, he spends his last years, varied by the summer residence at Mickleham.

The one serious drawback was his health. His attacks of gout are of course not diminishing in frequency or severity ; while indigestion gives him uneasiness on its own account. His stomach and liver are much impaired. He was all his life very temperate ; for many years he scarcely ever indulged in alcoholic drinks. Latterly, he took a fancy to the Scotch ale called Alloa ale ; this was what he used at his own table. Having regard to his gouty framework, the doctors of our day would have recommended to him Scotland's still more peculiarly national form of alcohol.

During these last six years of his life, he wrote comparatively little for the public ; not for want of will and purpose, but from diminishing strength and the increased pressure of his office work. His private social influence was subject to no abatement. As the adviser of the small band of philosophical radicals, in and out of Parliament, he was still of the greatest value to the cause of political progress.

A few words may be expended on his chief friends for these years. Of those already mentioned, the Grotes, Black, Hume, the Austins, Strutt, Romilly, Charles Villiers (his brother, Hyde, died in 1832), M'Culloch, Fonblanque—continued their intimacy to the last. Brougham's assiduity is even more conspicuous than before, and furnishes us with a number of letters of the highest interest. In his Chancellor days, he occasionally drove down on a Sunday to Mickleham.

With Henry Bickersteth we shall find the mutual attachment growing ever stronger. He used to take a house at Mickleham, to be near Mill during the holiday rambles. The reader of the two volumes of his Biography, when informed of his being offered the Mastership of the Rolls, is startled to find that Mill, whose name had not occurred previously, is the man whose judgment he sought before he could bring himself to accept. On the other hand, Bickersteth was Mill's counsel in the composition and style of his last work, the *Fragment on Mackintosh*, and induced him to make many alterations in the way of softening its tone.

The elder Mr. Marshall of Leeds, who came into Parliament for Yorkshire in 1826, and projected *the Parliamentary History and Review*, was in the Mill circle. He kept a large hospitable house in the West-end: we find Macaulay frequenting his parties. His second son, John, became member for Leeds, and and was also, I believe, one of Mill's visitors. The third son, James Garth Marshall, was member for Leeds in 1847, and was a friend of John Mill; I can remember meeting him in the India House.

Sir William Molesworth came up to London, in 1833, as member for the eastern division of his own county, Cornwall. He had few or no acquaintances in London, till he took the

Extract of a letter, May 28, 1831.—"Yesterday I dressed, called a cab, and was wheeled away to Hill Street. I found old Marshall's house a very fine one. He ought, indeed, to have a fine one; for he has, I believe, at least, thirty thousand a year."

pportunity that the House of Commons afforded of making
up to Grote, who got leave from Mrs. Grote to bring him to
he house. Mrs. Grote made a great deal of him, and he
soon got to know all the Grote circle, including the Mills.
His predilections were to radicalism and scepticism, so that
he had not to learn anything fundamental from his new
associates. By his own account, he got his scepticism at the
University of Edinburgh, where he spent two years; (this
was in the Twenties). He became one of Mill's most devoted
followers. He struck Mill greatly both for ability and for
having the courage of his opinions. He showed his zeal in
the unmistakable form of founding, at his own cost, the
London Review.

Dr. Neil Arnott was on intimate terms with Mill for the
years we are now entering upon. The acquaintance had not
begun long before 1830, and was probably a consequence of
his recently acquired reputation. The expository success of
the " Elements of Physics" published in 1827, is to this hour
without a parallel in the literature of science. The book, I
know, was greatly admired both by Mill and by Grote, and
led them to desire the acquaintance of the author. Arnott
was born not far from Montrose, when James Mill was attending the Academy there as a youth of fifteen. In the middle
of the week, when Mill would deviate from the line of his walk
home on Saturday and back to school on Monday, he and
Hume could vary their rambles by going south on the coast
road towards Arbroath. About three miles from Montrose
they would pass the farmhouse belonging to Arnott's father,
situated near the middle of the picturesque bay of Lunan, a
delightful afternoon excursion. Arnott spent only his childhood there, his father having gone to Aberdeen when he was
about eight years old: but he had sufficient memories to
interchange with Hume and Mill, when they reverted in conversation to their native locality. Probably he met Hume in
the circles of his patients, and was taken by him to Mill. His

conversation was sufficiently intellectual and scientific to be enjoyed by the whole set ; and he had a powerful scheming mind, extending to social philosophy, as well as to mechanics. He was of the sanguine temperament, full of hopes for the future of mankind, although his projects were often quixotic. He was latterly medical adviser both to Mill himself and to the family.

Fonblanque became Editor of the *Examiner* in 1830, and lifted the paper to its great eminence as a liberal weekly. His closest connexion was with John Mill, who was for several years a regular contributor of his. Fonblanque had previously contributed to the paper, as well as to the *Morning Chronicle* and to the *Westminster Review.* By his own account, he assisted Black in the *Chronicle* from 1821 to 1824, and wrote most of the articles on the Unpaid Magistracy.

Among the visitors to Mill, and the associates of his Sunday walks, for several years, was a barrister named Hogg ; the author of a *Life of Shelley*, and husband of the widow of Captain Williams who was drowned along with him. His son was a pupil with Coulson. Hogg seemed to have had objectionable points, and, before Mill died, the two had quarrelled ; the only case that I know of Mill's quarrelling with any one that had ever been his friend.

M'Culloch, the political economist, settled in London, on being made professor of Political Economy in University College, in 1828 ; after the frustration of Jeffrey's purpose to endow a chair in Edinburgh University, and to give him the first appointment. Mill no doubt took the lead in nominating him to University College.

Mill was usually joined in his long Sunday walk with some of his associates. He had cultivated the power of prolonged walking as necessary to his health , and John and the rest of the children were habituated in like manner. The Sunday excursions were sometimes very long indeed. I have heard it said that the party kept on foot from ten to four, and, after

nner, again for several hours.   Even the younger men spoke
 the fatigue as sometimes beyond endurance.   For some of
e last years in London, Coulson, Peacock, M'Culloch, and
ogg, were members of the regular walking party.   At Mickle-
ım, Sharp was a near neighbour, and John Mill considered it
part of his good fortune to listen to the conversation of his
ther and Sharp during their walks.

INDIA CHARTER RENEWAL.

1830—1833.

By an Act of Parliament passed on the 20th of August, 1833,
e East India Company received the final modifications of its
ınstitution, being deprived of the last remnants of its trading
ivileges.

The published proceedings connected with this great revolu-
ɔn bring Mill into the foreground, as the spokesman and
lviser of the Court of Directors, and afford the only means
e have of clearly understanding the official influence that he
tercised in the government of India.

By the Act of 1813, the Company had a renewal of its
ɔwers, with the loss of its India Trade.   That Act was to
:pire in 1834; so that, notwithstanding the deafening thunders
˙ the Reform agitation, the terms of the further prolongation
˙ the Company's government had to be considered by Parlia-
ent.

The mercantile public was not disposed to consent to the
ɔntinuance of the trading powers of the Company in any
ıape; and a severe struggle was impending.   The main fight
ɔok place some time previous to the introduction of the Bill
ı 1833.   In the Committees of Parliament, and in the corres-
ɔndence between the Government and the Court of Directors,
ıe ground was so effectively cleared as to leave little to the
ebates at the different stages of the Bill in the two Houses.

During the session of 1829, there was a rush of petitions from all the great centres of trade and manufactures, directed against the renewal of the Company's charter; the petitioners being opposed, not merely to the continuance of the Company's remaining monopoly—the China Tea trade—but to the retention of the India government in its hands.

Such was the strength of the hostile current, that the leaders of both parties looked upon the surrender of the tea monopoly as a matter of course. They were equally unprepared to transfer, at that moment, to the crown, the government of India.

The campaign opened in the end of 1830; while the Duke of Wellington was minister. In February, Committees were appointed in both Houses of Parliament—"to enquire into the present state of the affairs of the East India Company; and into the trade between Great Britain and China".

These, and all the subsequent Committees that the frequent dissolutions of Parliament in the next two years, required to be appointed afresh, were, in the Commons at least, unusually large; amounting to forty or fifty members. They had to include the leading men in the house, and a large representation of the centres of commerce.

The first Committees were cut short by the dissolution of Parliament on 24th July, caused by the death of the King. No others were appointed that session. A good deal of evidence was accumulated; the opposition to the Company being of course fully heard.

On the 12th October, the same year, the correspondence between the Government and the Company began in a conference held at Apsley House; the Duke and Lord Ellenborough (President of the India Board) met the Chairman and Deputy-Chairman of the Court of Directors; when the Duke with his usual curtness intimated that the Company was to be continued in the government of India, but with the loss of the China tea monopoly. The chairs reported the conversation to the Court of Directors, and a brief minute was

prepared on the 20th, bringing forward the fact of the insuffi-
ciency of the territorial revenue alone to meet the expenses of
government; there being a deficit of £800,000, at present
met by the China trade.

At the meeting of Parliament in Feb., 1831, a Select Committee of the House of Commons was again appointed. It
consisted of forty members to begin with; others were subsequently added. Earl Grey was in power, and Charles Grant
(afterwards Lord Glenelg) was President of the India Board,
and conducted all the negotiations with the Court of Directors,
and finally carried the Bill through Parliament. His name of
course headed the Commons' Committee; others were Lord
Althorp, Marquis of Chandos, Lord Morpeth, Sir James
Mackintosh (who now held an office in the India Board), Lord
Ashley, Joseph Hume, Labouchere, Poulett Thomson, Charles
Wood, Goulburn, John Marshall, &c. In April, Parliament
was dissolved. In the middle of June, the Committee was
reappointed much the same as before, 36 members to start with.

Before this third Committee, in August, Mill was examined
through eight sittings, on the India Revenue. This had been
his own special department, from his appointment in 1819, till
he became Chief Examiner in 1830.

In India, the main source of Revenue is the Land Tax;
and Mill describes minutely the machinery for collecting the
tax. He is asked if the Land Tax is a good one, and answers,
Yes; as far as this source goes, the people of the country
remain untaxed. The difficulties lie in the collection, and
these are discussed before the Committee at great length. The
chief problem that arose was due to the position given to the
so-called Zemindars by the Cornwallis Settlement of 1793; a
celebrated instance of mistaking the character of the pro-
prietary rights of the apparent owners of the soil. The
cultivators of the soil are called Ryots; they pay the government tax to the Zemindars, who are charged by the authorities
to a certain amount. The Ryots had a hereditary right to the

soil, subject to the payment of the tax, but the Zemindars
under the settlement were able to encroach upon those rights
and when the Company had its eyes once opened to the
blunder that had been made, various devices were resorted to
to prevent the rights of the Ryots from passing away ; and the
manipulation of those devices seems to have been one portion
of Mill's official duty for several years.   The principal remedy
was for the Company to purchase the land from the Zemindars,
whenever any of them were obliged to sell it, and to re-settle
the Ryots in their old hereditary rights.   Many regulations had
to be framed in carrying out this purpose, all coming within the
years when Mill was in charge of the Revenue Department.
Officers in the Courts of Justice, and the servants of Collectors
of Revenue, had to be prohibited from being bidders at the sales.
Settlements on Zemindars, where fraud was discovered, had to be
revised by a Committee.   Overcharges to an enormous amount
were discovered.   Directions were issued to resist the increased
demands of the Zemindars, from the extension of the poppy
cultivation.   Payment in kind was discouraged.

The third day's examination was opened with a question as
to the increase of the comforts of the people.   He replies, he
had conversed with many persons on this subject, and got
opposite opinions.   The sitting was next occupied with what
was termed the Village Settlement : under which the Ryots
were taxed by the head man of the village, a personage that
also needed looking after.   Here is one suggestion of Mill's
own :—" It has occurred to me, and instructions to that effect
have been conveyed to India, that the collector, in making his
bargain with the head man, should, previously to assigning him
the privilege, make him give in a schedule of the mode in
which he meant to distribute the assessment, and, having
obtained this statement, cause it to be fixed up in the village
itself, to be seen by every inhabitant of the village, with an
invitation to the people to make any remarks that might occur
to them."   The village settlements occured in the Presidency of

Fort William and the provinces. The discovery had been only recently made, that in a considerable district, the assessment was too high, and instructions, more or less peremptory, had been sent to take care that no more than the rent is exacted. Also it was recommended to the Madras Government that the Ryot's assessment should be fixed for a number of years.

The fourth day was taken up with a general discussion of the revenue system of India, which, if it could be limited to Rent, Mill had pronounced the best in the world.

On the fifth day, he is subjected to considerable badgering by the Committee on the Land Tax, on the merits of which they did not seem to agree with him. The other great sources of taxation were Salt and Opium; these could not be dispensed with; but the Company, on principle, had remitted a great number of petty taxes.

The cross-examination goes on for another day on the instructions to collectors. On the day following he is called to give an account of the fluctuations of Revenue in different provinces. The eighth day is occupied with the costs of collection of the salt and opium duties. Instructions had been issued to make every improvement in the modes of collection. There is then a long argument about a permanent settlement with the Ryots. In conclusion, he is asked his opinion as to the opening up of government employment to the natives. He does not think much good would come of it; better "to teach them to look for their elevation to their own resources, their industry, and economy". Petitions sent from India, he says, do not represent the general language of the country. As a final home thrust, he is asked if a person could form a judgment of the natives without being personally acquainted with them. Replies—" If the question refers to myself, I am far from pretending to a perfect knowledge of the people of India ".

It was during the heat of the Reform Bill discussions in the

Commons, that this examination took place; and the Committee was again cut short by the dissolution of Parliament following on the rejection of the Bill by the Lords. On the opening of the session, in January, a fourth Committee had to be appointed, with the understanding that it should subdivide itself, and take up the subject in six branches separately and simultaneously. Mill is summoned again; and examined in four departments. Under one head—denominated General—he describes the whole machinery of government, both at home and in India; and is questioned more particularly as to the constitution of the India administrative body. He disapproves of the present allocation of duties to the Governor-General. He would have a Legislative Council constituted by four persons thus :—one acquainted with the laws of England; one selected from the most experienced of the Company's servants; one, a native of the highest character and qualifications; and one, a person thoroughly versed in the philosophy of men and of government. As to the question of representative institutions for India, he pronounces a decided negative. He condemns the secret system at home (working through a Secret Committee of the Court of Directors) as of very little good. The sederunt of this special Committee included Sir James Macdonald, Marshall, Labouchere, Lord Sandon, John Wood, Lord Cavendish, Sir R. Inglis.

Before another Sub-Committee—(Grant, Shiel, Serjeant Wilde, O'Connell, Bonham Carter, Ewart, Lord Milton), he is examined on the Judicial System, and goes over its defects, namely, the combining of criminal and civil causes, and the system of appeals. He urges oral pleadings; would give power to the judges to call the witnesses; and enjoins attention to the customs of India.

Under the sixth branch of India business, called Political or Foreign, he is examined in presence of Mackintosh (in the chair), Wynn, Bulwer, and Macaulay. This is the department of the protected or dependent states, which he describes in the blackest colours. The British power protects native rulers from insurrection, the old standing refuge of oppression, and yet cannot compel them to govern well. Certain precautions are taken by way of exerting some influence on the native ruler, which are minutely described, but are wholly insufficient. Public opinion at home is opposed to absorbing these states ; but the sooner the intermediate plan is done away with, the better.

Being asked as to the most desirable frontier, he says there is nothing now between us and that, but the territory of Runjeet Sing. If threatened by the Russians on the north-west frontier, we should be obliged to take possession of the country to the foot of the hills. Runjeet Sing occupies the Punjaub : the boundary between him and the Hill States is not very definite.

Before another Sub-Committee (Frankland Lewis, Strutt, Sir Charles Forbes, Stuart Wortley), he again undergoes an examination on the Salt and Opium monopolies. This is on the 28th of June. On the 15th August, an official letter is sent in to the Committee, giving full details of the Land and other Taxes. The drafting of this would fall to Mill. The side observations are sometimes curious. He defends the pilgrim tax from the charge of identifying the British Government with idolatry. He avers that the licensing of stews is not authorizing them, but rather lessening evils that we cannot prevent. On the tobacco tax, he does not mince his opinion of the injuriousness of the article itself.

So much for the Parliamentary Committees. Another line of operations had to be carried on meanwhile, in the shape of correspondence between the Court of Directors and the Government, which really settled the terms of the new Bill. The lengthened arguments of the Directors were of Mill's composition, as a matter of course.

After the interview with the Duke and Lord Ellenborough, the chairs reported the result to the Directors, who agreed to

a minute on the subject. The change of ministry, however
made a new start, and Charles Grant now represented the
Government. The tug of war came in 1832. The prime
minister and Grant had an interview with the chairs, and
finally intimated the Government's decision, which was in
accord with the deliverance of the Duke in the end of 1830
Grant followed this up with a letter to the Chairman, contain
ing certain *hints*, as what the provisions of the Bill should be
To this, the Directors gave an elaborate answer. Knowing
that they could not maintain their monopoly, they contented
themselves with disabusing the public of the supposed advan
tages of an open trade, in reducing the price of tea, and in
affording new marts for our manufactures ; the peculiar cir
cumstances and policy of China constituting an exception
to all the rules of commercial policy. The more serious part
of the case was the future administration of the Company
under the new circumstances. There would be, for one thing
the difficulties in remitting money for home use. Still more
serious was the deficit to be made good, upon which a very
protracted controversy arose. The first letter of the Directors
contains a strong passage on the necessity of a sufficient
security to the Proprietors, "to compensate the Company for
the services which they have rendered, for the risks which they
have run, and for the sacrifices which they are called upon to
make, &c.". A farther point to be argued was the indepen
dence of the action of the Court of Directors, which was
seriously infringed by Grant's proposals. A long argumentative
letter from Grant (12th Feb., 1833) meets the Directors point
by point, and winds up with the ultimatum of the Government
To this the Court of Directors replies on the 27th, with great
elaborateness ; the longest and most masterly performance in
the whole controversy. With justice, does Tucker, one of the
Directors, in a motion at the Court of Proprietors, use these
words :—"Although our letters to the President of the Board
of Commissioners, &c., are distinguished for their ability, for

their clearness, their candour and truth, their conciliatory tone and spirit, and statesman-like views, as well as for their successful refutation of that specious and imposing, but unsatisfactory reasoning, which characterises the letters of Mr. Grant, &c."

The Bill is introduced, in the first session of the Reform Parliament, and is criticized at the India House as it advances. Grant and Macaulay are its sponsors in the Commons. The main provisions pass with no trouble : the debating chiefly turns upon the questions of the church establishments in India ; the Directors opposing their increase, but in vain.

It may seem a little strange that Mill, whose views on Trade were of the most advanced school, should be exerting himself heart and soul to counter-argue the demands of the trading community on this occasion. The reason can easily be gathered from the perusal of his evidence. The mercantile interest could not see, in the light of an official, the very stagnant condition of the native population in India ; and seemed to believe that, but for the obstruction of the Company's Government, there would be a great and sudden development of industry—exports and imports—to the benefit of the home producers.*

I now proceed with the records of the successive years.

1830.

In April was published Sir James Mackintosh's *Dissertation on Ethical Philosophy*. It appears that before the date of

* The foregoing history brings before us with tolerable vividness the nature of Mill's occupation as an India Official. A scrap of paper lying before me will further assist by a concrete example. The paper is a message drawn up to be sent to some person in the office, I cannot say who, it runs thus :—

" I have spoken to the Chairman respecting Major Ellwood's Case. He will make up his mind next week.

" Fletcher and I have gone carefully through the last Revenue Draft (Madras) publication, copies of it had been distributed among his friends. Mill at once put down his remarks upon it, intending them to appear as letters to the author. The publication was, however, delayed; and Mackintosh died on the 22nd May, 1832. The form taken by the remarks was then felt to be unsuitable, and nothing farther was done for a year or two. A remark of Mill's, in conversation, is remembered—"I must touch up Mackintosh before I die". The fulfilment of the wish was the "Fragment on Mackintosh". A specimen of its contents has already been given; its general plan will be described afterwards.

The article that Mill was induced, by great pressure, to contribute to the *Westminster Review*, after it had passed into Colonel Thompson's hands, was on the Ballot, and appeared in the July number of this year. It occupies 39 pages. It is a vigorous handling of the stock arguments against the Ballot protesting, nevertheless, at the outset, that the allegations o the opponents "bear upon them the broad appearance of mere pretexts; the sham pleas, which are invented and set up, as often as men are summoned to defend opinions, which they have adopted and are determined to maintain, from other considerations than those of their truth, or falsehood".

His first topic is the argument from the legitimate influence of property. He describes in glowing colours what he calls the

and made a few immaterial alterations When Mr M'Culloch has seen it, purpose giving it to the Chairman.

"The other Madras Draft will probably go into Committee on Wednesday next.

"There are no fresh arrivals in Revenue Department. Lord Hastings is a Paris. Buckingham has been sent home.

"J. M "

But now turn the other side of the slip. There is a closely written disserta tion entitled, "Reasons to shew that the Christian Religion was not intended to guide or influence the actions or happiness of this life; that its sole object is the future life". I need not quote the reasons. I merely wish to illustrate the transitions of Mill's employment during the long days at the India House.

moral influence of property, and never hesitates to avow the opinion that the government of the world must always be in the hands of the rich; but they must be under motives to gain the good-will of the community. The ballot does not interfere with riches legitimately used. It interferes solely with the employment of wealth to coerce the wills of men by fear.

He spends several pages in repaying with interest the common charge against the Ballot, of making men mendacious. Taking his usual high ground of the sacredness of the trust committed to the voter, he denounces unfaithfulness to his trust as treachery of the very first water. It follows that the man that brings motives to bear upon the voter to make him betray this trust, is himself criminal in the highest degree.

"Observe the horrid spectacle; two sets of men, the one comparatively rich, the other poor, so placed with respect to one another, that they act upon one another, for mutual corruption; that they gain their ends upon one another, only by a renunciation of the most sacred obligations, and the commission of the greatest crimes; that, in order to have inward peace, in such a course of acting, they must succeed in obliterating every trace of the higher morals from their minds. The sense of obligation to the community to which they belong, the regard due to a trust, are not compatible with their situation. The men who have occasion for the prostitution, the perjury, the faithlessness of voters, and the most perfect indifference on their part to the interests of their country, must beware how they appear to have any regard for morality before such persons, or any regard for country."

"The prostituted voter, we said, is less criminal, than his corrupter. Not only is he less criminal in the principal act; the being to a great degree the passive tool, the other the active agent; his crime being single, that of the suborner multiplied in every individual whose villainy he has secured; he is also less criminal in the circumstances of his act, they almost all in his case being extenuating, almost all in his suborner's case aggravating circumstances, of the guilt."

For what is the object of the suborner? "Take one of the men whose object is mere vanity—the distinction of being a member of parliament. Is there anything, in this petty, vulgar, motive, to extenuate the guilt of an enormous crime? The motive of that proportion of candidates who seek admission for the sake of plunder, is itself wicked, and of course adds to the wickedness of the conduct by which the admission is procured."

"Another tremendous accusation lies upon the class of suborners. They are the class by whom chiefly the moral character of the voting classes is formed. The opinions which they spread of what is honourable, and what dishonourable, become the governing opinions. But the habits of thinking, about what is right and wrong, what is shameful, what the contrary, diffused among any people, constitute the moral character of that people."

Among the opponents of the ballot in parliament are those who say—"they hope not to live to witness the time, when Englishmen shall not have the spirit to deliver their vote in the face of day. It would be as honest, and about as wise to say, they hope not to witness the time, when every Englishman shall not have his carriage and pair. If they were to say, which would be the only thing to the purpose that they hoped not to live to see the day when an Englishman would not go to the hustings, and fearlessly vote for the man of his choice, without regard to the dictation of any person upon earth; the falsehood of the pretext would be too glaring to be successful, even in a country where as much is done by hypocrisy as in England."

Towards the close, he expresses more fully his view of the importance of bringing proper motives to bear upon men of property.

"Men of property love distinction; but the distinction of property, where it is not connected with political power, o

trongly associated with the idea of it, is insignificant. The
,reat desire of men of property, therefore, always will be for
he distinction connected with public services. But, if they
iad an adequate motive for the acquisition, in a superior
legree, of the high mental qualities, which fit men for the
lischarge of public duties, it cannot be doubted that they
iave great, and peculiar advantages, for the accomplishment
)f their purpose. Other men, even those who are not confined
o mechanical drudgery, are under the necessity of employing
he greater part of their lives, in earning the means either of
ubsistence or independence. The men who are born to a
)roperty which places them above such necessity, can employ
he whole of their lives in acquiring the knowledge, the talents,
ind the virtues, which would entitle them to the confidence
)f their fellow citizens. With equal motive, and superior
idvantages, they would, of course, in general, have superior
iuccess. They would be the foremost men in the country, and
o they would be esteemed."

He backs himself up by his favourite Plato, who enunciates,
is a maxim :—'A man has peculiar advantages for attaining
he highest excellence of his nature, when he is above the
iecessity of labouring for the means of subsistence.'

" The man who is placed in these circumstances," he con-
inues, " has not only the whole of his time to bestow, in early
ife, upon the acquisitions which fit him for the business of legis-
ation and government; he alone, and not the man without
ortune, who is still engaged in other pursuits, can bestow his
ime and attention, undivided, upon the public services with
which he is intrusted. Our opinion, therefore, is, that the busi-
iess of government is properly the business of the rich ; and that
hey will always obtain it, either by bad means, or good. Upon
his every thing depends. If they obtain it by bad means, the
;overnment is bad. If they obtain it by good means, the
;overnment is sure to be good. The only good means of
)btaining it are, the free suffrage of the people."

Such are a few morsels from a once famous article. The positions were afterwards re-stated and argued by Grote, in his Ballot Speeches, with a degree of fulness that hardly left anything to the oratory that eventually succeeded in carrying the measure.

This article was afterwards reprinted as a twopenny tract, in a series of political tracts, edited by Roebuck, which I shall have occasion to refer to.

A letter from Mill to Macvey Napier on the 8th July, relates primarily to the filling up of a scholastic appointment in India, for which he desires Napier to look out a fit person. He appends some observations on University College, which have a more general interest. The appointing of Leonard Horner, as paid principal or head of the college, with no teaching duty, was a well-meant step on the part of the Council, but it was found to work very ill. Mill writes with some bitterness—

"I cannot close without saying a word about the University. The general meeting terminated better than I expected , and at any rate did no harm, which I feared it would do. But still it has left us in the same perplexities in which it found us. Brougham called here this morning to talk about the subject, and after being with me for an hour has just left me. The warden (though personally far more sinned against than sinning) is the grand source of difficulty; for in the state of hostile feeling among them it is vain to expect that the machine will work well—and there is the less hope of it, that it is the rooted opinion of the warden, that there is but one cure for all the evil, and that is, giving plenty of power to him. Brougham with sincere friendship for him, did not conceal from me his wish and his hope, that his friends would prevail upon him to resign. This I can mention to you in confidence; because I know the same is to a great degree your opinion as well as mine. And yet I should dislike to give any appearance of victory to those Professors who have

23

arried on a disreputable war against him; and in this respect
differ from him radically—that he has the interest of the University deeply at heart—they have shown that they had not. I
do believe (and I am grieved to say it) there is not a man
among them who, if his own interests were perfectly detached,
would care if it was burned to the ground to-morrow."

Place's MS. history of the College discloses another em-
broilment, happening this year, with reference to the Junior
School in the College.   This was not at first a part of the
College system.   The want of such a school was soon felt;
and as the buildings when complete would contain good
accommodation, a scheme for instituting it was put forward by a
number of the Proprietors, who subscribed the necessary funds
to begin with.   Mill was one of these subscribers, together with
Brougham, Lord Auckland, Hallam, Goldsmid, Dr. Lushington,
and others.   " The subscribers laid their scheme before the
Council of the University, proposing that they should take the
school under their patronage, and offering in that case to
place the nomination and power of removal of the Head-
Master in their hands, in order that no part of the system of
the school should be contrary to the principles upon which the
University has been founded. The Council approved of the plan,
accepted the offer made to them by the subscribers, and confirmed the appointment by the subscribers of the Rev. Henry
Browne of Corpus Christi College, Cambridge, to the office of
Head-Master."   Mr. Browne's programme, however, provided
for the opening of the classes each day with prayer and reading
of the scriptures.   This was a violation of the College's fundamental principle of religious neutrality, and could not escape
without remark.   Place is furious, and preserves a letter that
he wrote to Colonel Jones, containing these expressions :—
"Am I to believe that Mr. Mill was one of the schemers—
one of those who submitted his [the proposed head master's]
scheme to the Council, one of the Council who approved of the
scheme, &c., &c.   Above all, am I to believe that he is party

to this obnoxious prospectus ? Did he who wrote the memorable and admirable essay 'Schools for All, not Schools for
Churchmen only,' did he do all these things that Mr. Browne
might be warranted to set up a London University School for
Churchmen only? No, he did no such things." Place
addresses a similar letter (date given, 9th July, 1830), to Henry
Warburton, a sure sympathiser on such a point. Notwithstanding Place's strong remonstrance, the Prospectus passed in
this form with Horner's approval. I should doubt whether the
matter had received the full consideration of the subscribers and
the Council; and I presume the practice would not be long
continued.

After the three days of Paris (27th, 28th, 29th July), John
Mill went there in order to have personal interviews with the
chief actors. An interesting letter to his father is preserved ;
but I prefer to give it among my reminiscences of John Mill
himself. The French upturn added fuel to the English flame ;
and attracted the regards of the Reform party. John Mill,
from this time forward made French politics a special study,
and, I may say, a business. His father of course followed the
events with keenest interest.

Four months pass without any known event. The usual
holiday at Mickleham occurred in the interval ; and possibly
was occupied with the first draft of the observations on Mackintosh. Every such holiday had its appointed task ; only less
severe as the hand of time was telling upon the physical
vigour.

The 1st of December, this year, is the date of Mill's promotion to be head of the Examiner's office, through the retirement of his senior, William M'Culloch. His duty now was,
not to prepare despatches in any one department, as he had
hitherto done, but to superintend all departments—Revenue,
Judicial, Political, and General.

I had heard from various quarters that M'Culloch's reputation as an administrator was very high; his despatches

being accounted perfect models, and even superior to Mill's. It turns out, however, that these encomiums, although repeated by different persons, are all traceable to one source, namely Horace Grant, an official in the Examiner's office, who earned a well-merited reputation by a series of Education books, very much in advance of the time. Grant was one of John Mill's intimate friends, and was held in high esteem by him in every way I became acquainted with Grant, on one of my first visits to John Mill in the India House, and met him very frequently; I could not but regard him as an able man. I learn, however, on good authority, that James Mill was the means of withholding from him an increase of salary that the Directors would otherwise have been willing to allow; a proof of a want of perfect understanding between the two, which requires us to discount any unfavourable estimate that Grant might form of his official chief.

It strikes us as a curious coincidence that M'Culloch's retirement should take place just as the Company's Government was beginning its troubles; the intimation of the Duke having only then been received at the India House. Was this from an opinion felt by M'Culloch himself, or by the Directors, or by both parties, that Mill was the man to bear the brunt of the coming struggle, in other words, to prepare the defences of the Company against the pending attack? It was the head Examiner whose part it was to give shape to the views and arguments of the Court of Directors, and M'Culloch's retirement made the work fall on his successor.

One thing is certain, that Mill acquired a very great amount of influence and authority with the Court of Directors. It is doubted whether any one before or since obtained the same share of their confidence. It has been said that, he being dead when the Macaulay Commission brought over their new Code for India, the Directors could not trust their own judgment so far as to put it in force.

Mill had been one of the original members of the Athenæum Club, founded in 1824, the chief projector being, I am told, John Wilson Croker. This year the building was ready, and it was resolved to add 100 members to the Club. Mill was one of the Committee appointed to make the selection. This would scarcely be worth mentioning, but that it recalls a curious remark that I heard John Mill make. He said that he was elected to the club by this Committee; and but for that would never have been admitted at all: having already excited a sufficient amount of personal dislike among some of the members to ensure his being blackballed. This would seem to show that mere party feeling went to greater lengths then, in excluding men from the Athenæum, than it would do now. I am not aware of any offence that Mill can be supposed to have given to individuals in 1830, that would suffice to blackball a man in the present day.

In the *Autobiography*, John Mill states that the divergence between him and his father had become so great about this time, that he refrained as much as possible from talking on the subjects wherein they differed. He adds—" Fortunately we were almost always in strong agreement on the political questions of the day, which engrossed a large part of his interest and his conversation". He might have added, to the other questions of the day, the crisis in the India House, which made a great part of his work for two or three years. It must often have been the topic of their talk as they walked to and fro together between Queen Square and Leadenhall Street.

John gained a step by his father's promotion.

1831.

The Grey Ministry is now in power; Brougham is Chancellor, and is more anxious than ever to consult Mill on all emergencies. The extant letters to him, which are our most valuable documents for the remaining years, commence at this date.

Mrs. Grote has a memorandum for the 24th January.

"Mr. Mill (James) has had a baddish spell of gout. Confined for two weeks, and is a good deal reduced. He is now become 'Chief Examiner' at the India House. We dined with him in Queen Square on Sunday, 9th January, and in consequence of his pressing request that George would put forth some thoughts on the Essentials of Parliamentary Reform, he consented to employ the ensuing three weeks on the task."

The first letter to Lord Brougham is dated 5th February, and explains itself.

"QUEEN SQUARE, *5th Feby*, *1831.*

"MY DEAR LORD,

"Understanding by what passed between you and Lord Lansdowne last night, that you are maturing a plan about Emigration, I think I ought to make you acquainted, more distinctly than I have yet been able to do in conversation, with my views on that subject. You will take them, as they are meant to be offered, as items of the account which you cast up to make your own conclusion.

"First of all, I am anxious to know what scheme you have for preventing the influx of Irish; as without that, no void, by means of emigration, can be effected.

"I saw, the other day, that you immediately seized my idea of the necessity of comparing the sum necessary for the emigration of a family, and the fund which would suffice to give perpetual employment to the man, hence maintenance to the family. It is seldom considered how small that sum is a year's wages to the man, with a small addition for stock, the whole £50 or £60, would suffice.

"Two answers are ready, but neither, I think, of much weight.

"The first is, that you get rid of a breeding pair. True

but you also get rid of the capital which maintains them ; and by that means do not alter in the least the ratio of you population to your capital, either for the present moment, o for the future. The family in question, if breeding at home instead of the colony, would breed in a certain ratio to the supposed fund of £50 or £60 ; but every other family breed in exactly the same ratio, and that whether the family i question emigrates or remains at home.

" The other answer is, that though £50 or £60 would give your man perpetual employment at home, he will nevertheles be maintained in idleness. But I think we ought not to legislat upon such a principle as this ; that we must send away our popu lation, and the funds requisite for employing and maintainin them at home, because we have not the sense or the virtue t set them upon productive labour.

" I mention these things with the brevity of hints which t others would require much expanding, because your mind wi readily catch the meaning, and follow out the consequences.

" There is another consideration, more obvious, but whic is of some weight ; that the poor rate is paid out of income the money raised by loan for emigration, is a deduction from the capital of the country.

" I cannot forbear saying one word more on the subject o putting to labour the persons maintained at the public expense I perfectly agree with you that an effectual scheme to tha effect could not at present be brought forward, even by ministry with hopes of success. But much good would be done b prompting fit persons in both houses of parliament, to broac the subject, to create familiarity with the idea of it, the goo effects of it, and the feebleness of all objections. I am pe suaded that a ministry desirous to do more than circumstance will admit of their doing immediately, might in some suc ways make great preparation for their different objects ; and b taking a judicious share in such preliminary discussion strengthen the proper bias without committing themselves.

" We must have future conversations upon a point which I
as glad to find both you and Lord Lansdowne regarded so
vourably last night; I mean the choice of *managing* vestries
o I think I would call them rather than *select*), by the rate-
ayers of the parish. Something of this sort is indispensable,
r any tolerable management of the parochial fund. And I
ink that Parish Managers, and District Managers, constituted
on some such plan, and a sphere of action well defined for
em, would be a resource, which we may rue the want of, in
any emergencies which the present state of the world is not
likely to produce.

" I am, my Dear Lord,

" Faithfully yours,

" J. MILL.

The Lord Chancellor."

This letter shows him still in Queen Square. In a few
onths, he is at Vicarage Place, Kensington, in the detached
lla now called Maitland House.

On the 14th of Feb , he writes again to Napier on the filling
 of the appointment that he had formerly written about ; and
plies to suggestions about reprinting some of his Encyclo-
edia articles in the new edition (the Seventh) which Napier
 now editing. He also gives a more favourable account of
.orner's relations with parties at University College.

It appears to have been some time in March, that, in con-
quence of great pressure exerted upon Grote in the city, to put
mself forward as member, a consultation was held at Mill's
ouse to consider the matter. "After some hours it was
ecided that Mr. Grote would *not* come forward."

Our next document is also a letter to Napier, on the 1st
ne, still about the same appointment, on which the vacilla-
on of Lord Ellenborough had given needless trouble in the
ffice. He recurs to University College, retracts all that he
ad said about the better working of things. He had been

absent from the Council from illness, when he last wrote, and did not know the state of the facts. He now finds " that all the old causes of evil were in strong operation ; they have been met with no consistent measures of counteraction, and much more wisdom is needed now to combat with all the difficulties than I see any chance of being applied to them ".

In the month of August, he undergoes his eight days' examination before the Committee of the House of Commons, on the whole subject of the India Revenue.

A letter to Lord Brougham, on the 16th September, is our best indication of his views when the Reform Bill was in the depths. The point of time was, when the Bill had got through Committee in the House of Commons, and was down for the third reading (19th September). It was safe in the Commons—and the question uppermost in the country was, What will the Lords do?

" MICKLEHAM, *15th Sept,, 1831.*

" MY DEAR LORD CHANCELLOR,

" I have been down here for a few weeks, otherwise I should have endeavoured to get in contact with you before now. Whenever I am anxious about public matters, it always does, and always did do me good, to converse with you. I am angry, when I hear so much stir about the Lords. Sharp and I at our walk the other day met Denison, who said—would you really make fifty peers ? A fearful measure—death-blow to the peerage ! Very well, said I, and if the peerage will so have it, who is to blame ? What I want the Ministry to do—is to give out—fairly to proclaim—that they will *not* be defeated by the Lords ; that will do—the Lords are not wanting in that kind of wisdom which is called *sapere sibi.* That is truly my opinion. If they know you are determined, they will know what is proper for them to do. Croker and Peel are much more anxious to have you out than to defeat the bill—the last is their pretext.

"I shall be in town in a fortnight—when I shall be anxious to obey all your calls. You, I apprehend, will not get from town this year at all. When the bill comes into your house if I am in town I think I shall be present at the 2nd reading though I have not heard one debate these 20 years. Grey. Lord Plunkett and yourself, I wish to be the only speakers on your side. What havoc! What a waste of strength! But you must speak to those without and those who are to come. You must endeavour to make every sort of right, and sober, but deep, and manly sentiment strike root, so as not only to live, but yield fruit.

"About Peace (without which there is no salvation) it delights me to think how strong your feelings are. You are half a Quaker, and I am all but a whole one. India, its judicature altogether, or rather its government altogether, is a subject about which I should have to talk to you for a month There I am sure I can talk to you with advantage; because I can save you an infinite deal of pain in getting at the evidence on which you should build. I take the liberty in the meantime to entreat you, though you keep your ear open, to give it in trust to nobody till I have ground myself into it. The subject is of vast importance, and sound opinions about it seem to me to be not only rare, but absolutely wanting. The Lord be with you, prays fervently

"Your devoted

"J. MILL."

Place writes a long letter to Grote on the Reform crisis as it stood, on the 26th October. A short extract will show that he consulted Mill at every turn. "I had a long conversation with Burdett this morning, who seems well disposed to do anything and everything to obtain the Bill; and Mill, in reply to a note of mine, says, 'Your advice to the people who talk to you is the best possible. I saw Beauclerk and Perry to-day and am rejoiced to find that Sir Francis consents'."

1832.

The month of May of this year saw the crisis of the Refor[m] struggle.

I came across a reference to a deputation to Lord Brougha[m] which was headed by Mill; the purpose being to strengthe[n] his hands in the great contest in which he had a leading offi[-] cial part. Having mislaid the document, I cannot supply th[e] exact date or the terms of the address.

I shall have to review the peculiar influence exerted by Mi[ll] in the history of the Reform movement from the Peace to i[ts] consummation in the passing of the Bill. In the great agon[y] week, from Wednesday, 9th, to Wednesday, 16th May, his allie[s] and lieutenants play a conspicuous part. In the popul[ar] demonstrations that carried the day, we must count Franc[is] Place, George Grote, and Joseph Parkes, as chief among thos[e] that—

> Ride in the whirlwind and direct the storm.

Some particulars of the history of this momentous week ar[e] quoted in the Appendix.

The following letter to Lord Brougham is full of interest, an[d] tells its own tale, without comment.

"MICKLEHAM, *3rd Sept., 1832.*

"MY DEAR LORD CHANCELLOR,

"The subjects to which your letter adverts have bee[n] so much in my mind, that I have twenty times been tempte[d] to write to you—and only withheld by the fear of doing an[y] thing to interrupt the little time you have to repair the wea[r] and tear you sustain the rest of the year.

"Nothing can be conceived more mischievous than th[e] doctrines which have been preached to the common people, a[t] Birmingham and elsewhere. At a late meeting of the Unio[n] Attwood held forth for hours, giving an exaggerated descriptio[n] of the misery of the people, from low wages; then telling the[m]

that the only cause of low wages is the government, and whenever government does its duty, wages will be high. And the
rest of the Orators were in the same strain. ·I was enraged at
Black for republishing this atrocious stuff. The newspapers
should suppress all knowledge of these rascally meetings, by
abstaining from the mention of them.

"The nonsense to which your Lordship alludes about the
rights of the labourer to the whole produce of the country,
wages, profits, and rent, all included, is the mad nonsense of
our friend Hodgkin, which he has published as a system and
propagates with the zeal of perfect fanaticism Whatever of it
appears in the *Chronicle*, steals in through his means, he being
a sort of sub-editor, and Black not very sharp in detecting—
but all Black's own opinions on the subject of property are
sound.

"These opinions, if they were to spread, would be the
subversion of civilised society; worse than the overwhelming
deluge of Huns and Tartars. This makes me astonished at
the madness of people of another description who recommend
the invasion of one species of property, so thoroughly knavish,
and unprincipled, that it can never be executed, without
extinguishing respect for the rights of property in the whole
body of the nation, and can never be spoken of with approbation, without encouraging the propagation of those other
doctrines which directly strike at the root of all property.
There is a certain Macqueen of Bedford who has put forth a
pamphlet, recommending, without shame, that the ounce of
gold shall be coined into five sovereigns; that is that every
pecuniary contract in the nation shall be violated; in other
words, that one of the parties to every such contract shall be
robbed for the benefit of the other. If a man preaches this
doctrine without seeing what it is, he is below being treated
with by argument; if he preaches it, knowing what it is,
hanging, a thousand times repeated, would be too small a
punishment for him. I understand the Tory prints generally

are recommending this pamphlet. And upon the subject generally, the *Chronicle* has not been perfectly pure. The articles, however, in which any tampering with the currency has been spoken of as anything of a remedy, have all been written by Parkes of Birmingham, and let in by Black's softness both of head and temper. I have talked with him very roundly upon that subject, and his opinions are good, as far as he understands them, which is not far enough to save him from delusion. Unluckily, I am now able to see him but seldom; and then the influence of the people continually about him, gets the better of mine.

"I should have little fear of the propagation among the common people of any doctrines hostile to property, because I have seldom met with a labouring man (and I have tried the experiment upon many of them) whom I could not make to see that the existence of property was not only good for the labouring man, but of infinitely more importance to the labourers as a class, than to any other. But there are, in our circumstances at present, aids of that propagation, which may operate deplorably : one is that which I have just now mentioned, the robbery recommended through a depreciation of the currency ; the other is, the illicit cheap publications, in which the doctrine of the right of the labouring people, who they say are the only producers, to all that is produced, is very generally preached. The alarming nature of this evil you will understand when I inform you that these publications are superseding the Sunday newspapers, and every other channel through which the people might get better information. —I had been wondering for some time what made the *Examiner* speak of Lord Althorp so often in the tone of vituperation. Hearing that the Editor was going to Brighton, I got him to make a stop here on his way down, when he told me this, and that they considered Lord Althorp had not dealt fairly by them, or his own promise. I am sure it is not good policy to give the power of teaching the people exclusively to persons violat-

ing the law, and of such desperate circumstances and character
that neither the legal nor the moral sanction has sufficient hold
upon them.   The only effectual remedy is to remove the tax
which gives them this deplorable power.   Surely it ought not
to be said of your government that it is so void of resource as
to be unable to spare or to replace a tax of this amount, producing such consequences.

——"The resolution which seems to be taken to allow no merit
to our Society [Useful Knowledge], is most perverse.   Because
in one series of our Publications, there has been a superabun-
dance of things, but little practical, all that we have done
purely practical in other things is overlooked, and our character
given from the former.   We must, however, as you say,
endeavour at the practical even there.   But they are little
aware how difficult it is to get treatises of the kind they think
of; for though subjects upon which everybody writes and
talks, there are few people who can write and talk upon them
instructively.   It has been a source of great regret to me that
for the last twelvemonths I have been able to give so little
attention to the Society.   And till our Indian questions are
settled, which I hope will be next year, I shall continue to
have drudgery for every moment of my time.   But I am most
anxious to take a greater share in the labours which already
have done so much good, and for which there will long
continue to be so much occasion.

"What you say too about war is most important.   The
desire, so often expressed, that we should interfere to establish
good government all over the world, is most alarming, and if
assented to in any degree would lead to the worst of consequences.   The business of a nation is with its own affairs.
That is not only the general rule, but one to which it is not
easy to conceive a case of exception.   At all events, in the
present state of Europe we have nothing to do with any other
affairs but our own.   We have suffered enough by mischievous
interference.   Let us not again embark easily in that folly.

Besides, I am fully satisfied that the good of mankind in the largest sense, is more interested at the present moment, in the peace of England, and that of France, the two countries from which improvement emanates, and which will rapidly improve, if they keep free of war, than in re-establishing what they call the independence of Poland, or giving a particular Sovereign to Portugal, ten times told.

"I am ashamed of having prated to you so long—but, having once begun, I could not easily stop.

"I am, my dear Lord,

"With fervent wishes for your health and prosperity,

"Ever yours,

"J. MILL."

In a letter from the Governor General of India (Lord William Bentinck) to Mrs. Grote, there is a reference to Mill, in Lord William's usual strain of compliment and respect.

"I will not trouble you with my 'parish affairs'. From Mr. Mill, did an extraordinary curiosity so prompt you, you can learn much more of Indian affairs, than from me. I read his evidence with great pleasure, and much more profitable instruction, I suspect, than the E. I. committee. You mentioned his approbation of my administration. None could gratify me more, because he is one of the very few who can form a correct judgment."

The passing of the Reform Bill saw many of Mill's friends elected to Parliament. Grote came in for the city of London; Strutt for Derby. Hyde Villiers, was already in Parliament, and Secretary to the India Board, but died in the end of 1832. His brother Charles was first elected to Parliament, in 1835, for Wolverhampton, which he has continued to represent throughout his long and honourable career. Charles Buller, was member for Liskeard, in Cornwall, and retained his seat for life; he died prematurely, in the end of 1848. The old

Marshall retired : his second son John came in, with Macaulay as a colleague, for Leeds. The eldest son William had been in the House from 1826, to 1831, for a succession of places, but he is not in the Reform Parliament.

Mill was very anxious to get a seat for Charles Austin ; and strongly urged Hume to recommend him to Bath. Every one looked foward to Austin's career as one of extraordinary brilliancy, likely to end on the woolsack. Nevertheless, he remained out of Parliament, and devoted his energies to making an enormous fortune at the bar. I shall never forget John Mill's exclamation once when Grote told him that he had met Austin at dinner, and that he was launching forth in admiration of certain things in the New Testament. The contrast with his views in other days must have been very marked.

Roebuck was selected by Hume for Bath, on the recommen dation of Mr. Andrew Bisset.

We should not close the record of the year without noting the death of Bentham, on the 6th of June. His last illness was watched by his friends while the Reform struggle was at at its climax ; and John Mill did not fail to provide a worthy commemorative notice in the *Examiner*.

1833.

The Reform Parliament meets. Grote loses not a moment in giving notice of a motion for the Ballot.

Mrs. Grote tells us :—" In the beginning of 1833 Mr. and Mrs. Grote dined in Threadneedle Street with William George Prescott; his other guests being Henry Warburton, John Romilly, Joseph Hume, and James Mill. After some discussion it was settled that Mr. Grote should be the person to undertake the Ballot question in the ensuing session of Parliament."

Meantime the pressure of India affairs is coming to the intensity pitch. Mill had only a few days given him, in the

month of February, to prepare the final answer of the Court
of Directors to Grant's elaborate reply to their first paper.

There are two letters to Dr. Thomson, requesting him to
recommend a professor for the Elphinstone College, Bombay.
The second of the two (13th July), informs us that "the member
for Derby (Strutt) is coming down to spend to-morrow with
me," that is to be a Sunday visitor at Meikleham, as he often
was. This expression occurs :—" My head is full of India
bills, and has room for nothing else ".

The reader of Trevelyan's *Life of Macaulay* will be familiar
with the course of the India Bill in Parliament ; Macaulay
having delivered one of his greatest speeches in the debate on
the second reading. It was in that speech that he made the
following reference to Mill :—" Of all the innumerable specu-
lators who have offered their suggestions on Indian politics,
not a single one, as far as I know, however democratical his
opinions may be, has ever maintained the possibility of giving,
at the present time, such institutions to India. One gentleman, extremely well acquainted with the affairs of our Eastern
Empire, a most valuable servant of the Company, and the
author of a *History of India*, which, though certainly not free
from faults, is, I think, on the whole, the greatest historical
work which has appeared in our language since that of Gibbon,
I mean Mr. Mill, was examined on this point. That gentleman is well known to be a very bold and uncompromising
politician. He has written strongly, far too strongly I think,
in favour of pure democracy. He has gone so far as to maintain that no nation which has not a representative legislature,
chosen by universal suffrage, enjoys security against oppression.
But when he was asked before the Committee of last year,
whether he thought representative government practicable in
India, his answer was, ' utterly out of the question '."

By the Act, now passed, it was provided that one of the
members of the Supreme Council in Calcutta, was to be chosen
from among persons who are not servants of the Company.

One of Mill's suggestions was tantamount to this provision ; qualified by the condition that the said member should be versed in the philosophy of men and of society.

The Government immediately put this appointment in Macaulay's view. The salary was ten thousand a-year. The appointment, however, lay, not with the Government, but with the Court of Directors. Grant (President of the India Board), on the part of the government, would support the appointment , but he expected violent opposition from the Company. He mentioned Macaulay's name to the Chairs, and they were furious ; knowing the course he had taken against them on the India Bill. This is from a letter on the 23rd Oct. In ten days the appearances are altered, and the account Macaulay himself gives of the situation is this :—

" We have a new Chairman and Deputy-Chairman, both very strongly in my favour. Sharp, by whom I sate yesterday at the Fishmongers' dinner, told me that my old enemy James Mill had spoken to him on the subject. Mill is, as you have heard, at the head of one of the principal departments of the India House. The late Chairman consulted him about me ; hoping, I suppose, to have his support against me. Mill said, very handsomely, that he would advise the Company to take me ; for, as public men went, I was much above the average, and, if they rejected me, he thought it very unlikely that they would get anybody so fit."

We have seen that Mill was a friend of Zachary Macaulay, and although the families did not come together, Mill's relationships were well known to the household. (*Life*, Vol. I., p. 186, 1st ed.). In the interval between the appointment to India and his setting out, Macaulay frequently saw Mill at his house. John Mill remembered his father earnestly counselling him to keep to the line of an " honest politician ".

The only letter to Lord Brougham this year, is one of condolence for the loss of his brother James.

" MY DEAR LORD CHANCELLOR,

. "I have been in many minds about writing to you. My first impulse was to tell you how much I sympathize with you. And then I was afraid I should only be unreasonably officious. However, I must and will write. The death of any person, whom I have known so long, and known to possess so many amiable qualities, would have affected me. But when I think of the intimate and affectionate union in which he and you have lived from your boyhood, I conceive most feelingly the state of your mind, and pity you from the bottom of my heart. I would not venture thus to speak, but that the long personal attachment I have felt to you, and the share you have always shown I had in your regard, makes me think I have a right to the freedom of an old friend. The emotions of sorrow time will assuage, and the heavy calls of duty to which you must attend, will be a diversion to your thoughts. But alas ! the Deceased occupied a place about you which no body else can fill. No man can share your couusels as he did. That is a loss irretrievable.

" It is a great consolation to me to know you have been with your mother on this trying occasion. At her time of life such a blow as this falls with terrible weight. Your presence alone can support her. I trust you will be able to leave her, when you are forced away, in some degree of tranquillity.

" I hope you duly consider one duty, the care of your health. I know not when the time was, in the history of our species, that more depended on the health of one man, than depends at this moment on yours. The progress of mankind would lose a century by the loss of you. Think what that is !

" I hope you will not feel this as an intrusion. When it will be any gratification to you to see me, after your return, it will be a great satisfaction to me to come to you, and to talk with you about doing good to the world, which you

ave more deeply at heart than any other man I am acquainted
ith.

"Most affectionately and respectfully yours,
"J. MILL."

Mention of James Brougham is made by Jeffrey, "Cock-
urn's Life," II. 94.

1834.

We have very little to record for this year.

Among the great reforms carried through Parliament this
ession, was the Poor Law Amendment Act, with which Mill
rongly sympathized ; while John wrote strongly in its favour.
he Act, however, incurred the displeasure of the *Times*, which
ist then turned against Lord Brougham, and was attacking
im furiously. The following sentences show the form of
tack. "The *Times* for 15 years praised, supported, or it
ou will, patronised his Lordship, so long as we supposed Lord
rougham to be actuated by honourable and elevated notions,
uided by fixed and enlightened principles, aspiring to power
rrough none but direct and manly means, disposed to use it
irtuously. . . . We withdrew our friendship on finding it
estowed unworthily." This attack was the occasion of the
ollowing letter.

"MICKLEHAM, *27th Aug., 1834.*

"MY DEAR LORD CHANCELLOR,

"I am induced to write to you at present by what I see
a the newspapers. I had observed by the *Chronicle* which
lone I see down here, that the *Times* was barking at you,
s it had been doing before I left town. I asked for some of
ie particulars from my son, who came down on Saturday, and
e gave me such an account of the extent to which that paper
as carrying its outrages, as induced me to get him to send me
own a parcel of the recent numbers. I know no instance of such

gross abuse. Denying one's talents, making one out to be a driveller, and a fool, I have had some experience of, and it touched me very slightly ; because I had evidence enough that better judges than my assailants did not think me so. But it is much harder to bear the sort of moral charges brought by the *Times* ; and I know not well how I should have felt under them. You, however, have one enormous advantage in this respect. Your life has not been so obscure, that there can be anything now to discover about you. There is not a reflecting man in the civilized world who has not made up his opinion of your character ; from which few will be turned by a revolution in the language of the *Times*, which no man alive ascribes to the love of telling the truth.

"I have been induced to touch on this subject by my fear, not that any undue impression would be made on you by the powerless hostility of the *Times*, but lest others, many of whom will feel more for you than you do for yourself, should make you think the matter more serious than it is. My opinion is, that it does you no harm whatsoever. The motive of the *Times*, I infer with certainty, is duly appreciated. The *Chronicle* of yesterday says a pertinent thing enough. What is the reason that the hostility of all who prey upon the public, and fight for noxious privileges, is steadily against you, but that they reckon upon you as the steady, and thank God, the powerful friend of all that is good in government ? If they believed you unsteady and deceitful, they would have better hopes of you. It is only necessary that you should go on in your own course ; doing all the service to good legislation which you can, and when you are impeded, making it at all events known, how much more you would have done, if you had not been prevented ; and you will most effectually baffle and disgrace your enemies of all sorts and sizes. Many motives are obviously enough imputed to the *Times* : your advocation of the Poor Law Bill ; your efforts to get repealed the taxes on newspapers, and others. But, I doubt not there is something more than this. The

Times (drolly to be sure, but pretty evidently) have been assuming to be really the governing power in this country, and to overawe even the Ministry. They, therefore, cannot endure the idea of having a man at the head of a Ministry, who is made of stuff not to be dictated to by a newspaper. They want a Ministry of whom they may boast (by insinuation at least) that it is a tool of theirs—and then they will sell thousands of papers. It agrees with this theory of mine that you and Lord Althorp are the objects of their attack.

" I am amusing myself during these holidays with looking over a thing, which, if I can get it put in order while here, you may hear something more of. When Mackintosh's *Dissertation* first appeared, indeed before it was published, I had prepared some strictures upon it, chiefly with a view to expose his perversions of the principle of utility, and indeed the manner in which he had smattered with ethical science to evil purpose altogether. But I had written it in the form of letters to himself; which would not do, when he was dead; and with an asperity, which I would not find in my heart to use with a man who was just dead, and who could not stand up in his own defence. The papers thereupon lay by till now. But I could not help feeling that something useful might be done in removing confusion from men's minds on that important subject, of which Sir James's book is a wonderful example, and in showing the misfortune of men's deluding themselves with unmeaning words of which Sir James's book is not less an example.

" I am sorry for what you say about Lord Auckland. I must hear you speak on the subject of individuals, whose character I can but partially know. But the thing is of first-rate importance ; and every thing should be done to keep Lord William there. Cameron has been down with me for some days, mainly with a view to go into the details of his magnificent charge. He views it with the proper spirit. And I doubt not India will be the first country on earth to boast of a system of law and judicature as near perfection as the circumstances of the people would admit.

"I am, my dear Lord Chancellor,

"Most respectfully yours,

"J. MILL."

It was this summer that the *London Review* was projected.* With the Fragment on Mackintosh, it made up Mill's chief occupation, so far as we know, for the remaining two years of his life.

1835.

For this year our information is very full. Of the articles written for the *Westminster Review*, four are published in the course of the year. There is an unusual number of interesting letters to Lord Brougham, besides other indications of the current leading events, including the attack of illness that proved the beginning of the end.

Some interest may attach to the certificate that he gave his son James, in compliance with the forms prescribed by the East India Company for admission to the service of the Company. I presume it was by an exceptional privilege, that the Court of Directors accepted a certificate from a candidate's father.

* The following is the account given in the *Autobiography* "One of the projects occasionally talked of between my father and me, and some of the parliamentary and other Radicals who frequented his house, was the foundation of a periodical organ of philosophic radicalism, to take the place which the *Westminster Review* had been intended to fill · and the scheme had gone so far as to bring under discussion the pecuniary contributions which could be looked for, and the choice of an editor. Nothing, however, came of it for some time . but in the summer of 1834, Sir William Molesworth, himself a laborious student, and a precise and metaphysical thinker, capable of aiding the cause by his pen as well as by his purse, spontaneously proposed to establish a Review, provided I would consent to be the real, if I could not be the ostensible, editor. Such a proposal was not to be refused , and the Review was founded, at first under the title of the *London Review*, and afterwards under that of the *London* and *Westminster*, Molesworth having bought the *Westminster* from its proprietor, General Thompson, and merged the two into one."

"I certify that my son, James Bentham Mill, received the early part of his education, corresponding to what is usually received at school, in my house, and under my eye, myself being his principal teacher, and that it comprehended the usual subjects, Latin, Greek, Mathematics, Geography, and History—that he afterwards entered the University of London, in which he studied during the whole of four years, attending the Latin, Greek, and Mathematical classes, and for two years, the class of Natural Philosophy, the class of Chemistry, the class of Logic, and the class of Jurisprudence; and that since he left the University, the whole of his time, an interval of about two years, has been employed in prosecuting his studies at home, under my superintendence, improving himself in his knowledge of Latin, Greek, and Mathematics, and reading such books as I recommended to him, giving to me regularly an account of what he read, sometimes orally, sometimes in writing. I add the expression of my belief that he will be found a well-educated youth. And I cannot be mistaken in affirming that all his habits at present are good; that he is laborious and steady, of a calm and considerate disposition, and free from vice, as far as I know, of every kind.

"INDIA HOUSE, *7th June, 1835.*"

This is well known to have been a very stormy year in politics. The Peel Government had given place to the Melbourne Reform Ministry. There were four great measures pending, which the advanced reformers were bent on securing—Repeal of the Taxes on Knowledge, the Ballot, Reform of the Irish Church, and Municipal Reform. The first was postponed by the Chancellor of the Exchequer, Spring Rice—to the great disgust of the Radicals. The second, the Ballot, was opposed by the Ministry, although commanding a good support in the House. The third, the Irish Church, the Government undertook to deal with, but, in so doing, brought about a collision with the House of Lords, which raised the political excitement the year to its climax. The Municipal Reform Bill was also ie of the government measures.

The first number of the *London Review* was published in pril, and opened with an article by Mill on the " State of the ation ".

The purpose of the article is to place before us a view of ie present state of the country as boding for the future. The iost remarkable circumstance is the strength of the spirit of :form. The men whose boast and glory had been that they ere the general enemies of reform, have been compelled to eclare themselves its friends. The predominant influence of ie country—intellect and property taken together—is with ie reformers. The Tory party have changed their language nd their name. They lately tried the experiment of a general lection, which only showed more decisively the strength of ie reforming impulse ; and this notwithstanding that the power f intimidation and bribery, which is allowed by the present lectoral system, was exerted to the utmost.

The author then remarks upon the extraordinarily short time iat has sufficed for the growth of the spirit of reform. It is ut a brief interval since Sir Francis Burdett was expelled from ristocratic society, and since to be called a Benthamite exposed man to be cut in the street by the friends of the aristocrats. t cannot, then, be long ere the new spirit show material results.

It is a curious enquiry, what has been the agency of this reat change. Not the newspapers, for these have generally een very backward and unsteady in their advocacy. Not the irger periodicals, which are unsuited to the populace, and ddressed to the aristocratical classes. The real agency has een the spontaneous reflections of the middle class ; based, in great measure, on the observation of the way that Hume's ersistent exposures were received in the House of Commons.

Will this spirit be permanent? The answer depends on hether any good is to come of it. Well, as the Ruling Few have not yet been made to disgorge their spoil of the Many, good must come when that operation is accomplished.

The author here resumes his former expositions of the attitude of the Ruling Few to the subject Many ; setting forth the arts adopted, the support rendered by the union of Church and State, and by the class of Lawyers. By a threefold cord, the doom of mankind might have been sealed, but for printing and the reformation of Luther.

To come down to the actual situation. Formerly the opponents of change were divided into anti-reformers and half-and-half reformers. The first of these two are extinct ; they are incorporated with the others, without relinquishing their old modes of warfare. The thorough reformers have been rendered disreputable by the name " radicals " ; they are represented as desiring the destruction of government and religion, or else as so stupid as not see that what they desire amounts to that. The force of this calumny is now nearly spent. Who is to judge of what is good or bad in political institutions ? Is it the majority of those that defame the thorough reformers ? These are no more to be trusted than the majority of the people at large. If it is the wise few among them, then there is also a wise few outside of them. Defamation is not discussion. Government is no less government when it is better adapted to its ends ; religion is no less religion when it is purified from the defilements of selfish interests.

To show the differences of opinion as to abuses, the author refers to the master abuse—the want of freedom of election. This, opponents say, is an advantage ; the Reform Bill is now to be taken as *final*, it is on that view that Sir Robert Peel has declared his accession to it—a declaration that gives the measure of the man.

The author then dwells upon the necessity of the two things —secret voting and short parliaments.

Reverting to the junction above mentioned of anti-reformers and moderate reformers—the new moderates and the old—he shows how the classes respectively preponderate in the two Houses; and then addresses himself to the course proper to be pursued by the little band of genuine reformers. They are in a position where they may render incalculable good. They should not aim at office; the time is not come for a partial union with either parties of the moderates. Yet, it will be the interest of every minister to have them for him rather than against him. Their vocation divided itself into two paths of exertion. The one is to make it the interest of every ministry to be the author of reforms. The other is to be the champion of the philosophical principles of government. There has been no example in Parliament, of a man worthy of this function, since the short period when Ricardo lifted his head. The absence of men to stand up for principles has been so complete that a faction has been created against it.—" We believe it would be impossible to assemble an equal number of tolerably educated men, in any other part of the civilised world, among whom it would be fashionable to set reason at defiance, and to profess to act in contempt of her dictates ". There is a set of harsh phrases, serving each of them as a wrapper for a little parcel of sophistry. " Not speculation but practice," " wisdom of ancestors," " Institutions," and so on. The exposure of these sophistries would be a source of popular instruction of the highest importance.

The true reformer should farther signalize himself as the champion of property, as in the case of the attack on the fund-holders. Also, care should be taken to prevent injury to life-interests, a principle lately violated in the cry against the holders of crown pensions. Then comes the abolition of the tax on corn : the abolition of the malt tax would operate in the wrong direction.

Among detached incidents occurring to rouse the attention of reformers, the author refers to an insolent answer of Sir Robert Peel to the question of Mr. Wakely—whether the inhabitants of St. Margaret's parish were to have the choice of

their rector. Sir Robert observes, in the true style of o
Tory insult, "the inhabitants would not be put to that trouble
Education of course demands to be considered. Finall
the Colonies must be ranked as one grand cause of the oppre
sion of the English people. So long as a colony fails to defr.
its own expenses, it is hurtful to the mother country.

In the same number of the *Review* Mill contributes a
article on the Ballot, in the form of a Dialogue. It was
reply to a systematic attack on the Ballot in the *Edinbur.
Review* for January, 1833. The Speakers are—a Farmer, wl
has been enfranchised, but feels himself in the power of h
landlord; a Squire, who stands up for that state of things; ar
a Schoolmaster, who argues down the Squire, to the satisfactic
of the Farmer.

The following letter to Lord Brougham appears to have bee
written in June.

"VICARAGE PLACE, KENSINGTON,
" THURSDAY.

"MY DEAR LORD,
"Isaac Tomkins has shewn me the MS. of a secor
part of *Thoughts on the Aristocracy;* and has allowed me
shew them to you. I assured him I could take that freedo
with you.

"If you ask me what I think of them, I answer, they a
so much like the matter of certain musings I have had of lat
that I could almost believe they were written by myself, yet
wonder at the boldness of Friend Isaac.

"What he says of the Ministry, and of their position,
their inclination and their powers, cuts home so deeply, becau
it is so true. The people, however, must be made to und
stand, that it is to themselves they must look for reforms,
they would have any. And Isaac Tomkins is rendering
service of infinite importance by beginning the work.

"I tell him, it is a long and severe warfare in which he is engaging. But Isaac is made of good stuff. He says he knows by experience what perseverance can do in a good cause ; that he is old enough to remember the commencement of the endeavours which ended in the emancipation of black men from white, under less favourable circumstances than efforts can now be made to emancipate low-born men from the high-born ; and that, great as that object was, it sinks into nothing compared with this.

"I do not think Isaac's ambition is ill-placed, and I do not think he is insensible to the glory of annexing his name to the work, as that of Luther to the emancipation of all men from the domination of priests. These emancipations are the things to get permanent glory by, and Isaac Tomkins knows it.

"I am, my dear Lord,

"Most sincerely yours,

"J. MILL."

In the July number of the *London Review* appears the notable article on "The Church and its Reform".

In the article, in the previous number, on the State of the Nation, the author had reserved the consideration of the two great provinces of abuse—Law and Religion. The present article is devoted to Religion.

He begins with quotations from Jortin, and from Bishop Watson, in favour of a sweeping reform in the English church. Watson's expressions are a little remarkable. A reformer of Luther's temper, he says, would, in five years, persuade the people to compel the Parliament to abolish tithes, to extinguish pluralities, to enforce residence, to expunge the Athanasian Creed, to free Dissenters from Test Acts, and the ministers of the establishment from subscription to articles. After forty-four years, only one item has been scored—the repeal of the Test Acts.

The time is come for considering what might be done by a well-ordered and well-conducted clergy. The author proposes first to illustrate the nullity of the present ecclesiastical establishment in respect of good, and its power in the production of evil. The world needs no information respecting the abuses of the Romish church. The English clergy embraced the Romish machinery very nearly as it stood : the same orders of priests, with the same monstrous inequality of pay ; the same course of clerical service, doing little more than translate the Mass-book ; while the English clergyman is less devoted to the concerns of his office than the unmarried Romish priest. Can anything be a greater outrage upon the sense of propriety, a more profligate example of the contempt of public good, than to see a concatenation of priests, paid, in proportions, ranging from the height of princely revenues, down to less than the pay of a common footman ? The work performed for this pay exhibits, in the extreme, the opposite vices of extravagance and deficiency.

The author undertakes to maintain these two propositions :— First, the services that are obligatory, and are regularly performed, are Ceremonies, from which no advantage can be derived. Second, that the services that might be efficacious in raising the moral and intellectual character of the people, are purely optional, are performed always most imperfectly, and in general not at all.

He remarks first on the *Sunday Service.* The repetition of forms of words tends to become a merely mechanical operation. The formularies themselves are of the nature of mere ceremonies. Of the repetition of Creeds, in particular, the best thing that can be said is that it is purely ceremonial. If it is not so, it is far worse ; by the habit of affirming as fact what is not a fact, a habit of insincerity is engendered that may pander to every other crime. The Collects may be classed with the Prayers ; the whole together is either meaningless or a great deal worse. The essence of the religious sentiment is a steady conception of an Almighty Being of perfect wisdom and goodness. The Church of England presents a Being very imperfect in both attributes. This strong statement the author supports chiefly by the character and composition of the prayers. Telling God unceasingly of our wants implies that he needs to be told of them. Asking him continually to do things for us, implies our belief that otherwise he would not do them; that is, our belief either that God will not do what is right if he be not begged and entreated to do so, or that, by being begged and entreated, he can be induced to do what is wrong. Then as to praise, what use can there be in telling the Divine Being that he has such and such qualities, as if he was likely to mistake his own qualities, or that he is delighted in listening to his own praises. The Divine Author of our religion everywhere indicates his opinion that prayer is nothing but a ceremony. He nowhere lays stress on prayer as a duty. With his usual condescension to the weakness of his countrymen, he does not reprobate the practice, but by placing it among the vices of the Pharisees, he indicates what he thought of it. In the Sermon on the Mount, all prayer is reprobated but secret prayer, and even that is not recommended. Jesus never himself makes a prayer on a public occasion; his expression— your Father knoweth what things ye have need of before you ask him—is a distinct declaration that prayer is a ceremony only. It is self-evident that to offer petitions to the Divine Being with the idea that they will have any effect is to suppose the petitioner wiser than his Maker.

As to the rest of the Sunday service, where is the use of a priest to read a chapter of the Bible which every head of a family does at home? Why read particular chapters only? Then the Communion Service is considered, among Protestants, as a ceremony. According to Bentham's showing, it was never intended to be permanent, even as a ceremony, and it is particularly ill-fitted for that use.

Next comes the Sermon, the only thing not essentially ceremonial, but liable to become not only ceremonial like the rest, but mischievous.   One great feature of sermons consists in praise heaped unceasingly on the Divinity, with condemnation heaped as unceasingly on the Personification of Evil, as if there could be any one not already prepared to bestow laudatory epithets upon God, and opprobrious epithets on the Devil, as far as his powers of language would permit.   Another grand class of Church-of-England sermons is occupied with praise of the Church and abuse of Dissenters ; converting religion, which ought to be a principle of love, into a principle of hatred.   Is this a morality fit to be promulgated in every parish in the kingdom ?   The author here adduces a charge of the then Archbishop of Canterbury, when Bishop of London, which Bentham had already overhauled, and where Dissenters were treated as " enemies " and men of " guilt ".   Is not this Antichrist ?

Another class of sermons is the controversial ; those that undertake to settle points of dogmatic divinity.   It is the opinion of rational men, that for ordinary congregations, such discourses can be of no use, and have a tendency to be hurtful. They put undue stress on points of belief that are not necessary   They lower man's ideas of the Divine character ; they suborn belief, and create in the hearers a habit of dealing dishonestly with their own emotions.   This is nearly the most immoral state of mind that can exist in a human being.   The Church of England teaching, in a vast amount, has this tendency.   Oh, for a Pascal !

Leaving other subdivisions of sermons, the author comes to the moral.   Though a man of the proper stamp would have other and more effectual means for making good moral impressions, yet a discourse of the right sort, delivered on the day of rest to the assembled parishioners, would have happy effects. It would establish pure ideas of the moral character of God, a matter neglected or trampled upon in the Church of England religion.   It is childish to call the Almighty benevolent, and ascribe to him actions that are the reverse; or to call him wise, and represent him as moved by considerations that have weight only with the weakest of men.

The author directs particular attention to the notions propagated as to punishment after death.   Punishment is in itself undesirable, and it is to be applied in the smallest quantity possible. The prevailing doctrine of future punishments reduces the Deity to an atrocious savage.   Not only is the punishment excessive, it is also useless, being applied when the time of action is gone by.   Proximity of punishment is necessary to its efficacy.   Hell-punishment is not derived from Scripture, as might be proved by particular evidence.   In the view of Butler, the individual will pass into a future life with all his acquired habits and dispositions, and be under a corrective regime, which will bring him right in the end.

Next to the propagation of correct notions of the Supreme Being, is the stimulation of kindly and generous feelings, and of the desire of doing good; guarding against misleading affections; above all impressing parents with the right course to be taken in the education of children.

Such, however, is not the character of the moral sermons of the Church of England.   The author professes to have heard many of these, and to have found them to consist of vapid commonplaces, given in vague and vapouring phrases.   He has often asked himself, after hearing such a sermon, whether any human being could have received one useful impression from it.   He allows that the church has produced sermons of great controversial ability, but all defective in moral teaching.

So much for the regular service.   There remain the special ceremonies of Baptism, Marriage, and the Burial of the Dead; which are all dismissed as worthless, and, in the case of baptism, vicious from doctrinal error.

The author admits that there are good men among the working clergy, but they are the small number, and their energies are wanting in system.   They are not instructed in the art of doing good.   Is it any wonder that, among a people improving in intelligence, the clergy have lost their influence? And if so, what is the use of them?   The population have chosen other guides.   The Dissenters give evidence that they are in earnest about their religion.   The Establishment is the natural sink of the indifferent, and of those whose lives are too scandalous for any other Christian society.   The Church of England exists merely as a state-engine; a willing instrument of those that hold the powers of government, to assist in abusing these.   It is worthy of remark that the drunken and pauper part of the population cling to the church.

Having gone thus far, the author finds it advisable to mitigate the clamour that is likely to be raised by such plain speaking; and he proceeds to adduce, as authorities on his side, Dr. Middleton and Jeremy Taylor, which, however, bear chiefly on the intolerance and bigotry of the church.   The author adds, of himself, that the clergy of the church have sworn to stand still, and therefore detest all those that go on. The search after truth bodes them evil, and all their art is employed to prevent it.

So much for the evils; now for the remedy.   By certain changes, far from violent, the church might be made an instrument of good.   The first thing would be a more equal distribution of work among the clergy, by equalizing parishes. Next, to secure men of good education and character, they should receive sufficient pay.   Then comes the question—who is to appoint them?   The author does not pronounce decisively on this point, but assumes the difficulty to be not insurmountable.   He considers the best modes of superintendence, whether by individuals (bishops) or by assemblies, as in Scotland.   He allows that the Scotch system has worked best, but favours a modified system of personal inspection.   Instead of having great lords to do the work, he would have inspectors at, say, £1000 a-year; the highest pay of the parish priest being £500: all pay being by salary, instead of by estates; a system that he strongly condemns. He inclines to think that laymen would be preferable for the work of inspection : there would be no questions as to the adherence of the clergy to dogmas ; it being a fundamental of the scheme that the inculcation of dogmas should be forbidden, as suborning belief, and tending to make men liars. On this topic the author enlarges by referring to the history of the church, and its persistent opposition to all enquiry. He quotes the reprobation of Locke by Copleston, for disrespect to the opinions of the church, and illustrates the degradation of the mind of the clergy by copious extracts from the *Dunciad.* He also returns to his old charges against the church for neglecting education until it became a piece of tactics ; when, by coupling it with religion, they made sure that it should be in their own hands.

He repeats, from the positive or constructive side, that ceremonies and dogmas should be dispensed with. This would make a truly Catholic church : all would share in its services ; it would be the true idea of a State religion. · The addresses of the clergy would have no other object than to assimilate the minds of the hearers to Him who is the perfection of wisdom and benevolence. This would be the true plan for converting Dissenters ; there would be no schism, when men had nothing to scind about.

The work of the clergy would thus consist in supplying all possible inducements to good conduct. No general rules could be given for the work, but tests might be applied for results. Such would be—premiums for the minimum of crimes, of lawsuits, of pauperism, of ill-educated children. The assembling of all the families on the Sunday, clean and well-dressed, has an ameliorating effect. Besides addresses of a purely moral kind, instruction in science and useful knowledge would be of great service. Even branches of political science might be introduced ; such as political economy and the conditions of good government. Some of the elements of jurisprudence would be valuable; to teach the maxims of justice and the theory of protection of rights.

These would be the more serious occupations of the **day of rest**. There should also be social amusements of a mild character, such as to promote cheerfulness rather than profuse merriment. Sports involving bodily strength, are not well adapted to promote brotherly feelings; their encouragement in antiquity had in view the urgency of war. Music and dancing would be important. It would be desirable to invent dances representing parental, filial, and fraternal affections; and to avoid such as slide into lasciviousness, which the author is always anxious to repress. Quiet and gentle motions, with an exhibition of grace, are what would be desired. To keep everything within the bounds of decency, the parishioners would elect a master and a mistress of ceremonies, and support their authority. A conjoint meal on Sunday would have the happiest effects; being a renewal of the *Agapai*—love feasts—of the early Christians; but with the exclusion of intoxicating liquors.

The author finally disposes of the objection—How is all this to be done? If there are as many people in earnest about religion as there are who pretend to be, all the difficulties would be overcome.

We should not have been astonished at such a paper proceeding from Bentham, whose studies in Theology were extremely limited. But Mill had a complete Theological education, under able masters; and his reading in the subject even in his later years was very considerable. His exegesis of the New Testament in regard to prayer, is somewhat surprising. That he could have supposed it possible, in the course of a few years, to unlearn the whole of the Christian traditions, and to re-model the entire ritual upon the basis of a Religion of Natural Theism, is more wonderful still. Judging from the point of view of our time, he has even mistaken the lines of the future modification of our Theological and Ecclesiastical framework. It is in the highest degree improbable, from present appearances, that the State will continue to uphold a parochial system for any purposes unconnected with purely secular business.

The article, with all its ingenuity, will have to be remanded to the list of Utopias, among which it will deserve perusal for its constructive suggestions.

The immediate effect of such an outspoken criticism of the Church was to damage the circulation of the *Review*. The editors were more careful for the future, but they could not recover the ground that was lost; and the suspicion of its irreligious tendency was never effaced.

The following letter refers to a set of Lectures on Political Economy, prepared by William Ellis, and, at Lord Brougham's suggestion, delivered to popular audiences throughout the country. They were circulated gratis to the Mechanics' Institutions. I can remember receiving a copy for the Aberdeen Institution, of which I was Secretary. A subsequent letter alludes more fully to the incidents connected with them.

'' INDIA HOUSE, *8th July, 1835.*

" MY DEAR LORD,

" I have made arrangements, which I shall be unable to alter, for going out of town on Friday afternoon. But I consider that as of little consequence ; because I know well what to expect from the Lectures ; and should eagerly give my assent to whatever may be deemed the best mode of using them. Is anybody known who could be used as an itinerating lecturer ? I have a high opinion of what may be done by that means, with such lectures as you can make. It would be good to think of the means of having a set of Lecturers. It would not be difficult to have men of tolerable capacity trained to be good readers ; and that, with discreet conduct and gentleman's manners, would suffice.

"I am, my dear Lord, with admiration of your ceaseless efforts,

"Most faithfully yours,

"J. MILL."

Our next intimation gives the date of his chest seizure. Lord William Bentinck had just come from India, and Mrs. Grote was displeased that he had not yet paid her a visit.

"KENSINGTON,
"SATURDAY, *15th August, 1835.*

"MY DEAR MRS. GROTE,

"I hasten to exonerate Lord William, who is wanting in no point of respect in regard toward you. The last conversation I had with him, which is the only one I have had with him alone—after a hundred questions about you—he said, 'I shall go down to-morrow to see her at Dulwich'. And he seemed rather disappointed when I told him he would not find you. I won't tell you all he says about you; it would make you too vain. He is going for a few months to some watering-place in Germany. Indeed, I am afraid, he is gone. If he is not, I should like you to call upon *him*. He is a man worth making much of, I assure you. When I consider what he is, and what he has done, in a most important and difficult situation, I know not where to look for his like.

"I was seized, the beginning of this week, with a spitting of blood, and have been ordered to keep since in perfect quiet, and not to speak. We have got the better of the hemorrhage, I think, for the present, and I venture to go this afternoon to Mickleham. I shall send for Myrtle in the beginning of the week, and, as soon as it is safe for me to venture motion, I shall get on her back.

I pity the purgatory of poor Grote. I imagine, however, from what I read in the ministerial papers, that the H. of C. will pretend the Corporation Bill is still worth having, notwithstanding its murder by the Lords, and that the House will be

up soon.   After Lyndhurst's clause about the freemen, I should
be glad to know what there is good in the Bill?

"I am, my dear Madam,

"Most truly yours,

"J. MILL."

'Myrtle' was a horse that Mrs. Grote lent him for several
summers during his stay at Mickleham; his powers of walking
being of late reduced by general weakness.

His arrival at Mickleham made a sad impression on the
household.   A lady, still living, the daughter of Professor
Wallace, was then on a visit, and remembered his entering the
house.   He was scarcely able to speak, and his only words
were—"Give me some marmalade and some milk".   The
family remember sending to the neighbours to get some cold
meat, as he could not endure anything hot.

This was but the consummation of his down-hill career.   In
the spring, he had mentioned to Romilly and Strutt, who had
been dining with him, that he had suffered much the previous
winter from sick headache.   He had also an attack of gout in
the eyes, of which we can dimly imagine the horrors.

Dr. Arnott thought he might still recover.   Sir J. Clark, a
better authority on lung disease, never thought so.   Arnott used
to attribute the growing obstruction of his lungs, to the dust on
the road to Mickleham, on which he had two three-hour
journeys a week, on the top of the coach, for several months
in the year.   There can be no doubt, however, that much
deeper causes were at work.

A fortnight later, he writes to Lord Brougham.

"MICKLEHAM, *August 29, 1835.*

"MY DEAR LORD,

"I take the liberty of requesting that you will be so
good as allow Mr. Bracken to see you.   He is the gentleman
about whom I have spoken to you before, the late partner of
our friend James Young in the House at Calcutta, the misfor-

tunes of which have reduced him from affluence to absolutely nothing. His wish is that you would speak of him to Lord Auckland (as he has now made up his mind to go back to India) with such recommendation as you may think his may require. It will speak to Lord Auckland's feelings, I am sure.

"You are fighting, my dear Lord, a noble battle, the consequence of which will be long-lived glory, while I have been only fighting with disease. I have an up-hill fight of it, as well as you.

"I am, my dear Lord,

"Most respectfully yours,

"J. MILL."

Prostrate as he was, he rouses himself to pen the following energetic epistle, also to Lord Brougham :—

"MICKLEHAM, 5th October, 1835.

"MY DEAR LORD,

"Nothing ever was more ridiculous than this attempt to make a plagarist of you for the Lectures of Mr. Ellis, which were written for the sole purpose of being delivered by himself in the City of London Literary Institution, where my son tells me that he heard the first lecture; when Mr. Ellis, before beginning to read it, told his hearers that his sole object was to lay before them the doctrines of the science in the plainest manner he had been able; that he had aimed at no originality; that he had taken the doctrines, and sometimes even the words, as he had found them in the most approved books. You heard of these lectures for the first time from me, I having mentioned them casually in one of our conversations about the time. It so happened also that a person whom you know had read your discourse (not then printed) on the Study of the Physical Sciences to a Literary Society at Manchester; and it immediately occurred to you that he might very usefully read these same lectures to the same Society, if Mr. Ellis would part with them for that purpose, which he very readily did. They were afterwards lent to Mr. Leonard Horner, for the purpose of being read either by himself, or somebody else (I forget which), at some Institution in Edinburgh. And they have been read, chiefly through your recommendation, in several other places. My son has undertaken to send this history to Black, and if he puts it in, the truth will be known. As for M'Culloch, he has a knack at finding people stealing from him; though there is nothing in him to steal; for all that he has, which is sound, is either the opinion of some other previous writer, or an error. But this shows that your enemies are hard driven to find a subject of attack.

"As to the subject of your former letter, which you sent me from Althorp, it did not tell me anything but what I was in some degree prepared for. I knew, in a general way, the feeling of your former colleagues towards you; but I pretty strongly trusted in their cowardice. I did not think they would *dare* to go on without you. For though weak men never like to have a strong man among them, I did not imagine they were so utterly blind to their own weakness. But all that is necessary for you is to have patience. Your merits are not forgotten, as will appear when the time comes. Changes are not far off. To be sure, the baseness of the treatment you have met with is not common, except among Whigs, not making an exception of Tories. I have been reading, while down here trying to get back a little health, Coxe's Life of Marlborough, which, if you have not already done it, you should read. It throws much light on our history; but, above all, on the trade of calumny in the hands of our leading factions. The extent to which it was carried against him most was equalled by the malignity both of Whig and Tory. He never gained a victory which was not made a charge against him. And it is melancholy to contemplate in his case the power of a calumniating press, when employed and seconded by leading parties, or a leading party in the State. It succeeded for a time in dimming the lustre even of Marlborough's glory; enabling his enemies to turn him out of all his employments, after making him odious to the Queen, and actually to trample upon him in the dirt.

" I am very happy to find you at Brougham, where you will enjoy the quiet you are in need of. I hope you will remain long enough, to let your mind settle into its habitual state, after the circumstances of excitement in which for some late years you have been placed; and to reflect on what it will become you to engage in, when parliament meets. As for the Ministers, they are taking holiday; and will not bestow a thought upon the measures of next Session, as usual, till within a fortnight of the meeting of Parliament, when they are in such bustle, that they cannot think at all; and then have no wish but that parliament will be kind enough to indulge them in doing nothing, and then they may please both the Lords and the Court. That would be heaven to them. That will make opening for you; and I hope you will be prepared to make use of them with dignity and efficiency. They may count upon the support of parliament for another Session, I think; but neither the parliament nor they should count much longer upon the silence of the people. And parliament now is afraid of the people; though we must have the means shortly of making the people's voice a better security. By-the-bye, what is your opinion of the operation of the Corporation Act, even as it is hacked and hewn, on the choice of members of parliament? Will it give us liberal members? I have thought but little on the subject. But Joseph Hume, whom I was accusing here the other day of having, with the Ministers, submitted too tamely to the dictation of the Lords, maintained that a great deal would be gained in the power of choosing liberal members. I wish it may be so. But we must have a better House of Commons before much will be done.

" I am, my dear Lord, with the greatest regard,
      " Ever truly yours,
            " J. MILL."

After staying out the autumn at Mickleham, he returns to London ; but is unable to resume office work. His active career is ended, and all that remains is a few months of suffering and gradual decay.

The October number of the *London Review* contains an article on Law Reform.

This is an article of forty pages, but largely made up of extracts from great authorities to show the defects of the Law. Lord Erskine, Sir Samuel Romilly, and Lord Brougham's speeches are laid under contribution for the purpose. The author's own exposition is occupied with urging the three grand requisites—a Code, a proper distribution of Judges, and the taking of the evidence of parties orally in the court.

" Such is the compass of law reform. It is all contained in three essential particulars :—expressing the law as it ought to be expressed ; employing judges to do the judicial business of the country where they can do it to most advantage ; prescribing to them the mode of inquiry which leads with most certainty, and least trouble, delay, and expense, to the knowledge of the truth.

" That they are simple means, that they are efficient means, and that all other means are bad in comparison, is among the clearest and most infallible of the deductions of common sense.

" It is very evident, however, that they must be conjoined, in order to the attainment of the end to which they are directed. No one, and no two of them, without the other, will answer our expectation.

" Suppose we have the law expressed, as it ought to be expressed ; but judges employed and distributed in the barbarous and irrational manner in which the men doing judges' work in England are distributed and controlled, and doing it with the detestable procedure which they use ; it cannot be doubted that the improved expression of a law administered by such instruments would go a very little way towards affording us the un-

speakable benefits of good judicature.   The delay, the expense,
and even the uncertainty, would be very little diminished.

"Again, suppose we had judges well supplied and placed, both
for the original and appellate jurisdiction, but acting through
an abominable procedure, and with a law abominably expressed,
it is obvious under what disadvantages these judges would necessarily act, and to what an extent they would be hindered
from affording to the community the benefit of a good administration of justice.

"As these three things, had in perfection, are indispensable
for a good administration of justice, it is obvious what must be
the effect of trying to do without them, by making repairs on
the despicable instruments which exist.   Repair them as long
as you please, you will have nothing but a pair of Sir John
Cutler's stockings after all.   Touch this thing or the other thing
in all your ill-contrived judicial establishment, it is an ill-contrived
judicial establishment still.   Rectify some of the vices of your
system of written pleadings, it is a system of written pleadings
still, and thoroughly ill-adapted to the end we desire to attain.
In regard to codification, doing this piecemeal is something
like a caricature of reason.   If a mass of ideas, all in disorder,
are to be methodized so that they may be expressed with the
greatest brevity and accuracy, you must take them all together ;
you cannot detach a portion, and say, we will order these ; because the order proper for them depends upon the order which
is proper for all the rest.

"We do not, however, though we think this a most important
principle, undervalue the efforts of those who have pushed the
work of codification in a less perfect manner.   They saw that
in the benighted state of mind of those on whom the decision
still depended, the proposition to systematize and accurately
express the whole law would be regarded as something frantic,
while that of working upon a part would at any rate obtain a
hearing.   That hearing was, at all events, a good thing.   It
tended to familiarize to all men's minds the subject.   It tended

to make them acquainted with the reasons for and the reasons against codification ; the clearness and cogency of the one, the miserable imbecility of the other. This process happily is going on ; and we expect shortly to hear a call for general and comprehensive codification, as irresistible as that which has given us, at last, a commencement of parliamentary reform."

We have next in order of date a characteristic letter to his son, James, who was studying in the East India Company's College of Haileybury, with a view to the India Civil Service.

"MICKLEHAM, *18th Oct., 1835.*

"MY DEAR JAMES,

"John will call and order your waistcoat to-morrow, and you will have it in a day or two.

"I was much pleased to see you had the highest mark in everything last month. You must strive hard to have the same in the remainder.

"The difficulties you are in about the fate which awaits you in point of honours can only be met by your utmost exertions. He who works more than all others will in the end excel all others. Difficulties are made to be overcome. Life consists of a succession of them. And he gets best through them, who has best made up his mind to contend with them.

"I do not like to give you any instructions about your Essay ; both because it would not be fair towards those with whom you have to contend, and because I am desirous to see what you yourself make of it.

"Do not allow yourself to be taken in, as many people are, by an ambiguity in the word *property*. Englishmen in general incline to think that where property is not entire, especially in the land, there is no property. But property may be as perfectly property, when it includes only part, as when it includes the whole. There is no doubt that the ryot has a property in the soil, though it is a limited property. There is also no doubt that the government has a property in the soil, that also limited—the one property limited by the other.   It is therefore a case of joint property.   Hence the controversies.

" My complaint is not removed.   The lungs are now pretty clear, but the cough remains ; and the coming winter keeps up alarms.   However, I must take all the care I can.   The rest here are all well   And we shall move to town as soon as the weather becomes cold.   We have had H. Bickersteth and Lady Jane for several days of last week.   And his conversation is always an enlivener.   I am the better for it.

"Yours truly,

"J. MILL."

During the previous session of Parliament and the winter following, up to the assembling of the Houses in 1836, Roebuck brought out a series of remarkably vigorous pamphlets, entitled " Pamphlets for the People ".   The greater number he wrote himself : others were contributed by his brother-in-law, Mr. Thomas Falconer, now a County Court Judge in Wales, and for a time Sub-Editor of the *London Review*, and the *London and Westminster*.   A third contributor was A. H. T. Chapman. William Allen wrote on Church Establishments in reply to Dr. Chalmers.   The pamphlets came out weekly, at the cost of 1½d.   They were an attempt to break down the newspaper stamp, which the Whig Government would not abolish. Several were exclusively devoted to the subject of " Taxes on Knowledge".   All the questions of the day, including Municipal Reform, were successively handled.   The House of Lords had a considerable space devoted to it.

It was a part of Roebuck's plan to provide cheap issues of important political articles, and several of Mill's Encyclopædia and Review articles were printed.   The Ballot article (Westminster) was sold for 3d.; the Dialogue, for 2d.; Colony, Jurisprudence, and Education, for 4d. each.

The circulation of the tracts is stated to have reached ten thousand.

1836.

In the *London Review* for January, comes out a paper entitled "Aristocracy". The chief point of passing interest attaching to it, was the treatment of the House of Lords question, which had so largely engaged the attention of Radical Reformers during the preceding year.

He begins with the remark that the advocates of Aristocracy, by a common device when a bad thing has to be vindicated, labour to confound inequalities of fortune with aristocratical privileges. Of inequalities of fortune in themselves, Reformers were far from thinking evil. The good effects of these are to furnish leisure for intellectual attainments, and for cultivating the elegancies of life. But by inequalities are meant those that are the natural result of the laws of accumulation, not the unnatural results of coerced inheritance. Enormous fortunes in the hands of a small class, are adverse to both intellect and elegance. Such persons are neither intellectual nor encouragers of intellect. Besides, they are corrupters of taste, isasmuch they making cost the standard. Who but people whose taste is gone would have thought of erecting, in one day, a triumphal arch? A man might as soon ornament his drawing-room with thumb-screws and bootikins. Music is not so easily spoiled; but it is the rich man's concern that it should not go down to his poorer neighbours. And so, just because strolling musicians have become good performers, was war declared against them. In painting and sculpture, the taste of the man of wealth is pure selfishness. Instead of encouraging new pictures, he carries home old ones, and shuts them up from inspection. Our aristocratic Legislature gave £11,000 for two Coreggios, when £20,000 was all they had to spare for education, and when they could not relieve us from the taxes on knowledge.

The author next handles severely the style of social intercourse arising from overgrown wealth. It is voted ungenteel to be the introducer of a serious subject; the frivolity in conversation is proverbial and notorious. It is made up of two tones; mockery and vehement admiration. What is desirable above all things in society is a spirit of mutual benevolence; the tone of scorn and mockery is destructive of this.

"It is thus evident, that society derives no improvement from the style of conversation and social intercourse which take place in a class of men of overgrown wealth. It is, on the other hand, the main cause why the state of intellect, of morals, and of taste, is in this country at the low point at which, in each of these respects, it remains; nor will there be any change for the better, till the influence of that class ceases to be predominant." These consist in one or other of the three things—money, dignity, power. Money privileges arise from an undue share of the government, by which are gained sinecure offices, and exemptions from taxes. Rank or dignity in a few necessarily supposes degradation in the rest; and a degraded community is not an object of comfortable contemplation. The motives to the highest degree of well-doing in every line are then most operative when this well-doing leads to the highest distinction. Artificial ranks are a contrivance to prevent the *præmia virtutis* from being at the highest.

But of all kinds of privilege, the most important is political power. The sole reason of political authority being the good of the community, any portion not answering this end is noxious. To set up men by giving them powers to be used for their own advantage, at the expense of the rest of the community, is to set up a body of enemies. The greatest mischief of all is to give such men legislative powers. In England, nearly one half of the legislative power is placed in the hands of men who, by the tenure on which they hold it, are of necessity converted into a body of enemies. The great object of their dread is every approach to good government. "The existence of this power is an evil, so great, that all other grievances in the state sink into nothing compared with it. That a clear-sighted and resolute people will not always endure it, is not to be feared; but how long it may contrive to carry on its work, by fair words, and by little concessions, well-timed, it is not easy to foresee: especially so long as those who take the lead of the people in opposing them, afford them so much encouragement, by the faintness of their desire for the progress of good government, and the feebleness with which they urge even the reforms which they approve."

The House-of-Lords question was the question of the day. The author proposes as a remedy the following plan. "Let it be enacted, that if a bill, which has been passed by the House of Commons, and thrown out by the House of Lords, is renewed in the House of Commons in the next session of parliament, and passed, but again thrown out by the House of Lords, it shall, if passed a third time in the House of Commons, be law, without being sent again to the Lords."

In case the Lords refuse their consent to the measure, he recommends the House of Commons to proceed a step farther, and declare that bills, as passed by themselves a certain number of times, and at certain intervals, are law. This resolution the people would hail with transport, and make the enactments laws by their obedience; and from that moment the House of Lords is blotted out. What could they do? The Judges would follow suit; or if they did not, they could be replaced by those that would.

According to Lord John Russell, followed by his Attorney-General (Campbell), there is no occasion for any reform of the House of Peers; the Lords, they say, will grow wiser. What if these authorities are mistaken? It is not ignorance that is the source of the evil, but a much deeper cause—every man's preference of himself to another. If this could be got over, all government would be unnecessary.

Another pretence for delaying the reform of the Lords is that they will grow wise enough to see the danger of resisting the will of the people. But what reformers object to is the state of perpetual excitement that would be necessary ; a state, so far as it goes, of anarchy. The people can act only in two ways ; by violence, or by the prospect of violence, so near as to be terrifying. Is it not better to withdraw the necessity of the Lords' consent to a measure, after a certain number of refusals ?

In thus limiting the power of the Lords, in one way, the author would add to it in other ways where the mischievous use of it could be prevented. He would give peers the right of being elected to the Commons. This he thinks would be a stimulus to the education of the whole class ; and would supply motives to cultivate the good opinion of the people. The consequence would be an increase in their opportunities of rising to be the foremost men of the state, and an increase in the happiness attaching to their position.

Finally, " we shall be told, that, by this reasoning of ours, we destroy the foundation of monarchy as well as aristocracy ". In reply, the author points out the difference of the reasons for the two institutions. The greatness and the glory of a king depend upon his people ; he is identified in interest with them. In England, it is a fact that our kings made the blunder of linking themselves with the aristocracy. The aristocracy after making them dependent upon themselves, have made a stalking horse of them. The power of the sovereign has been converted into their power ; no wonder they like it. But till that was brought about, how did they behave ? They were the king's antagonists and his oppressors ; and it was only by the aid of the people that he could make head against them. The Stuart contest showed the king that he could not rule but in subservience to parliament. He has since put his neck into the collar of the aristocracy. But the interest of a king is not irreconcilable with the interests of his people, and it is not yet proved that his office is an unnecessary one. A first magistrate is necessary. The question is whether he should be hereditary, or elective. With a hereditary rule, talent is a matter of chance ; with an elective, a high degree of talent is tolerably certain. Yet, as he must govern in subservience to parliament, and must choose ministers agreeable to parliament, he cannot go far wrong, and talent is not of much importance. In these circumstances, there are very solid advantages on the side of the hereditary principle. If the chief magistrate is to be elective, the choice must reside either in the parliament or in the people. If by parliament, the consequence would be a great development of faction, to the detriment of attention to business. The choice of the people is perhaps less pregnant with evil ; but the agitation and ferment would be in every way unfavourable.

"If ever the King of England becomes clear-sighted enough to see that he has been very ill-advised, in leaning upon a corrupt aristocracy, and a corrupt church, as the two crutches without which he could not stand ; and that he may rest with assurance on the solid advantages to the people, inherent in his office; he will occupy a far more exalted station in the social union than he has hitherto done. He will feel that he reigns in the reason and understanding of his people ; which is a more steady reliance, than that reigning in their hearts, which he has hitherto heard so much about, and to so little purpose."

The article was immediately reprinted as a cheap Tract in the Roebuck series of reprints. It was not so immediately popular as Roebuck's own writing ; but it must have obtained a considerable circulation.

In the same number of the *Review* is a Dialogue—"Whether Political Economy is useful," which, like the one on the Ballot, has the author's usual terseness, and a respectable command of the arts of Dialogue, which comparatively few have wielded with any great success for didactic purposes. This is his last work.

All that remains of the narrative is to present a few fragmen-

tary indications of the closing months. In January, he writes
one of his vigorous and sympathetic epistles to Lord Brougham,
now severed for good from the Whig Ministry, and thereby
placed in a new and anomalous position.

"KENSINGTON, *14th January, 1836.*

"MY DEAR LORD,

"I have not been on good terms with myself for some
time, for delaying to write to you. But really, besides the
aversion to do anything, which this illness has left behind it,
I know not what to say. I was out of the way and knew
nothing but the lies of the newspapers. I was also told that
your doctors thought, when you went out of town, you had
better not be pestered with letters. However, there is a talk
within the last few days, in the newspapers, which has roused
me. Though I know, in a general way, that there were feelings
which ought not to have existed, I still believed that things
would come round. If I can at all believe what is confidently
rumoured, I must now give up that expectation. I know not
how all this will end. I cannot augur well of it. People, who
certainly have no strength to spare, do not seem to me to act
wisely, when they throw away the best part of what they have.

"With respect to yourself, I am doubtful whether they have
not done you a service, rather than an injury. They do not
know your internal resources, either for personal happiness, or
for commanding the attention either of the present, or of future
generations. After having shown yourself *facile princeps* in the
contentions of public assemblies, it now remains to show what
you can be in the quiet walks of literature. Having written
more than any other ten men on the spur of the occasion, I
wish you now to begin something which you may labour with
all your care. Among various subjects I have thought of for
you, I am most in favour with a history of your own times.
This you could do with infinite advantages ; and though, in
doing it faithfully, you would have to say things not pleasing
to existing individuals, this would to a great degree be remedied

by reserving the work for posthumous publication. When one is about to bestow on the world κτῆμα ἐς ἀεί—it is of little importance whether they get it ten or twenty years hence.

"I am going on towards recovery. I am allowed to go out in mild days into the garden, and they tell me that, if I take care till the good weather comes, I shall be well again. I hope that you will return to town quite restored.

"I am, my dear Lord,

"With great and unalterable regard,

"Ever yours,

"J. MILL."

On the same day Bickersteth writes with reference to his accepting the office of Master of the Rolls :—"I have had a severe struggle to make myself submit, and without the support of your opinion, I scarcely think that I should have succeeded. . . . It will be a great comfort to me when I can have an opportunity of talking matters over with you. I shall endeavour to find one as soon as possible."

The belief in his final recovery lasted a good while longer. The next document from his hand is dated 9th March. His son James had received his appointment to the India Civil Service, and had gone out to India. His departure was the first break in the family, and much was made of him in the way of correspondence on the part of the others. His father undertook to contribute to the monthly letter, and the first contribution is an interesting glimpse into the domestic interior. I give it entire.

"LONDON, 9th March, 1836.

"MY DEAR JAMES,

"I begin my first monthly epistle, which I hope will find you comfortably employed at Calcutta, after a prosperous voyage. We thought a good deal about you, till you were gone. We looked out very eagerly for a north wind. The first intelligence George and Derry (Henry) brought me every morning was, which way the wind set; and there were plenty of conjectures about what you might be doing; Geordie in particular has a vehement propensity to determine the unknowable.

"John is still in rather a pining way; though, as he does not choose to tell the cause of his pining, he leaves other people to their conjectures. As for myself, I am going on much as when you saw me, not going back, but going very slowly forward. As I found I was not getting strength, and was not likely to get it, unless I had more exercise in the open air than I could take by walking, I have been compelled, though sorely against my will, to hire a chariot for a month; and I go out with one of the three little ones, for two or three hours every day. The rest of us are all well; and more or fewer of them will write to you.

"We should have been beginning by this time to talk of Mickleham, but for the state of my health, and the badness of the house, which puts all in uncertainty and restrains the imagination. We do not think much about it. The lessons go well on. I have not yet resumed my hearing of them; but John hears them and gives me a highly favourable account. As soon as I get a little strength (for I am so weak that everything is still a burthen to me) I shall set seriously to work on Logic with Derry. I think he will penetrate it rapidly; and it will be of immense importance to him: it will give clearness and force to his intellect to a wonderful degree.

"We have made a revolution with respect to the garden, which I think will be of advantage. I have made an annual bargain with a nurseryman who is to keep it in order, and keep it full of everything for a certain sum. We are to have the walks all turned, and the box new arranged; and I suppose I must go to the expense of some new gravel to make it look fresh. We shall be very smart, and wishing you here to see our smartness. We have had three new fruit trees, to replace those decayed ones you may remember, near the bottom of the garden. One is a nectarine, I think, and the other two are peaches, and one is christened after you, and called James.

"There is nothing yet decided about the railway at Mickle-ham, but we are still in danger. I wish we could light upon a snug, warm house, in which I could live with safety.

"And so much for the first epistle.

"Sis felix, et ne sis indignus ut sis.　　"J. Mill."

In the letter to James from the next brother, Henry, we have a few additional particulars of interest. Henry writes, 5th April : "I believe it is chiefly owing to this bad weather, that we have no better news to tell you of my father, but we have this now to cheer us, that we *must* be coming to something better. The low miserable kind of torpidity, which he has had, during which he told Lord and Lady Langdale he was in a state which he could not have conceived before to be possible he could exist in, a total lack of ideas, when the mind was looking out on nothing, a mere empty space, a chaos, is more I believe the doctors think, distressing at the time, than of any material influence in retarding convalesence."

Again, in the same letter:—"I have been reading to my father when out in the carriage for his airing, a pastoral, in Scotch by Allan Ramsay, called the 'Gentle Shepherd'. My father thinks it the most beautiful pastoral in any modern language. In these drives we often go to Wandsworth and Richmond, and I always think of you and our walks to Mickleham, as we pass that willow tree at the bottom of Richmondhill. My father got tired of Swift's Lilliput and Brobdingnag, and he said I read it so ill, that unless the subject was so interesting as to take his attention from my reading, he could not bear it ; but reading against the sound of the carriage wheels, for two hours and a half, I should not mind, if I had the consolation of giving any pleasure, but in addition to my sore throat, I have the satisfaction of being reminded at every turn that I am giving pain, instead of pleasure."

He made an effort to contribute to the next letter to James, and wrote the following sentences, which may be given as his last composition. " I would not let this opportunity pass without saying a word to you. But as the rest, I suppose, have told you all the incidents, and I am worn out writing to the Governor-General and Macaulay and Cameron, I shall reserve my contribution till the next time. My great complaint now is weakness, but that is extreme and most distressing. How-ever, they say that needs but a little time and good weather, which has hitherto been wretched."

A month later, Henry writes :—" Last night as we, 'Geordie and I' were sitting up in my father's room, George after a long silence, suddenly said, ' I hope James (I suppose John's being unwell put it into his head) is well '. My father directly said, ' So do I, George, but I have no right to think about it, and therefore I do not think about it ; I do not know anything about it, and so I ought not to think about it : but when the time comes to write to him, poor fellow, and to let him know that we do not forget him, then I like to think of him, and then I do think of him.' These were his words, but this morning he says, we must beg you to excuse him for not writing to you, he feels so weak and so great an aversion to writing at all."

A letter written in July lets us see him as the end drew near. " We had all of us been led to believe that my father could not live, for a week before he died, so that we were somewhat prepared, at least as much prepared as one can be for a thing which seems so distressing, as to be impossible to happen. You will be less prepared for it than we were, but you will not have had the torment of seeing him get weaker and weaker every day, seeing too that we knew it perfectly ; and although he seldom said anything about it, never by way of complaint, yet he sometimes, when he thought he should not recover, used to say to me or George that he would very willingly die, if it were not that he left us too young to be sure how we should turn out."

On the 13th June, Place wrote to Mrs. Grote :—" Stayec too long with poor Mill, who showed much more sympathy anc affection than ever before in all our long friendship. But he wa: all the time as much of a bright reasoning man as he ever wa, —reconciled to his fate, brave, and calm to an extent whicl I never before witnessed, except in another old friend, Thoma: Holcroft, the day before and the day of his death."

This was ten days previous to the end.

John was at Brighton for his own health during his father'; last illness ; but wrote assiduously to Henry, to know whethe his hurrying back would be of any use. " As to my father tell me as fully as you can how he is, both as to his illnes itself, and as to spirits, and what you think would be pleasantes to him ; not what he would wish or say out of kindness to me.

The last phase of his illness was bronchitis ; he sank awa on the afternoon of Thursday, the 23rd of June. Mrs. Grote remarks as a coincidence :—" At the very hour during whicl Grote was delivering this speech on the Ballot, his great menta teacher and friend, James Mill, was passing away from amongs us. He died without any pain or struggle, of long-standing pulmonary phthisis. Grote was much affected by his loss though we were aware that it was imminent for several month before it happened."

He was buried in Kensington Church. Of the friend present at the interment, Molesworth was one of those mos notably overcome with grief.

CHAPTER VIII

REVIEW OF LATEST WRITINGS:—POLITICAL
ECONOMY: ANALYSIS OF THE HUMAN MIND:
FRAGMENT ON MACKINTOSH.

MY notice of these works must necessarily be brief; yet,
to pass them over entirely would leave a feeling of
incompleteness in the biography of their author.

POLITICAL ECONOMY.

This work, first published, as we have seen, in 1821, went
through three editions, and was not afterwards reprinted. The
author's purpose in writing it is thus expressed :—

" My object has been to compose a school-book of Political
Economy, to detach the essential principles of the science from
all extraneous topics, to state the propositions clearly and in
their logical order, and to subjoin its demonstration to each.
I am, myself, persuaded, that nothing more is necessary for
understanding every part of the book, than to read it with
attention ; such attention as persons of either sex, of ordinary
understanding, are capable of bestowing."

He apologizes for not quoting authorities as he proceeds,
and remarks—" I cannot fear an imputation of plagiarism,
because I profess to have made no discovery ; and those men
who have contributed to the progress of the science need no
testimony of mine to establish their fame ".

Nevertheless, the subject was one that he had often written
upon, and he could not pass through his mind any depart-

ment of Social Philosophy without impressing his individuality upon it. The terse and clear expository handling was a novelty, in form at least ; and there were not wanting novelties in the substance. The principle of Population was for the first time urged in the pressing and practical form that John Mill afterwards iterated. The following sentences will exemplify what is meant.

"If we may thus infer that human happiness cannot be secured by taking forcible methods to make capital increase as fast as population ; and if, on the other hand, it is certain, that where births take place, more numerous than are required to uphold a population corresponding to the state of capital, human happiness is impaired, it is immediately seen, that the grand practical problem is, To find the means of limiting the number of births. It has also appeared, that, beyond a certain state of density in the population, such as to afford in perfection the benefits of social intercourse, and of combined labour, it is not desirable that population should increase. The precise problem, therefore, is to find the means of limiting births to that number which is necessary to keep up the population, without increasing it. Were that accomplished, while the return to capital from the land was yet high, the reward of the labourer would be ample, and a large surplus would still remain."

Another point of originality was the doctrine of the unearned increment. This came under Taxation. We have seen his view as to the India Land Tax. Where land, however, has become private property, the State cannot without injustice tax landlords out of proportion to their stake in the community. But when, without any exertion on their part, the progress of society adds to the value of their land, there is no injustice in appropriating this increase for the good of the community at large.

"That rent, which is bought and sold ; that rent, upon which the expectations of individuals are founded, and which, therefore, ought to be exempt from any peculiar tax, is the present rent; or at most the present, with the reasonable prospect of improvement. Beyond this, no man's speculations, either in making a purchase, or in making provision for a family, are entitled to extend. Suppose now, that in these circumstances, it were in the power of the legislature, by an act of its own, all other things remaining the same, to double that portion of the produce of the land which is strictly and properly rent: there would be no reason, in point of justice, why the legislature should not, and great reason, in point of expediency, why it should avail itself of this, its own power, in behalf of the state; should devote as much as might be requisite of this new fund to defray the expenses of the government, and exempt the people. No injury would be done to the original landowner. His rent, such even as he had enjoyed, and to a great degree such even as he had expected to enjoy it, would remain the same. A great advantage would at the same time accrue to every individual in the community, by exemption from those contributions for the expense of the government, to which he would otherwise have had to submit."

One better versed than I am in the doctrines and history of Political Economy, could no doubt mention many other points characteristic of the work and its author. I believe, however, that I have noticed two of its greatest specialities.

ANALYSIS OF THE HUMAN MIND.

Although I am better qualified to speak of the author's greatest work of a purely philosophical kind, the scope of this Biography forbids the amount of exposition that would be necessary to do it justice.

It was a part of his early ambition, dating from his attendance on Dugald Stewart's Lectures, to contribute to the advancement of Mental Philosophy. His numerous and heavy labours in other regions prevented him, till late in life, from entering upon the task. His severe logical discipline was an important preparation; and the *Analysis* is signalized, among other merits, by the careful definition of the terms employed. This, however, was not enough. The field of mental facts had to be long and continuously reflected on; and previous writers had to be carefully studied. Here, his opportunities were somewhat deficient. The space of time devoted to the work (1822-29), after deducting the other claims on his attention, was barely enough for so great a task; and, in point of completeness, the result is manifestly inferior to the treatises of Reid and Stewart, and somewhat on a par with the Lectures of his own Edinburgh contemporary, Thomas Brown. In precision, and in thoroughness of grasp of fundamentals, it excels them all.

The chief merit that the author himself would have claimed for the work, is the carrying out of the Principle of Association, as it had been put forward by Hartley and Gay, who immediately preceded him. It must be remarked, however, that the first and more obvious application of this principle, namely, to the explanation of the Intellectual faculties and processes, is entirely wanting. A fundamental mistake clouded all this part of the subject. The distinction between contiguous association, and the resuscitation of ideas from resemblance, is essential to drawing the line between Memory and Reasoning; and this distinction Mill failed to make. He allowed that there was such a thing as association by Resemblance, but looked at the facts so slightly as to suppose that it was a mere case of repetition. His account of the Intellectual faculties is meagre in the extreme; and, in dealing with Abstraction and Reasoning, he discusses rather the logical than the psychological aspects. Indeed, a considerable portion of the work should have gone to make up a treatise on Logic.

The use actually made by him of the principle of Association, was to resolve our complex feelings or emotions, into simple or elementary feelings; and to show that many of the states commonly recognised as simple, such as the Affections, the Æsthetic emotions, and the Moral Sentiment, are in fact compound. As an incidental consequence, he dwells upon the enormous possibilities of education, in the sphere of the feelings.

He starts from our Pleasurable and Painful Sensations, as the groundwork, and shows how association connects these in our minds with their causes. From actual sensations and their actual causes, we come, by repetition, to form ideas of these sensations and of their causes. We then contemplate the sensations and the cause of them as past, and as future. Out of these conjunctions, arise our ideas of Wealth, Power, Dignity, and their contraries. When our fellow-creatures are contemplated as causes of pleasures and pains, we contract feelings towards them, corresponding to what are termed social affections; as Friendship, Kindness, Family, Country, Party, Mankind. A like explanation applies to the objects called Sublime and Beautiful, in which the author follows in the train of Alison's well known theory of Beauty.

Next comes the explanation of the Will. Pleasures and Pains are the motives to our actions ; whether simple states, or the various compounds of these, expressed by Wealth, Power, Dignity, Love, &c.

He considers that he has now prepared the way for the great ethical problem of the Moral Sense, which he undertakes to resolve into the elementary states of the mind, as already reviewed. He accounts for the Virtues, by showing them to be means to the more primary ends of securing pleasures and warding off pains ; Prudence, operating in this way, as regards ourselves, and Justice and Benevolence, as regards others. The grand difficulty here is to account for seeking other men's pleasures, or to trace to self-seeking causes, our Disinterested Benevolence. Reciprocity goes a good way, and is adduced accordingly.

A long chapter on the mechanism and growth of the Will concludes the work; and, for the state of physiological and other ·knowledge at the time, is remarkably able and original.

The salient merit of the treatise is the demonstration of the compound character of many of the states formerly accounted simple. The author was not uniformly successful here, although he did a great deal. His basis was too narrow. Sensation does not cover the whole field of our primitive sensibilities; we have primary emotions also, as Fear, Love, and Anger: the attempt to resolve these into Sensations, and their causes, is a failure. Without taking them into the account, neither Beauty nor the Moral Sentiment can be satisfactorily explained.

I have not space for more minute criticism. The work is one that will long be read by students in philosophy. The statements are so concise and clear, and the illustrations so good, that the author's strong points can be seized with very little effort; and his defects are too obvious to do any harm. A perusal of his chapter on the Social Affections is sufficient to disabuse the mind of a prejudice—industriously circulated against philosophers of his school, from Hobbes to Bentham— of slighting the private affections, in aiming at a lofty regard to the public weal. The section on the Family affections is replete with the ideal of perfect domestic happiness: and, if the author did not act up to it, as he did to his ideal of public virtue, the explanation is to be sought in human weakness and inconsistency.

A FRAGMENT ON MACKINTOSH.

The motive to the composition of this work is stated in the Preface. It was the belief that the confusion into which Mackintosh, in his Dissertation, "had thrown the science of Ethics, was calculated to do great injury to the minds of such young inquirers as might resort to his work for instruction; and my fear that the puffing, on the part both of himself and his friends, which had so successfully served the author through life, and the reputation he thence enjoyed, would procure a temporary and unfortunate celebrity to a deleterious production."

After a short chapter setting Mackintosh right upon the primary notions of Ethics, he enters upon the treatment of Hobbes, whose character and philosophy Sir James had condemned—for its dogmatism, its coldness, its striking the affections out of human nature, its pure selfishness, and so on.

The looseness of the author's mode of making good these accusations makes him an easy victim to Mill's ruthless criticism. The severity reaches its climax in dealing with Mackintosh's remarks referring to Hobbes's followers—"not to mention Mandeville, the buffoon and sophister of the alehouse; or Helvetius, an ingenious but flimsy writer, the low and loose moralist of the vain, the selfish, and the sensual". A writer that could indulge in this style must not complain of Mill's treatment. "He shall have judgment without mercy that hath shewed no mercy." Mill's vindication of these two writers is masterly, as we may suppose. His incidental remarks on Mackintosh himself include the following observations, which sum up one of the worst accusations against him—his pandering to popularity.

"They were two writers of name. It was, therefore, in Sir James's way, to tell us how well he was acquainted with them. They were also two very unpopular names. It was therefore also in Sir James's way to give them a dash of his black brush. He knew with whom it would be popular to speak ill of them. He therefore looked out for disparaging epithets; any would do, so be they were strong enough. So down went 'the buffoon and sophister of the ale-house,' and 'flimsy writer, the low and loose moralist of the vain, the selfish, and the sensual'. By these few words Sir James proves that he was unacquainted with the writings which he thus traduces. No man who was acquainted with them would have chosen such terms to express himself in; however much he might have dissented from what is contained in them. For not only have they no appropriateness to the faults that are in the writings, or have ever been imputed to them ; but they do not even point in that direction."

The next chapter is on Butler. "Sir James glories in heaping praise on Butler." The ethical doctrines of Butler, both as presented by himself, and as handled by Mackintosh, are criticised to exhaustion. Such remarks upon the commentator as the following crop out, in endless variety of form:—

"There is not one of the more complicated phenomena of the human mind of which Sir James has more in his brain than a confused shadow of an idea. He is therefore constantly mistaking one thing for another." Again—"There is no more certain test of an understanding which has no force in it, than the facility with which it is taken in by a truism." "Sir James's inaccuracy in the use of words is a phenomenon." "It is for the benefit of exemplifying strongly to the young, the tendency of vague and circuitous language, in philosophy, that there is any use in attending to Sir James."

But by far the most elaborate chapter on the work is the vindication of Bentham. This occupies 180 pages. As Mackintosh had included, in his strictures on Bentham, a reference to his supposed disciples as well, Mill was personally implicated, and therefore had to answer for himself as well as for Bentham. The importance of the chapter is not limited to chastising Mackintosh ; it is a valuable aid to the understanding of Bentham's whole method of working. The shower of sharpest sleet is only too incessant. Sir James, he says, begins with a panegyric on himself. He is willing to put his courage and honesty to the severest test, in speaking of Bentham. What was the call for this ? "As Sir James was not going to praise, but to help in disparaging, an unpopular writer, he had nothing to fear." This was not quite correct. Sir James had nothing to fear from general society ; but he had some knowledge of the sharpness of weapon and power of arm that could be counted on in Bentham's defence ; and there he had some cause to fear.   Hence we are astonished at the recklessness of his language against the Bentham set : " braving vulgar pre-judices " ; " seeking distinction by singularity " ; " clinging to opinions because they are obnoxious " ; " wantonly wounding the respectable feelings of mankind " ; " looking down with pity, if not contempt, on the profane multitude ".   Before hitting anyone so hard, Mackintosh should have been quite sure that he had no friends.

Mill takes up all these offensive epithets piecemeal, in a way that the curious reader must see for himself.   A very small specimen of a long book is all that can be admitted here ; and I must economize farther, by asking that the reply of Mill to Macaulay on " Government," already cited, p. 231, be taken also as an example of the style of the " Fragment ".

All Mill's friends that I have ever conversed with, regretted the asperity of his language towards Mackintosh.   John Mill would have probably reprinted the book, but for this circumstance. It had been read over in MS. to Bickersteth, who had sug-gested a good deal of softening, and his suggestions were, I understand, for the most part adopted.   Still, as it stands, the amount of provocation given would not justify to the ordinary reader such perpetual nagging.   Not that such a strain is unfamiliar in polemic warfare.   Far worse severities of language have been perpetrated thousands of times.   The error in Mill's case lay in not recognizing the fact that the opinions of the great majority cannot, with impunity, be spoken of without much greater self-restraint on the part of a member of the small minority.

CHAPTER IX.

CHARACTER AND INFLUENCE.

THE ample exhibition of Mill's character in the course of the narrative now brought to a close, and the copious citation and abstract of his own writings, can leave little to be said in illustration of his mind as a whole. Nevertheless, a general summing-up may be of service in bringing to view points that have escaped mention, and in leaving a more compact and portable impression of the man.

As to *physique*, Mill was of the middle stature, 5 ft. 8 in. His figure was symmetrical, and well knit; the muscular proportions perfect for activity, without approaching the athletic extreme. In complexion, he was fair, without sickly whiteness, and without pink; the hair light, the eyes light grey. The form of the face may be judged of from the portrait, taken when about fifty; large head, massive forehead, straight nose, projecting eyes.

The play of the features I can fancy only by the resemblance of the children. John had manifestly his mother's aquiline form of face; yet I remember once walking with him in Piccadilly, when we accosted Sir David Brewster, who, on being introduced, exclaimed, " I'd have known ye from yer faather ". The sprightly mobility of feature, the sparkling, genial glances of the eye, with the special individuality of grouping, must have belonged to the father, and been inherited by the son.

He had a full, strong, clear voice—which his son did not have.

The general temperament was of course nervous, but not unbalanced by vigour in the other functions, especially the muscle. The nutritive powers could not have been originally deficient; they stood out marvellously well, considering the strain put upon them. Yet, it was there that weakness first crept in. In early youth, or middle age, he contracted the disposition to gout, which afflicted him through life, and turned to phthisis at last. No one will be unprepared for the conclusion, that the amount of work that Mill went through was too much for the human constitution at its best.

When we enquire into the proportions of his mind, we discover that he was, like the younger Pitt, chiefly a compound of Intellect and Will. The Emotions were not wanting, but they were not the dominant interest; they were servants and not masters. Intellect was the foremost fact, Will the second, Emotion the third.

Avoiding useless refinements, and the affectation of a systematic analysis that could not be made intelligible in few words, I will at once speak to the peculiarities that help to resume the biographical facts.

First then as to the characteristics of his Intellect.

That his Intellectual powers were of a high order is attested by the work that he achieved. That his special characteristics were such as we denominate by the terms scientific and logical, is also apparent. His training in science was not even the highest that the time could have permitted; he had, nevertheless, imbibed the scientific methods to a degree beyond most of the professed votaries of science. In other words, he had thoroughly mastered Evidence, and all the processes subservient thereto. His training was aided by the old logicians, and by the best models of clear reasoning that the philosophical literature of the past could afford.

Logic, with him, was not merely corrective; it was made a means of suggestion or invention. He was a master of the art of exhausting the logical implications of doctrines; more especially the obverse implications. Who but he (and Bentham) would have included, among the abuses of the Press, undeserved praise? Mackintosh attempted to overthrow his theory of Government by the remark, among other things, that a nation might both mistake its interest, and be hurried by passion to act against it. Says Mill:—"Does it, according to his logical head, follow, that because a nation may sometimes mistake its true interest, therefore its best security for good government is not to be found in effecting an identity of interests between those who govern, and itself?"

As a fallacy-crusher, he had no equal but Bentham. The war against vague phrases, sanctified by usage, by sentiment, and by class interests, was a life-long occupation to both. Their writings are among the small number that possess this characteristic in an eminent degree; while the best subsequent examples have been in a great measure stimulated by them.

Mill's early studies and tastes, the accidents of his career, and the circumstances of the time, conspired to make him, above everything else, a political and social philosopher. He was thoroughly acquainted with all the best writings, ancient and modern, on the theory and practice of politics; and he knew enough of history to check theories by experience. His knowledge of English history in particular, his constant observation of the course of English politics, and, finally, his occupation in connexion with the Government of India, are to be counted among his qualifications for acting as an adviser in the critical emergencies that occurred in his life-time. While, in a great degree a pupil and follower of Bentham in Law and Jurisprudence, he was vastly Bentham's superior in Politics strictly so called. Of the literature of Political Philosophy, Bentham knew almost nothing; his reading in History was very limited; and he became a politician quite late in the day, and plunged headlong into extreme views, in maintaining which, to be sure, he was able to make mincemeat of the apologies for things as they were. Mill, I take it, while so daring as to be accounted

revolutionary, was really the safest politician of his age.   In
the first French Revolution, no such man was to be found.

His fertility of mind went beyond the question of government, to all the regions of the Social Science, including Political
Economy.   In many things he was, of course, a learner under
Bentham, but not a mere learner.   He devised expedients of
his own ; and his judgment of Bentham's plans was wholly
unfettered, and was all the more valuable in the cases where
he gave them his unqualified concurrence.

He was a man of strong Will, in the best sense of that somewhat indefinite phrase.   The basis of will is necessarily the
active temperament ; and Mill was, by nature, a truly energetic
character.   Activity was natural to him ; he would never be
found lounging and musing in idleness.   But Will, in the
highest sense, is activity confined to proper channels, by a few
great leading motives ; these having their source in the feelings,
regulated by the intellect.   It is when a man has conceived
some great ends of life with such intensity that they engross all
the available active energy, that he is said to have Will in the
higher meaning of purpose, persistence, steadiness of pursuit,
as contrasted with intense fits of desultory application.

Mill had formed for himself, at an early age, his ideals of
pursuit.   He conceived a certain ambitious future in the employment of his high intellectual powers ; and, he combined
with this, a wish to contribute something to the welfare of
mankind.   He would not sell himself for the rewards of party ;
he had taken his measure of the grovelling dishonesty of mere
partizanship.

It is a consequence of the determined pursuit of one or two
all-comprehending ends, that a man has to put aside many
claims of mere affection, feeling, or sentiment.   Not that he is
necessarily devoid of the warm, social emotions : he may have
them, in fair measure; not, however, in an overpowering degree.
It is that they stand in his way to other things ; and so are, on
certain occasions, sacrificed ; leading thereby to the reproach

of being of a nature hard and unfeeling. Such was Pitt, and such was Mill. They had their friendships, their attachments, and their hours of sociability; but they would not be called sociable men, in the sense commonly received. Mill had warm friendships, and was true to them; a feature that we expect in a man of the best type of will. Such a one is faithful to all his engagements; and his way is, not to incur more than he can meet. Mill was thus with his friends: he failed, in some particulars, though not in all, with his family; the size of which his son considers to be his one fatal imprudence.

He acquired very naturally the habit of proscribing sentiment, when he found it interfering with people's greatest good. The liberal politics of such men as Godwin and Leigh Hunt was marred by super-sentimentalism.

It was impossible for any one that conceived such a high ideal of human improvement, to miss seeing the importance of Truth, not as an end in itself—this the philosophy of Utility does not admit—but as a means possessing the very highest degree of urgency. To test all assertions by adequate evidence, to extricate the truth from involvments of imperfect language, to push inquiry by every method, these are prime essentials of human progress. Of equal necessity is the removal of all checks to the liberty of expressing opinions. If these objects have the importance that Mill attributed to them, his labours for their promotion would alone entitle him to be accounted a benefactor of the race.

The biographical narrative makes sufficiently apparent his self-denying life. While the demands upon his energies for his private needs were at the very utmost, he was an active fellow-worker with the philanthropic band that abolished slavery, ameliorated the horrors of our prisons, and began the general education of the people. He declined the public importance that his labours might have brought him, in order to bestow it upon others who needed the stimulus.

Every man that promotes great changes must lay his account

with hostility, more or less bitter and pronounced. How to deal with opponents is one of the most difficult points of ethics. We cannot be the friends of a cause, without being the enemies of its enemies. If they fight, so must we; if they pass from argument to invective, calumny, and the infliction of personal injury, we must make reprisals. Yet, it is impossible to carry this far, without the malignant passions coming into play; and thus the best and holiest of men fall into the employment of weapons that in principle they disapprove of. The use of strong language must be judged by the provocation. Mill, all his life, waged a war against those that he considered enemies of human welfare. He often gave vent to strong language; but never to coarse invective. The cause that he fought under was public and not personal. He never said anything so severe as has fallen from Lord Shaftesbury. He had his feelings of natural resentment; but there is no proof that he indulged in the vice of malignity, or resentment for its own sake. The emotions that were his solace and his reward were the social and not the anti-social. He could not help disapproving of a number of people—disliking some, and despising others; yet he made ample allowance for circumstances, and did not press severely upon individuals, except on public grounds.

His strong feeling of independence, for which he endured so much toil, was not, to my knowledge, accompanied with any haughty, Pharisaical pride. I do not think that he was either proud or vain, in the common acceptation of the terms. Some have said that he was approachable by flattery; who is not? But, unless I had had personal observation of the conduct that has been so interpreted, I could not undertake to say what it amounted to.

Many marked traits of amiability, pure and simple, could be cited from his daily life. Besides his friends, among men of intellectual standing, the sharers of his opinions, he could take interest in people without much intellect, if they had goodness

of heart. He cherished the associations and the companion
of his early days. He loved Scotch songs ; his musical tast
not being very deep. He delighted in the birds that fed i
his garden ; he was once very indignant with John Black fc
scouting away a blackbird. He cherished flowers, and enjoye
rural surroundings ; and carried this sentiment so far as t
object strongly to his Mickleham valley being spoiled by th
Epsom railway. Notwithstanding his indisposition to com
municate the detailed incidents of his early career, he coul
speak of his struggles, in general terms, with much feeling.

He was scrupulously attentive to the manners and refinemen
of good society. He dressed carefully ; being what is terme
a "natty" man. His fine figure was not thrown away. Th
first thing that Lord William Bentinck remarked upon, to Mr
Grote, after becoming acquainted with him, was his gentlemanl
bearing. In spite of all that is said of his arrogant manne
he made his way in society, and gained over people hi
superiors in rank.

I have trusted entirely to eye-witnesses for the account c
his powers in conversation, and his sway over the minds c
youth. Whether, as John Mill said, he was pre-eminentl
adapted for a prime minister, he was at all events a born leade
—a king of men.

As a writer, his style has been found fault with, especially b
Bentham ; who spoke of the History in particular, as abound
ing in bad English. The fact I believe to be that, although h
took great pains to get rid of Scotticisms, he did not attain
mastery of good English idiom. A Scotchman may possibl
become a writer of pure English, but either he must leav
Scotland early, or he must drink very copiously from the pur
wells of English Literature. John Wilson, Thomas Campbell
Byron, and Lockhart, were never reproached for writing ar
un-English style. Even Jeffrey had very little remains of th
Scotch. But not merely had Mill to listen to Scotchmen for

good part of his life ; his studies also led him to a number
of Scotch authors—Hume, Millar, Ferguson, Adam Smith, and
Robertson.*

So far as I am able to judge, there are comparatively few
un-English modes of expression in his later writings.   One
peculiarity of his that may be noticed is the old-fashioned use
of the negative—I know not, I see not—for I do not know, I
do not see.   I think the Scotch are specially addicted to this
form ; English writers now-a-days use it very seldom.   Curiously, the earliest specimen of John Mill's writing that has been
preserved begins—" We know not ".

Irrespective of the point of idiom, Mill is a careful, correct,
and perspicuous writer.   His grammar is, to my mind, less
often at fault than his son's.   His sentences are generally well
marshalled, and easily disclose their meaning.   The arrangement into paragraphs, is seldom defective.   His sense of what
was requisite to lucidity never deserted him.

It is needless to remark that his composition was essentially
cast for scientific subjects.   He had practised narrative style in
his long historical work, and attained a certain success ; but it
was not carried to the pitch of art.   The truth is, although a
man of great general accomplishment, language was not his
forte.   It is curious to compare him even with Bentham in this
respect.   Not only was Bentham educated in the circles whose
conversational English is of standard purity, being in fact the
standard itself, thereby securing the correctness of his idioms ;
he was, in addition, a man of a natural literary endowment.

* Hume was one of the most careful of writers ; he was long out of Scotland , he had a good literary taste ; and yet his style is spoken of by Walter
Bagehot in the following terms : "Hume is always idiomatic, but his idioms
are constantly wrong ; many of his best passages are on that account curiously
grating and puzzling ; you feel that they are very like what an Englishman
would say, but yet that, after all, somehow or other they are what he never
would say ,—there is a minute seasoning of imperceptible difference which
distracts your attention, and which you are for ever stopping to analyse".   This
criticism helps us to understand how it was that Mill's expressions offended the
ear of Bentham.

His copiousness of language would have set him up in a literary profession, and might have even obtained for him a place among our English classics. Speaking roughly, I should say that the vocabulary at his command was twice as abundant as Mill's. His philosophy was unfavourable to the fullest exercise of the gift; but, within the limits allowed, he was an admirable writer. Whatever he attempted he did well. His chief display, in addition to his expositions of his own subjects, was in wit, humour, and invective; in all which he was a master. Mill occasionally tried his hand in the same regions, but with little success. He had the disposition to be witty and humorous; but wanted the resources of language and the play of fancy. His power lay in sarcasm and invective; there he achieved something considerable. Yet, the terrific onslaught of Bentham in those works that hung fire from dread of prosecution, was far beyond Mill's literary capacity.

There remains now only one other topic—the nature and extent of the influence exerted by Mill in the political movement crowned by the Reform Bill of 1832.

REFORM MOVEMENT.

It is unnecessary for the purpose we have in view, to go farther back than the Peace, in order to trace the streams of Liberal politics then existing, and to note the swellings of the current from that time onward. Three-fourths, or four-fifths of the influences that brought about Reform may be supposed to have had their origin since 1815.

Among the best known facts of our political history is the Reform movement that followed the American Revolution, which led to various motions in Parliament by Pitt himself; there being a network of societies in the country for promoting the object. It was in 1783 that the Duke of Richmond published his programme—universal suffrage, annual parliaments, and electoral districts—which became the watchwords of the Reform societies. The French Revolution came ; and with it Pitt's Tergiversation and the State Trials, aimed at suppressing the agitation everywhere.

In 1793, Grey made his famous speech on the Aristocratic composition of the House of Commons. In 1797, he moved again in the House of Commons, and was supported by 91, against 256. This was the last of the Whig motions on Reform for many years. The subject was left to the so-called Radicals, till Lord John Russell took it up in 1819.

The Reform Societies were never entirely silenced by prosecution A small number of energetic publications continued to flow from the press during the first fifteen years of the century. Criticism of the Government, in Parliament and out of it, maintained the conviction that there was something rotten in the state. Let us recall a few of the particulars.

What we should desire in a complete history of English opinion or Reform, would be to indicate the various authors of that opinion, the views promulgated, and the extent of their reception in the successive years. For we find that, among the genuine Reformers, the doctrines were more or less conflicting and their influence mutually destructive.

The sympathizers with the French Revolution had to suffer the furious attack of Burke. This brought to the front the writings of Paine, whose influence both in America and England was very great. The sale of the " Rights of Man " in England has been estimated at hundreds of thousands. It was the gospel of the absolute equality of men, as proclaimed at the French Revolution, and was largely embraced here as in France, by the down-trodden many. Paine's religious scepticism, announced in the " Age of Reason," had numerous followers in the lower orders, as Voltaire had among the higher, in the beginning of the century. These were the classical works of Radicalism, and were in continuous demand among an intelligent portion of the working classes.

For the first third of the century William Cobbett was a thorn in the side of the governing powers, and could have been an influential agitator, but for his pig-headedness and crotchets. For a time, he was the ally of the Westminster Radicals. The following extract from his Memoirs, by Huish, describes the connexion.

"Cobbett was now an inmate of Newgate (1804). . . . Many of his old friends deserted him, but on a sudden he acquired new ones, by altering the tone of the sentiments which he had been accustomed to use. Amongst those new friends was Sir Francis Burdett, whom he had generally treated with an unbecoming severity, but who now suddenly became the object of his warmest panegyric. Sir Francis often visited him in Newgate, where the party frequently consisted of four of the most notorious characters of the times—Sir F. Burdett, Major Cartwright, Henry Hunt, and W. Cobbett. It was in this conclave that the affairs of the nation were canvassed with a degree of perseverance and acuteness superior to anything which had ever taken place before, and which may be said to have laid the foundation of many of those great political events which were afterwards recorded in the annals of the country.

"The intimacy between him and Burdett was maintained until the month of February, 1817, when it was suddenly cut short, and no intercourse afterwards took place between them, even up to the time of Cobbett's death."

Of the quarrel, Cobbett speaks thus :—

"I was attacking him at the time ; I was accusing him distinctly of having abandoned the reformers in the months of February and March, 1817 ; I was laying it upon him with a heavy hand. I was telling him that I would bring him down, though it might cost me about ten years to do it."

Cobbett's Register, started in 1802, was continued through all sorts of fortunes and misfortunes till his death in 1835. A historian of the present day would hardly wade through his sixty volumes, notwithstanding their close bearing on the current of political events. The sale was always counted by thousands.* A selection of papers from the Register, in six closely printed volumes, affords ample material for Cobbett's political opinions, and for exemplifying his peculiar style.

From the time of his alliance with Burdett, he advocated radical reform of parliament, reduction of taxes, abolition of sinecures, and so on. He carried on an everlasting warfare about the national debt, and especially abused Peel's resumption of cash payments. He blamed the paper system for all the distresses of the nation. He charged the farmers with folly for their protection clamour, and bade them look to his reform of the monetary system to get better prices. He was always furious against Malthus, "that shallow and savage fellow, with his project for what he calls checking population". The bad condition of the labourers (he said) was wholly due to the National Debt. All attempts to amend the Poor Laws he treated with contempt. Scarlett's Bill of 1821, he called a bill to check the breeding of labourers, lest the land should not yield enough to feed them. The old Poor Law he called "That wise, humane, and just code". "Let those volumes of the Register (now 38) say whether the great and ever-prevailing burden of complaints has not been the ruin, the starvation, the degradation of the English labouring-class by the means of co-operating with an infernal paper money system." "I am convinced that paper money, large farms, fine houses, pauperism, hangings, transportings, leprosy, scrofula, and insanity, have all gone on increasing regularly together." He explains at length how all this happens.

In a letter addressed to Sir F. Burdett, 22nd May, 1822, he declares it to be unjust on the part of the Landlords to hold tenants to their leases under the present circumstances.

"No tenant *can possibly* have seen or thought of, what he was really doing when he contracted to pay rent for the use of

* In a passing reference to Cobbett, in 1817, Bentham speaks of his circulation of 60,000.

a farm in this kingdom at this time ; and, as the casualty which has arisen *could not possibly* be in his contemplation when he made the contract, the contract is not binding in *conscience*, and ought not to be binding in *law*."

In 1823, he indulges in a long tirade against Ricardo, " on his Proposition for Dividing the Land, in order to pay off the National Debt ". The same year, he frantically abuses Wilberforce, for creating sympathy towards the West India negroes, to the neglect of the home labourers. " The devil a bit do you make any comparison between the lives which the Blacks lead, and the lives which the White labourers lead."

In 1824, he is found denouncing manufactures as " one great cause of pauperism and of the degradation of the people". The funding system is credited with all the misery following out of them, as well as " Malthus and his crew of hard-hearted ruffians ".

These few specimens from only one volume of the Selections (6th) are of use in recalling to mind the perilous stuff that Cobbett spread broadcast for so many years. He had his followers and readers in all the large towns. I can remember his name as a household word before the Reform Bill. His " Register " and " Twopenny Trash " found their way into the shops of the working men. During the Reform agitation, he made a lecturing tour extending to Scotland, and it was a great disappointment to me, that he did not come to Aberdeen. His abuse of the Whigs, however, was a jarring note, when the nation was in earnest to unite for some measure of reform. He succeeded in getting into Parliament, but showed his characteristic incoherence and whims, by speechifying against the admission of the Jews. He required at all times a broad surface for his copious hatreds ; and was true to only one idol, himself.

Another noted agitator of the period covered by Cobbett was Henry Hunt, or, as he was called—Orator Hunt. His

extraordinarily chequered and eccentric career was recorded by
himself during the leisure of his $2\frac{1}{2}$ years' imprisonment for the
Peterloo affair.   Although some of his statements want checking, his narrative is a part of the history of the Radical
movement.   His biography begins to be interesting when,
about 1800, he was converted to Radicalism by a Henry
Clifford, and taken down to Horne Tooke's Sunday gatherings
at Wimbledon.   There he professes to have met the disaffected
politicians of London and Westminster, among whom he
mentions Place and Burdett (Place himself says he had not
exchanged a word with Burdett before 1807).   He spoke much
like Cobbett of the contemptible Westminster junto—meaning
Place, Burdett, and the rest.*   He made various attempts to
get into Parliament.   He marred Hobhouse's candidature for
Westminster in 1818, and let in the Whig candidate.   From
August, 1819, dated his two and a-half years' imprisonment.
Cobbett and he co-operated for a number of years, but when
Hunt was elected for Preston in December, 1830, Cobbett,
who had himself been once rejected for Preston, vilified him
considerably.   He failed in Parliament, chiefly by his abuse of
the Whigs, and praise of the Tories, which made him suspected
of being a Tory in Radical clothing.   In his last years he set
up a blacking manufactory.   He also introduced his "roasted
corn," as a substitute for coffee, which was intended as a hit at
the revenue.   These articles became a part of his own notoriety,
and a handle for the ridicule of opponents.   Bentham took
O'Connell to task for joining in that form of vulgar abuse.
" Should you ever again have occasion to speak of Henry
Hunt, I hope you will not again bring it up against him, as if
it were a matter of reproach, that he sells Blacking or anything
else , for, besides that there is no harm in selling Blacking, the

---

* In speaking of the period of the Horne Tooke gatherings, he says, "At
this time there was in fact very little disinterested patriotism amongst the working classes of the community".   Place, from still better knowledge, came to
the same conclusion.

feeling thus betrayed belongs not to us democrats, but to aristocrats, who make property (and that more particularly in a particular form, the immoveable) the standard of opinion."

Cobbett and Hunt stood very nearly equal in Bentham's opinion. "Hunt and Cobbett I contemplate with much the same eye, as the visiters of Mr. Carpenter, the optician, contemplate the rabid animals devouring one another in a drop of water. Hunt I never saw, nor corresponded with. Cobbett I saw once at the house of a common acquaintance; and, without so much as the shadow of a dispute, half-an-hour sufficed me for seeing him exactly as he is. As a speaker, Cobbett, they say, is nothing; Hunt very great. His moral character nothing has changed, nor presents a probability of changing; his intellectual character has received prodigious improvement. In the city of London, his influence has, of late, exercised by means of his speeches, become very considerable." This was in 1828.

Bentham having said that the people, if possessed of the suffrage, would choose persons of fortune and influence, rather than "such men as Hunt and Cobbett"; Cobbett retorted by calling Bentham the "antediluvian lawyer"; his invention being evidently at fault for an epithet.

In the publication called the "Black Dwarf," edited by Thomas Jonathan Wooler, from 1817 to the end of 1824, Radicalism was kept within more reasonable bounds, although there was no sparing of the rod in dealing with kings, aristocrats, and borough mongers. It is all but certain, that Major Cartwright was the pecuniary prop of the periodical; the radicalism was exactly of the Major's type, his name was everywhere throughout, and it died with him. More respectable still, it struck up a connexion with Bentham, no doubt through the Major. It contains several direct contributions from Bentham, as well as numerous selections from his writtings. Besides this, Wooler obtained permission to reprint in a series of separate numbers the Parliamentary Catechism as well as numerous selections from his writings. The paper attacked Malthus, but allowed letters in reply. Republicanism, after the American type, was its creed.

In the person of George IV., the attack of the extreme radicals on kingcraft was all too easy; and Wooler fulminated from Warwick gaol (where he was made to spend a year) against the trade. One of his letters "From the Black Dwarf to the Yellow Bronze in Japan" is headed "Failure of Kingcraft in some nations—Advice to such kings to look out for other Business," &c.

Here is a chance quotation giving the programme of the paper :—"If I were to go to sleep I should dream of strange matters for England—such as the erection of a monument to the memory of the brave and virtuous Riego !—a Reform of Parliament—a reduction of the debt—a revision of the public expenditure on the North American scale—the triumph of liberty on the Continent—the annihilation of the Turkish power—the consolidation of the liberties of Greece—the restoration of the tranquillity and happiness of Ireland—and certain other matters which I should think desirable for the benefit of the human race ;—but as I am awake, few of these things are likely to delight me—yet there are hopes of Greece, and the Continent may be roused from its fretful lethargy. The age is certainly improving in knowledge ; and knowledge is power with rational beings. So that, in a few years, the people of all countries may see that they can do without *their keepers*, and paying them their wages, may bid them be off to the moon, or elsewhere, where insanity is the order of the day."

The issue for October, 1824 (it began weekly, but the Six Acts compelled it to change to a monthly), announces the death of the Major. At the end of the year, the editor closes his labours. This is his pathetic farewell.—"In ceasing his political labours, the Black Dwarf has to regret one mistake, and that a serious one. He commenced writing under the idea that there was a PUBLIC in Britain, and that public devotedly attached to the cause of Parliamentary Reform. This, it is but candid to admit, was an error. Either there is no public, or that public is indifferent upon the subject. . . ."

For outspokenness and audacity, none of the radical agitators came up to Richard Carlisle, who was proportionally honoured by the Attorney-general of the time. Republican, Atheist, and Malthusian—he affronted at once the three most powerful objects of the country's veneration. Such advocacy of popular principles as his could have done little for the cause, where so much that was obnoxious went along with it. His mission was to afford a test case of Liberty of Thought; and, in that view, the advanced liberals stood up for him. Bentham came forward in his behalf. John Mill's first appearance in print was to denounce the prosecution of him and his wife. I have reason to believe that he received substantial aid in his long imprisonments from the Bentham circle.

Among the advocates of progress, at the epoch under review, a distinguished place must be assigned to William Godwin. His great work "Political Justice," came out in 1793. It was a splendid ideal, or political romance, and may be fitly compared to the Republic of Plato. It set people thinking, made them dissatisfied with the present state of things. It was the basis of Shelley's Creed; Jeremy Bentham's "Not Paul but Jesus," contributing to the superstructure,

Godwin's name would be ever famous in history, were it only for the part he took in defeating the Government prosecutions of Horne Tooke, Hardy, Holcroft, Thelwal, and others, twelve in all, in 1794. His letter to the *Morning Chronicle*, on the charge of Chief-Justice Eyre, wakened up the public mind so effectually, that all the trials ended in acquittals. Had these men been sentenced, liberty in England might have been as disastrously suppressed as it was in Scotland by the different issue of the prosecutions of Muir and Palmer.

Although thus capable of being a great political power, Godwin did not occupy himself with political writing in any form between 1815 and 1832.

The London newspaper press falls under the retrospect that we are now occupied with. But the organs more specially devoted to Liberalism—the *Chronicle* and the *Examiner*—have been sufficiently noticed in our narrative.

Something remains to be said on the *Edinburgh Review*, as an agent of progress. I do not think that Mill, in his merciless criticism of its ambiguous utterances, made the full allowance for the good that it really achieved. He pronounced it too exclusively the organ of the Whig Aristocratical party in Parliament. No doubt, many of its political articles had no larger aim than to see the restoration of that party to power. Yet, to the credit of Jeffrey it must be stated, that he constantly protested against this narrow view. That he admitted so many of Mill's articles showed that he was not a narrow-minded editor. But we find him again and again remonstrating with the defenders of pure Whiggism. I have marked many such passages in Cockburn's Life, and must make room for one. Cockburn speaks :—

" Then, as to home politics, his opinions were in substance just those of the Whig party ; but with this material qualification, that he was one of those who always thought that even the Whigs were disposed to govern too much through the influence of the aristocracy, and through a few great aristocratical families, without making the people a direct political element. He stated this view in the following letter to Mr. Horner, 26th October, 1809. 'In the main, I think our opinions do not differ very widely ; and, in substance and reality, you seem to me to admit all that I used to contend with you about. In the first place, you admit now that *there is* a spirit of discontent, or disaffection if you choose to call it so, among the people, which must be managed and allayed, in some way or other, if we wish to preserve tranquillity. And, in the next place, you admit that the leading Whigs belong to the aristocracy, and have been obliged to govern themselves a great deal by the necessity of managing this aristocracy. Now, all I say is, that there is a radical contest and growing struggle between the aristocracy and democracy of this country ; and agreeing entirely with you, that its freedom must depend in a good measure on their coalition, I still think that the aristocracy is the weakest, and ought to give way, and that the blame of the catastrophe will be heaviest on those who provoke a rupture by maintaining its pretensions. When I said I had no confidence in Lord Grey or Granville, I meant no more than that I thought them too aristocratical, and, consequently, likely to be inefficient. They will never be trusted by the Court, nor cordial with the Tories ; and, I fear, unless they think less of the aristocracy and its interests and prerogatives, they will every day have less influence with the people.' "

In 1810, he wrote an article on the State of Parties (No. 30), in which these views were strongly pressed. Addressing Horner, as a typical Whig, he calls it the article " which you all abused—and which I consequently think the best of all my articles, and the justest political speculation that has appeared in our immortal journal ".

It is quite true that some more energetic impetus was wanted to bring on the great revolution ; but it would be a mistake and an injustice to deny to the *Edinburgh* a fair share in the preparation of the public mind for the final results. The powerful attacks on abuses by Sydney Smith, the eloquence of Jeffrey, the energy and flow of Brougham, and a host besides, were in the right direction, notwithstanding all that Mill had to say against the ambiguity and the truckling of not a few of the articles.

We turn next to review the influence of the large towns under their local leaders. Westminster would of course be first; but the only thing left to remark upon respecting it would be its action upon the other towns. In the columns of the *Black Dwarf*, may be seen the assistance given to Birmingham on various occasions. At a meeting in connexion with the state prosecutions, Feb. 26, 1818, the Resolutions to be submitted had been drafted by Bentham.

The importance of Birmingham in the Reform struggle gives it a title to priority of mention among the great English towns. In Mr. J. A. Langford's *Century of Birmingham Life*, may be found some particulars as to the movement there. On the 17th June, 1812, there is a meeting of artisans to consider how to express gratitude "to those gentlemen of Birmingham who have so laudably exerted themselves to restore the suspended trade, and also to those who have so benevolently subscribed to the relief of the poor of this town". The author remarks—"It is the first instance we have of the artisans taking any part in public life—unless we look upon their doings at the riots of 1791 as having a prior claim".

The "great political agitation which produced the Political Union, and ended in obtaining the Reform Bill of 1832, was begun amid obloquy, opposition, and persecution, and had to endure many years of toil and suffering before success was obtained. . . . In every town of importance, Hampden Clubs had been formed, for the purpose of creating a demand for reform, and educating the people in politics.

"In Feb., 1817, . . . the report of the secret committee of the House of Commons on the subject of these clubs was presented." The following is an extract describing their organisation and object.

"Whatever may be the real objects of these clubs in general, your Committee have no hesitation in stating . . . that in far the greater number of them, and particularly in those which are established in the great manufacturing districts of

Lancashire, Leicestershire, Nottinghamshire, and Derbyshire, and which are composed of the lower order of artisans, nothing short of a Revolution is the object expected and avowed.

"On the professed object of their institution [Parliamentary Reform], they appear to be in communication and connexion with the club of that name [Hampden Club] in London." *V B*

The first meeting at New Hall Hill (famous in the Reform crisis) was on 23rd Jan., 1817. The attendance was not alarmingly great; 10,000, including women and children, being the estimate. A Petition to the House of Commons was resolved on, and the populace dispersed quietly.

A more formidable meeting was held on 19th July, 1819, when Sir Charles Wolseley was elected "Legislatorial Attorney and Representative" to the town. This was a great step, and alarmed the Government. The leaders at the meeting (Cartwright and Wooler were there) were indicted, and brought to trial in London, in August, 1820. A shopkeeper, George Ragg, was brought to trial at Warwick Assizes for selling Carlisle's *Republican* and other obnoxious publications, including a number of the *Black Book*. The chairman of the New Hall Hill meeting, George Edmonds, was tried at the same Assize, and fined and sent to Warwick jail. In spite of all this, the organisation of the Birmingham Political Union went on, and was conducted by able and discreet leaders. On the 14th July, 1823, the "Birmingham Union Society of Radical Reformers" gave a grand dinner to Henry Hunt, then in the zenith of his popularity.

On Dec. 14, 1829, "when hundreds of the inhabitants were shivering by their cold firesides, Mr. Attwood, with Mr. Scholefield and 14 other gentlemen, met at the Royal Hotel. They were called together by a circular, 'signed by six tradesmen'. This little meeting then founded 'The Political Union for the Protection of Public Rights'. They adjourned till the Monday following, when they met at the Globe (now the Clarendon), Temple Street. Mr. Attwood again presided, and he, in

conjunction with Mr. Charles Jones and Mr. T. C. Sa
submitted the rules of the Union. They were adopted ar
signed by 28 persons ; and it was resolved that they should 1
submitted for the approbation of the people."

The newly organised Union at once commenced to act upc
public opinion. On the 25th Jan. following (1830), a meetii
was attended by about fifteen thousand ; G. F. Muntz in tl
chair. Attwood spoke and explained the objects of the Unio
On the 17th May, was held another great and enthusiast
meeting. On the 16th August, there was a meeting to expre
joy at the three days in France. Joseph Parkes is fir
mentioned as present at this meeting.

What follows is incorporated in the history of the Refor
Bill struggle, and need not be repeated.

A good history of the Manchester movement has been pr
vided in Archibald Prentice's *Historical Sketches and Person*
Recollections. Manchester came forward in the days of Horr
Tooke, and had a Constitutional Society presided over by M
Thomas Walker, the leading citizen of the time. In the ye
of the State Trials, he and six other persons were indicted fi
conspiracy. Law (afterwards Lord Ellenborough) was pros
cutor, and Erskine conducted the defence. The tri
completely broke down, from the bad character of the princip
witness. Thomas Walker had been marked out for prosecutic
by his staunch adherence to Liberal principles, and by tl
ascendancy he had gained in Manchester, through leading tl
successful opposition to Pitt's " Fustian Tax ". He was mac
" borough reeve " of the town, the only constituted authori
that it then possessed ; and was in high esteem with all tl
great Liberal politicians of the country. He died in 1817.

The radicalism of Manchester seems to have slumbere
without being extinguished. It awakened in 1812, and receivi
a farther impetus in 1815. The Corn Laws was the fi
question that stirred the community. " In 1817, a small ba1

(including Prentice) had begun to write in Cowdroy's paper, previously containing, like the other local papers, little that was not gleaned from the London journals." "Party spirit was no less virulent in 1817, than it had been in 1794." "The whole aspect of society was unfavourable. The rich seemed banded together to deny the possession of political rights ; the poor seemed to be banding themselves together in an implacable hatred to their employers, who were regarded as their cruel oppressors. Out of this bitter antagonism there seemed to be no other result than some great and destructive convulsion. . . .

". . . The events of 1819 showed that there was some fructification of the seed that had been sown, and revived the hopes of the previously almost despairing."

In January, 1819, Hunt made a public entry into Manchester from Stockport. His presence had a stirring influence. The radicals took to military drilling, without arms. This brought down the Royal Proclamation against military training, seditious meetings, and the election of legislatorial attornies (like Wolseley at Birmingham). The excitement became intense, and, on the 16th August, was held the meeting of 60,000 persons at St. Peter's Field, at which took place the military attack with a view to capture the ringleaders ; eleven persons being killed, and six hundred wounded. " Yet," says Prentice, " radicalism was not extinguished, not even damaged, by the compulsory calm. Instead of great meetings, where noisy braggarts usurped the place due to the intelligent and thoughtful men who represented the better part of the industrial classes, there were the little congregations of the workshop and at the fireside, at which the principles of representation were calmly discussed, and comparatively sound opinions formed, as to what ought to be the real objects of a government."

In 1821 was started the *Manchester Guardian*, which soon rose to be a first-class Liberal organ ; and under it, the Liberal movement became naturally more and more enlightened.

On the eve of the Reform Bill, in 1830, Cobbett gave Lectures in Manchester. , While he talked a great deal of Political Economy, his hearers remarked two omissions—the monopoly of the corn-growers, and the want of adequate representation in the House of Commons.

Prentice was in London, in 1831, during the Reform crisis, and, to his great gratification, succeeded in obtaining an interview with Jeremy Bentham. He makes the recital of the incident an opportunity of testifying to the good he had received from Bentham's writings. " When I had taken my station in the ranks of those who were combatting for reform, and, as I believed had been instrumental in popularising some of his doctrines, and thereby rendering them, in my comparatively narrow sphere, the guiding principles of many ardent friends of liberty, my feeling of reverence for the great apostle of reform did not wear off. . . ."

I am not able to refer to any histories of other great English towns, during the Reform period. Similar causes were everywhere at work, and the effects were much the same in kind, although various in degree and in circumstances. At the Reform crisis, every town, large and small, was up and doing, from whatever source the inspiration had come. Respecting one great industrial centre, Newcastle, I have been informed by Mr. Holyoake, that the determination to accept nothing short of the ten-pound franchise, was due to the resolution formed there. The twenty-pound figure was in favour with the Whig leaders, and might have been accepted, but for Newcastle.

A few remarks on Edinburgh will complete the survey. The fitting words are supplied by the biographer of Charles Maclaren, the founder of the *Scotsman*.

" It was in the year 1816 that the idea of starting an independent newspaper in Edinburgh originated. The political terrorism which overspread the country towards and after the close of the war had permeated society ; and the ruling powers carried their paralyzing and repressive influences into almost every sphere of public action. The local press was utterly abject ; no Edinburgh paper could be found independent or courageous enough to expose almost any sort of abuse, however flagrant, if in doing so there was the slightest risk of giving offence in high quarters."

" Efforts at reform and liberation were suppressed, either by an abuse of the law, as in the cases of Muir, Gerrald, and others, or more generally and effectively by a rigorous social persecution—the man who questioned whether all things were for the best was socially, professionally, and commercially discredited. The Whig landed gentry, a small but powerful body, and a brilliant band of Whig lawyers, almost alone maintained a good testimony. The mercantile class was then small in Scotland, and even there there was almost universal fear and quaking."

Maclaren's "calm, clear, forcible expositions of political questions as they arose, told steadily and rapidly on the public mind. With all deference to the good work done by the *Edinburgh Review* in its own sphere, it was the *Scotsman*, through the articles of Mr. Maclaren, that first spread or popularised Liberalism in Scotland. The *Review* was a sort of bishop over the few faithful—the *Scotsman* was a missionary to the many unconverted."

The influence of Mill began at an early stage in the Reform movement, and is thus described by Roebuck :—" When, however, after 1812, the question (of Parliamentary Reform) again became a topic of discussion, and the Radical reformers began to stir, the persons who at that time led them, more especially in the city of Westminster, adopted that exposition of principles on this subject which may be found stated with great precision as well as brevity by Mr. James Mill, the historian of British India, in the article ' Government ' in the Supplement to the *Encyclopædia Britannica*. The whole doctrine of natural right was discarded, together with the principle of individual representation; and an extensive constituency was now demanded, because by this means alone, as the Radical reformers asserted, the interests of the people and their representatives could be made identical, and an honest as well as intelligent government obtained through representation." This was previous to the publication of any of Mill's articles, and must have been the result of his talk with the Westminster politicians. At this stage, Bentham had his Plan of Parliamentary Reform written, but not printed. The discarding of the doctrine of natural rights was a great clearance of the ground; it removed a source of weakness and misgiving from the cause. The defenders of things as they were had to equip themselves with a new set of reasons; and were easily worsted when the appeal was made to argument.

Before Mill's "Government" article was written, Bentham's Reform Catechism appeared (1817), and was a powerful engine on the side of Radicalism. There was, however, a want of tact and discretion in proceeding at once to the extreme of Universal Suffrage. There was, for such a reasoner as Bentham, something even worse. He had coupled with the universality of the suffrage, the universality of a certain modicum of Education; yet in working with Burdett and Cartwright, he allowed the demand for the suffrage to precede the education.* Mill laid down principles that would ultimately conduct to universal suffrage; but, for the present, he looked to the enfranchisement of the middle class. He and Bentham

---

* Bentham's education test was given in the enumeration of exceptions, or as he called them, *defalcations*, under Universal Suffrage. One of the admissible defalcations was *Non-readers*. Bentham, however, considered that any one could overcome this defect by three months' application of evening leisure; an assumption in the teeth of all reasonable probability.

If education was proper to be considered as a preliminary to Universal Suffrage, the conditions to be required could not be less than these two. First, a national education, under which every child had to be at school for a given number of years Second, a cheap and wholesome newspaper press, such as was possible only after the abolition of the newspaper stamp duty.

were equally strenuous for the ballot; but his advocacy was probably the chief cause of its adoption by the advanced reformers.

The immediate effect of the article on " Government " must have been considerable; yet without turning up the files of the contemporary newspapers and political periodicals, it could not be definitely stated.   The other *Encyclopædia* articles, such as Colonies, Liberty of the Press, would still farther contribute to lay the enlarged foundations of political right.   But, it was in the *Westminster Review*, that he did most to give both impetus and direction to the Reform movement.   John Mill says :—" At this period, when Liberalism seemed to be becoming the tone of the time, when improvement of institutions was preached from the highest places, and a complete change of the constitution of Parliament was loudly demanded in the lowest, it is not strange that attention should have been roused by the regular appearance in controversy of what seemed a new school of writers, claiming to be the legislators and theorists of this new tendency.   The air of strong conviction with which they wrote, when scarcely any one else seemed to have an equally strong faith in as definite a creed; the boldness with which they tilted against the very front of both the existing political parties; their uncompromising profession of opposition to many of the generally received opinions, and the suspicion they lay under of holding others still more heterodox than they professed; the talent and verve of at least my father's articles, and the appearance of a corps behind him sufficient to carry on a Review; and finally, the fact that the Review was bought and read, made the so-called Bentham school in philosophy and politics fill a greater place in the public mind than it had held before, or has ever again held since other equally earnest schools of thought have arisen in England."

Roebuck adverts to the same influence in the following terms :—" The anomalies to be found in every part of our constitution were assailed continually, and not without effect,

by a large class of systematic and acute reasoners on the science
of government, whose unsparing criticisms, and accurate and
often profound deductions, were not always refuted by those
who argued in support of things as they were, and who, by
appeals to the beneficial working of the system, sought to repel
the hostile inferences of a severe and inexorable logic.   The
class of reasoners, called at this period Radical reformers, had
produced a much more serious effect on public opinion than
superficial inquirers perceived, or interested ones would
acknowledge.   The important practical effect was not made
evident by converting and bringing over large numbers of
political partisans from one banner or class to another, or by
making them renounce one appellation and adopt another ; but
it was shown by affecting the conclusions of all classes, and
inducing them, while they retained their old distinctive names,
to reason after a new fashion, and according to principles
wholly different from those to which they had been previously
accustomed."

It is evident that Mill got hold of the more intelligent minds
of the growing middle class in our great centres of industry.
To them his views and reasonings were adapted in many ways.
He seconded their natural demands for better government and
better legislation to suit the extension of manufactures and
commerce, which must have suffered grievously from the bad
administration of justice ; and insisted on their having a share
of political power for their own defence.   His principles were
wide enough to include the lower orders in the suffrage, but the
extension must be gradual and accompanied with the spread of
education.   He differed from the Cobbetts and the Hunts, in
taking securities against ignorance and brutality, and in holding
out no delusive promises of raising wages by the instrumentality
of legislation.   He and his son were alike distinguished both
for their sympathies with the working class, and for refusing to
feed them with false hopes.

The ten-pound franchise hit very closely Mill's idea of the

first step in Reform. In Grote's pamphlet, published at his
instigation, entitled *Essentials of Parliamentary Reform,* the
proposal was to enfranchise about a million of voters ; and the
calculation was that so much could be effected by a pecuniary
qualification of £100 a-year (income). Of course the Ballot
was an essential in his eyes ; but this could not be extorted
from the legislature of the time.

Had Mill not appeared on the stage at the opportune
moment, the whole cast of political thinking at the time of the
Reform settlement must have been very inferior in point of
sobriety and ballast to what it was. His place could not have
been taken by any other man that we can fix upon. Bentham,
without him, would not have sufficed for the crisis. If privilege
had been confronted with French Revolution theories of the
Rights of Man and absolute equality, the various classes of the
community might not have been got to co-operate with that
harmony and unanimity which gained a bloodless victory over
an obdurate aristocracy. Even Macaulay's advocacy of the
Reform Bill, which was perhaps the most impressive of any,
was matured by his having to pass through the Mill schooling,
which he pretended to despise and refute. Indeed, but for his
early contact with Mill's disciples at Cambridge, he might have
sat by the side of Peel, or at all events have been the supporter
of some minimum compromise that would have baulked the
popular wishes with safety, and postponed for years the results
achieved in 1832.

APPENDIX

APPENDIX.

APPENDIX.

A. (p. 19).—*Mill's reading in Edinburgh.*

Professor Masson has recently extended his researches into the musty records of the Edinburgh University Library, and has sent me a few additional jottings of the books taken out by Mill from the General Library during the last of his three years as a student of Arts, and his first of Divinity. They are almost exclusively philosophical works :—Origin of Language, Vol. II.; Harris's Philological Inquiries ; Hume's Essays, Vol. I.; Anarcharsis, Vol. IV.; Stewart's Elements (only just published); Ferguson's Morals ; Harris ; Beattie's something or other.

B. (p. 151.)—*Bentham on Romilly.*

The following unpublished letter of Bentham (to Place) gives his opinion of Romilly in the most unreserved way, and is very interesting. It was written immediately after Romilly's death (6th Dec., 1818).

"My acquaintance with Romilly commenced in 1784 or 5, he being then young at the Bar. On my return from Russia, early in 1788, it ripened into intimacy, which continued without interruption or coolness till his death, notwithstanding the divergency of our declared sentiments in party politics, and the part which I declared to him my having taken in opposition to him in his quality of candidate for Westminster . . .

"No sooner had I got from the printer any one of my works—and a multitude there has been of them, which, for some reason or other never saw till long afterwards, if ever, the public light—than a copy went to Romilly of course. My manuscripts were equally at his command. . . .

". . . When he declares himself, as he does everlastingly, full of doubts, he worships himself in public for the learning and anxiety which generated them, and considers his duty as fulfilled. . . .

"Notwithstanding our intimacy, such was our local distance, so distractive our respective occupations, we saw one another but seldom. Having travelled through that vast volume of mine intituled *Church of Englandism,*

&c., he sent for me, and pronounced these very words : 'Bentham, I am as sure as I am of my existence that, if you publish this, you will be prosecuted ; and I am as sure as I am of my existence that, if you are prosecuted, you will be convicted. There is scarce a sacrifice that I would not make rather than that you should publish.' Not but that he agreed with it in every tittle, and declared it to several persons the most captivating book he ever read. He suggested precautions which for some time were observed, but have for some time been discontinued."

Bentham adds, in his own hand :

"His sentiment in favour of the cause of the people went as far as ours. By avowing them in public, he should do harm (he said) to himself, and no good to the cause."

C.—*The Reform agony week.*

On Monday, the 7th May, Lord Lyndhurst, in the House of Lords, carried his destructive amendment to the Bill, by 151 to 116. On Wednesday, the 9th, Lord Grey resigned. The king sent for Lyndhurst, who of course referred him to the Duke of Wellington ; and the Duke was occupied for several days with his fruitless attempts to form a ministry. In the meantime, the country had information on Tuesday, of the hostile vote of the Lords ; and every succeeding day added intensity to the popular fury. One of the first fruits was the addition to the Political Unions of a vast number of the more cautious and pacific citizens, many of them wealthy, who had hitherto kept aloof from agitation. Monster meetings were held, and resolutions passed of the most menacing kind. Petitions to the House of Commons to stop the supplies were general : the Manchester petition being the first to reach the House. The Birmingham Petition broadly insinuated that an appeal to arms was in store. Resolutions to pay no more taxes became the order of the day. The provincial deputations in London met the London Unions, and the common ardour was thereby increased. It was in the face of this growing conflagration, that the Duke was negotiating to form a Ministry. Authorities are divided as to what particular phase of the terrible agitation first arrested his hand. There was, of course, the likelihood, amounting almost to a certainty, of a hundred thousand men in arms marching to London, to be joined by a larger number there. There was also the misgiving as to the military, with which Somerville's narrative respecting the Scots' Greys has made us familiar.

Great probability, however, attaches to the influence of a more specific move, with which Francis Place is identified, as chief instigator. On Saturday, the 12th, every blank wall in London was covered with a placard bearing these words ;—Go for gold—and stop the Duke. The effect is said to have been electric. A run upon the banks began. On Monday, it was believed that the Duke had actually formed a cabinet, and the Bank of England was besieged the whole day ; upwards of half a million of coin was carried off in a few hours. The same evening, the petitions for stopping the supplies poured into the House of Commons, and the excitement of the House was increased by the double stimulation. On Tuesday, the 15th, the demand upon the Bank went on with increased violence ; but, in the afternoon, there was news that the Duke had failed, and that Earl Grey had been sent for—which was confirmed by his moving the adjournment of the House of Lords till Thursday. On Wednesday, the spread of the information had a tranquillizing effect, and was just in time to save the credit of the country.

Without farther preface, I give a letter from Place to Grote, written on Tuesday evening.

"Charing Cross, *15th May, 1832.*

"My dear Sir,

"We may now sing, 'Glory to God in the highest,' the Bill is won, the *people's* Bill, by the *people's* minister, and all this without the aid of the City of London—'Life and Fortune' men.

"You and I can afford to differ, and may perhaps improve each other by differing. I expected a short denial from you in the *Standard.*

"Just at the time the *Standard* was publishing your—what shall I call them—oh ! arguments, to prove that '*Go for Gold*' was *no go at all*, came a Great man, who, seeing the Placard in my room, pointed at it and exultingly exclaimed 'that's the Settler ! *that* has done it '. This he said in the presence of a gentleman whom he had never before seen. When the gentleman had retired, he told me how the Placard and some other *little* things had worked out the reformation. He (the Great man) feared a hitch : a very extraordinary one, and promised, if there should be one, to come to me again. It is now eleven, P.M., and he has not been, I conclude that all is right ; I shall see him again in the morning. The great man came to me, from other 'great men,' to ascertain my opinion of the chance there was the excited people would become quiescent on the return of Lord Grey, &c., &c.

"I pledged my existence for their acquiescence and peaceable demeanour, if Lord Grey and Lord Althorpe would declare in Parliament that the Bill would be carried unmutilated.

"Now—pray recollect—that '*Go for Gold*'—was only an enlivener, that I said it would send the Bank to St. James's—and we should have Lord Grey and the Bill.—It has done its duty.

"Yours truly,

"Francis Place.

" 16th May, 9 A.M.—When I look at the City news in the *Chronicle* and see what is said of the conduct of the Bank Directors—and couple that with the results which the great man showed me, I am mightily pleased at what has been done. Anything, everything, was to be risked, rather than have the Duke.

" '*Go For Gold—and Stop The Duke'*

is my motto."*

The *Standard*, in discussing the placard, had addressed a strong appeal and remonstrance to Grote, as a banker, for countenancing such a perilous move Grote published, next day, in the *Standard* and in the *Times*, a strong letter of disapproval of the step, which is what Place alludes to. In the previous October, when the Lords had rejected the Bill, on the second reading, Grote felt that there remained nothing but the appeal to force, and expressed to Parkes the embarrassment of his position. He said—" I myself find it very difficult to steer my course, in my present commercial station for I cannot possibly embark in any measures pointing directly to the employment of force, without altogether losing my character in the commercial world, and I therefore feel myself precluded from taking any prominent part in the guidance of the projected Political Union here. Men more forward and more free to act than I am, must undertake the conduct of this Association."

The event proved that Place's placard was a wise move. It was understood that the king was exceedingly sensitive to the views of the " City " ; and, therefore, nothing could have been conceived so well calculated to produce on him a speedy impression, as the run upon the bank. The refusal of taxes, the stoppage of the supplies by the House of Commons, would have been slower in operating ; armed insurrection would have been a work of some time : while the collateral consequences of each of these measures would have been no less disastrous than the run for gold.†

Now as to the share of Parkes, in the week's proceedings. Joseph Parkes, known to his contemporaries as " Joe Parkes," was a solicitor in Birmingham previous to the passing of the Reform Bill ; afterwards he

---

* In his MS., Place is in doubt whether he should tell who the "Great man" was. He actually puts down a name, and then scores it out. It is possible, however, to see that the name was " Hobhouse", and what he says, otherwise, shows plainly enough that he was meant

† Doubleday, in his *Life of Peel*, says—" It is known that these placards were the device of four gentleman, two of whom were elected members of the reformed parliament Each put down £20." That Place would not act alone, in such a daring venture, I fully believe. He was not a man that thought lightly of revolution. Grote, in writing to Parkes, after the October crisis, makes this remark—" Place is not in good spirits, he appreciates the mischief of riot and commotion more highly than even I do ".

settled in London, and had, as a part of his business, the management of the elections of the Whig party. He was ultimately rewarded with a lucrative post in the Court of Chancery. In a long letter to Mrs. Grote at the close of the terrible week, he thus describes his adoption into the family —"Sincerely I say it, Bowring's introduction of me to Bentham, and Gregory's to George Grote and Mill, created all the power and courage I have brought to bear in favour of the people." We ought to have had from himself direct a full account of what he did and witnessed during those perilous days. From the general history of the time, and from his correspondence with the Grotes, may be gleaned the following facts.

It was, of course, as leader and representative of the Birmingham Union that Parkes made his mark. The chairman of the Union was Thomas Attwood. He and Parkes were the two chiefs by pre-eminence. The excitement at Birmingham, on Tuesday the 8th, by the news of Lyndhurst's amendment, may be imagined ; but it was the announcement of Lord Grey's resignation, which came on Thursday morning, that led to decisive action. A meeting was convened at three o'clock that afternoon at Newhall Hill, at which resolutions were passed, and a deputation appointed to proceed to London the same night. Parkes was in this deputation. His operations on Friday and Saturday I know only in a general way. They would consist in consultations with the London Union, and with the Parliamentary and other Leaders of the Reform Party. On Saturday morning, he writes a note to Grote in these words :—"Beach and I mean to dine with you at six at Dulwich if you are disengaged. Nicholson and many city men say you *must* be returned in a new Parliament. I shall be in the city about 2 or 3. The zeal of the people exceeds all expectation. We shall do the business." The business, however, was not done yet. On Sunday, Parkes posts to Birmingham, to add fuel to the fires there. He arrives at his own door at six on Monday morning. In one hour, he tells us, "I sent letters and expresses to all the towns within fifteen miles, directing meetings to be instantly held by beat of drum and bells, and their addresses to be expressed back to me by *four* that afternoon. In that hour, between six and seven, the inhabitants of the whole town of Birmingham were tumbling into the streets, and the bells clamming. At seven I started in a chaise and four (the horses decorated with blue ribbons) to Attwood's cottage." Attwood's family expected nothing but warrants for high treason. A great meeting was convened, of course. The deputation returned the same evening to London. "During the whole day we told the people that they *might* have to make great sacrifices, and to contend for their liberties—that life and property must be respected. Our arrival in London, and subsequent proceedings here, you know well. Lord Durham told us last night, at a meeting of good men at Ellice's, that "the country owed Reform to Birmingham, and its salvation from revolution to the *last* stroke." The letter was written on Friday the 18th, when all had become serene. The remaining sentences of interest are these :—" If we had been over-reached this week by the Boroughmongers, I and two friends should have *made* the Revolution, whatever the cost. I had written to General J——, and had got a cover to Colonel N——, and would have had both in Birmingham, and a Count Chopski (a Pole), by Monday ; and I *think* we could have prevented anarchy, and set all right in two days. I have had great advantage in seeing behind the scenes."

In the interim, Parkes had been again to Birmingham. On Tuesday evening, when the Duke's failure was known, Parkes and Green were off, reaching Birmingham on Wednesday morning. A meeting was held the same day ; a memorial to Lord Grey was agreed upon, and a deputation of five left for London the same evening, Parkes being one. Thursday saw the famous interview of the King with Lords Grey and Brougham, when he gave a written consent to create Peers. On Friday, it was known that this process was unnecessary. The House of Commons was quieted on the eve of a new Reform debate, by the news that the Bill was safe. This was at six o'clock in the evening, and the crisis was over.

D.—*Notices of Mill from personal knowledge.*

Macaulay, in a letter written after hearing of Mill's death, says—

" I have been a sincere mourner for Mill. He and I were on the best terms, and his services at the India House were never so much needed as at this time. I had a most kind letter from him a few weeks before I heard of his death. He has a son just come out, to whom I have shown such little attentions as are in my power."

In the *Morning Chronicle*, Black penned an appropriate memento ; partly biographical, partly eulogistic. The valuable portions for us are those where he gives his own impressions of Mill, as the result of long familiarity.

" We have heard Mr. Mill speak with great warmth of the impression which the writings of Plato made on his youth, and it is probably through some such influence, that he seems to have been led at an early period of his life to regulate his conduct strictly according to an elevated ethical standard. With him principles were not suffered to remain unapplied. He allowed no opportunity of doing good to escape. He had constantly present to his mind the idea that the moment a man comes to be occupied only with himself, he sinks nearly to the level of a brute, and his life was an effort to ameliorate the condition of his species, to diffuse knowledge

and virtue, and contribute to swell the amount of human happiness.
Whenever he came in contact with a young man of good dispositions and
abilities, he exerted himself to place him in a situation in which he might
have a sphere of usefulness suited to his character and qualifications.   At a
time when Mr. Mill had a growing family, with an income of not more
than £300 a-year, derived from his literary labours, he possessed great
influence with most of the distinguished men of the day, and of that
influence he availed himself, by allowing no opportunity to do good to
those whom he believed to be deserving men to escape him.   The secret of
his influence with the government may be of use to literary men, who in
general, from their profuse and irregular habits, are in dependent circumstances, and driven by their necessities to solicit accommodation from the
rich men with whom they are in habits of intercourse.   By a system of
rigid economy, Mr. Mill was at all times perfectly independent, and he
never approached any man with a solicitation for himself individually.

"Mr. Mill was eloquent and impressive in conversation.   He had a
great command of language, which bore the stamp of his earnest and
energetic character.   Young men were particularly fond of his society, and
it was always to him a source of great delight to have an opportunity
of contributing to form their minds and exalt their characters.   No man
could enjoy his society without catching a portion of his elevated enthusiasm.
Many of the men in whom the country now places its warmest hopes
benefited largely by the enlightened society of Mr. Mill.   He watched the
progress of a promising young man with intense interest, and we shall
never forget his grief at the premature death of the virtuous and accomplished Mr. Eton Tooke, the eldest son of Mr. Thomas Tooke.   High as
were the intellectual qualities of Mr. Mill, he was still higher in his moral
capacity.   He was an utter stranger to the selfishness which, whether
coarse or coated over with a polish, enters so largely into the character of
too many English gentlemen, and communicates such apathy and indifference to it."

In a touching conclusion, Black says :—" The writer of this brief notice
is one of the many who owe a deep debt of gratitude to James Mill, who
assisted him at a time when he had few friends."

In the *Examiner*, Fonblanque wrote —

" With profound grief we have to record the death of one of the first
men of our time ; the loss of one of our master-minds, of one that has
given the most powerful impulse, and the most correct direction to thought.
Wherever talent and good purpose were found conjoined—the power and
the will to serve the cause of truth—the ability and the disposition to be
useful to society, to weed out error, and advance improvement—wherever
these qualities were united, the possessor found a friend, a supporter to

fortify, cheer, and encourage him in his course, in James Mill. He fanned every flame of public virtue, he strengthened every good purpose that came within the range of his influence. His conversation was full of instruction, and his mind was rich in suggestion, to a degree that we have never found equalled. His writings, with all their solid value, would convey but an imperfect notion of the character and powers of his mind. His conversation was so energetic and complete in thought, so succinct, and exact *ad unguem* in expression, that, if reported as uttered, his colloquial observations or arguments would have been perfect compositions His thoughts, conveyed to paper, lost some of the excellences we have mentioned. Yet his works will be stores of valuable doctrine, to which we shall often repair for instruction. It was hardly possible for an intelligent man to know James Mill without feeling an obligation for the profit derived from his mind. That mind is now lost to us, but *quidquid amavimus, quidquid mirati sumus manet, mansurumque est in animis.*"

Underneath the above, is quoted an appreciative notice from the *Globe.* One sentence brings out a special point, not adverted to by the others. "He was retiring in his habits, and seldom took part in any public proceedings, though he took a lively interest in all proceedings for national and social improvement. . . ."

I cannot refrain from adding to these obituary notices the eulogy written by Grote many years afterwards. I may remark by way of preface that Grote's references to Mill in conversation were very frequent, and always in terms of deep veneration. He never mentioned his name without "Mr.," which is, by common usage, omitted in speaking of the dead. He often adverted, in tones of wonder and reproach, to the public neglect and forgetfulness of a man that he himself accounted the greatest intellect that he had ever encountered. Fortunately, the thought occurred to him, when he undertook to review the younger Mill's *Hamilton*, that the moment was opportune for giving expression to what he felt regarding the elder. I must give the passage in full.

" While speaking about the general merits and philosophical position of Sir William Hamilton, we have hitherto said nothing about those of Mr. Mill. But before we proceed to analyse the separate chapters of his volume, we must devote a few words to the fulfilment of another obligation.

" Mr. John Stuart Mill has not been the first to bestow honour on the surname which he bears. His father, Mr. James Mill had already ennobled the name. An ampler title to distinction in history and philosophy can seldom be produced than that which Mr. James Mill left behind him. We know no work which surpasses his *History of British India* in the main excellences attainable by historical writers ; industrious accumulation, continued for many years, of original authorities ; careful and conscientious criticism of their statements ; and a large command of psychological analysis, enabling the author to interpret phenomena of society, both extremely complicated, and far removed from his own personal experience. Again, James Mill's *Elements of Political Economy* were, at the time when they appeared, the most logical and condensed exposition of the entire science then existing. Lastly, his latest avowed production, the *Analysis of the Phenomena of the Human Mind*, is a model of perspicuous exposition of complex states of consciousness, carried farther than by any other author before him ; and illustrating the fulness which such exposition may be made to attain, by one who has faith in the comprehensive principle of association, and has learnt the secret of tracing out its innumerable windings. It is, moreover, the first work in which the great fact of Indissoluble Association is brought into its due theoretical prominence. These are high merits, of which lasting evidence is before the public ; but there were other merits in Mr. James Mill, less publicly authenticated, yet not less real. His unpremeditated oral exposition was hardly less effective than his prepared work with the pen ; his colloquial fertility on philosophical subjects, his power of discussing himself, and of stimulating others to discuss, his ready responsive inspirations through all the shifts and windings of a sort of Platonic dialogue—all these accomplishments were, to those who knew him, even more impressive than what he composed for the press. Conversation with him was not merely instructive, but provocative to the dormant intelligence. Of all persons whom we have known Mr. James Mill was the one who stood least remote from the lofty Platonic ideal of Dialectic—Τοῦ διδόναι καὶ δέχεσθαι λόγον—(the giving and receiving of reasons) competent alike to examine others, or to be examined by them on philosophy. When to this we add a strenuous character, earnest convictions, and single-minded devotion to truth, with an utter disdain of mere paradox, it may be conceived that such a man exercised powerful intellectual ascendancy over younger minds. Several of those who enjoyed his society—men now at or past the maturity of life, and some of them in distinguished positions—remember and attest with gratitude such ascendancy in their own cases : among them the writer of the present article, who owes to the historian of British India an amount of intellectual stimulus and guidance such as he can never forget."

We are interested in seeing the terms employed by Lord Brougham, in speaking of his greatest friend. The eulogy is sufficiently strong. It is given in the Introduction to his Speech on Law Reform (Feb. 7, 1828) as printed in the luxurious four-volume Edition of his Speeches, published 1838. In the eleven volume edition of his works (1855-60), two volumes

are devoted to a selection from the Speeches.* The speech on Law Reform
is curtailed to the Peroration ; and the Introduction is gone. The latest
edition of the works (1872) is a reissue of the edition of 1855-60, "without
any material change ". The eulogy of Mill is thus dropt out from what
may be considered the permanent or standard edition of Brougham's collected writings. I here reproduce it from the complete edition of the
Speeches.

" The school of Mr. Bentham has numbered among its disciples, apostles
of his doctrine, others of eminent merit, of whom unhappily death, by removing one of the chief, enables us to speak, however difficult it may be to
speak of him as his great merits deserve. When the system of legal polity
was to be taught, and the cause of Law Reform to be supported in this
country, no one could be found more fitted for the service than Mr. Mill ;
and to him more than to any other person has been owing the diffusion of
those important principles and their rapid progress in England. He was a
man of extensive and profound learning, thoroughly imbued with the
doctrines of metaphysical and ethical science ; conversant above most men
with the writings of the ancient philosophers, whose language he familiarly
knew ; and gifted with an extraordinary power of application, which had
made entirely natural to him a life of severe and unremitting study. His
literary pursuits had originally directed him chiefly to subjects conected
with moral and political philosophy ; but his attention being drawn, somewhere about 30 years ago, (1808 or 1809), to the writings of Mr. Bentham,
he speedily devoted to their study the greater part of his time; and, becoming acquainted with their celebrated author, was soon received into his entire
confidence, and co-operated with him until his decease in the propagation
of his philosophy.† It is in the valuable dissertations which Mr. Mill contributed to the *Encyclopedia Britannica* that the fruits of his labours in this
field are stored for public use ; and no one can rise from the perusal of
them without being convinced that a more clear and logical understanding
was never brought to bear upon an important subject, than he lent to the
diffusion of his master's doctrines. His admirable works on the Principles
of Political Economy, and of Moral Philosophy, entitle him, perhaps, to a
higher place among the writers of his age ; but neither these nor his *History
of British India*, the greatest monument of his learning and industry, can
vie with his discourses on Jurisprudence in usefulness to the cause of general
improvement, which first awakened the ardour of his vigorous mind, and

* The Preface says—" The selection of the Speeches was for the most part
made by friends who were well acquainted with the history of the time, and in
whose judgment reliance could be placed "

† To his son, Mr. John Mill, we owe the preparation of Mr. Bentham's
second work, the *Rationale of Evidence*, which is admirably executed.

on which its latest efforts reposed. His style was better adapted to didactic works, and works of abstract science, than to history ; for he had no powers of narrative, and was not successful in any kind of ornamental composition. He was slenderly furnished with fancy, and far more capable of following a train of reasoning, expounding the theories of others, and pursuing them to their legitimate consequences, than of striking out new paths, and creating new objects, or even adorning the creations of other men's genius. With the single exception that he had something of the dogmatism of the school, he was a person of most praiseworthy candour in controversy, always of such self-denial that he sunk every selfish considera- tion in his anxiety for the success of any cause which he espoused, and ever ready to the utmost extent of his faculties, and often beyond the force of his constitution, to lend his help for its furtherance. In all the relations of private life he was irreproachable ; and he afforded a rare example of one born in humble circumstances, and struggling, during the greater part of his laborious life, with the inconveniences of restricted means, nobly main- taining an independence as absolute in all respects as that of the first subject in the land—an independence, indeed, which but few of the pampered children of rank and wealth are ever seen to enjoy. For he could at all times restrain his wishes within the limits of his resources ; was firmly resolved that his own hands alone should ever minister to his wants ; and would, at every period of his useful and virtuous life, have treated with indignation any project that should trammel his opinions or his conduct with the restraints which external influence, of whatever kind, could impose.'

I will finally advert to some recorded sayings of Bentham, which are in the highest degree depreciatory of Mill's motives as a democratic politician. These sayings are given in Bowring's *Life*, among the memoranda of Ben- tham's conversations. On being quoted, in an article on Bentham in the *Edinburgh Review*, they drew forth from John Mill an indignant letter of repudiation. From this letter I give the following extract :—

"The Reviewer, quoting from the *Memoirs*, says, ' Bentham said of Mill, that his willingness to do good to others depended too much on his power of making the good done to them subservient to good done to him- self. His creed of politics results less from love for the many than from hatred of the few. It is too much under the influence of social and dissocial affection.'

"What is here promulgated as Bentham's deliberate judgment, was never, I will venture to affirm, believed by any human being who had the smallest knowledge of Mr. Mill.

"I know not how a biographer is to be justified in giving publicity and permanence to every idle word which may have been said to the prejudice of others, under some passing impression or momentary irritation. It would, besides, be easy to show, that the reports of Bentham's conversations contained in the Biography, abound in the inaccuracies which are to be expected when things carelessly stated by one person, are afterwards noted down from memory by another. But whatever Bentham may really have said, when a statement so injurious to another is made on his authority, justice to that other imposes the necessity of declaring what the *Memoirs* amply confirm, that among Mr. Bentham's eminent intellectual endowments, capacity for judging of character was not one. The manner of his intercourse with others was not favourable to his acquiring a real knowledge of them ; and his warmest friends and admirers often lamented that his opinion of men depended less on their merits than on accidental circumstances, and on the state of his personal relations with them at the time. On no other principle can I account for his expressing any opinion of Mr. Mill bearing the complexion of that quoted in the Article.

"It imputes to Mr. Mill, as the source of his democratic opinions, the vulgarest motives of an unprincipled demagogue ; namely, selfish ambition, and a malignant hatred of the ruling classes. Now, there was perhaps no one man among Mr. Mill's contemporaries, holding similar opinions to his, who stood more manifestly clear from even the suspicion of these motives.

" He could in no way hope for 'good to himself' from the opinions he professed. In many respects they stood in the way of his personal interest. They deprived his writings of the countenance of either of the great parties in the state, in times when that countenance was much more important than it now is, and when he might have obtained it as easily as many others did, who had not a tithe of his talents. Even had his opinions become predominant, which he never expected would be the case during his life, he would, as he well knew, have reaped no personal benefit from them ; and assuredly, the time when he embraced democratic doctrines, was a time when no person in his senses could have entertained the smallest hope of gaining anything by their profession.

"As for 'hatred of the few,' the phrase seems introduced solely to round an antithesis. There never was a man more free from any feelings of hatred. His hostility was to institutions and principles, not to persons. It was his invariable doctrine that the ruling individuals were not intentionally bad, nor in any way worse than other men. Towards some of them he entertained strong feelings of personal friendship. A certain asperity, no doubt, appears occasionally in his controversial writings ; but it proceeded from no private motives :—the individuals against whom it showed itself never injured him, never wounded his vanity, or interfered with his interests ; his path and theirs never crossed. It has been shown in the highly honourable acknowledgment recently made by Mr. Macaulay, how far Mr. Mill was from retaining any grudge, even when he *had* been personally attacked, and with a severity which the assailant himself cannot now approve. Mr. Mill never wrote severe things of any one but from honest conviction, and in the exercise, as he believed, of a duty; and the fault, if fault it be, is one which we of this age may view with leniency, when we see how often the absence of it has no better source than incapacity of earnest feeling on any subject not personal."

The remainder of the letter is occupied with refuting Bentham's insinuation of ingratitude on the part of his father. The narrative in the text containing all the facts he adduces in answer to this groundless accusation.

The following sentences, also given by Bowring, from Bentham's conversations about Mill, are a curious study.

"He will never willingly enter into discourse with me. When he differs he is silent. He is a character. He expects to subdue everybody by his domineering tone—to convince everybody by his positiveness. His manner of speaking is oppressive and overbearing. He comes to me as if he wore a mask upon his face."

The apparent contradiction of being at once silent and an oppressive talker, we may reconcile by supposing that the occasions and persons addressed would be different. Of course, Bentham saw him in his usual vein before a mixed company; and seemed to disapprove of his manner of laying down the law to people generally. The silence and the mask would be as regards Bentham himself, and must appear strange when we know of the thousands of animated discussions that the two must have maintained together. The only possible meaning that we can attribute to the words is, that Mill employed tact and reserve in dealing with Bentham's very peculiar temper, and did not contradict him when it would have been of no use; while he would not affect to agree with him when he disagreed. Bentham was in temperament warm and effusive; his play of humour covered a soft and affectionate nature. But this did not incline him to enduring personal attachments, without perfect agreement in all his opinions and projects.

To complete the testimonies to Mill's power as a converser, I add the few expressive sentences from his son's delineation :—"I have never known any man who could do such ample justice to his best thoughts in colloquial discussion. His perfect command over his great mental resourses, the terseness and expressiveness of his language and the moral earnestness as well as intellectual force of his delivery, made him one of the most striking of all argumentative conversers : and he was full of anecdote, a hearty laugher, and when with people whom he liked, a most lively and amusing companion. It was not solely, or even chiefly, in diffusing his merely intellectual convictions that his power showed itself . it was still more through the influence of a quality, of which I have only since learnt to appreciate the extreme rarity that exalted public spirit, and regard above all things to the good of the whole, which warmed into life and activity every germ of similar virtue that existed in the minds he came in contact with : the desire he made them feel for his approbation, the shame at his disapproval ; the moral support which his conversation and his very existence gave to those who were aiming at the same objects, and the encouragement he afforded to the faint-hearted or desponding among them, by the firm confidence which (though the reverse of sanguine as to the results to be expected in any one particular case) he always felt in the power of reason, the general progress of improvement, and the good which individuals could do by judicious effort."

E.—*Mill's Commonplace Book.*

Mill's Commonplace Book, in four vols., presented by his son to the London Library, is interesting as a clue to his studies. He must have been, all his life, very assiduous in copying extracts from the authors that he read ; and the general course of his reading is thus brought clearly before us. Like most men, even the most erudite. he had certain leading topics always in view. These I will shortly indicate.

I may remark that his reading embraced, besides English, three languages—Greek, Latin, and French · in each of which he was perfectly at his ease. He also knew a little of Italian and Spanish.

Foremost of all the topics is the subject of the Liberty of the Press. On this he has accumulated opinions and illustrations from the wide compass of ancient and modern literature. The general drift is, of course, in favour of Liberty, with practical refutations of the various subterfuges for evading the application of the principle.

As might be anticipated, a nearly, if not quite equal, prominence is given to the topic of Government, especially with reference to the necessity of popular control. Citations from history, from philosophers, statesmen, and miscellaneous writers, are directed against the mischiefs of unchecked authority, and the necessity of representative institutions. A number of hard hits against Aristocracy in particular are got out of Aristotle, Tacitus, Shaftesbury, Harrington, Adam Smith, Turgot, Fénélon, Burke, D'Alembert, Gibbon, Mackintosh, Madame de Stael, Rochefoucauld, Pilati.

The way that Governments produce and foster vices in the people is largely illustrated from the Greek and Roman writers, as well as from moderns.

A considerable mass of citations refer to Religion, mostly, of course, in the controversial point of view. The theologians quoted are Chillingworth, Butler, Clarke, Jeremy Taylor, Tillotson, Warburton, Smith, Jortin, Campbell (George), Bossuet (his early favourite), Conyers Middleton, Barrow, Bishop Watson, Paley. There is a good deal from Hobbes, Bayle, Hume, and Bacon. So also Locke, Swift, Montesquieu, Boileau, Burke, Berkeley, S. Johnson. Ancient writers are largely cited in connection with the same fertile topic.

A favourite subordinate position is Theory or Speculation *versus* Practice, in which he brings a mass of authorities to check the overweening presumption of the "practical" man. One of his last writings in the *London Review* was a Dialogue on this subject.

A collection of extracts on Fallacies and Popular Errors of all sorts—Political, Religious and others—could have been anticipated.

A good many citations have reference to Law, Judges, and Law Procedure.

His reading was evidently not extensive in the Belles Lettres. His Greek authors were Plato, Aristotle, Thucydides, Demosthenes, Isocrates, Lucian, Xenophon, Herodotus, Plutarch, Dionysius of Halicarnassus; the poets he may have read in his early days, but not latterly; Aristophanes and Euripides are quoted for political allusions. Cicero, Seneca, Quintilian, Pliny, Tacitus, come up; Livy is scarcely adduced, but Horace and Juvenal are not unusual. Terence appears once or twice.

The French authors are numerous, and many of them are often cited :— Bayle, Voltaire, Montesquieu, Turgot, Condorcet, D'Alembert, Madame de Staël, Bossuet, Pascal, Condillac, Volney, Helvetius, Rousseau, Fénélon, Montaigne, Tracy, Molière, Boileau, De La Rivière, Raynal, Cabanis, De Retz, Arnauld. The reference to poetry is usually with a view to some political doctrine.

There is a notable absence of patristic and middle age literature. The Fathers and the Schoolmen are alike unrepresented.

The English authors are, of course, the most numerous; but the references to them are limited by the lines of study. Of a few, great use is made. Hume is often cited, but not so often in philosophy as for politics. Johnson's writings are largely quoted from. Burke is also a chief resort. Gibbon is liberally drawn upon. Milton's prose is oftener used than his poetry. Then we have Bacon, Hobbes, Locke, Adam Smith, Shaftesbury, Algernon Sidney, Temple, Bolingbroke, Harrington, Chesterfield. The great English Divines of Liberal tendency I have already mentioned. I add among the promiscuous references—Raleigh, Sir T. More, Beaumont and Fletcher, Dryden, Pope, Swift (a favourite), Burnet (History), Fielding, Butler (Hudibras), Littleton (Persian Letters), Sterne, Cowper, Robertson

(History), Blackstone, Paley, Sir J. Reynolds, Mitford (Greece), Dr. Donne, Horne Tooke, Peter Pindar, Burton (Anatomy of Melancholy), Sir W. Jones, Beattie, Erasmus Darwin, Arthur Young, North's Lives, Horace Walpole, Roger L'Estrange.

Great use is made, as we have formerly seen, of Fra Paolo's History of the Council of Trent.

The absence of the lighter literature is conspicuous everywhere. The citation of poets is for purposes other than purely literary.

A. KING AND CO., PRINTERS TO THE UNIVERSITY.

CPSIA information can be obtained
at www.ICGtesting.com
Printed in the USA
LVHW060426110222
710847LV00005B/11